Frontispiece. Top: Roosevelt Lake. View of unidentified archaeological
              sites along the north shore of Roosevelt Lake, below the
              high-water mark (courtesy of the U.S. Bureau of Reclamation,
              Arizona Projects Office).
              Bottom: Horseshoe Reservoir. View of the Mercer Ruin in
              the foreground with the Horseshoe Reservoir floodpool in the
              background (courtesy of the U.S. Bureau of Reclamation,
              Arizona Projects Office).

ORME ALTERNATIVES:

THE ARCHAEOLOGICAL RESOURCES OF ROOSEVELT LAKE AND HORSESHOE RESERVOIR

Volume I

Prepared for

The United States Bureau of Reclamation

As part of

The Central Arizona Project

By

Steven L. Fuller
A. E. Rogge
Linda M. Gregonis

With reviews by

Robert C. Euler, Stephen Plog, Dwight W. Read

Submitted by

Cultural Resource Management Section
Arizona State Museum
The University of Arizona

June 1976

Report submitted in final fulfillment of Contract No. 14-06-330-14

ARCHAEOLOGICAL SERIES NO. 98

ABSTRACT

The Orme Alternatives Project, which is part of the U.S. Bureau of
Reclamation's Central Arizona Project, was implemented in order to examine
possible alternatives to the proposed Orme Dam and Reservoir. As reported
by Canouts (1975), the proposed Orme Reservoir Project would have an extremely
adverse impact upon the cultural resources of central Arizona. Therefore,
the Bureau of Reclamation contracted the Arizona State Museum to evaluate
the impact of two partial alternatives. One alternative would consist of
raising Roosevelt Dam, on the Salt River, 30 feet and thereby increasing
the size of Roosevelt Lake by approximately 12.7 square miles. Combined
with the first alternative would be a second alternative which would consist of raising Horseshoe Dam, on the Verde River, some 140 feet and enlarging Horseshoe Reservoir approximately 7.8 square miles. It was felt
by the participants in the project that the kind of data required to evaluate the relative impacts upon cultural resources of these various projects
could be obtained through a 20 percent probabilistic sample. The goals of
the Orme Alternatives Project were, then, to conduct sample surveys of the
Orme Alternatives project areas and to make statistical predictions on the
quantity, extent, and nature of the archaeological resources affected by
proposed reservoir enlargement. These predictions can then be compared to
the Orme Reservoir 100 percent site data.

Chapters 2, 3, and 4 present background studies for the general
Orme Alternatives region. Included in these chapters are general discussions of the environmental settings, the range of resources available to
aboriginal inhabitants of this region, the history of archaeological and
ethnological research in the Tonto Basin and Verde Valley, and a synthesis
of the culture-history of these two basins.

Chapter 5 reviews the implementation of the sample survey and provides raw data on the results of the survey. Basically, the survey consisted of a disproportionate stratified random sample. At Roosevelt Lake,
29 sites were recorded in the 20 percent surveyed portion of the project
area. At Horseshoe Reservoir, 64 sites were found in the surveyed area.
This total of 93 sites represents a range from small limited activity areas,
such as agricultuaral check dams, to large pit house villages and multi-
story pueblos.

The central concern of the project, constructing parameter estimates
of total sites and man-days which can be compared to the 100 percent Orme
Reservoir data, is contained in Chapter 6. Using a combined ratio estimation procedure, it is possible to make estimates of the total number of
sites within both project areas as well as the total number of man-days
necessary for collection of the total data from all of these sites. The total
number of sites at Roosevelt Lake and Horseshoe Reservoir is estimated to be

374 with a possible range from 287 to 461 (at a 70 percent confidence interval). The total data recovery man-days is estimated to be 121,700 with a
range between 79,900 and 175,400. In order to aid in the evaluation of
the precision and adequacy of this sample projection, the Orme Alternatives
sample design was utilized in a simulation experiment with the Orme Reservoir
100 percent data. Three hundred samples were selected using an interactive
Fortran IV program for each of eight different sampling frequencies. Basically, the simulation shows that the precision of the combined ratio estimate
increases regularly with sample size but the absolute size of the standard
error may never become small if the data are highly skewed.

Chapter 7 presents an analysis of settlement variability between the
Horseshoe Reservoir data and the data collected at Roosevelt Lake. Broken
down into habitation and non-habitation components, as well as into three
time periods, the data are analyzed in terms of density, degree of aggregation, site size, and spatial patterns. For the sake of comparison,
these analyses are also performed on the Orme Reservoir data and on the
Vosburg Locality data from just below the Mogollon Rim (Chenhall 1972).
In this sense, quantified settlement information is available along a
transect from the Mogollon Rim area (Vosburg), through the Transition
Zone (Roosevelt Lake and Horseshoe Reservoir), and eventually to the
Sonoran Desert (Orme Reservoir). No satisfactory explanation of the variability among these settlement data has yet been achieved.

Chapters 8, 9, and 10 are essentially the management chapters of
this report. Chapter 8 discusses the significance of the Orme Alternatives
resources within a framework of historical, scientific, social, and monetary
perspectives (cf. Scovill and others 1972). The Orme Alternatives resources
are then compared with the Orme Reservoir resources in terms of these categories of significance. The conclusion is that both the Orme Alternatives
resources and the Orme Reservoir resources are definitely of significance.
However, several aspects of this study, some quantitative and some qualitative, indicate that the Orme Alternatives resources are of greater significance.

Based on the parameter estimates and the evidence for the significance of the Orme Alternatives resources, it is concluded that the alteration of Roosevelt Lake and Horseshoe Reservoir will have an adverse impact
upon the resources. This impact is estimated to be of a degree which
should be avoided. Although avoidance and protection of the Orme Alternatives resources is recommended, two alternative mitigation actions are
discussed. Total data recovery costs are estimated on the basis of formulas generated for the Orme Reservoir Project (Canouts 1975). A total
data study program for the Orme Alternatives resources is estimated to
cost $81,904,100 with a possible range from $53,772,700 to $118,044,200.
Since the time and money for such a massive project is probably unobtain-
able, an adequate data study program based on a probabilistic sample of the
Orme Alternatives resources is recommended as a mitigative action if data
recovery becomes necessary. Based on a 50 percent sample, adequate data
recovery and study costs would be $40,952,050 with a possible range from
$26,886,350 to $59,022,100.

Chapter 10 contains a preliminary research plan which outlines some of the immediate goals of any data recovery program. The first step in such a program would be the completion of the survey (the remaining 80 percent) so as to provide an accurate frame of elements to be sampled during an excavation and data recovery stage.

Appendices to the Orme Alternatives report include a ceramic analysis of site surface collections made during the 20 percent sample survey (Appendix I). This analysis was utilized to make temporal and cultural inferences regarding these sites. Appendix II contains three "peer reviews" of the Orme Alternatives manuscript. These were solicited from Robert C. Euler of the Grand Canyon National Park, Stephen Plog of Southern Illinois University, and Dwight W. Read of the University of California, Los Angeles. These reviews are provided in order to present independent, and hopefully unbiased, assessments of the technical and managerial aspects of this report. Appendix IIIA and IIIB (Volume II) contain the descriptions and maps for the 93 sites recorded during the Orme Alternatives 20 percent survey. Copies of Volume II which contain these descriptions will only receive a limited distribution in order to protect these resources. Additionally, Figures 6 to 13, which are site location maps in Chapter 5, are deleted from most copies of this report.

ACKNOWLEDGMENTS

As is usually the case, this report represents more efforts than just those of the authors. Our first thanks go to the gatherers of the data, crew members Peter Coston, Terrill Nickerson, and John Roney, who adapted remarkably well to a Lower Sonoran summer.

Of course, no data would have been collected unless the Bureau of Reclamation, Arizona Projects Office, had agreed to sponsor the survey of these two reservoirs. We thank the personnel of that office for not only sponsoring the project, but also for their cooperation in providing background information, in making a helicopter available for a one-day reconnaissance, and especially for allowing us an extra eight months for report preparation.

The personnel of the Cultural Resource Management Section of the Arizona State Museum also deserve our sincere thanks. Linda Mayro, Project Director for the Orme Alternatives Project, made our jobs easier by coordinating certain support services, taking care of all of the administrative paper work, keeping us from exceeding our budget, and for providing us with valuable feedback on all aspects of the report. Lynn S. Teague and Mark Grady, who were heads of the Cultural Resource Management Section at various times during the project, should also be acknowledged. Additionally, Lynn read and commented on several portions of the report and Mark initiated the agreement with the Bureau of Reclamation. R. Gwinn Vivian was principal investigator of the Orme Alternatives Project.

Chapter 6, the statistical evaluation of the sample survey, results from the input of many individuals. Those who read the chapter and provided valuable comments include: Donald G. Callaway, Department of Anthropology, the University of Arizona; Ronald Schoenberg, Department of Sociology, the University of Arizona; David Marks, Agricultural Experiment Statistics Lab, the University of Arizona; David Hurst Thomas, the American Museum of Natural History; and Dwight W. Read, Department of Anthropology, University of California, Los Angeles. Also of help during the preparation of the simulation section of Chapter 6 was Larry Manire of the Data Processing Section of the Arizona State Museum; and Anique George of the Department of Anthropology, the University of Arizona. Larry was especially helpful, as he wrote the computer program for the simulation phase of the project. Also to be thanked for lending us help and expertise are David E. Doyel, Larry Hammack, and W. Bruce Masse of the Arizona State Museum. Without their help and knowledge of central Arizona ceramics, we would have had difficulty making sense of our sherd collections.

Robert C. Euler, Grand Canyon National Park, Stephen Plog, Southern Illinois University, and Dwight W. Read, University of California, Los Angeles, all deserve special acknowledgment for their participation in this project. Not only are their reviews (Appendix II) very constructive and useful, but their willingness to produce such reviews within a tight time frame is especially appreciated.

We also benefited from our participation in a Central Arizona Ecotone Project symposium held in Black Canyon City (Arizona) in October, 1975. We thank Carol S. Weed and George J. Gumerman of Southern Illinois University, Carbondale, for inviting us as well as for providing portions of their own reports.

And finally, the people who actually produced this report should be singled out for their ability to take our drafts and translate them into this final copy. Virginia Diebold, Melinda Curry, Sue Ruiz, and Carole McClellan all took part in the typing of this report. Gayle Hartmann, who edited the report, was especially talented in her ability to take half-thoughts and give them meaning. Charles Sternberg drafted all of the maps and should be commended for translating field maps and rough sketches into these fine illustrations.

CONTENTS

FIGURES

TABLES

Chapter 1

INTRODUCTION

The estimated cost of mitigating the loss of archaeological resources if the proposed Orme Reservoir were to be built at the confluence of the Salt and Verde rivers has been calculated at more than 22 million dollars (Canouts 1975). As part of an attempt to explore possible alternatives to the Orme Reservoir Project, the Arizona State Museum entered into a contract with the Bureau of Reclamation to investigate the resource potential of two alternative reservoir sites (Figure 1). Both of these alternatives, the enlarging of Theodore Roosevelt Lake and the enlarging of Horseshoe Reservoir, are being considered as possible components of the Central Arizona Project. The following report, in partial fulfillment of the contract between the Arizona State Museum and the Bureau of Reclamation, is a discussion of the Orme Alternatives archaeological resources, including their description, their significance, their cost of mitigation, as well as discussions of the cultural-environmental backgrounds of both reservoir sites.

Project Location

One half of the Orme Alternatives consists of raising the crest of Roosevelt Dam some 30 feet and therefore the height of Roosevelt Lake the same amount. The other half of the alternatives consists of raising Horseshoe Dam 140 feet; this would raise Horseshoe Lake's high-water mark some 140 feet. Roosevelt Lake is in Tonto Basin, a broad, crescent-shaped, intermontane valley in central Arizona (Figure 2). The northwest arm of the basin is drained by Tonto Creek. The Salt River drains the eastern arm of the basin. Roosevelt Dam, constructed between 1906 and 1911, is at the confluence of these streams, and the lake formed behind the dam covers a considerable portion of the valley floor in the lower part of the basin. The Mazatzal Mountains form the western boundary of the Tonto Basin, and the rugged Sierra Ancha Mountains form the northern boundary. Lesser ranges encircle the basin on the east and south sides. The Roosevelt Lake area is about 50 air miles east-northeast of Phoenix (Figure 1) and is described in detail in Chapter 2.

Horseshoe Reservoir is located in the middle of the Lower Verde some 35 air miles north-northeast of Phoenix (Figure 1). The Verde River Valley, which is the drainage just to the west of the Tonto Basin, can be divided into three sections: upper, middle, and lower (Figure 3). These terms have been used somewhat inconsistently in the archaeological literature. In order to avoid confusion, the following definitions, which correspond to those used by Shaffer (1972: Map 3), will be adopted.

1

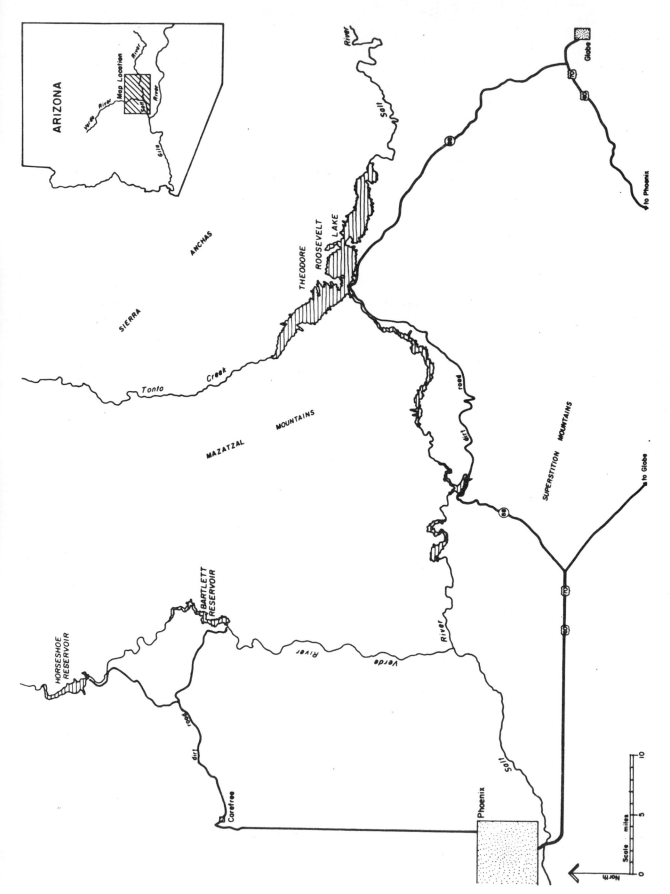

Figure 1. A Locational Map of Roosevelt Lake and Horseshoe Reservoir

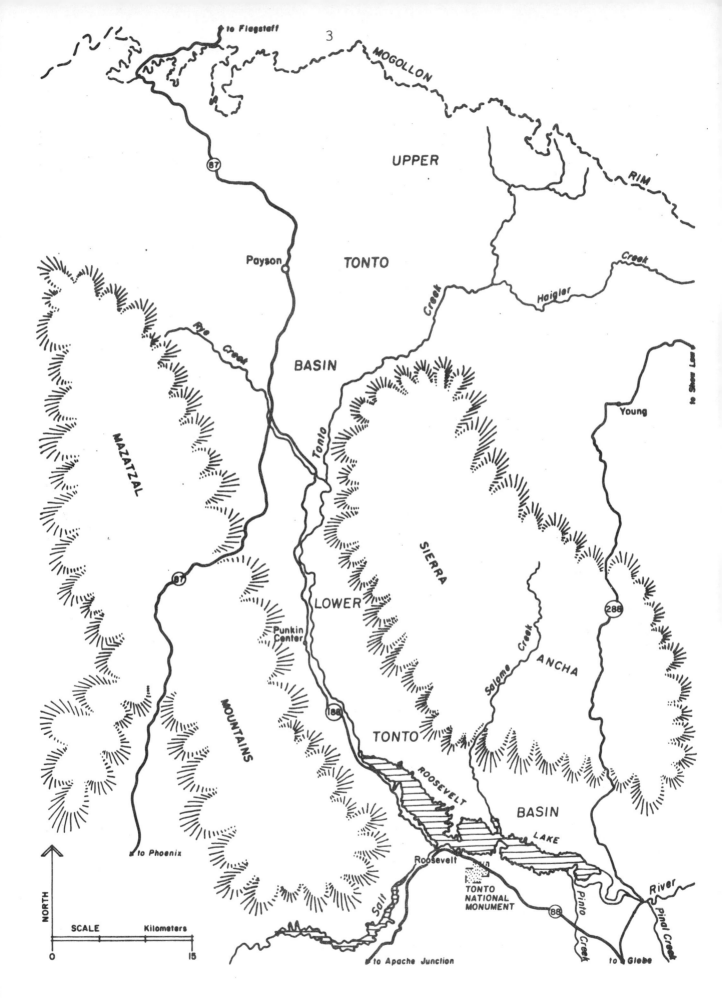

Figure 2. Divisions of the Tonto Basin.

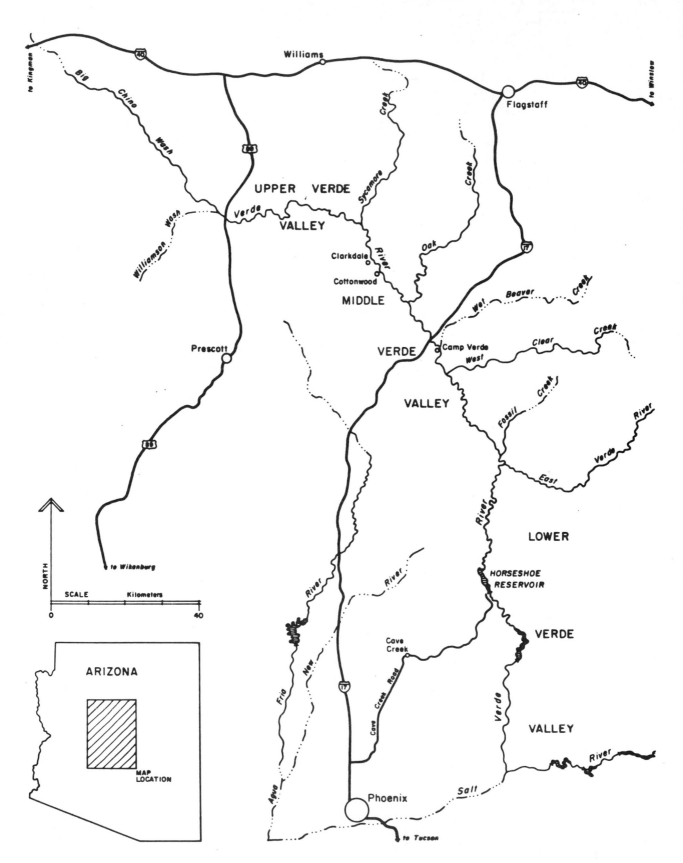

Figure 3. Divisions of the Verde Valley.

The Upper Verde Valley consists of the northwest-southeast-trending Chino Valley. At the confluence of Big Chino Wash and Williamson Wash the Verde River turns and flows almost due east for about 20 miles through a narrow canyon. It then turns southeast again and flows through a broad valley referred to as the Middle Verde Valley. Entering the Verde Valley from the east are several major tributaries including Sycamore Creek, Oak Creek, Beaver Creek, and Clear Creek. About five miles south of the confluence with Clear Creek, the Verde Valley narrows and remains relatively narrow to its junction with the Salt River. This final section is referred to as the Lower Verde Valley. Entering from the east are Fossil Creek, the East Verde River, and another Sycamore Creek (Figure 3). The Horseshoe Reservoir area is described in detail in Chapter 2.

Project History and Implementation

The Orme Alternatives Project was conceived of jointly by the Arizona State Museum and the Bureau of Reclamation in early 1975. Field work was initiated on June 9, 1975, and continued through July 25, 1975, as specified in the contract. As determined by the Bureau of Reclamation, the National Forest Service, and the Arizona State Museum, a 20 percent sample of the total, direct impact area was surveyed with a primary goal of determining the potential impact upon the cultural environment that would result if Roosevelt Lake and Horseshoe Reservoir were raised. The survey areas investigated by the Arizona State Museum are discussed in more detail in Chapters 2 and 5 and Appendices IIIA and IIIB. In order to conduct this study, a field team consisting of one Supervisory Archaeologist (Steven Fuller) and three archaeological crew members (Peter Coston, Terrill Nickerson, and John Roney) was utilized. More exact figures concerning the field time and man-day figures is provided in Chapter 5. During this field phase, research was initiated in Tucson by a research team consisting of the Project Director, Linda Mayro, and two Research Archaeologists, A. E. Rogge and Linda Gregonis. Analysis and report preparation were begun immediately after the termination of the field work by a research team consisting of Fuller, Gregonis, Mayro, and Rogge. This phase was completed in February, 1976.

Research Orientation

In addition to the primary goal of determining the amount and nature of impact that would be rendered to archaeological resources by the alteration of Roosevelt and Horseshoe dams, it was also felt that such a study could contribute something positive to archaeological research. However, as a result of the limited amount of archaeological investigations that had been conducted in the immediate area of the two reservoirs, the research investigations are, by necessity, rather exploratory in nature. It was decided early in the project that to set up a research design based on the deductive testing of certain hypotheses would constitute an overzealous activity at this point. Instead, our research goals are focused on three general problem orientations. The first will be an investigation of problems concerning the description and recognition of the local cultural historical sequences. The background history of archaeological research in the region is provided in Chapter 3, and Chapter 4 discusses the actual culture-histories of the two project areas. The second problem area will be an analysis of the relationship between environmental variability and archaeological manifestations, including a discussion of the concept of the central Arizona transition zone as an explanatory device for subsistence-settlement patterns. This relationship is dealt with exclusively in Chapter 7. The third problem domain will be a methodological study of sampling procedures. This focus not only contributes to a current methodological "issue" in archaeology, but the satisfactory resolution of this problem in regard to Orme Alternatives will provide a more accurate, more responsible estimate of the total number and character of sites as derived from the 20 percent sample. Chapter 5 discusses the actual sampling design developed for the Orme Alternatives 20 percent survey. Chapter 6 evaluates the sample and presents a statistical prediction of the total number and variability of sites in the two project areas. Chapter 9 utilizes these sample predictions in estimating a total cost of data recovery from the predicted number of sites while also making recommendations for protection of these resources.

It is hoped that a preliminary examination of these three problem domains will enable more systemization in the conduct of future archaeological research in the Roosevelt and Horseshoe vicinities. Perhaps, then, the statement of logically-derived hypotheses will be more feasible, making possible the ultimate objective of explaining the similarities and differences of this archaeological record.

Chapter 2

ENVIRONMENTAL CONDITIONS

The following discussion of environmental conditions within the
Roosevelt Lake and Horseshoe Reservoir localities emphasizes aspects of
physiography, hydrology, faunal and floral distributions, and local climates. The brief discussions of these environmental variables is considered necessary for a fuller understanding of the various prehistoric
and historic occupations in this region. Undoubtedly, prehistoric
Indians, and Anglo-Americans alike, have utilized these areas in order to
exploit or extract certain energies from the natural environment. However, the emphasis placed on specific constellations of resources has
varied through time and among cultural groups. In the case of prehistoric
cultures, these exploited energies were in the form of available wild
plants and animals as well as the soil and water resources necessary for
agricultural practices, while the historic Anglo inhabitants of this region
have largely been interested in the grazing resources as well as the min-
eral resources available. A better understanding of these man-land relationships is one of the goals of this project.

Besides discussing the environments in both of the reservoir areas,
a section of this chapter comments on aspects of historical disturbance
affecting the natural environments of these two reservoirs.

Roosevelt Lake Section

Physiography

The portion of Arizona that lies between the Colorado Plateau
Physiographic Province and the Basin and Range Physiographic Province has
been labeled the Transition Zone (Wilson and Moore 1959) and is characterized by canyons and large structural troughs such as the Tonto Basin.
The Roosevelt Lake area is mainly in the lower Tonto Basin, although it
extends some 15 miles up the Salt River arm. This latter zone has sometimes been referred to as the Roosevelt Basin, although it is best considered as an extension of the Tonto Basin (Steen and others 1962: 3).

The geologic history of the basin has not been exhaustively studied.
According to Barsch and Royse (1971), it is a typical down-faulted, sedi-
ment-filled basin and range trough lying between uplifted mountain ranges.
To the southwest are the Mazatzal Mountains and to the northeast are the
Sierra Anchas. Both ranges are oriented northwest and southeast are com-
posed largely of Precambrian granite, gneiss, shist, and metasediments.

Occasional Tertiary volcanic flows are exposed. It would appear that
this vulcanism preceded the structural formation of the Tonto Basin trough
as no volcanic materials are found interbedded with the basin-fill deposits (Barsch and Royse 1971: 10). The basin fill sediments consist of
sandstone, siltstone, claystone, conglomerate, marl, gypsum, diatomite,
caliche, and pyroclastics, thus representing fluvial, lacustrine, colluvial, and alluvial depositional environments. Exposed sections of these
sediments exceed 1,000 feet, and it is probable that they extend several
times that distance into the subsurface (Barsch and Royse 1971: 62). On
the basis of fossil evidence, these beds generally date in the Pliocene
epoch of the Tertiary period (2-12 million years B.P.), although the
youngest are probably Pleistocene and the oldest are possibly late Miocene
(12-23 million years B.P.) (Royse and others 1971: 12-13).

The post-basin-fill history of the Tonto Basin is largely erosional
in nature. As a result of climatic oscillations, several periods of
erosion and alluviation have contributed to a landscape primarily consisting of elevated benches and floodplains (Barsch and Royse 1971). Two
types of benches are described: one is a river terrace and the other is
a pediment terrace. The former results from downcutting of the main
stream and its tributaries which leaves the old floodplain dissected and
elevated above the new channel. These old surfaces parallel the present
course of Tonto Creek and slope down-valley at the same gradient as the
active stream (Barsch and Royse 1971). Seven of these alluvial terraces
have been identified for the Tonto Creek drainage, each of which represents a separate climatic interval. The Slate Creek terrace is the only
one that can be positively identified as being in the Roosevelt Lake
project area.

The other type of bench, or pediment-terrace, should not be confused
with pediments but rather should be considered as pediment-like features
(Barsch and Royse 1971: 69). This term should be used so as to differ-
entiate between the original concept of pediments as piedmont plains cut
into hard, crystalline rocks and similar piedmont features that are cut
into relatively soft, basin-fill sediments (Barsch and Royse 1971: 69).
As with river terraces, these pediment-terraces have been left elevated
at many levels as a result of successive downcutting of the drainage
system. Five pediment-terraces have been defined for the Tonto Basin.
It is suggested that pediment-terraces were formed under arid or semi-
arid conditions and that river terraces were formed during the humid intervals of the Pleistocene (Barsch and Royse 1971: 72-73).

Within the project area there are alluvial river terraces both
along the Salt River and Tonto Creek arms of Roosevelt Lake, and pediment-
terraces between the alluvial river terraces and the Sierra Ancha and
Mazatzal mountain fronts. In addition to these bench-like physiographic
situations are extensive areas of active floodplain deposits. These
include the Tonto Creek floodplain, the Salt River floodplain, and numerous medium-sized floodplains within the tributary drainages that flow into
the Tonto Basin. A final physiographic subdivision includes those steep

slopes that mark the division between the various terrace levels. These
talus slopes and escarpments are easily distinguished by their slopes of
over 10 percent. Basically, these physiographic subdivisions roughly
correspond with the four sampling strata defined in Chapter 5, "The
Survey."

Hydrology

The Roosevelt Lake area is in what is called the "Central Highlands
Water Province" (Ligner and others 1969: 475-476), a region transitional
to the Colorado Plateau Uplands Province and the Basin and Range Lowlands
Province. In general, these provinces correspond to Fenneman's (1931)
physiographic provinces and, more specifically, to Wilson and Moore's
(1959) Transition Zone. Portions of the Salt River and Tonto Creek
drainage systems are contained in the Roosevelt Lake project area.

Tonto Creek, which flows into the northwest arm of the lake, drains
the extensive Tonto Basin from northeast of Payson to where it now enters
Roosevelt Lake. Most of the stream-flow in this almost perennial drainage originages in the upper basin which has a drainage area of 675 square
miles. During the period between 1942 and 1970, the average annual stream-
flow was 110 cubic feet per second (hereafter cfs). In 1956, a total of
17,120 acre feet of water passed the gauging station, while a maximum
annual flow of 224,500 acre feet has been recorded. A daily maximum of
53,000 cfs was recorded on September 5, 1970, and a minimum flow of 0 cfs
has been recorded occasionally. Broken down seasonally, Tonto Creek
shows a biseasonal stream-flow peak with the period of December-April
showing the most activity. The maximum monthly activity is in March with
an average of over 16,000 acre feet. A secondary peak occurs in August
and September with August showing a monthly average of over 7,000 acre
feet. May through July represents a dry period for Tonto Creek; June only
averages less than 1,000 acre feet. Tonto Creek flows on the average of
97.4 percent of the time making it a seasonal stream. All of the preceding data on Tonto Creek's hydrological characteristics have previously
been presented by Schuman and Thomsen (1972: 13-17). It should also be
noted that none of the tributary drainages in the lower Tonto Basin are
perennial. Rather, they usually only flow ephemerally after cloudbursts
and extended periods of steady rainfall.

The Salt River is decidedly perennial drainage comprising one of
the major systems in central Arizona. Data collected from 1913 to the
present time at a guaging station just upstream from Roosevelt Lake indicate that this 4,306 square mile drainage basin contributes an average
discharge of 852 cfs or 617,300 acre feet per year. An extreme high
discharge of 117,000 cfs was recorded August 5, 1911 (U.S. Department of
Interior 1974: 155). Unlike Tonto Creek, the Salt River's seasonal variation indicates that a single major stream-flow peak occurs between February and May with 65 percent of the annual flow passing the gauge during

this period. June and July are the months of least stream-flow with August and September registering only slightly more (Dunbier 1968: 89).

One point that should be emphasized is that these two drainages in the Roosevelt Lake area are highly irregular and are not easily amenable to patterning. The annual runoff for the entire watershed above Roosevelt Dam may be as high as 2,650,000 acre feet or as little as 162,000 acre feet (Dunbier 1968: 82).

Vegetation

In general terms, the survey area around Roosevelt Lake is part of the Lower Sonoran Life Zone (Merriam 1890) and consists of a predominately desertscrub vegetation type which extends up the major valley bottoms into this highland province. The consistency of desertscrub vegetation is broken by the presence of riparian and mesic-adapted plant communities in certain locations. The former is due to the presence of the Salt River at the eastern end of the reservoir and Tonto Creek at the northwest end. The latter situation appears to be a result of both the presence of man-made Roosevelt Lake and ephemeral washes extending back from the lake.

On the floodplains, at both ends of the reservoir, a desert riparian woodland predominates with such species present as cottonwood, walnut, seep willow, desert broom, desert willow, tree tobacco, datura, and tamarisk, an introduced species.

In some places bordering the deciduous woodland zone and in other places intergrading with it are mesquite bosques. The predominance of mesquite is also found in an almost continuous ring around Roosevelt Lake. While mature mesquite trees provide an almost continuous overstory, the understory is entirely composed of grasses in the better-developed bosques.

Away from the floodplain and areas immediately adjacent to the lake, the plant communities are made up of various combinations of small leaf trees, scrubs, cacti, and various annuals. The primary plants in these areas are mesquite, creosotebush, blue paloverde, yellow paloverde, various chollas, prickly-pear, sahuaro, various acacias, jojoba, Mormon tea, gray-thorn, hackberry, and canotia.

In some otherwise typical desertscrub communities at the west end of the lake, in the shadow of the Mazatzal foothills, were observed some woodland and chaparral species such as juniper, scrub oak, sotol, and yucca. In general, these plants were found on north-facing slopes.

A complete list of plant species recorded at Roosevelt Lake is presented in Table 1 along with an indication of which ones are of some economic value to aboriginal populations.

Table 1

Plant Species Observed at Roosevelt Lake

Common Name	Scientific Name	Common Name	Scientific Name
Cottonwood*	Populis fremonti	Sahuaro*	Carnegiea gigantea
Tamarisk	Tamarix pentandra	Chainfruit cholla*	Opuntia fulgida
Sycamore	Plantanus wrightii	Staghorn cholla*	Opuntia versicolor
Walnut*	Juglans major	Christmas cholla*	Opuntia leptocaulis
		Prickly-pear*	Opuntia Engelmannii
Mesquite*	Prosopis juliflora	Buckhorn cholla*	Opuntia acanthocarpa
Catclaw*	Acacia greggii	Teddy bear cholla	Opuntia bigelovii
White-thorn*	Acacia constricta	Hedgehog cactus	Echinocerus sp.
Mimosa*	Mimosa sp.	Barrel cactus	Ferocactus sp.
Blue paloverde*	Cercidium microphyllum		
Yellow paloverde*	Cercidium floridum	Desertbroom	Baccharis sarothroides
Gray-thorn	Condalia sp.	Brittlebush	Encelia farinosa
Lyceum (squawberry)*	Lyceum berlandieri	Paper daisy	Psilostrophe sp.
Hackberry*	Celtis reticulata	Tree tobacco*	Nicotiana glauca
Scrub oak*	Quercus turbinella	Seep willow	Baccharis glutinosa
Juniper*	Juniperus sp.	Mistletoe	Phorandendron sp.
Mormon tea*	Ephedra trifurca	Ragweed	Ambrosia sp.
Canotia	Canoita holancantha	Arrowweed	Pluchea sericea
Creosotebush	Larrea tridentata	Desert willow	Chilopsis linearis
Jojoba*	Simmondsia chinensis	Globe mallow	Sphaeralcea sp.
Sotol*	Dasylirion wheeleri	Senna	Cassia sp.
Soaptree yucca*	Yucca elata	Snakeweed	Gutierrezia sp.

*plants of primary economic importance

Faunal Resources

The faunal observations made while surveying the Roosevelt Lake project area should be considered biased and unrepresentative of the entire range of faunal populations. This is in large part due to the fact that most of the desert fauna avoid excessive activity during the heat of the summer day. Unfortunately, the survey team could not schedule its activities to coincide with faunal activities.

Mammals observed during archaeological studies included white-tailed deer, mule deer, cattle, coyote, jackrabbit, cottontail, racoon, ground squirrel, and mice.

Avifauna sighted by the survey crew included Gila woodpecker, Gambel's quail, buzzard, cactus wren, mockingbird, owl, pelican, dove, hawk, and heron.

Reptiles included diamond-backed rattlesnake, an unidentified non-poisonous snake, and various lizards.

Other fauna that have been observed in the general vicinity (Dickerman 1954) include rock squirrel, chipmunk, pocket gopher, porcupine, gray fox, ring-tailed cat, badger, skunk, bobcat, mountain lion, and javelina.

No information is available on native aquatic species, though it is presumed that this perennially-watered valley maintained a variety of such species in pre-reservoir times.

Climate

It should be emphasized that in any study of plants, animals, or the earth's surface, the climate is an important controlling factor. Many of the variables that are described in this chapter are largely dependent upon the present climatic regime--one that can be projected back in time in a very general sense for some 2,000 years (Bryan 1925). Such a projection does not preclude microclimatic shifts or oscillations, although such shifts in the Lower Sonoran Desert would probably only affect the density of certain species rather than cause replacements of one species for another or one community for another (Goodyear 1975). Oscillations of this type are generally believed to have taken place on the Colorado Plateau (Hevly 1964; Schoenwetter 1962) and, by inference, are suggested for the Salt River Valley (Weaver 1972). In any case, no major climatic or biotic changes have been documented for the Southwest for the past 8,000 years (Martin 1963).

The climate in the Roosevelt Lake area is semi-arid and characterized by hot, dry summers and mild winters. To best represent the

climatic particulars of this area, data from the Roosevelt 1 WNW climatic
station (Sellers and Hill 1974: 412) as well as the Reno Ranger Station
(Sellers and Hill 1974: 408) are compared. The former station is located
in the town of Roosevelt on the south shore of the lake and the latter
station is located one mile south of Punkin Center, in the heart of the
Tonto Basin. The Roosevelt station is at an elevation of 2,205 feet, and
the Reno Ranger Station is at an elevation of 2,420 feet. Both climatic
summaries represent data from the 30 year period between 1941 and 1970.
During this period, Reno reported a mean annual precipitation of 16.75
inches, while Roosevelt recorded only slightly less with 14.15 inches.
Both stations receive their moisture during two distinct rainfall seasons.
Most of the summer precipitation results from turbulent, summer afternoon
thunder showers that are common between July and September. Despite the
frequency of this storm build-up, relatively little moisture falls due to
the height of the cloud bases as they roll off the top of the Sierra Anchas
and Mazatzals. The winter precipitation spans the months between December
and March and accounts for approximately one-half of the total. Because
this moisture is derived from frontal storms originating in the Pacific,
and is dependent upon the storm-track's position, the annual variation is
quite significant. At Reno Ranger Station, only an insignificant portion
of the precipitation falls as snow and when it does, it immediately melts.

The temperatures at these two stations show similarities in the
maximum readings while showing some variability in the nightly lows. At
Roosevelt, the annual mean temperature is 68.1° F., while the Reno Ranger
Station records an annual mean of 65.5° F. In the summer, the high temperatures at both stations hover around 100° F., although highs over 110° F.
are not uncommon. Summer lows range from 65° F. to 75° F. The winter
maximum temperatures are generally in the 50s and 60s at both stations,
although readings above 70° F. are experienced in every month of the year.
The winter lows at Reno are generally below or near freezing, while those
at Roosevelt are moderated by the proximity of Roosevelt Lake which seems
to create certain aspects of a maritime climate. This effect is particularly exemplified by comparing the annual mean lows at these two stations;
Roosevelt registers an annual mean low of 52.2° F., while Reno is significantly lower at 50.5° F. It would seem obvious, then, that the natural
effects of nightly cold air drainage are cancelled out to some degree by
the residual warmth radiated by the water in Roosevelt Lake. The frost-
free period at Reno lasts from the end of March to the second week of
November—a span of some 225 days. The frost-free period at Roosevelt
lasts for more than 300 days and is one of the longest in the state of
Arizona. Surely this latter figure does not represent the pre-reservoir
conditions in the Tonto Basin. The frost-free period at Reno Ranger
Station probably better represents actual conditions for this area.

Horseshoe Reservoir Section

Physiography

As discussed for Roosevelt Lake's physiography, this area of the lower Verde River is also part of the Transition Zone that separates the northern Colorado Plateau Physiographic Province from the southern Basin and Range Province. The Horseshoe Reservoir area, like the Tonto Basin, is a typical, down-faulted trough where the Verde River opens up below its central, canyon-like region.

Very little geological work has been conducted, or at least published, in this lower Verde Basin, and much of the following discussion is an abstraction of the author's observations in light of what has been published for the Tonto Basin and other central Arizona basins. In reference to the Tonto, Chino, Payson, Safford, and Verde valleys, Royse and others (1971: 8) state that all of these basins are late to middle Tertiary in age and have common physical characteristics.

Bordering the sediment-filled lower Verde Basin are the Mazatzal Mountains to the east and a smaller, unnamed range to the west. For the most part, these uplifted mountain blocks are composed of Precambrian granite, gneiss, shist, and metasediments, although Tertiary and Quaternary basalt flows are fairly common.

The basin-fill sediments consist of various lacustrine and fluvial materials including limestones, marls, conglomerates, siltstones, claystones, and diatomites. Although dates and depths are not published for these sediments, it is assumed that they correspond generally with those already discussed for the Tonto Basin.

More specifically, this portion of the lower Verde River valley consists primarily of floodplain deposits, river terraces, and pediment-terraces. Additionally, colluvial deposits generally mark the breaks between the various terrace levels. At the north end of the project area, where the Verde River empties into Horseshoe Reservoir, the survey zone intersects with the present, active floodplain of the Verde River. Immediately above the floodplain are various river terraces marking the presence of former river floodplains. Beyond the river terraces, and sometimes intergrading with them, are the pediment-terraces that extend from the edge of Horseshoe Reservoir to the foot of the Mazatzal Mountains to the east. The last physiographic subdivision consists of the steep erosional and talus slopes that mark the escarpments between various terrace levels. These later physiographic features are especially evident along the west side of the project area where the linear distance between the mountain tops and the valley floor is generally abbreviated. For the most part, these subdivisions roughly correspond to the three sampling strata that are defined in Chapter 5, "The Survey."

Hydrology

The Horseshoe Reservoir area is also in the Central Highlands Water Province (Ligner and others 1969: 475-476). Although the drainage basin of the Verde River above this reservoir (5,872 square miles) is somewhat larger than the upper Salt River watershed, the generally lower elevations which comprise this region make for a lower average discharge for the Verde. Over the 28 year span between 1945 and 1973, the Verde averaged 482 cfs and 349,200 acre feet per year. An extreme high discharge of 81,600 cfs was registered on December 31, 1951, although an estimate of 100,000 cfs was made for a flood in March, 1938. A minimum discharge of 61 cfs was recorded on July 18, 1958, therefore making the Verde River a perennial stream (U.S. Department of Interior 1974: 177).

Seasonal characteristics of stream-flow are not as clearly defined for the Verde River as they are for the Salt and Tonto drainages. However, a glance at yearly data for the period between 1945 and 1965 (U.S. Department of Interior 1954, 1964, 1970) indicate that the Verde is characterized by a pattern of bi-seasonal stream-flow. It appears that the highest discharge occurs between December and March, while a secondary peak in flow occurs in August and September. The months of June and July represent the period of least flow. As for regularity, the Verde is only slightly less irregular than the Salt River, having a maximum runoff of 1,107,000 acre feet per year and a minimum of 185,000 acre feet. These later figures represent the Verde's discharge at its confluence with the Salt River (Dunbier 1968: 84).

Vegetation

The Horseshoe area is similar to the Roosevelt area in that it, too, is within a finger of Lower Sonoran Desert that extends upstream into a transitional zone. In general terms, the project area can be considered as consisting of two distinct plant communities. At the north end of the survey area, where the survey contour intersects with the Verde River, the vegetation is typically riparian with cottonwood, sycamore, willow, tamarisk, cat tails, and some reeds dominating the picture. Interspersed with this community and on the slightly elevated areas within the flood-plain zone are several areas of mesquite bosque which consist almost entirely of mature mesquite with a ground cover of unidentified grasses.

Where the survey area coincides with the elevated benches around Horseshoe Reservoir, the vegetation is an almost homogeneous mixture of little leaf trees, scrubs, and cacti. Efforts at breaking this zone down into the more classically-defined desertscrub plant communities fail as the vegetative associations form a somewhat blurred mosaic in these areas. Communities can be differentiated locally on a very small scale, though these variations do not appear to be patterned in respect to topography. Subtle soil changes are suggested as accounting for this slight variation.

Plants in this zone include mesquite, catclaw acacia, white-thorn acacia, squawberry, hackberry, paloverdes, creosotebush, jojoba, gray-thorn, ocotillo, brittlebush, prickly-pear, cholla, sahuaro, and other small cacti. Scattered junipers were noted in one portion of Ister Flat at the northeast corner of the project area. This area, however, was generally dominated by an otherwise typical desertscrub plant association. A complete list of plant species recorded at Horseshoe Reservoir is presented in Table 2 with indication of those plants that may have been of economic importance to aboriginal populations.

Faunal Resources

Because of the same adverse factors that were noted in the Roosevelt faunal observations, this discussion of animal populations and distributions is also limited and biased.

Mammalian fauna observed during the archaeological survey included mule deer, coyote, wild burro, cattle, cottontail, jackrabbit, javelina, and white-tailed deer.

Avifauna observed included night hawk, owl, Gambel's quail, red-tailed hawk, bald eagle, buzzard, cactus wren, dove, heron, and crow.

Western diamond-backed rattlesnakes and various lizards made up the reptilian observations.

Climate

The climate for the Horseshoe Reservoir area is similar to the Roosevelt Lake area in that both are in a semi-arid zone characterized by hot summers and mild winters. Precipitation figures available from Horseshoe Dam represent the 23 year period between 1948 and 1970 (Sellers and Hill 1974: 266). This station is at an elevation of 2,020 feet. Because temperature data are not available from Horseshoe Dam, those data for Cave Creek are presented (Sellers and Hill 1974: 143). This later climatic station, which is at an elevation of 2,120 feet, is also in a valley and is some 25 miles to the southwest of Horseshoe Dam Reservoir. These data from Cave Creek represent only 12 years (1950-1961) and, therefore, should be considered somewhat insufficient.

During the years 1948-1970, Horseshoe Dam reported a mean annual precipitation of 14.18 inches. Almost half of this total falls during the months of July through October as a result of the annual "monsoon" system that brings in moist, heated air from the Gulf of Mexico. Generally, this moisture falls from afternoon thunderstorms that build up daily over the highlands to the north, east, and west of the lower Verde Valley. A secondary precipitation peak occurs between December and March as a result of frontal storms sweeping across California and Arizona from the Pacific Ocean.

Table 2

Plant Species Observed at Horseshoe Reservoir

Common Name	Scientific Name	Common Name	Scientific Name
Cottonwood*	Populis fremonti	Sahuaro*	Carnegiea gigantea
Tamarisk	Tamarix pentandra	Prickly-pear*	Opuntia Engelmannii
Sycamore	Plantanus wrightii	Christmas cholla*	Opuntia leptocaulis
Willow	Salix sp.	Buckhorn cholla*	Opuntia acanthocarpa
Cat tail	Typha sp.	Staghorn cholla*	Opuntia versicolor
Reeds	Phragmites communis	Chainfruit cholla*	Opuntia fulgida
		Teddy bear cholla	Opuntia bigelovii
Mesquite*	Prosopis juliflora	Hedgehog cactus	Echinocerus sp.
Catclaw*	Acacia greggii		
White-thorn*	Acacia constricta	Snakeweed	Gutierrezia sp.
Mimosa*	Mimosa sp.	Desertbroom	Baccharis sarothroides
Blue paloverde*	Cercidium microphyllum	Fairy duster	Callindra eriophylla
Yellow paloverde*	Cercidium floridum	Brittlebush	Encelia farinosa
Gray-thorn	Condalia sp.	No name	Lippia wrightii
Lyceum (squawberry)*	Lyceum berlandieri	No name	Janusia gracillis
Hackberry*	Celtis reticulata	No name	Aloysia wrightii
Juniper*	Juniperus sp.		
Mormon tea*	Ephedra trifurca		
Creosotebush	Larrea tridentata		
Jojoba*	Simmondsia chinensis		
Ocotillo*	Fouqueria splendens		

*plants of primary economic importance

The temperature data from Cave Creek indicate that the annual mean is 68.2° F., the annual mean high is 83.1° F., and the mean low is 53.4° F. In the summer, the temperatures range from around 70° F. to well over 100° F. in the afternoon. An extreme of 115° F. has been recorded. In the winter, the high temperatures are generally in the 60s and the lows in the mid-30's. A record low of 19° F. has been recorded. No data are available on the frost-free period at Horseshoe Lake or Cave Creek, although a 330-day growing season is the average recorded at Bartlett Dam on the lower Verde River (Sellers and Hill 1974: 92). This latter figure surely represents the moderating effects of Bartlett Lake's warm waters much in the same process as discussed for Roosevelt Lake.

A Comment on Historic Modification

This project, like the Orme Reservoir survey (Canouts 1975) emphasizes those relationships that can be seen between cultural data (the sites and artifacts) and their environmental surroundings. Through the study of interactions between such variables, it is hoped that an understanding can be developed concerning questions of how and why cultures adapt to their respective environments. It should be obvious that the methods discussed above can be most successful if a valid transformation can be made between what appears as today's environment and what can be assumed to have existed during earlier occupations of any such area. This transformation is difficult to make for the Roosevelt and Horseshoe areas. It is readily apparent that some historic disturbance to the environment has taken place at both areas, as both have hosted man-made reservoirs for at least several decades.

The lower Tonto Basin has been the scene of Theodore Roosevelt Lake and Theodore Roosevelt Dam since completion of construction in 1911. Information as to the appearance of the basin before inundation is virtually nonexistant. It is likely, however, that dam construction was not the first phase of historic disturbance in the area. When the Tonto Basin was first settled in the late 1870s, the basin was reputed to have grass as high as 4 feet.

Later in the 19th century, the Salt arm of the basin was utilized by Anglos for grazing and wheat farming (Bandelier 1892), while the Tonto arm was reported to be the home of farmers who grew vegetables and grazed some livestock (Bourke 1891). It is likely, therefore, that pristine conditions were long a thing of the past by 1911. Since 1911, Roosevelt Lake has had an apparent erosional effect around its perimeter due to wave action and water level fluctuation. Although erosion is easy to see and document, the effects of the lake on vegetation are harder to isolate, though they are probably significant. Today, a border of mesquite and other mesic-adapted plants form a buffer zone around the high water mark of the reservoir which stands out in stark contrast to the typical desert-scrub plant assemblages at levels above the artificially raised water table. The effect beyond this buffer zone has probably been less direct, although influences caused by the large quantity of humans and grazing animals that now frequent the area should be better understood. In any case, quantitative data concerning Roosevelt Lake's environmental disturbance are sadly lacking.

The amount of historic disturbance to Horseshoe Reservoir's natural environment is probably of a lesser magnitude and is not as obvious as that noted for the Roosevelt area. Horseshoe Dam was completed in 1947, thus producing the relatively small lake that backs up the Verde River for some five miles. Again, historic disturbance is suspected for the area long before the construction of the dam. Mindeleff (1896) reports that in the 1800s, during his travels, the Verde River Valley was already overgrazed and dissected because of it. He also notes that agricultural interests in the valley were robbing stone from the ruins in order to construct water control features. The presence of Horseshoe Reservoir has undoubtedly affected the vegetation around the high water mark as there is presently a strip of dense mesquite bordering the lake. Away from the lake, the vegetation appears to be relatively undisturbed. A factor contributing to this situation is that very few people utilize this area today.

In summary, we can assume that the present environments within the two project areas are not quantitatively representative of what was utilized by prior inhabitants. In many cases, qualitative discussions of environmental surroundings are probably acceptable for this particular stage of this study. However, strong correlations between sites and vegetative species should be avoided for the present time. Future survey and mitigative phases of this project may, however, attempt to solve such problems concerning this transformation between the present and past environmental conditions.

Chapter 3

HISTORY OF ANTHROPOLOGICAL RESEARCH
IN THE TONTO BASIN AND THE VERDE VALLEY

Three Generations of Archaeological Research

The amount of archaeological research that has been done in the Tonto Basin and the Verde Valley is meager compared to many other areas of the Southwest. Nevertheless, the history of this research can be divided into three intellectual generations. Archaeologists of each generation made different assumptions, deemed different problems significant, and considered different sets of variables important for understanding the prehistory of the area. These generations correspond roughly to continent-wide shifts of research emphases that have been recognized by others who have reviewed the history of American archaeology (for example, Moore 1973; Willey and Sabloff 1974). These generations overlap somewhat in time but provide a useful framework for reviewing the history of research in the Tonto Basin and Verde Valley.

The first generation of research dates from about 1880 to 1910. During these 30 years, a series of extensive surveys was completed. The second generation can be divided into two phases. The early phase, primarily in the 1930s, continued to emphasize survey work, but major excavation projects were completed in both the Tonto Basin and the Verde Valley. During the 1940s, virtually no archaeological research was conducted in either area. A second phase of the second generation of research began in about 1950 and continues to the present time. A few additional surveys have been made and numerous small excavation projects, stimulated for the most part by salvage requirements, have been completed. Both phases of the generation are linked by a common research goal which is the definition of the time depth and spatial variability of archaeological remains in order to construct regional cultural-historical sequences. However, some of the most recent research projects have operated only partially under the time-space paradigm of the second generation. They have also been guided in part by the research orientation of the third generation. This most recent generation, which is still in its infancy, is focusing on processual problems and, in particular, seeks to understand the dynamic relationships between prehistoric populations and their environments.

The First Generation: Early Extensive Surveys

Willey and Sabloff (1974) have identified the period from 1840 to 1914 in the history of American archaeology as a "classificatory-descriptive" period, but this label may be somewhat misleading. Schuyler (1971) has argued that any history of archaeology, such as that of Willey and Sabloff, which segments this history into an initial period of speculation, a middle period of description and classification, and finally a period of explanation is not very accurate. Moreover, this approach to history is biased to the extent that all previous research is judged by current standards. A more useful approach is that used by Moore (1973) who emphasizes the intellectual integrity of each period of research. He characterizes each period as a community of scholars that defined its own set of significant research problems and also its own set of standards for description, classification, and explanation.

In his analysis of the history of archaeology in America, Moore (1973) identified a period from 1860 to 1935 when archaeology was done by a community of scholars affiliated with the American Anthropological Association. Since anthropology was established as an academic discipline in the United States only in the 1880s and 1890s, the first members of this community were not professionally trained as anthropologists. However, their common interest consisted of a desire to develop a unified comprehensive approach to the study of mankind. Archaeology was only part of this approach and, as such, was expected to contribute to finding answers to general anthropological questions. The two main problems focused on by archaeologists during this time period were continental in scope. One problem was to determine man's antiquity in the Americas. The other involved comparing the variability of archaeological remains from the three major regions that had been identified. These regions were the eastern United States with its mounds, Mexico and Peru with their monumental stone structures, and the Southwest with its cliff dwellings and pueblos. The ultimate goal of defining the evolution of aboriginal technology, social institutions, and other customs was never achieved. This paradigm faded as it was gradually replaced by more regionally restricted questions.

Archaeologists who have reviewed the history of Southwestern archaeology have recognized that the nature of archaeological research changed significantly around 1880 (Taylor 1954; Brandes 1960; McGregor 1965; Martin and Plog 1973: 3-34). The subsequent period is often described as the one in which "scientific" archaeology began. Taylor (1954) also characterized the archaeology of this period as being an extension of ethnological research, and as mentioned above, Moore further (1973) argued that this was true of all archaeology in the Americas at this time. In the Southwest the relation between ethnology and archaeology was particularly close because many aboriginal sociocultural systems continued to function; thus, archaeology was commonly viewed as ethnology projected into the past (cf. Longacre 1970b). Taylor also described the archaeologists of this period as working with the assumption of a single prehistoric Pueblo culture and being unconcerned with temporal distinctions. The following generation of researchers reversed this view and instead sought to define variability in time and space. However, research done by the first generation of researchers in both the Tonto Basin and the Verde Valley indicates that they did recognize regional differences in architecture and artifacts within the Southwest and even posed questions concerming such dynamic processes as the establishment and abandonment of sites through time.

During the first generation of research, the Tonto Basin and Verde Valley area were visited by only three professional archaeologists. In addition, an active amateur, Edgar Mearns, who worked as an Army doctor at Camp Verde from 1884 to 1888, investigated the archaeology of the Verde Valley. This research of the professionals was done under the auspices of two institutions located in the eastern United States. The Archaeological Institute of America sponsored the survey of the Tonto Basin and the extreme lower section of the Verde Valley made by Adolf Bandelier. Surveys of the Verde Valley by Cosmos Mindeleff and Jesse W. Fewkes were sponsored by the U.S. Bureau of American Ethnology. Prior to the advent of this first generation of research, information about the ruins of the Southwest had been recorded only haphazardly by explorers and Army officers. Bandelier, Mindeleff, and Fewkes were among the first people to do archaeological research in the Southwest as a full-time occupation.

From 1880 to 1886 Bandelier undertook a vast survey of much of the Southwest. He visited most of New Mexico, central and southern Arizona, and northern Chihuahua and Sonora. As part of this project, he visited the Tonto Basin and the lower Verde Valley in 1883. His approach, like that of other researchers of this time period, was to visit some of the sites within any given area, then classify them according to their architecture, size, location, and the artifacts associated with them, and then compare them with other areas. In the Tonto Basin Bandelier (1892: 420-435; 1970: 112-127) recorded agricultural features such as irrigation ditches and gridded gardens. In the lower Verde Valley he discovered more canals and features he called artificial tanks (currently recognized as ball courts). He also visited cliff dwellings constructed of stone masonry (now within Tonto National Monument) and a type of site he called checker-board sites. These checkerboard sites were surrounded by cobble walls and contained rooms built of boulder masonry. He had found this type of site only in the Mimbres and middle and upper Gila River valleys to the south and east. He subdivided this type into sites with a central roomblock, and those with rooms scattered throughout the area enclosed within the compound wall. Bandelier considered the possibility that these various types of sites represented a developmental sequence but was unable to document any temporal differences. After examining the pottery at the various types of sites he concluded that they had all been occupied by one culture. He did report that a few sites on the lower Verde, in the vicinity of Fort McDowell, contained sherds quite different from the pueblo style of white and red with black decoration and that architecture was sometimes of adobe construction rather than stone. These sites were similar to sites found in the deserts to the south, so he hypothesized that the lower Verde Valley was a boundary between northern and southern tribal ranges. He supported this hypothesis by citing a legend of the Pima Indians who lived in the southern desert. The legend asserted that the Pimans had formerly waged war with another tribe located in the Verde Valley.

Mearns (1890) did excellent archaeological research as an amateur. He recorded the location of more than 100 sites, most of which were in the middle Verde Valley, and made limited excavations in a few sites including Montezuma Castle. He was the first to recognize that the ruins of the Verde Valley were "highly diverse in form, style, material, and location," but he nevertheless asserted they were the product of one race.

By the early 1890s when Cosmos Mindeleff (1896) surveyed the Verde Valley from its confluence with the Salt River north to Camp Verde, he and his brother Victor had been working for a decade in the Southwest for the Bureau of American Ethnology. He had made an extensive study of the pueblo architecture of the Colorado Plateau and had also visited sites in the southern deserts of Arizona. He recognized considerable differences between the ruins of the two areas and knew that some of this variability could be attributed to environmental differences, such as lack of building stone, but felt this was not an entirely adequate explanation (Mindeleff 1896: 187). Subsequently, he went to the Verde Valley with the explicit purpose of trying to document a transition zone between the northern and southern areas.

Besides various types of habitation sites, he recorded field houses, irrigation canals, gridded gardens like those Bandelier saw in the Tonto Basin, and reservoirs like those Bandelier described in the lower Verde Valley. Mindeleff hypothesized that these features might have been trashing floors. He remarked that in all his earlier surveys he had never encountered the type of habitation site which he called boulder-marked sites. These were evidently similar to those that Bandelier had referred to as checkerboard sites.

Despite the number and diversity of sites, Mindeleff concluded that the occupation of the valley had not necessarily been a long one. He explained much of the diversity in terms of functional and environmental differences. For example, he saw temporary field houses as contemporaneous with habitation sites and reasoned that masonry pueblos could be built only in areas where suitable building stone outcropped. He was also developing a theory, based on contemporary pueblo myths, which hypothesized that slowly migrating clans could generate a large number of sites in a relatively short time (Mindeleff 1900). Mindeleff also argued that the occupation had been late. Research on the Colorado Plateau had led to the definition of a developmental sequence for ceremonial rooms or kivas. They had originally been round but later had become square or rectangular, as in the modern Hopi and Zuni villages. None of the sites that Mindeleff visited in the Verde Valley contained any evidence of round kivas, so he inferred they were late.

Mindeleff had recognized one temporal trend which was that of increasing aggregation of population. He hypothesized that aggregation occurred in response to defensive needs. In its ultimate stage, this trend had, according to Mindeleff, resulted in only three large pueblos

being occupied in the section of the river he had surveyed. One of these
(now known as the Mercer Ruin—O:14:1 ASM) is located just north of where
Horseshoe Dam was later built. Mindeleff concluded that the ruins of the
Verde Valley were essentially of the puebloan type and the western boundary of the pueblo area would have to be sought elsewhere.

Fewkes made a brief survey of the upper middle Verde Valley in 1895
as part of his ethnological and archaeological study of the Hopi Indians
and their history. In his first report of this expedition he essentially
agreed with Mindeleff's interpretation of the prehistory of the Verde
Valley (Fewkes 1898). He published a second report more than a decade
later after having acquired more experience with the archaeology of
southern Arizona (Fewkes 1912). As a result he began to change his interpretation of the Verde Valley ruins. He still referred to the area as a
frontier of the puebloan area, but he concluded that the ruins of the
region also exhibited many similarities with areas to the south and west.
Therefore, the Verde Valley was also a frontier for the culture whose
homeland was in the Phoenix area. Fewkes continued to believe all the
ruins were relatively recent, but he had begun to recognize the probability
of more time depth and even considered the possibility of a pre-pueblo
culture that archaeologists were then speculating about.

The growing appreciation of regional and temporal differences sig-
naled the end of the first generation of research. With the development
of techniques to measure time depth more precisely, the time-space paradigm
was born.

The Second Generation: Space-time Surveys and Excavations

Willey and Sabloff (1974) have identified the period in the history
of American archaeology from 1914 to 1960 as the classificatory-historical
period. They divide the period into two parts. The first dates from 1914
to 1940 and is characterized by an emphasis on chronological concerns.
During the second part, in addition to chronology, a concern with context
and function also developed. This second phase seems to represent increasing dissatisfaction with the space-time paradigm and a search for a different framework to organize archaeological research.

Moore (1973) has identified the period from 1920 to 1965 as one in
which American archaeology was done by a community of scholars who budded
from the American Anthropological Association and founded the Society for
American Archaeology. As a result, their research became less oriented
towards general anthropological questions and instead was guided by a
paradigm based on the chronological method. In its most general form,
this method rests upon the two basic concepts of cultural area and cultural
period. The assumption is made that areas occupied by people possessing
the same culture will exhibit similar archaeological evidence, and that
through time the cultures of these regions will develop and change.
Evidence of these changes will be reflected in the archaeological remains.

Historical reviews of the local history of Southwestern archaeology after 1910 have tended to recognize smaller time periods, and each reviewer has stressed changes in research emphasis (Taylor 1954; McGregor 1965; Longacre 1970b; Martin and Plog 1973: 3-34). Since they all recognized an early interest in chronology followed by a general broadening of research interests, the definition of a two-part second generation of research from 1910 to the present seems to be a useful framework.

The development of the chronological method which influenced the way archaeology was done throughout the Americas took place to a large extent in the Southwest. N. C. Nelson (1914, 1916) initiated the practice of serrating sherd collections by means of stratigraphic excavation procedures. These techniques were applied by Kroeber (1916) and Spier (1917) to site survey projects near Zuni in western New Mexico and by Kidder (1924, 1931) to a major excavation project at Pecos Pueblo in eastern New Mexico. A third dating technique which is very precise but more limited in its range of applicability is dendrochronology. It was developed into a functional archaeological tool in the Southwest during the late 1920s by Douglass (1929). By the end of that decade a time-space framework known as the Pecos classification (Kidder 1924) had been outlined, and the research goal of most Southwestern archaeologists in the following decades was to "fill in the gaps" in local culture histories (Taylor 1954).

Another difference between the first and second generations of research was their institutional basis. As the second paradigm was being formed, local archaeological research institutions were formed. The University of Arizona established an archaeology department under the direction of Byron Cummings. In addition, privately funded research institutions played a major role during the second generation of research. Harold Colton organized the Museum of Northern Arizona at Flagstaff, Arizona, and Winifred and Harold Gladwin established the Gila Pueblo research institution at Globe, Arizona. Most of the research done in the Tonto Basin and the Verde Valley during this period was directed from these institutions.

During the first phase of this generation of research, the Gladwins organized a vast survey of the entire greater Southwest. The Tonto Basin and Verde Valley were surveyed as part of this project. Colton had initiated an intensive survey in the immediate vicinity of Flagstaff, but as the survey expanded, some sites were recorded in the Verde Valley by Museum of Northern Arizona archaeologists. Colton published his first synthesis of northern Arizona archaeology in 1939 (Colton 1939) and updated it in 1946 (Colton 1946).

Other minor surveys were carried out in the Verde Valley by graduate students in conjunction with their thesis research (Jackson 1933; Allen 1937). Some minor excavations were also made. King excavated a small cliff dwelling on Sycamore Creek (reported by Dixon 1956) and an aboriginal salt mine was investigated by Morris (1928). Cummings made limited test excavations at the Mercer Ruin (reported in Jackson 1933) and directed the excavation of the King Ruin on Chino Wash in the upper Verde Valley (reported in Spicer and Caywood 1936). Two major excavations were made in the middle Verde Valley in conjunction with the U.S. Civil Works Administration program. Caywood and Spicer (1935) excavated and stabilized a large pueblo which has been designated Tuzigoot National Monument, and the project also involved the excavation of a small pit house site and survey of sites in the surrounding area. Jackson and Van Valkenburgh (1954) directed the excavation of the cliff dwelling at Montezuma Castle National Monument (also cf. Kent 1954).

In the Tonto Basin, Haury (1932) excavated a Hohokam village while working for Gila Pueblo. Gila Pueblo also sponsored limited excavation at Rye Creek pueblo in the upper Tonto Basin, but a report of this excavation was never published (cf. Gladwin 1957: 310-317). Haury (1934) also tree-ring dated several cliff dwellings located in the Sierra Ancha Mountains about 15 miles northeast of the basin.

The methodology used by archaeological surveyors during this period was to visit as many sites as possible of all types, sizes, and conditions, and make a collection of sherds found on the surface of these sites. Other information about architecture and artifacts was recorded when available, but analytical emphasis was placed upon the sherd collections. The dating techniques that had been developed led to the definition of pottery types on the basis of manufacturing technique, vessel form, and particularly on color and style of decoration. These types proved to be useful in dating the sites on which they occurred. In addition, groups of similar pottery types were used to define archaeological cultures.

It was during this generation of research that the northern culture recognized by first generation archaeologists came to be known as Basket-maker-Pueblo or Anasazi. The southern culture was named the Red-on-buff or Hohokam culture. The Mogollon culture was also being defined in the mountains of east-central Arizona and western New Mexico. However, the archaeological sites of the Tonto Basin and the Verde Valley were recognized as not fitting neatly into any of these three major cultures. They seemed to represent mixtures of traits from all these areas. Because of this, the Gladwins designated the Tonto Basin as the homeland of a culture which they called Salado. Colton originally referred to the culture of the Verde Valley as the Los Reyes branch of the Mogollon, but later called it Southern Sinagua because of its affinities to another "mixed" culture was to be found in the headwater region of the Agua Fria and Verde rivers. They referred to it as the Prescott culture.

The construction of Roosevelt Dam began in 1906, and by the time the Gladwins surveyed the Tonto Basin many sites had been flooded. Nevertheless they located 180 sites and by detailed analysis of their pottery collections they were able to define three temporal periods where Bandelier had not been able to document them. They dated these periods from about A.D. 1100 to 1400. They explained the initiation of the changes in artifactual and architectural styles which defined each period as being due to a migration of

people into the basin. The homeland of the immigrants was hypothesized
on the basis of similarities of pottery styles. The Gladwins suggested
that the first migration which had led to the creation of the Salado culture had come from the upper Little Colorado and San Francisco river
valleys to the north and east. Because of similarities to pottery types
in the Hopi area to the north, the last two phases were hypothesized to
have resulted from migrations from this area.

In addition, the Gladwins noted that a Hohokam plainware, known as
Gila redware, was often mingled with the Salado types. This was interpreted as evidence for continuing influence from areas to the south.
Haury's excavation of the site known as Roosevelt 9:6 (1932) showed that
pure Hohokam sites were present in the basin during the Colonial Hohokam
period which was dated prior to A.D. 900.

The Gladwins' survey of the Verde Valley from its junction with the
Salt River north to the mouth of Sycamore Creek (near Clarkdale, Arizona)
resulted in the recording of 185 sites. They assigned each of these sites
to one of four prehistoric cultures or to the historic Apache occupation.
Each of the four prehistoric cultures was hypothesized to be the result
of an invasion or some other sort of influence from either the north, east,
south, or west. Because of a general scarcity of painted sherds, which
had become the real key to dating a site, they were unable to order these
cultures in a well-defined sequence.

A decade later when Colton (1939) summarized what had been learned
about the prehistory of the Verde Valley, he was able to state that the
valley had been occupied at least from A.D. 700 to 1400. The early end
of the sequence was poorly understood but two late foci or phases were
defined. The Honanki focus was dated from A.D. 1100 to 1300 and the Tuzigoot focus from A.D. 1300 to 1400. The excavations of Tuzigoot and Montezuma Castle provided much of the evidence for defining these periods.
Colton's scenario of the prehistory of the Verde Valley hypothesized that
at the early end of the sequence Hohokam people had lived as irrigating
farmers on the valley bottom next to the river. Separated by an unoccupied
zone, the Southern Sinagua had lived on the edge of the valley and had
practiced rainfall farming. During the 11th century the Hohokam were
occupying sites as far north as Flagstaff, but by A.D. 1100 the Sinagua
began invading the valley bottom and eventually drove the Hohokam out.
They themselves abandoned the valley three centuries later. By the time
Colton (1946) revised the prehistory of the Verde Valley, enough additional
information had been gathered to allow him to define four foci earlier than
the Honanki focus.

As World War II approached, and throughout its duration, the pace of
archaeolgoical research slackened. When research resumed, the general
time-space paradigm continued to provide the orientation for research in
the Tonto Basin and Verde Valley, but the character of research projects
did shift. The most common type of project during this second phase was
the small salvage excavation. In general the results of these projects

were used to modify and refine the phase definitions provided by earlier research, but some projects have also investigated problems involving settlement patterns and subsistence systems. Arguments about pottery classifications, phase definitions, dating of phases, and the nature of interregion influence represented by pottery types were common and remain as problems today.

During the second phase of research in the Tonto Basin one major excavation project was completed at Tonto National Monument (Steen and others 1962). Work actually began in 1940 but was interrupted by World War II. The excellent preservation at these cliff dwellings provided clues about traits of the late Salado culture that were seldom preserved in open sites.

In 1954 Olson and Olson (n.d.) recorded 55 sites during a survey of parts of the upper Tonto Basin and the East Verde River Valley. The survey was made for Paul S. Martin of the Chicago Field Museum of Natural History who was completing his research program in west central New Mexico. However, Martin decided not to move his archaeological program to the Tonto Basin. In 1967, the Museum of Northern Arizona surveyed other localities within the upper Tonto Basin and East Verde Valley in order to clear the right-of-way for expansion of the Tonto Forest Seismological Observatory. Forty-nine sites were discovered and recorded (Kelly 1969).

Several small salvage excavation projects have been completed in the northern Tonto Basin since 1960. In 1962 Olson (1971) excavated two sites with cobble-outlined rooms. Hammack (1969) excavated four similar sites in 1966. In 1971 Haas (1971) excavated the Ushklish Ruin, a colonial Hohokam site that also exhibited many Anasazi traits. As part of this same salvage project, Huckell (1973b) excavated a preceramic lithic work area that was assigned to the Chiricahua stage of the Cochise hunting and gathering culture that had been defined in southern Arizona and dated about 5000 to 1000 B.C.

Two other projects have been completed just west of the Tonto arm of Roosevelt Lake. One was a site survey made in 1973 along the proposed realignment of Arizona Highway 87 (Arizona State Museum n.d.). Seventeen sites were recorded, most of which were identified as either Hohokam or Salado. In 1974 Raab (1974) briefly tested the edge of a Salado pueblo site located on the shore of Roosevelt Lake in order to assess the impact that would result from the construction of a boat launching ramp nearby.

In the summer of 1975, Arizona State University established an archaeological field school in the upper Tonto Basin with plans for conducting research in the area for several years.

In addition, thesis and dissertation research (Young 1967; Pomeroy 1974) has dealt with the classification of Salado pottery types. Other projects including surveys (Brandes 1957; Windmiller 1971, 1973; Grady 1974) and excavations (Windmiller 1972a, 1974a, 1974b, 1974c; Doyel 1974b, n.d.; McGuire n.d.) were not located in the basin proper but in the Globe area just to the south. However, research in this area is relevant to Tonto Basin culture-history because of the indication that the sequence of occupation in the area was continuous from the era of Hohokam dominance to the later period of Saladoan dominance. The earlier research by Gila Pueblo had indicated there was a gap between A.D. 900 and 1100 during which the area was abandoned.

During the second phase of the second generation of research in the Verde Valley more surveys and several small excavation projects were completed. While stationed at Montezuma Castle National Monument from 1946 to 1950 as a National Park Service employee, Schroeder (1947, 1948, 1949, 1951, 1960) conducted intermittent surveys in the immediate area. In 1955 Peck (1956) located 28 sites in the valley of the East Verde River in conjunction with his thesis research at the University of Arizona. Recently the Arizona State Museum (Canouts 1975) intensively surveyed the area at the junction of the Salt and Verde rivers that would be affected by the proposed construction of Orme Reservoir.

Minor excavation projects began in 1949 when Shutler (1950) excavated the Dry Creek site, a preceramic lithic site similar to the Hardt Creek site excavated by Huckell (1973b) in the Tonto Basin. He also excavated pit house sites, sites with surface wattle-and-daub structures, a small masonry pueblo, and a cliff dwelling (Shutler 1951). In 1956 Wasley (1957) excavated a pit house near Camp Verde as a highway salvage project. In 1957 and 1958 the Museum of Northern Arizona made excavations at three Hohokam sites in the middle Verde Valley, and Breternitz (1958, 1960) incorporated these data into a revised synthesis of middle Verde Valley prehistory. In 1967 Kayser (1969) excavated Screwtail Cave as a highway salvage project. This site, which consisted of three small rockshelters and a work area, was located in the Mazatzal Mountains which separate the lower Verde Valley and the Tonto Basin. In 1967 and 1968 the Arizona Archaeological Society, an amateur society located in Phoenix, mapped a 100+ room site known as Brazaletes Pueblo and excavated one room (Valehrach 1967; Valehrach and Valehrach 1971). The site is located on St. Clair Mountain about four miles south of Horseshoe Dam. Shaffer (1972), in conjunction with his thesis research at Arizona State University, has excavated a six-room boulder pueblo located about two miles south of Horseshoe Dam.

In general, this second phase of the second generation of research has refined the initial culture histories of both the Tonto Basin and the Verde Valley that were developed by the first phase of researchers, but has also raised many problems of interpretation that remain unsolved. Although hypothesized migrations, invasions, or waves of diffusion are still being argued about, they are no longer so readily accepted as the only explanation of the variability in the archaeological evidence. A return to a broader, more general anthropological research orientation is characteristic of some of the latest archaeolgoical research in the Southwest.

The Third Generation: Processual Problems

Willey and Sabloff (1974) have labeled the current period in the
history of American archaeology the explanatory period. They date its
beginning at 1960. It is obvious that earlier generations of archaeologists have been concerned with explaining the archaeological evidence
they discovered, and therefore, Willey and Sabloff's label is somewhat
inappropriate. It is just as obvious that the standards of explanation
have changed. Willey and Sabloff characterize this last period as being
influenced by the re-emergence of cultural evolutionary theory from within
anthropology, as well as systems theory and ecological theory from outside
the discipline. Increased emphasis on quantitative methods and rigorous
hypothesis testing procedures have been adopted in order to achieve the
new standards of explanation. The diverse interests of this still developing paradigm seem to be united by a common agreement that the definition
of processes rather than static descriptons constitute explanation (cf.
Simon 1962). Instead of describing the state of past cultures at various
points in time in terms of trait lists, as the time-space generation did,
this new generation attempts to discover the recipes or formulas, that is,
the processes, which can account for the changing characteristics of prehistoric societies. In addition, the process paradigm focuses on generalizable relationships rather than idiosyncratic or unique events.

Just as the application of the second paradigm to research in the
Tonto Basin and the Verde Valley lagged behind its development in the
greater Southwest, so has the third. No research guided exclusively by
the process paradigm has been done in either the Tonto Basin or the Verde
Valley proper. However, some recent process-oriented research has been
done in the immediately adjacent areas and it has implications for understanding prehistoric society-environment relationships in both the Tonto
Basin and the Verde Valley.

One example of this research is Kelly's (1971) effort to account
for changes during the 12th and 13th centuries in the Northern Sinagua
area as responses to a deteriorating environment. He argued that intitial
adjustments included changes in settlement locations and an aggregation
of population. New techniques of water control and terracing were also
adopted, but Kelly suggested that a point of diminishing returns was
eventually reached and the final adaptive response was abandonment.

Another example of this new line of research is an on-going survey
and excavation project being directed by Gumerman in the Agua Fria River
drainage just to the west of the Verde Valley (Gumerman and Johnson 1971).
It is essentially an attempt to explain the variability of archaeological
remains in the area on the basis of an ecological analogy. Biologists
have defined the concept of an ecotone as a transition zone between two
or more diverse plant and animal communities (Odum 1971: 157-159). Ecotones are usually quite narrow but can have considerable linear extent.
They contain species from all major communities which they border and
usually additional species limited to the ecotones. Not only are a greater

number of species found in ecotones, but the density of these species is usually greater than in neighboring major communities. This increased variety and density is labeled the "edge effect." Gumerman's research is based on the hypothesis that environmental ecotones are also cultural ecotones or transition zones, and as such they may display characteristics analogous to the edge effect. He feels this may account for regional variation in subsistence patterns, population density, and settlement patterns including defensive site locations. Doyel (1972) had developed a cultural ecological model based upon the concept of the edge effect for explaining the prehistoric changes that occurred in the Tonto Basin.

History of Ethnological Research

Two basic sources of ethnological information are available about the Western Apache and Yavapai who were living in the Tonto Basin and Verde Valley during historic times. One is the journals of early European explorers in the area and the other is ethnographic studies that have been made by anthropologists during this century. The history of contact with native people in this area has been summarized by Schroeder (1963) in a document prepared for a claim presented to the Indian Claims Commission.

Two relevant ethnographic studies were made in the 1930s. Gifford (1932, 1936) briefly studied the Yavapai of the Verde Valley area and Goodwin (1942) made a much more extended study of the Western Apache. These ethnographies provide a picture of hunting, gathering, and raiding societies that depended relatively little upon farming in apparent contrast to the prehistoric societies who occupied the area during the preceding millenium. Although a few sites recorded by various surveyors have been identified as Yavapai or Apachean, the archaeology of the historic period in the Tonto Basin and Verde Valley has never been intensively pursued.

Chapter 4

CULTURE-HISTORY OF THE TONTO BASIN AND VERDE VALLEY

Parts of the Tonto Basin and the lower Verde Valley were combined
into one archaeological survey project because of current water management planning requirements. Nevertheless, this constitutes a coherent
program of research in terms of the prehistory of the region. The
culture-histories of the Tonto Basin and the lower Verde Valley have not
yet been well documented, but available information indicates that the
history of occupation was similar in both areas (Figure 4). During early
historic times the region was occupied by semi-nomadic groups who depended very little upon farming. During late prehistoric phases both areas
were occupied by peoples whose culture has been described as a mixture of,
or peripheral to, the major Anasazi, Mogollon, Hohokam, and possibly
Patayan cultures that have been defined in the Southwest (McGregor 1956;
Willey 1966) (Figure 5). At an earlier point in time both areas were the
scene of a more nearly pure Hohokam occupation. Evidence of the prehistory
of both regions prior to this time is meager but suggests that hunting
and gathering societies may have been using the area for several millenia.

Relatively little recent archaeological research has been done in
either area (Olson 1963). This, plus the fact that the archaeological
evidence does not fall neatly into one of the major cultures that have
been defined in the Southwest, has perpetuated a certain amount of classi-
ficatory controversy. Major revisions of our current understanding of the
culture-history of both areas, as reviewed in this chapter, are to be
expected. The sequence of occupation in the Tonto Basin that was defined
by the work of Gila Pueblo in the 1930s remains the basic culture-history
outline for the area (Haury 1932; Gladwin and Gladwin 1935). Breternitz's
(1960) summary of the culture-history of the middle Verde Valley is the
best model of the sequence of occupation in the lower Verde Valley. The
small amount of research done in the lower Verde Valley itself indicates
that its local culture-history may be somewhat different from that of the
middle Verde Valley.

The Prehistory of the Tonto Basin

Although a substantial amount of evidence indicates that hunting
and gathering societies occupied the Southwest by at least 10,000 B.C.
(McGregor 1965; Willey 1966; Martin and Plog 1973), the earliest evidence
of occupation in the Tonto Basin discovered to date is that from the Hardt
Creek site (Huckell 1973b). This small preceramic site, which is located
in the upper Tonto Basin, was identified as belonging to the Chiricahua

33

34

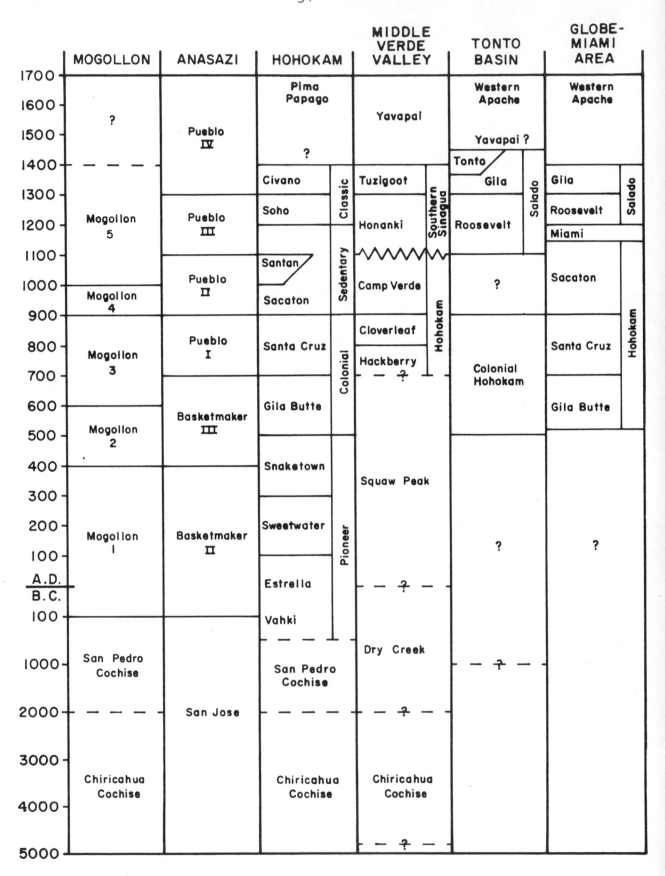

Figure 4. Prehistoric Cultural Sequences in the Southwest
(after Gladwin and Gladwin 1935; Breternitz 1960;
Doyel n.d.).

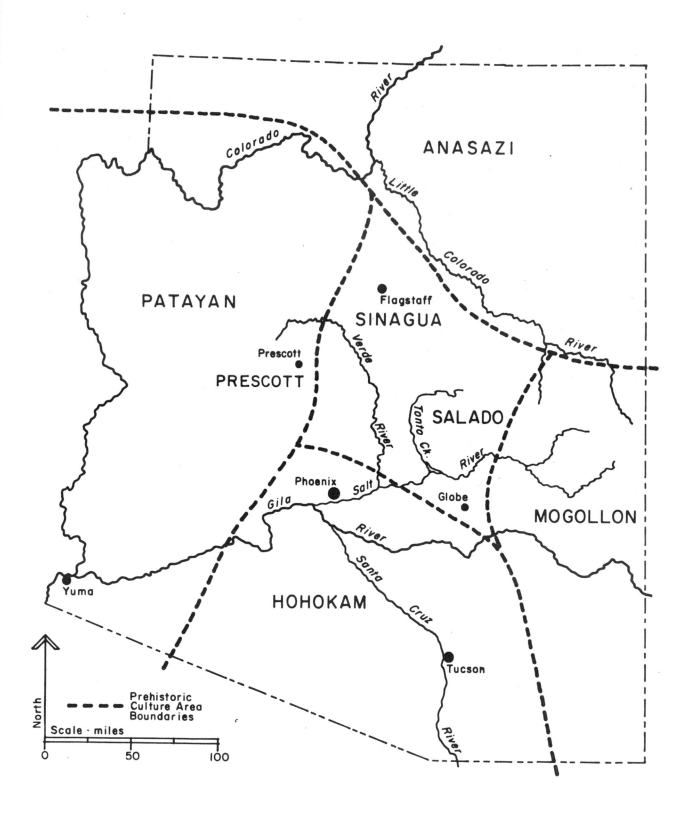

Figure 5. Extent of the Major Culture Areas in Arizona.

stage of the Cochise culture. The Cochise culture was originally defined in southeastern Arizona as a regional variant of the Desert culture tradition, which has been recognized throughout the western United States. The chronology of the Chiricahua stage is poorly documented, but Huckell suggests that the Hardt Creek site was occupied sometime between 5000 and 1000 B.C. The lithic debris at the Hardt Creek site indicates that the site was a processing station where only a few tasks, such as woodworking, hide processing, and tool manufacture and repair were performed. Huckell has located what he feels is probably a contemporaneous base camp a quarter of a mile to the south of the Hardt Creek site. It is possible that much of the archaeological evidence of this early time period has been deeply buried, but no systematic search for sites of this period has ever been made (Steen and others 1962: 4).

The next evidence of occupation is contemporary with what has been defined as the Colonial period of the Hohokam sequence in the Gila-Salt Basin. The Colonial period as now defined is composed of two phases (Haury 1945). The Gila Butte phase is generally dated from A.D. 500 to 700, and the Santa Cruz phase dates from A.D. 700 to 900. Two sites dating to the Colonial period have been excavated within the Tonto Basin. These sites provide the first evidence of the sedentary occupation of the basin.

Haury (1932) excavated Roosevelt 9:6, a site located in the lower basin on the south bank of the Salt River. He excavated 14 pit houses, one brush kitchen, one boulder-outlined room related to a later pueblo located nearby, two trash mounds, two cremation areas, and several outdoor firepits. Stratigraphic overlapping and trash fill indicated that not all the houses were absolutely contemporaneous, but on the basis of the types of houses and red-on-buff pottery, Haury assigned them all to the Colonial period. The Gila Butte and Santa Cruz phases had not been defined at the time of the excavation, but a few black-on-white trade sherds from the Anasazi area indicated the occupation at Roosevelt 9:6 was contemporaneous with Basketmaker III-Pubelo I.

Haas (1971) excavated the Ushklish Ruin, another Colonial period site, which is located about 30 miles to the northwest of Roosevelt 9:6 in the upper Tonto Basin. The preliminary analysis of this project indicated that it was occupied during the Santa Cruz phase. About a third of the site had been destroyed by road construction, but 12 pit houses, seven cremations, one burial, and 30 outdoor firepits were still complete or partially intact. The architecture and artifacts from this site were much less homogeneous than those from Roosevelt 9:6. This increased variability was attributed to Anasazi influence.

Haury hypothesized that the homogenity at Roosevelt 9:6 and other Colonial period sites was due to a colonization from a common center of origin in the Gila-Salt Basin. He argued that through time, as local adjustments and contacts with surrounding cultures were made, cultural traits would become more heterogeneous. If Roosevelt 9:6 is essentially a Gila Butte phase site, the evidence from the Ushklish Ruin would support his hypothesis. Walnut Creek Village, located about 30 miles northwest of Roosevelt 9:6, is another late Colonial period site that is characterized by artifactual and architectural heterogeneity that was attributed to interaction between Hohokam and Anasazi groups (Morris 1970). If Roosevelt 9:6 was not occupied earlier than the Usklish Ruin and Walnut Creek Village, the heterogeneity of these more northern sites may simply be attributed to the fact that they were closer to the Anasazi frontier.

A recent Arizona State Museum (n.d.) survey in the Tonto Basin has recorded other Hohokam sites, but the surface evidence did not provide enough information to assign them to a phase. It is generally assumed that the Hohokam who colonized the basin also built the irrigation canals that have been identified in the area. In addition to farming, the Hohokam must also have made some use of the abundant wild foods that grow in the area.

The next certain occupation of the basin has been assigned to the Salado occupation which is generally dated from A.D. 1100 to 1400. This would imply that the basin was abandoned for about 200 years between A.D. 900 and 1100. Whether this gap is real or simply due to the lack of archaeological research is still a matter of debate. One pit house at a site in the northern Tonto Basin has been dated to A.D. 900 to 1125, but it was identified as belonging to the Southwestern Sinagua culture rather than the Salado (Hammack 1969). Recent research in the Globe area just to the south of the Tonto Basin indicates that the gap may not be real. A survey made by Brandes (1957) southwest of Globe recorded some 90 Salado sites. Some of the pottery collected from the surface of these sites was identified as Sacaton Red-on-buff, which is characteristic of the Sedentary period as defined and dated to A.D. 900 to 1100 in the Gila-Salt Basin. Other surveys and excavations have recovered further evidence of some sites being occupied in the area between A.D. 900 to 1100 (Windmiller 1971, 1972a, 1973, 1974a, 1974b, 1974c; McGuire n.d.). Recently Doyel's (1974b, n.d.) excavation of eight sites along Miami Wash has yielded good evidence of a continuous sequence of cultural phases dating from approximately A.D. 500 to 1400. In particular, he defined a Sacaton phase as dating from A.D. 900 to 1150. During this period Hohokam groups apparently lived in small sites near major drainages. The period from A.D. 1150 to 1200 has been designated the Miami phase. It is characterized by small sites containing surface and possibly pit room architectural units groups within a compound wall. Determining whether a similar continuity of occupation occurred in the Tonto Basin itself remains a problem for future research.

The Saladoan occupation of the Tonto Basin was originally defined by the Gladwins (1935), who hypothesized a sequence of three phases based upon their survey data. They dated the first phase, which was called the Roosevelt phase to A.D. 1100 to 1250. Pomeroy (1974) and Doyel (n.d.) have argued that the pottery types that characterized this period, Roosevelt Black-on-white and Pinto Polychrome, actually do not date earlier than A.D. 1200. Doyel dates the Roosevelt phase in the Miami-Globe area to

A.D. 1200 to 1300. However recent research by Arizona State University in the Vosberg district, which is located about 35 miles northeast of the Tonto Basin, indicates that Pinto Polychrome, Gila Polychrome, Salado Red, and Salado White-on-red were being used in this area by A.D. 1100 (Chenhall 1972: 50). Because no Roosevelt phase sites have been excavated within the Tonto Basin, the chronology of this phase remains problematical.

During the Roosevelt phase, sites in the Tonto Basin were small. They typically had from 6 to 20 boulder-outlined rooms surrounded by a boulder wall that is usually referred to as a compound wall. The boulders that outline the walls evidently served as foundation stones for two types of walls. One type consisted of cobbles laid with adobe mortar. Where evidence of cobbles and mortar is absent it is inferred that walls of wattle and daub were built on or against the foundation stones. The compounds are usually square or rectangular and vary from 20 to 50 feet or 6 to 15 meters on a side. The rooms are located randomly within the compound and often against the compound wall. Other traits that characterize the Roosevelt phase include three-quarter grooved axes, trough metates, one-sided manos, well-made, notched and indented-base arrowpoints, copper bells, ornaments of turquoise, bone and shell that was both carved and inlaid, and both extended inhumation and cremation burial within the compound.

The settlement pattern of the Roosevelt phase is not well understood. It is known that some sites of the phase are superimposed on Colonial Hohokam sites. Most of the sites are located on the valley floor on high ground above the river. It is assumed the Saladoans used the irrigation canals constructed by the Hohokam. It has been suggested that because the Gladwins recorded only 180 Salado sites within the basin that population density was low, but the incomplete nature of the Gladwins' survey is probably a poor indication of population size.

The origin of the Salado culture has been a subject of considerable debate. Roosevelt phase painted pottery, above-ground masonry architecture, and burial by inhumation have been recognized as Western Pueblo traits. Therefore a migration from the east or north is usually inferred. The Gladwins (1935) suggested that the upper Little Colorado and San Francisco river valleys were the home of these migrants, while Steen (Steen and others 1962) suggested the upper Gila River Valley. Schroeder (1953) has hypothesized a radically different origin for the Salado culture. Because two distinct manufacturing techniques were used in making the utilitarian plainwares that occur in Salado sites, Schroeder hypothesized that the Salado culture resulted from a blend of two distinct cultural patterns. Because the Salado lacked round kivas and flexed inhumations, he argued that the migrants did not come from the Anasazi area. Instead, Schroeder suggested that the coil-and-scrape pottery manufacturing tradition was brought in by migrants from the upper Salt River Area. To explain the presence of the paddle-and-anvil pottery manufacturing tradition, he inferred that a group, characterized by a blend of Sinagua and Hohokam traits, had migrated into the Tonto area from the south and west. In a later publication, Schroeder (1960) discussed a different hypothesis. He argued that the Gladwins' definition of the Salado was incomplete and had recognized only part of a much more complex pattern. Schroeder's latest scenario suggests that during the Salado period the indigenous people of the Tonto Basin accepted Sinagua traits from the East Verde River Valley and northern Tonto Basin area and possibly from the Mogollon-derived pueblos to the east.

Doyel's (n.d.) recent work just south of the Tonto Basin indicates that compound architecture and extended inhumation occur earlier than the characteristic early Salado pottery types, Roosevelt Black-on-white and Pinto Polychrome. He suggests that these earlier traits diffused from some southerly region before a migration of people from the east or north entered the Salado area.

In a different view, DiPeso has suggested that the development of Salado culture was the result of the creation of a pan-Southwestern trade network that was based in such sites as Casas Grandes in northern Chihuahua (DiPeso 1968, 1974; Young 1967).

It is obvious that the definition of Salado culture, let alone an explanation of its origin and development, is the subject of continuing debate (Lindsay and Jennings 1968). The excavation of early Salado sites in the Tonto Basin may help to resolve these problems.

During the (middle) Gila phase, which according to the Gladwins, succeeded the Roosevelt phase around A.D. 1250 to 1300, black-on-white pottery was no longer made, and Pinto Polychrome was replaced by a type called Gila Polychrome. Gila Polychrome has a very wide distribution throughout the Southwest and was made locally in other areas outside the Tonto Basin. Gila phase sites are characterized by small, boulder-outlined, contiguous room blocks located in the center of compound walls. Steen (Steen and others 1962) suggests that contemporaneous with these compound sites are other types of sites located on the edges of the Tonto Basin. These include large masonry pueblos located on ridge tops and cliff dwellings built in rockshelters. Because the Saladoan settlement pattern within the basin has never been adequately documented, this remains an untested hypothesis. The Gladwins hypothesized that the changes of the Gila phase were due to a migration of people from the Hopi area to the north. This hypothesis, which was based upon similarities of pottery types in both areas, remains mere conjecture. Doyel (n.d.) prefers to see the apparent diversification of settlement locations as reflecting the development of more effective use of the wide range of available environmental resources.

The Gladwins defined a third phase that supposedly developed in the Tonto arm of the basin. Sites of this phase were identified by the presence of abundant Jeddito Black-on-yellow ceramics and the appearance of Tonto Polychrome. Pierson (Steen and others 1962) argued that the Tonto phase as described by the Gladwins differed so little from the Gila phase that they should be combined. He then attempted to redefine a new Tonto phase. He assigned cliff dwellings and hilltop pueblos that were surrounded by walls to this phase. In addition, he maintained that Gila phase sites on the valley floor were used seasonally while farming. Steen (Steen and others 1962), on the other hand, suggested that some of the hilltop sites were of historic Yavapai origin. It is also possible that the hilltop sites may be related to the "redware-mountaintop-pueblo" complex which has been recognized but poorly defined in the area between the lower Verde and lower Agua Fria river valleys (Chenhall 1967: 53). Doyel (n.d.) has concluded that Pierson's redefinition of the Tonto phase is based upon too little data and he prefers to drop the third phase entirely and extend the Gila phase to A.D. 1400 or 1450 when the area was abandoned by sedentary farmers.

Seven sites that date to the time of the Salado occupation have been excavated in the Tonto Basin. The only one of these in the lower basin was the cliff dwelling in Tonto National Monument (Steen and others 1962); these have been dated to the 1300s. Because of excellent preservation, the excavation yielded not only information about architecture and artifacts but also about the plants and animals used by the Saladoans. The six other sites, which all contain evidence of 10 or fewer cobble-outlined rooms, are located in the northern Tonto Basin. Five of these sites could be dated on the basis of painted pottery types to the 13th century. The dominant plainwares at two of these sites were identified as Tonto Brown and Tonto Red, types commonly found on Salado sites (Olson 1971). However, the dominant plainwares at the other sites were identified as Verde Brown and Verde Red, and therefore, the sites were assigned to the Honanki phase of the Southern Sinagua sequence that has been identified in the Verde Valley (Hammack 1969). Because of the ambiguities inherent in the definition of the plainware types involved, the cultural affiliation of the northern Tonto Basin remains problematical.

All of the sites excavated in the northern Tonto Basin can be interpreted as sites of short term or seasonal occupation by dispersed small family groups. Hammack's (1969) analysis indicates that the activities performed at these sites were related to food growing, gathering, and processing. Excavations by Windmiller (1974a, 1974b, 1974c), McGuire (n.d.), and Doyel (1974b, n.d.) have revealed a similar settlement pattern to the south of the Tonto Basin. How these small sites relate to larger, apparently contemporaneous, Saladoan pueblos is unclear (Grady 1974). Several large Saladoan pueblos have been excavated in the Globe area such as Gila Pueblo (Gladwin 1957: 322-326; Shiner 1961; Young 1972); Besh-ba-gowah (Vickery 1939); and Togetzoge (Schmidt 1926), but very little information about these excavations is available.

One final problem concerning the culture-history of the Tonto Basin is determining why the area was abandoned by sedentary farmers around A.D. 1400 or 1450. A number of causes have been hypothesized, including nomadic raiders, climatic change, and internal strife, but none has ever been confirmed as a completely satisfactory answer.

Understanding the prehistory of the Tonto Basin, and in particular
the enigmatic Salado culture, remains a challenging problem for future
archaeolgoical research. The only hope for achieving this understanding
rests upon more complete documentation of what is left of the archaeological record in the Tonto Basin.

Lower Verde Valley Prehistory

No cultural sequence for the lower Verde Valley has ever been defined, but a seven-phase culture-history for the middle Verde Valley has
been outlined by Breternitz (1960). Although differences between the
prehistory of the middle Verde and lower Verde valleys are to be expected,
Breternitz's sequence should approximate the sequence of prehistoric phases
in the lower valley. Determining the magnitude of the differences between
the two areas can be accomplished only by more research.

The middle Verde Valley sequence begins with the Dry Creek phase.
The chronology of this phase is poorly understood, but Breternitz suggests
it may date from around 2000 B.C. to A.D. 1. Several "pre-pottery" sites,
which were apparently occupied sometime during this phase, have been recorded by Museum of Northern Arizona surveys, but the Dry Creek site is
the only one that has been excavated (Shutler 1950). Core and flake tools,
grinding stones, and fire areas at this site indicated that it had been
used as a work area where a limited range of activities had been performed.
No habitation structures were found. Shutler suggested the lithic tools
were similar to assemblages from the Chiricahua stage of the Cochise culture, but Breternitz (1960) argued that they also resembled artifacts of
the Amargosa culture, a regional variant of the Desert culture that had
been defined in the Mohave Desert.

Evidence of the second period, which is named the Squaw Peak phase.
is also very limited. It has been dated from around A.D. 1 to 700. Only
two excavated structures have been assigned to this phase (Breternitz
1958, 1960). Both were buried by later occupations and were discovered
only by chance. No other Squaw Peak phase sites have been recorded.
Houses of this period were shallow, round, or rounded rectangular, jacal
wall pit houses with one center support post. They were entered through
a ramp entryway on the east side and had sub-floor, bell-shaped storage
pits. Flat or basin grinding stones, oval manos, and flake knives-scrapers
characterize the tool assemblage of this period. Breternitz concluded that
there was not yet enough evidence to determine the cultural affiliation
of this phase.

The introduction of pottery making marks the beginning of the
succeeding Hackberry phase. Breternitz dated this phase from A.D. 700 to
800 but suggested that further research may show that pottery may have
appeared in the area as early as A.D. 500. This early pottery is of a
type known as Verde Brown. Because Breternitz concludes that Verde Brown

is a locally made variety of Gila Plain, a type common in the Hohokam area, he argues that pottery making was introduced by the Hohokam.

Only two excavated sites have produced evidence of the Hackberry phase (Shutler 1951; Breternitz 1960), but other sites have been recorded. Only one site yielded evidence of architecture. This one structure was described as a slab-lined pit house. At the other site only the lowest level of a trash mound was assigned to this phase. Cross-dates are based upon intrusive Snaketown Red-on-gray and Gila Butte Red-on-buff from the Hohokam area and Lino Gray and Lino Black-on-gray from the Anasazi area. Breternitz hypothesizes that the Hohokam entered the Verde Valley during this period, probably by way of the Agua Fria drainage rather than the more rugged lower Verde Valley.

The following Cloverleaf phase is dated from A.D. 800 to 900. Evidence of this phase also comes from only two excavated sites (Breternitz 1958, 1960), although survey data indicate there were other established villages along the Verde River during this time period. House floor plans of this phase were rounded rectangles or irregular ovals with short ramp entrances to the north, south, or west. Some houses had two support posts; others may have had four. The floors of some houses were raised and supported by notched stones exactly as at Roosevelt 9:6 in the Tonto Basin. Especially large houses have been interpreted as communal structures, but this inference has been challenged (Morris 1970). Canal irrigation may have begun during this period. Ninety-nine percent of the plainware recovered from sites of this phase was Verde Brown. Diagnostic intrusive types include Kana-a Black-on-white and Santa Cruz Red-on-buff. Other intrusive types include Deadmans Black-on-red, Black Mesa Black-on-white (late in the phase), and Snaketown Red-on-gray and Gila Butte Red-on-buff (which are problematical since they should antedate Santa Cruz Red-on-buff). Trough metates and rectangular manos replaced older types of grinding tools. Other artifacts characteristic of this period include pestle-pounders, basalt hoes, saws, and knives, slate palettes, uncarved stone bowls, basalt cylinders, stone rings and pendants, and shell bracelets.

The overwhelming similarities to other excavated Hohokam sites in the Gila-Salt Basin have been used to infer a colonization of the Verde Valley by Hohokam people at this time. Other excavated sites along the Agua Fria River to the west, which date to the same time period or even slightly earlier (Weed and Ward 1970; Weed 1972; Huckell 1973a), have also been interpreted as evidence of the movement of Hohokam colonies out of the Gila-Salt Basin.

The Camp Verde phase is dated from A.D. 900 to 1100-1125. Excavations at seven different sites have yielded evidence of occupations dated to this phase (Caywood and Spicer 1935; Wasley 1957; Breternitz 1958, 1960; Pierson n.d.). Two house types are reported for this phase. One is the typical two-post Hohokam pit house and the other is a four-post pit house. Large houses, which have been interpreted as communal structures, have been

recorded as well as Casa Grande type ball courts. Evidence of both cremations and extended burial has been reported. Throughout this phase
Verde Brown continued to be the dominant plainware, although Tuzigoot
Brown, Brown Smudged, Red, and Red Smudged began to appear during the
11th century. Verde Red-on-buff, which has been described as a local
imitation of Sacaton Red-on-buff, was the only local decorated pottery
of this phase. Diagnostic intrusive types were Black Mesa Black-on-white,
Black Mesa/Sosi Black-on-white, Tusayan Black-on-red, Tusayan Corrugated,
and Sacaton Red-on-buff. Snaketown Red-on-buff and Gila Butte Red-on-buff
sherds have also been found in early Camp Verde phase contexts. These
types are thought to date to earlier phases and this association has not
been explained.

The Hackberry, Cloverleaf, and Camp Verde phases represent an era
of increasing dominance of Hohokam traits in the Verde Valley. During
the 11th century, Hohokam traits occurred even further north than the
Verde Valley in the Flagstaff area (McGregor 1941). The nature of the
inferred colonization of the area by the Hohokam is unknown. Schroeder
(1960) has proposed the term Hakataya as a name for the indigenous basal
culture of western and central Arizona that produced a plain brown pottery
made by a paddle-and-anvil technique. Because of a dichotomy of traits
often present in the sites of these phases, such as two types of pit
houses and the presence of both cremations and extended inhumations,
Schroeder suggests that when the Hohokam entered the Verde Valley, they
and the Hakataya lived side by side in the same villages. Breternitz
reported that the ceramics and lithic tools from both types of houses are
essentially the same. Why the Hohokam entered the area, how they inter-
acted with the local populations, and why Hohokam traits seem to have
disappeared at the end of the Camp Verde phase remain unanswered questions.
During the last two phases of the culture-history of the middle Verde
Valley, there is no evidence of the presence of Hohokam people in the
area. Instead, it has been inferred that people of the Sinagua culture,
which has been defined in the Flagstaff area by Colton (1946), migrated
into the Verde Valley.

The first period of occupation by the Southern Sinagua is known as
the Honanki phase, and it is dated from A.D. 1100 or 1125 to 1300. The
architecture of this phase is characterized by masonry pueblos in open
areas or in cliff shelters (Fewkes 1898, 1912; Colton 1939; Jackson and
Van Valkenburgh 1954; Kent 1954; Dixon 1956), but one pit house with
partial masonry walls has been assigned to this phase (Breternitz 1960).
The well-known cliff dwellings of Honanki, Palatki, and Hidden House are
assigned to this phase, as well as the early occupation of Tuzigoot and
Montezuma Castle. Local plainwares of this period are Tuzigoot Red and
Verde Brown. Intrusive decorated wares are Flagstaff Black-on-white,
Walnut Black-on-white, Citadel Polychrome, and Tusayan Black-on-red. It
is believed that the Southern Sinagua practiced rainfall farming along
the valley edges and took over the canal irrigation systems that were
originally built by the Hohokam along the river. Extended inhumation
was practiced during this period. What became of the indigenous people

who have been labeled the Hakataya remains undetermined. Schroeder (1960) has suggested that the continuing use of Verde Brown pottery indicates their continued presence.

There is some information available from a few Honanki phase sites located in the lower Verde Valley. Brazeletes pueblo is a 100+ room pueblo that has been mapped and briefly tested by the Arizona Archaeological Society, an amateur group based in Phoenix (Valehrach 1967; Valehrach and Valehrach 1971). It is located on a mountain top about four miles south of Horseshoe Reservoir. The dominant plainwares that were recovered from the one room that was excavated were identified as Verde Brown and Verde Red. Because of this, the site was identified as belonging to the Southern Sinagua branch, but it was also reported that many of the artifacts recovered were typically Hohokam. The occupation of this site has been dated by ceramics to the Honanki and succeeding Tuzigoot phase.

Another Honanki phase site, Az. U:2:29 (ASU), located two miles south of Horseshoe Dam, has been excavated (Shaffer 1972). It was a six-room boulder-outlined pueblo located within a compound wall. Its occupation was dated by ceramics to about A.D. 1150 to 1225. Shaffer interpreted the site as a farming and gathering site, and also suggested that the evidence from this site indicated that interaction with the Hohokam did not cease at the end of the Camp Verde phase. He further suggested that the Honanki phase, in the lower Verde Valley, may not be the result of migration or diffusion from the Northern Sinagua area but rather of indigenous development out of the preceding Camp Verde phase.

One other excavated site, Screwtail Cave, is located in the Mazatzal Mountains just to the east of Horseshoe Reservoir (Kayser 1969). The site consisted of three small rockshelters and a work area. It was interpreted as a seasonally occupied gathering site which was used during the 10th through 12th centuries. It was postulated that from A.D. 900 to 1100 cultural affiliation was with the Hohokam and that after A.D. 1100 it shifted to the Salado of the Tonto Basin.

The surveys of Mindeleff (1896) and the Gladwins (1930) do indicate one prominent difference between the middle and lower Verde Valley sequences. Boulder-marked compound sites are commonly found in the lower valley but apparently not in the middle section. Because of the similarities between these sites and compound sites in the Tonto Basin, the Gladwins hypothesized a Salado intrusion into the lower Verde Valley.

The sites recorded by the Arizona State Museum survey at the proposed Orme dam site in the extreme lower Verde Valley were identified as basically Hohokam or Hohokam-Salado (Canouts 1975). Arizona State University surveys have also indicated that by the beginning of the Tuzigoot phase, the lower Verde Valley was dominated by Salado and Classic Hohokam influence rather than Sinagua (reported in Shaffer 1972).

A problem related to determining the cultural affiliation of the late prehistoric phases of the lower valley is the interpretation of the Classic Hohokam phases. The changes that characterize the Classic Hohokam have been attributed to an intrusion of Salado (Haury 1945), but Schroeder (1953, 1960) has hypothesized that the Southern Sinagua invaded the area. Documenting the prehistory of the lower Verde Valley during the post-A.D. 1100 period may help to resolve this problem.

The final phase that has been defined in the middle Verde Valley is the Tuzigoot phase. It dates from A.D. 1300 to 1400 or 1425. Excavated sites dating from this phase include Montezuma Castle and Tuzigoot. All other known Tuzigoot phase sites are large pueblos located either in cliff shelters or in the open. In the lower Verde Valley one probable Tuzigoot phase site, other than Brazeletes pueblo, is the Mercer ruin, Az. 0:14:1 (ASM). This site, which is estimated to have more than 200 ground floor rooms, was first mapped by Mindeleff (1896). Cummings made cursory test excavations in the 1930s (reported in Jackson 1933).

In the middle Verde Valley indigenous pottery types include Verde Brown, Tuzigoot Red, Tuzigoot Black-on-red, and Tuzigoot White-on-red. Other types recovered from these sites include Jeddito Black-on-yellow, Winslow Polychrome, and Prescott Black-on-gray. Extended inhumation continued to be practiced. The Tuzigoot phase is interpreted as a continuation of the Southern Sinagua occupation. The archaeological record in the middle Verde Valley ends around A.D. 1425. Why the prehistoric sedentary farmers left the area remains an unanswered question.

Ethnohistory of the Tonto Basin and Verde Valley

Ethnohistoric evidence indicates that the Yavapai occupied the lower Verde Valley and shared the Tonto Basin with some Western Apache bands. The relationship of these groups to the prehistoric inhabitants is only partially known. As was indicated above, the prehistoric sedentary farmers evidently abandoned the area around A.D. 1400 or 1450. The first Spanish explorer entered what is now Arizona in 1539. Virtually nothing is known about the intervening years, and because the historic record is so incomplete, very little is known about the subsequent half century or more.

One fact that does seem to be well established is that the Western Apache were not living in east-central and southeastern Arizona when the first Spaniards entered the area. Between 1539 and 1542 Spanish explorers made a dozen trips between the Salt River Valley and Zuni pueblo and reported that the area was unoccupied (Schroeder 1963: (V-A) 1). There are some references in historic documents to Apache in the Hope-Zuni area in the mid 1600s, but the Western Apache evidently did not move into east-central and southeastern Arizona much before A.D. 1700 (Schroeder 1963: (V-A) 11-15). Soon after this they began raiding Piman and Spanish settlements to the south.

Spanish explorers first visited the Verde Valley in A.D. 1583, 1598, and 1604 and reported meeting Indians in the area who were apparently Yavapai (Schroeder 1952a, 1963: (V-A) 1-3). Whether these historic Yavapai were descendents of the prehistoric farmers of the Verde Valley remains undetermined, and therefore, it is not known if the valley was ever actually totally abandoned. If they were descendents of the prehistoric populations, they had radically altered their life style.

The historic Yavapai roamed through 20,000 square miles of western and central Arizona. Their population density is estimated to have been only about one person per 13 square miles (Gifford 1936). They were divided into three or four major subdivisions each of which was composed of a number of semi-nomadic bands that lived mostly by hunting and gathering and depended relatively little upon farming. The Yavapai moved seasonally from the deserts to the mountains in order to gather wild foods as they ripened. In addition, they raided the Pima, Maricopa, and European settlements to the south, and the Walapai and Havasupai, their linguistic relatives, to the north. The Yavapai may have used the Tonto Basin prior to the arrival of the Western Apache, and almost certainly occupied all of the lower Verde Valley. The ethnographic evidence does indicate that there was an unoccupied strip of territory between the Pimans in the Gila-Salt Basin and the Yavapai to the north.

Controversy surrounds the identification of the historic aboriginal inhabitants of the Tonto Basin. The Pinal band of the San Carlos Western Apache group occupied the southernmost part of the basin and did some farming along the south bank of the Salt River (Goodwin 1942: 4; Schroeder 1963: (V-B) 23). The remainder of the basin was occupied by a group that is usually referred to in the historic sources as the Tontos or Tonto Apache. There has been considerable debate about whether these groups were Western Apache or Yavapai (cf. Corbusier, W. H. 1886; Gifford 1932, 1936; Goodwin 1942; Schroeder 1963; Brugge 1965; Corbusier, W. T. 1969). It is clear that the subsistence strategies and general sociocultural characteristics of the Western Apache and the Yavapai were very similar except for the fact they they spoke very different languages, and by the mid-1800s the two groups had intermarried extensively. This is probably one reason for the confusion about the identification of these groups.

The semi-nomadic lifeway of the Apache and Yavapai came to an end in the 1870s when all but a few resisters were forced onto reservations. The ethnographic information about the historic Western Apache and Yavapai occupation of the region may seem to be more complete than any archaeological evidence will ever be, and for some aspects of sociocultural systems, this is undoubtedly true. However, it must be remembered that the available ethnographic evidence is also often biased and limited. The major ethnographic studies of the Western Apache (Goodwin 1942, 1971; Buskirk 1949; Kaut 1957; Basso 1970) and the Yavapai (Gifford 1932, 1936) were all made more than 50 years after these Indians were forced onto reservations. These studies are often based on rememberances rather than observed behavior.

Archival research may reveal new historic information about the
ethnohistory of the area, but a largely undeveloped line of research is
historical archaeology. Very little work has been done with Yavapai or
Apache archaeology (cf. Olson 1955; Gerald 1958; Tuohy 1960; Longacre
and Ayres 1968; Wilcox n.d.), perhaps because the archaeological study of
nomadic societies is a difficult endeavor. Nomads usually accumulate
relatively little material cultre, and the materials they do manufacture
and use are discarded over a vast territory. The Yavapai and Apache often
lived in caves, or built domed wickiups that disintegrated rapidly. With
ruined masonry pueblos in the area to attract the attention of archaeologists, it would be easy to fail to observe the archaeological remains of
these groups. A better understanding of the nature of occupation in the
Tonto Basin and lower Verde Valley from A.D. 1450 to 1850 may depend upon
the development of methods and techniques which will allow archaeologists
to perceive, date, and analyze the archaeological deposits created by
nomadic societies.

Anglo Use of the Tonto Basin and Verde Valley

The Spanish conquest of the southwest began in the 1530s. In 1821
Mexico won her independence from Spain and took over control of the region,
but lost much of this territory in 1848 when the United States won the
Mexican-American war. Despite more than 300 years of European presence
in the Southwest, the Tonto Basin and Verde Valley remained unoccupied
by Anglos at the time of the American take-over. This situation changed
rapidly in the next 25 years. During the 1860s, three army posts were
established in the area including Fort McDowell in the lower Verde Valley,
Camp Verde in the middle Verde Valley, and Camp Reno in the eastern foothills of the Mazatzal Mountains (Schroeder 1963: (V-E)). From these posts
the army sent out campaigns to subdue the native Yavapai and Apache bands
that lived in the area. By 1875 the Yavapai and Apache had been forced
onto reservations (Spicer 1962: 251, 257).

Farming and ranching by Anglos in the Tonto Basin began in the late
1870s. Bandelier (1970: 110) reported seeing large ranches and wheat
farms along the Salt arm of the basin in 1883. Smaller ranches and vegetable and fruit farms were located along the Tonto arm (Bourke 1891: 145).
The construction of Roosevelt Dam began in 1906, and the lake it created
flooded much of the farmland within the basin.

Trapping was the earliest Anglo activity in the Verde Valley. This
was followed by mining which began in the 1860s (Mearns 1890: 6; Mindeleff
1896: 185). In the 1870s and 1880s after the Yavapai were relegated to a
reservation, Anglos moved into the region to farm, ranch, and cut lumber
(Mearns 1890: 6; Gladwin and Gladwin 1930: 165-167). Because the lower
Verde Valley lacks a broad floodplain and is subject to frequent flooding,
farming was always limited. Grazing cattle and sheep were the major economic activities pursued by Anglos. Although the number of people living

in the area was never large, Mindeleff (1896: 191) noted that by around 1890 the lower and middle Verde Valleys were already badly overgrazed.

Both the lower Verde Valley and Tonto Basin were included in the Tonto National Forest when it was established in 1905 (U.S. Department of Agriculture, Forest Service 1957). Since then the use of the area for recreational activities has been steadily increasing.

One result of the increasing Anglo use of the area has been the destruction of many of the archaeological resources of the area. Early settlers often robbed ruins for stone, built on ruins, reused prehistoric canals, and collected prehistoric artifacts for private collections (Mearns 1890; Bandelier 1970: 111-117). The first Anglo settlers also provided a market for prehistoric pottery, and the Yavapai and Apache dug in many ruins to collect vessels and exchange them for groceries (Schroeder 1960: 13). Evidence of pothunting has been reported by almost every archaeologist who has worked in the area. Increased recreational use of the area has led to more extensive pothunting. Because pothunters have recently begun using large earth-moving machines, the rate of the destruction of archaeological resources appears to be increasing rapidly.

Summary

The sequence of human occupation of the Tonto Basin and Verde Valley is only partially documented, but the information that is available does indicate that both areas experienced similar prehistoric, ethnohistoric, and historic occupations. Some evidence indicates both areas were used by hunters and gatherers as early as 5000 B.C. Sometime between A.D. 500 and 900 both areas were apparently colonized by Hohokam peoples from the Gila-Salt Basin. However, very little is known about the indigenous inhabitants of the area prior to this time. In the Verde Valley, Hohokam traits also characterize the period between A.D. 900 and 1100. Evidence from this time period is lacking in the Tonto Basin, but evidence from surrounding areas indicates the continued presence of Hohokam peoples in the area. Sometime around A.D. 1100, Hohokam traits disappeared and "mixed" cultures characterize both areas--the Southern Sinagua in the Verde Valley and the Salado in the Tonto Basin. Both of these cultures are poorly understood. The prehistoric sequence ends around A.D. 1400 or 1450 when these sedentary farmers abandoned the area.

Ethnohistoric evidence indicates the region was then occupied by Western Apache and Yavapai bands. Although these groups did some farming, they were heavily dependent upon hunting, gathering, and raiding, and thus their way of life contrasts sharply with the late prehistoric adaptation. Both groups were eventually forced onto reservations by the United States government in the 1870s.

Anglo use of the area continues to be mostly ranching, farming, and mining activities; however, the area has been increasingly used for recreation in recent years.

Chapter 5

THE SURVEY

As part of an effort to lend credibility to our survey predictions, as well as to fulfill contract stipulations, this chapter details the operational steps and rationale that formed the design of the sample survey. In addition to reviewing the central theories of survey sampling, the first section of this chapter describes how decisions were made in regard to our choice of sampling technique, sampling scheme, sampling fraction, and finally, the delineation of sampling units. The second section of the chapter discusses the implementation of the survey including site definitions, surface collections, site forms, survey techniques, recording procedures, and field logistical data. The final section of the chapter presents raw site survey data as well as a discussion of the categorical framework in which the sites were placed.

The Sample Design

The goal of this project was to evaluate the archaeological resources within those areas at Roosevelt Lake and Horseshoe Reservoir that would be flooded if the high water levels were raised. The contract stipulated that this analysis was to be made on the basis of an intensive survey of 20 percent of both direct impact zones. Therefore the project provided an opportunity to investigate some of the unsolved methodological problems of archaeological survey sampling. If further stages of this project should lead to a total survey of the area, it will provide an excellent opportunity to empirically test the adequacy of our sampling procedures.

By tradition, archaeological surveyors have been non-probabilistic "probers" or "purposive selectors" (cf. Cowgill 1975). Only in the past decade and a half have archaeologists begun to recognize that the intuitive grab or judgment sampling techniques of these strategies are, in many cases, neither the most appropriate nor the most efficient (Redman 1974: 5). They have come to realize that probabilistic samples are good methods of obtaining samples that reflect, within ascertainable limits, characteristics of entire populations. Probability samples are those samples in which every element in the population has been assigned, by means of some mechanical operation of randomization, a calculable, non-zero probability of being selected (Kish 1965: 20). Many types of probability sampling designs have been developed (cf. Hansen and others 1953; Cochran 1963; Kish 1965), and archaeologists have recently begun to test the efficacy of different designs for various problems and contexts (Mueller 1974, 1975b; Plog n.d.). The pattern that seems to be emerging is that for each situation some designs work better than others, but as yet, no reliable generalizations have been formulated that relate design efficacy to the nature of the population under study, its environmental setting, and the problems being investigated. Our goal was to devise a sample that would allow us to estimate with reasonable accuracy the quantity, nature, and significance of the archaeological resources within the direct impact zones of both reservoirs. In addition, our results are data that can be used in achieving the broader goal of defining generalizations about the efficacy of archaeological sample designs.

The results of a well-executed probabilistic sample should yield a great deal of information about the population under study, but in order to execute a probabilistic sample one must already have prior knowledge of many characteristics of that population. This apparent paradox results from having to make decisions during the planning of a probabilistic sample design about (1) sampling technique, (2) sampling scheme, (3) sampling fraction, and (4) sampling units (Mueller 1974: 28-30, 1975a: 37-38).

With regard to sampling technique, two choices are available--element or cluster sampling. Element sampling requires that the frame (that is, the list of items to be sampled) consists of all individual elements that are the subject of investigation. Since in most archaeological surveys the element of interest is the site, this would mean that a list of all sites in the population under study would have to be available. If such a list did exist there would be no need for the survey, unless, of course, more information was needed about those sites. As some of the archaeologists who first argued for the use of probabilistic sampling in archaeological research realized, archaeological surveyors are often forced to use a cluster sampling technique (Vescelius 1960; Rootenberg 1964). Several recent archaeological studies have emphasized the fact that the formulas that have been developed for use with element sampling techniques to estimate population parameters and the precision of those estimates (the variance and the standard error) must be modified for cluster sampling (Mueller 1974: 62-63, 1975a; Judge and others 1975: 86-88; Matson and Lipe 1975: 128-134; Read 1975: 54-58; Thomas 1975: 77-81). As a result, the cluster technique is associated with more complicated and more limited statistical analysis. Furthermore, if the data being studied are distributed in a clustered manner, which is usually true of archaeological data, less precise estimates of population parameters result (Kish 1965: 149-150; Blalock 1972: 527).

Our survey goals revolved around the location and description of sites, but we were able to define our sampling problem as one of determining site density and number of man-days required for data recovery per unit area. This meant that areal units rather than sites per se could be considered to be our sampling elements. Since a complete list of areal units could be listed we were able to use an element sampling technique rather than a more complex cluster technique (cf. Thomas 1975).

The choice of sampling schemes that can be combined with the element sampling technique includes simple random, systematic, and stratified schemes. These schemes are different procedures for determining which elements of the sample frame will be incorporated into the sample. A simple random scheme involves selecting the sample elements by some random process and is commonly done with a table of random numbers. With the systematic scheme the first element between one and n is selected by some random process and then every n^{th} element is selected, where n is the reciprocal of the sampling fraction. For example, in this case our sampling fraction is one-fifth or 20 percent. We would randomly choose a number between one and five and then choose every additional fifth element in the population. The stratified scheme involves dividing the elements of the sampling frame into two or more groups and then drawing an independent random or systematic sample from each group or stratum. Each stratum can be sampled equally, in which case the sample is called a proportionate stratified sample, or unequally, in which case it is known as a disproportionate stratified sample.

In designing the 20 percent sample for this project a disproportionate stratified random sample was selected. We intended to sample an approximately proportionate number of acres in each stratum, but because the areal units, which were the elements in the sampling frame, were of unequal size, the number of elements sampled per stratum was disproportionate. Compared to the simple random selection of elements, both systematic and stratified schemes insure a more uniform coverage of the frame, but stratification avoids theoretical problems involved in calculating the variance for systematic samples as well as problems created by unrecognized trends or periodicity that may be present in the population. There are reasons for suspecting that such patterns may often occur in archaeological survey data (cf. Judge and others 1975: 87; Matson and Lipe 1975: 131). In addition Plog's (n.d.) analysis of archaeological sampling strategies indicated that the precision of systematically selected archeological survey samples was unpredictably erratic. Stratification also allows the incorporation of prior knowledge about relevant variables, and when this results in dividing the population into groups that are relatively more homogeneous, greater precision of estimated population parameters follows.

On the basis of previous archaeological research in the general region and the results of a brief helicopter reconnaissance of both reservoir areas, it was decided that the units could be classified into microenvironmental categories that were probably differentially used in prehistoric times. These categories included (1) floodplains and lower river terraces, (2) gently sloping pediment-terraces (that is, less than 10 percent slope), and (3) steeply sloping zones (that is, greater than 10 percent slope). It was reasoned that the floodplain and lower river terraces would most likely be the areas where evidence of canals and Hohokam sites would be found. Gently sloping pediment-terraces would be a logical place for other habitation sites and evidence of water control techniques for rainfall farming. If any sites at all were located on steeply sloping areas, it was hypothesized that they would be sites of temporary seasonal food gathering and processing stations. Floodplains and lower river terraces were exposed only at the ends of each of the reservoirs. Since Roosevelt Lake has two arms, two floodplain and lower river terrace strata were defined--one on the Tonto Creek arm and one on the Salt River arm. Each of the sample units at each reservoir was then assigned to one of the defined micro-environmental strata. Our goal was to produce more internally homogeneous strata in terms of site occurrence which would, in turn, result in lower variance of population parameter estimates. Even if this did not prove to be true, it insured a more uniform sample of the survey areas than a simple random sample would.

The third choice to be made was that of the sampling fraction--the proportion of elements or clusters to be selected. Empirical results of archaeological surveys are inconclusive at this time but tend to indicate that an adequate sampling fraction may vary from 1 percent to 50 percent or even more depending upon the nature of the research situation and research problems (Mueller 1974: 30; Read 1975: 51). A sampling fraction of 20 percent was stipulated by the contract. The U.S. Forest Service, which administers the land upon which both Roosevelt Lake and Horseshoe Reservoir are located and is responsible for the archaeological resources, accepted this as a minimally adequate level of sampling at this stage of the project.

The selection of the size and shape of sample units was the last choice that had to be made. Empirical results of archaeological surveys are also inconclusive on this point but indicate that the usefulness of circles, quadrats, or transects varies with the goals and situations of surveys (Mueller 1974: 30; Redman 1974; Judge and others 1975; Matson and Lipe 1975; Plog n.d.). Virtually all archaeological probabilistic sample surveys to date have used these arbitrarily defined spatial units. Faced with the task of having to sample narrow, irregular strips surrounding two existing reservoirs, it was immediately apparent that it would be very difficult to impose any form of arbitrary grid of quadrats or transects over the area to be surveyed. In addition, simply locating any system of arbitrary units "on the ground" would be a time consuming process. A reasonable estimate for the amount of time required to locate and plot one unit might range from one-half to one man-day. At this rate our productive survey field time would be reduced by 13 to 25 percent. Because the Horseshoe area has never had section boundaries surveyed, the loss of productive field time would probably have been near 25 percent and perhaps even more. In light of these considerations we opted to try to define some type of natural units that could be recognized easily in the field.

Deciding upon the size of sample units for any particular sample design involves a compromise among considerations of statistical theory, the nature of the distribution of the data being sampled, and the economics of sampling procedures (Redman 1974: 19-20). Statistical considerations indicate that a larger number of smaller units lead to more accurate and precise results, but economic considerations tend to indicate that a smaller number of larger units would be less expensive to survey. The distribution of the data must also be considered because each sample unit should be large enough to produce enough information for analysis.

In regional survey projects such as this one, archaeologists have recommended the use of sample units that range in size from about 25 to 160 acres (Mueller 1975a). A typical size is a 500 m^2 quadrat (62 acres).

The natural sampling units that we decided upon were defined by intermittent tributary streams that were plotted on 7½ minute USGS quadrangle sheets. These cut the circular ring of the survey area surrounding the existing reservoir into 122 sample units at Roosevelt Lake (Figures 6-10*) and 54 sample units at Horseshoe Reservoir (Figures 11-13*). The high water line that formed the lower boundary of these units was clearly marked and the upper edge, which was the only arbitrary boundary, was extrapolated in the field from the quadrangle sheets with little difficulty. Acreage within each sample unit was estimated with a compensating polar planimeter. Two "runs" were made with the planimeter by each of two independent observers and the results averaged. The resulting estimates of the acreage of each primary sample unit probably averaged less than 5 percent error.

At Roosevelt Lake, the 12.7 square miles (32.9 km^2) that lie within the direct impact zone were divided into four strata as described above. Then using a table of random numbers (Arkin and Colton 1963), sample units were randomly selected from each stratum until at least 20 percent of the acreage of each stratum had been selected to be surveyed. See Table 3 for the sampling frame and randomly drawn sample. Each stratum contained from 15 to 48 sample units which averaged 67 acres (27.1 hectares) in size. Of the total 122 sample units, 24 were randomly selected as the units to be surveyed. They included 1,801 acres (729 hectares); this constituted a 22 percent sample of the area that would be flooded by the proposed 30 foot vertical increase in the high water level.

At Horseshoe Reservoir, 7.8 square miles (20.2 km^2) lie within the direct impact zone. Using the same procedure for defining naturally delimited sample units, 54 such units averaging 93 acres (37.7 hectares) in size were defined. These were grouped into three environmentally defined strata as discussed above. Each stratum contained 14 to 25 sample units of which three to six were selected as the units to be sampled by using a table of random numbers. Only in one case was a slight departure made from the resulting sample. Sample Unit 14 in Stratum 3 contained 18 acres, and was selected but never surveyed due to a lack of field time and access. Nevertheless, 171 acres or 25 percent of the stratum was surveyed in the remaining three sample untis, and therefore the stratum should be represented adequately. The total of 12 sample units randomly drawn covers 1,108 acres (449 hectares); this constitutes a 22 percent sample of the area around Horseshoe Reservoir that would be flooded by the proposed 140 foot vertical increase of the high water level. See Table 4 for the sampling frame and the selected sample.

*Figures 6 through 13 (pages 55 to 62) are deleted from most copies of this report in order to protect the resources from unauthorized disturbances.

Figures 6 to 13, the site location maps
that appear on pages 55 to 62, are deleted
from most copies of this report.

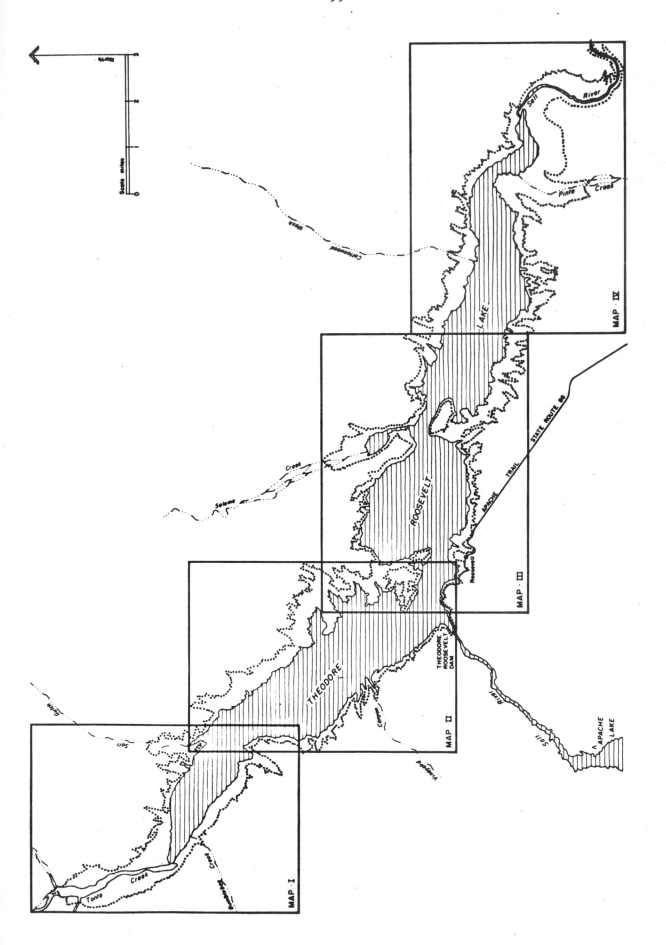

Figure 6. Roosevelt Lake: Map Key

56

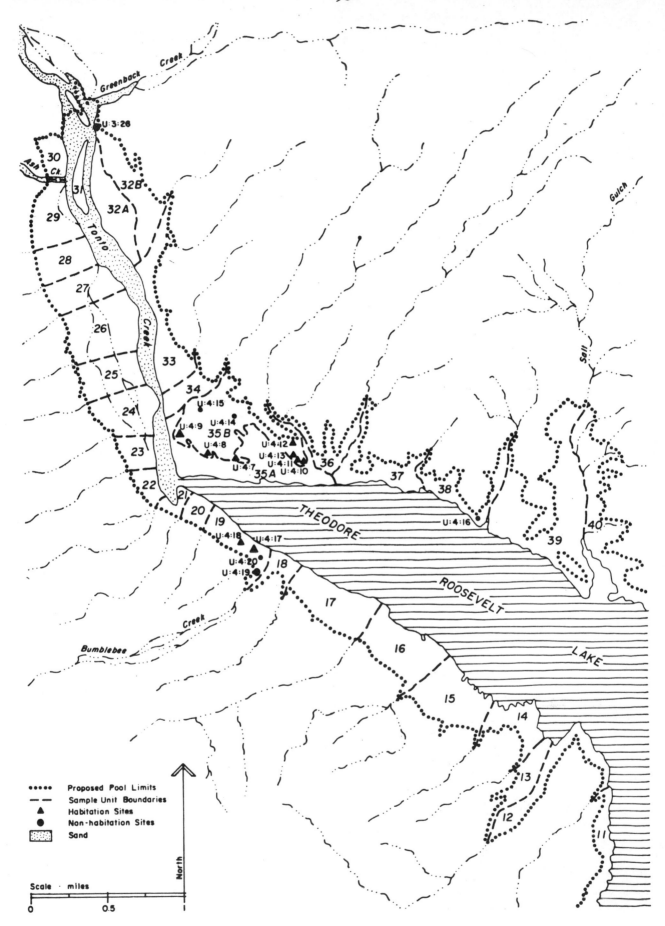

Figure 7. Roosevelt Lake Sites and Sample Units: Map I

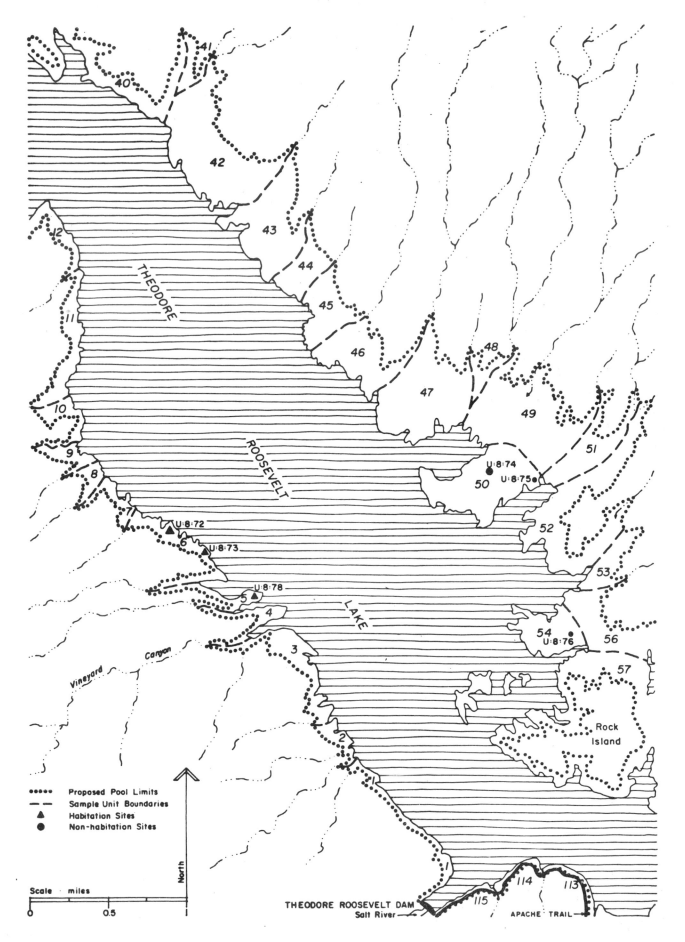

Figure 8.   Roosevelt Lake Sites and Sample Units: Map II

ROOSEVELT LAKE

THEODORE ROOSEVELT

Windy Hill

Salome Creek

Rock Island

APACHE TRAIL

North

Scale · miles

0   0.5   1

••••• Proposed Pool Limits
‒ ‒ ‒ Sample Unit Boundaries
●   Non-habitation Sites

50 U:8:74
52
53
54 U:8:76
56
57
58
59
60
61
62 U:8:75
64
65
66
67
68
69
70
93
94
95
96
96 U:8:71
97
98
99
100
101 U:8:70
102
103
104
105
106
107
108
109
110
111
112
113
114

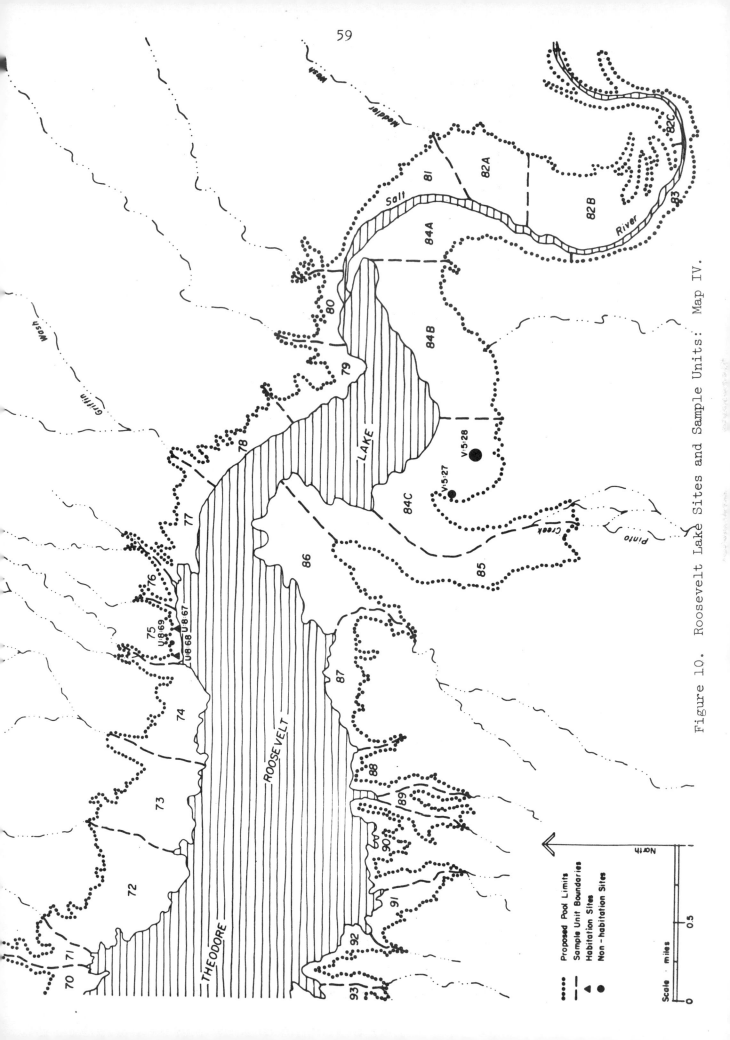

Figure 10. Roosevelt Lake Sites and Sample Units: Map IV.

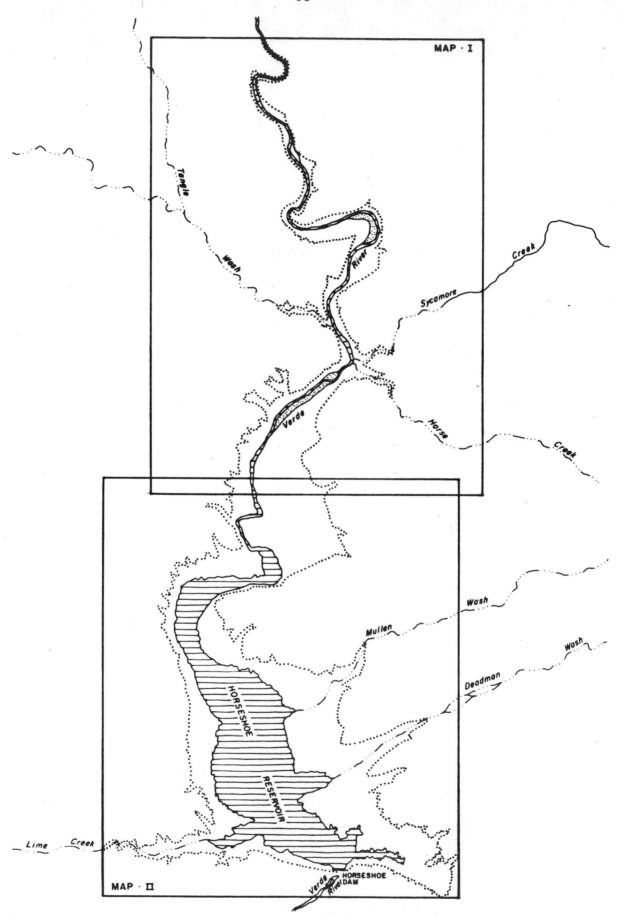

Figure 11. Horseshoe Reservoir Map Key

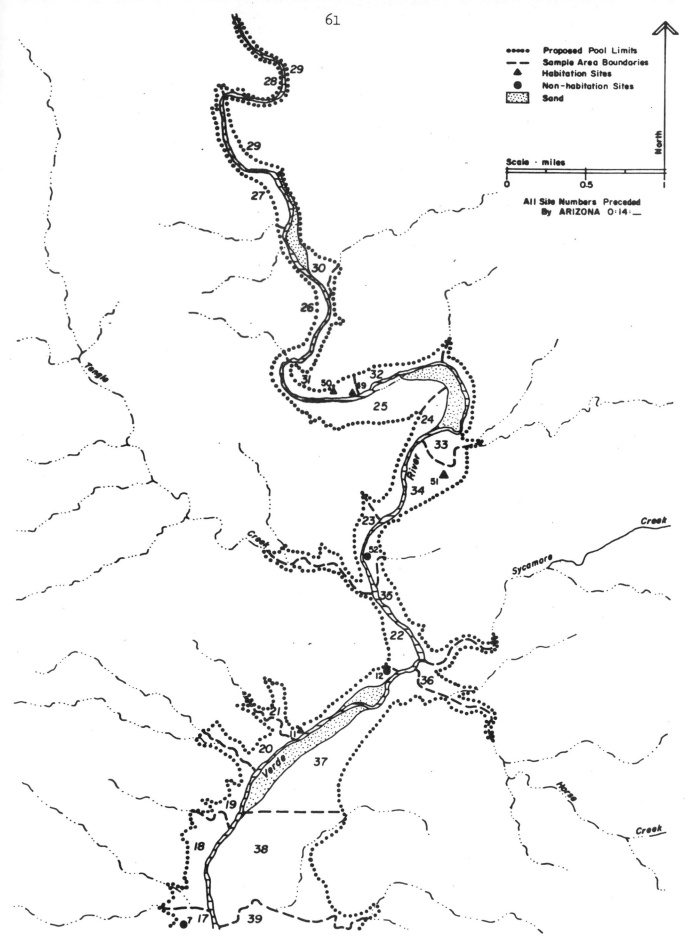

Figure 12.   Horseshoe Reservoir Sites and Sample Units: Map I.

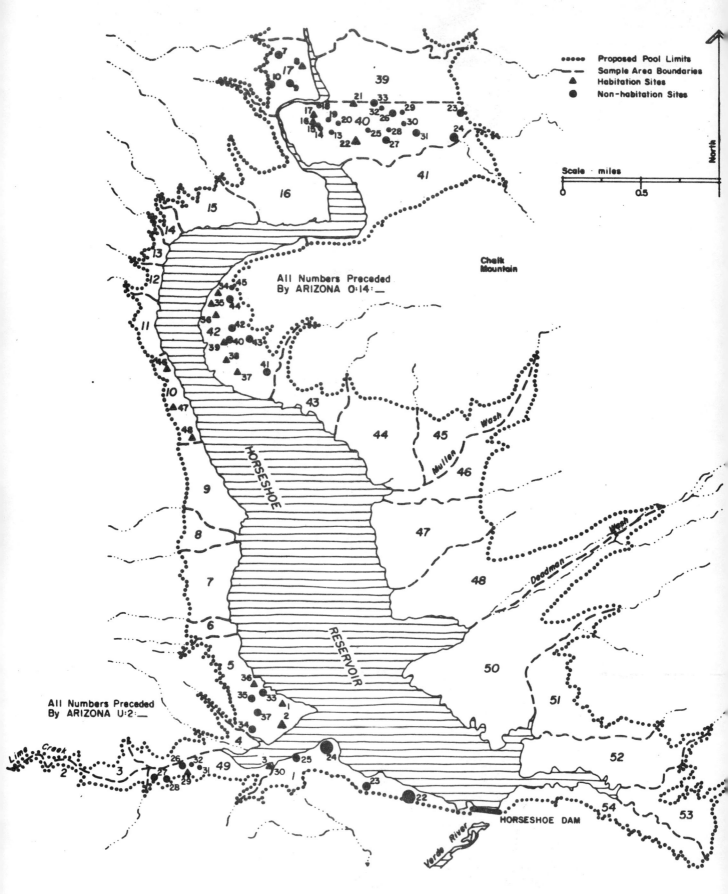

Figure 13. Horseshoe Reservoir Sites and Sample Units: Map II.

Table 3

Sampling Frame and Selected Sample for Roosevelt Lake Survey

Stratum 1. Floodplains and terraces, Tonto Creek arm			Stratum 2. Floodplains and terraces, Salt River arm		
Sequence Number	Sample Unit Number	Number of Acres (y_{hi})	Sequence Number	Sample Unit Number	Number of Acres (y_{hi})
1	19	45	1	77	49
2	20	17	2	78	62
3	21	11	3	79	87
4	22	22	4	80	53
5	23	30	5	81	106
6	24	72	6	82a	100
7	25	63	7	82b	181
8	26	108	8	83	44
9	27	62	9	84a	62
10	28	50	10	84b	187
11	29	65	11	84c	317
12	30	32	12	85a	218
13	31	17	13	85b	146
14	32a	71	14	86	146
15	32b	84	15		_157_
16	33	86			
17	34	36			
18	35a	_129_			

Stratum 1: $y_h = 1000$, $20\% \ y_h = 200$

Stratum 2: $y_h = 1915$, $20\% \ y_h = 383$

Sample Units Drawn Randomly (Stratum 1)

1	19	45
8	26	108
15	32b	_84_

$\sum_{n_h} y_{hi} = 237$

Sample Units Drawn Randomly (Stratum 2)

4	80	53
7	82b	181
12	84c	_218_

$\sum_{n_h} y_{hi} = 452$

Table 3 (cont.)

Sampling Frame and Selected Sample for Roosevelt Lake Survey

Stratum 3. Gently sloping pediment-terraces (less than 10% slope)

Sequence Number	Sample Unit Number	Number of Acres (y_{hi})	Sequence Number	Sample Unit Number	Number of Acres (y_{hi})
1	3	52	25	52	130
2	11	54	26	53	36
3	12	61	27	54	49
4	13	39	28	55	13
5	14	39	29	56	97
6	15	70	30	60	67
7	16	81	31	61	72
8	17	76	32	62	81
9	18	21	33	67	49
10	35b	138	34	69	67
11	36	42	35	70	89
12	39	202	36	71	53
13	40	164	37	72	167
14	41	26	38	73	147
15	42	170	39	74	107
16	43	90	40	87	89
17	44	38	41	91	48
18	45	47	42	93	67
19	46	75	43	94	38
20	47	154	44	98	61
21	48	25	45	99	80
22	49	179	46	100	113
23	50	101	47	101	85
24	51	66	48	109	35

$$y_{hi} = 3850$$

$$20\% \ y_{hi} = 770$$

Sample Units Drawn Randomly

2	11	54
10	35b	138
13	40	164
22	49	179
23	50	101
27	54	49
33	67	49
47	101	85

$$n_h$$

$$\Sigma y_{hi} = 819$$

Table 3 (cont.)

Sampling Frame and Selected Sample for Roosevelt Lake Survey

Stratum 4.   Steeply sloping zones (greater than 10% slope)

Sequence Number	Sample Unit Number	Number of Acres (y_{hi})	Sequence Number	Sample Unit Number	Number of Acres (y_{hi})
1	1	38	22	88	39
2	2	17	23	89	29
3	4	23	24	90	80
4	5	22	25	92	37
5	6	46	26	95	31
6	7	20	27	96	43
7	8	16	28	97	36
8	9	20	29	102	50
9	10	24	30	103	39
10	37	46	31	104	22
11	38	46	32	105	15
12	57	100	33	106	23
13	58	69	34	107	6
14	59	67	35	108	25
15	63	16	36	110	40
16	64	68	37	111	8
17	65	17	38	112	13
18	66	7	39	113	13
19	68	8	40	114	13
20	75	22	41	115	13
21	76	17			

$y_{hi} = 1383$

20% $y_{hi} = 277$

Sample Units Drawn Randomly

2	2	17
4	5	22
5	6	46
7	8	16
11	38	46
20	75	22
22	88	39
23	89	29
27	96	43
41	115	13

$$\sum_{n_h} y_{hi} = 293$$

Table 4

Sampling Frame and Selected Sample for Horseshoe Reservoir Survey

Stratum 1. Floodplains and terraces.			Stratum 2. Gently sloping pediment-terraces (less than 10% slope)		
Sequence Number	Sample Unit Number	Number of Acres (y_{hi})	Sequence Number	Sample Unit Number	Number of Acres (y_{hi})
1	22	52	1	1	109
2	23	49	2	5	143
3	24	44	3	6	27
4	25	99	4	7	92
5	26	19	5	8	40
6	27	28	6	9	90
7	28	8	7	15	75
8	29	18	8	16	144
9	30	16	9	17	85
10	31	24	10	37	177
11	32	25	11	38	311
12	33	36	12	39	204
13	34	73	13	40	253
14	35	39	14	41	197
15	36	48	15	42	185
			16	43	63
			17	44	59
			18	45	95
			19	46	117
			20	47	184
			21	48	256
			22	50	381
			23	51	163
			24	52	161
			25	53	144

$$y_{hi} = 578$$

$$20\% \; y_{hi} = 116$$

$$y_{hi} = 3755$$

$$20\% \; y_{hi} = 751$$

Sample Units Drawn Randomly

10	31	24
11	32	25
13	34	73

$$n_h$$

$$\Sigma y_{hi} = 122$$

Sample Units Drawn Randomly

1	1	109
2	5	143
5	8	40
9	17	85
13	40	253
15	42	185

$$n_h$$

$$\Sigma y_{hi} = 815$$

Table 4 (cont.)

Sampling Frame and Selected Sample for Horseshoe Reservoir Survey

Stratum 3. Steeply sloping zones (greater than 10% slope)

Sequence Number	Sample Unit Number	Number of Acres (y_{hi})
1	2	34
2	3	40
3	4	71
4	10	49
5	11	36
6	12	18
7	13	17
8	14	18
9	18	72
10	19	39
11	20	45
12	21	48
13	49	74
14	54	<u>124</u>

$$y_{hi} = 685$$

$$20\% \ y_{hi} = 137$$

Sample Units Drawn Randomly

4	10	49
12	21	48
13	49	<u>74</u>

$$\overset{n_h}{\Sigma} y_{hi} = 171$$

Field Methodology and Logistics

The Orme Alternatives survey was conducted under what could be considered the standard procedures developed by the Arizona State Museum. By this we mean that wherever feasible, the Orme Alternatives survey team utilized the Arizona State Museum standard site definition, collected surface artifacts in a manner so as to disturb the site minimally, recorded surveyed sites on the standard ASM site form, and performed the on-the-ground survey in a manner so as to record all possible site manifestations. In addition to elaborating on the methodological topics mentioned above, this section also presents certain logistical data.

Site Definition

The Arizona State Museum Site Survey Manual (Arizona State Museum 1974: 3) states that three tentative criteria should be utilized in the definition of any site: (1) it must exhibit definable limits in time and space; (2) it must contain more than one definable locus of past human activity; and (3) it should have an artifact density of more than five per square meter. It was soon apparent that the first two criteria were useful for the definition of cultural manifestations encountered during the survey. However, the third criteria proved to be totally unmanageable in regard to the sites that were encountered. In retrospect, only a minimal percentage of the 93 sites that were recorded would have qualified under this criterion. It is suggested that artifact density criteria should be field tested at the earliest stage of any project to see if it is, indeed, functional. If so, an estimation of density threshold should be determined on the basis of locally specific cultural manifestations.

Surface Collections

It is the general policy of the Arizona State Museum to avoid collecting artifacts from the surface of sites during the survey stage. The rationale behind this is that many archaeologists (cf. Schiffer 1972) feel that there is a significant spatial relationship between surface material and subsurface remains. Additionally, a large percentage of cultural remains in southern Arizona are only surface sites. Thus, unconstrained or uncontrolled surface collecting can render a bias to remaining materials that can never be totally absolved. One alternative to collecting is to identify materials while the site is being surveyed and recorded, thus negating the need for disturbing the site's archaeological context. Because of the suspected nature of ceramic materials from the Tonto Basin and the lower Verde River, we felt that subtle morphological differences exhibited in plain utility wares could be of use in the ultimate interpretation of such remains. It was also felt that such distinctions could not be accurately perceived in the field and that minimal surface collections should be made. In order to mitigate against excessive disturbance to the site's context, collections were made from previously disturbed (potted) areas when possible. When this was not possible, small collections were made from areas where potential disturbance was felt to be minimal. It should also be pointed out that systematic, unbiased, surface sampling of the sites, though a highly desirable goal (Redman and Watson 1970), was felt to be completely unreasonable within the project parameters. It was conservatively estimated that a truly random surface collection of artifactual material would take an average of one man-day per site. A total of 93 additional man-days would have added 63 percent to the field time and costs. An additional difficulty was that a significant proportion of the sites, especially at Roosevelt Lake, had been picked over by artifact collectors, thus rendering a bias to the remaining sample.

Site Survey Form

The ASM Site Survey Form is six pages in length. It has been used in its present form since 1973. Included in this form is locational and legal information, site descriptions, artifactual descriptons, environmental data, site conditions, research potential, mitigation estimates, and various maps. The questions posed by the survey forms are open-ended in order to provide the survey crew with the latitude to exercise their creative ability in discussing the full range of cultural-environmental relationships.

Survey Procedures

Except for the final two days of field work, the Orme Alternatives crew consisted of three crew members and one supervisory archaeologist. Despite logistical problems in reaching certain sample units, unusually heavy desert vegetation, and less than pleasant weather, the primary consideration was at all times to locate all evidence of past cultural activity and to record those manifestations that were considered of site status as discussed above. In order to accomplish this task, the four members of the survey team worked as a unit at all times. Actual field methodology consisted of walking back and forth across the sample units until it was assured that all sites were found. The width that was traversed by the crew varied according to vegetative cover and topography. In some places, a width of only 30 m could be surveyed on one pass. In other places, where the vegetation was minimal, as many as 150 m could be covered. Where vegetation was reasonably penetrable, we feel that virtually all archaeological sites were found and recorded. Where vegetation was barely penetrable, we feel that most sites were recorded, although the possibility exists that some cultural manifestations remain unnoticed.

Site Recording

Two general procedures were followed in recording sites. In some cases, sites were recorded immediately after discovery and in other cases, complete sample units were surveyed before returning to record any sites that had been noted. Generally, the decision between these two options was based on the variables of access, site density, time of day, site size, or site complexity. In any case, the decision was primarily based on the most economical use of field time. The actual recording of sites was conducted by all four crew members and individual duties were generally rotated. Thus, one person would work on collecting environmental data, one would work on the site and artifact descriptions, one would work on maps, and one would work on research potential, condition, site collections, and photography. Additionally, all sites were staked with a 1 inch by 2 inch wooden stake labeled with a metal tag indicating the site's field number. No sites were flagged in order to avoid drawing attention to them.

Field Logistical Data

At Roosevelt Lake, a total of approximately 1,801 acres was surveyed in 80 man-days. Of these 80 man-days, it is estimated that 68 were spent conducting actual field work, while the remaining were spent setting up and closing down operations at Roosevelt Lake and in Tucson working on field-related projects such as completing site forms and itemizing surface collections. Including this "down time," a total of 22.5 acres were surveyed each man-day. If only the 68 field days are considered, then 26.5 acres were surveyed each man-day. Using the 80 man-day figure, a total of 0.36 sites per man-day were recorded. The 68 day figure yields a total of 0.43 sites recorded per man-day.

At Horseshoe Reservoir, 1,108 acres were surveyed during a total of 66 field man-days. This latter figure was completely spent in the field and "down time" has not been calculated for the Horseshoe phase of operations. Thus, 16.8 acres were surveyed per man-day. This lower efficiency rate, in comparison to Roosevelt, is undoubtedly due to the higher incidence of site occurrence at Horseshoe--0.97 sites were recorded per man-day at Horseshoe.

Survey Site Data

The survey conducted at Roosevelt Lake, as part of the Orme Alternatives study, revealed a total of 29 archaeological sites, of which three are purely historic, 24 are purely prehistoric, and two represent historic and prehistoric activity. Considering that a total of 1,801 acres was surveyed intensively, the site density for the sampled portion of the project area is one site per 62.1 acres or 10.4 per square mile.

At Horseshoe Reservoir, 64 prehistoric sites were recorded and no historic sites were observed or recorded. Considering that 1,108 acres were intensively surveyed, the site density in the sampled portion of the area is one site per 17.3 acres or 37.2 sites per square mile.

Of this total of 93 archaeological sites, at least seven different
site types or categories are fairly evident. In many cases, a single
site may include several categories. The following discussion describes
these separate site categories and provides a cursory review of the range
of sites within each category at each of the reservoir areas. Additionally, two tables (Tables 5 and 6) are presented that illustrate which
sites are associated with the various site categories. In cases where
several categories were noted at one site, that site number is listed in
all relevant columns with an asterisk indicating such multi-listings.
The following paragraphs describe these categories.

Field Houses

The term field house, as used in this report, denotes a temporary
or non-permanent structure generally near an agricultural field. Whether
used for temporary habitation, as sun or wind breaks, or as storage units
is usually beyond the scope of survey investigations. Additionally, it
is conceivable that such structures are not entirely related to agricultural practices but may also be related to some other subsistence procurement or processing activities. The majority of these field houses consist
of one room, although two-room structures have been included in this category in certain cases (cf. Az. U:8:70, O:14:20). The sites also vary in
their wall construction techniques. Some contain what appear to be almost
full-height cobble walls that are now fallen (Az. U:8:75, U:2:23), while
others only consist of boulder outlines (Az. U:8:70, U:2:28). These later
structures are presumably the bases for jacal or brush walls. Only two
field houses were recorded at Roosevelt Lake (Table 5), while 23 were
recorded at Horseshoe Reservoir (Table 6). It should be noted that 11 of
the Horseshoe field houses were recorded with associated agricultural
features such as check dams and contour terraces.

Cobble Clusters

The term "cobble cluster" was used to define several amorphous site
features at both reservoir areas. For the most part, these consist of a
single layer scatter of river cobbles in a square of less than 4 m on a
side. They can be distinguished from agricultural rock piles as these are
not piled up and are frequently associated with small clusters of artifacts.
Five of these sites were recorded at Roosevelt Lake (Table 5) and two were
recorded at Horseshoe Reservoir (Table 6).

Agricultural Systems

The number and diversity of agricultural systems recorded was substantial, especially at the Horseshoe area. Following the terminology
proposed by Vivian (1975), the following agricultural features were recorded:

Table 5

Sites Recorded at Roosevelt Lake According to Category

Site Category	Sites
Field houses	Az. U:8:70, U:8:75
Cobble clusters	Az. U:4:14, U:4:15, U:4:16, U:8:74, U:8:76
Agricultural systems	Az. V:5:28*
Habitation: Pueblos	Az. U:4:7, U:4:8, U:4:9, U:4:10, U:4:11, U:4:12, U:4:13, U:4:17, U:4:18, U:8:68, U:8:72, U:8:73, U:8:78
Habitation: Pit Houses	Az. U:8:67
Middens	Az. U:8:69, U:8:71
Sherd and lithic scatters	Az. V:5:27*
Unknown	Az. U:4:20
Historic	Az. V:5:27*, U:5:28*, U:4:19, U:8:77, U:3:26

*indicates sites that are listed in more than one site category.

Table 6

Sties Recorded at Horseshoe Reservoir According to Category

Site Category	Sites
Field houses	Az. U:2:22*, U:2:23*, U:2:24*, U:2:26*, U:2:27, U:2:28, U:2:34, 0:14:12*, 0:14:7*, 0:14:13*, 0:14:14, 0:14:15, 0:14:18, 0:14:20*, 0:14:40*, 0:14:39*, 0:14:42*, 0:14:43*, 0:14:44*, 0:14:45, 0:14:23*, 0:14:25, 0:14:33
Cobble clusters	Az. 0:14:19, 0:14:26*
Agricultural systems	Az. U:2:22*, U:2:23*, U:2:25, U:2:28*, U:2:2*, U:2:35, U:2:37, 0:14:12*, 0:14:7*, 0:14:13*, 0:14:16*, 0:14:17*, 0:14:20*, 0:14:34*, 0:14:35*, 0:14:42*, 0:14:43*, 0:14:44*, 0:14:23*, 0:14:24, 0:14:27*, 0:14:33*, 0:14:47*, 0:14:48*
Habitation: Pueblos	Az. U:2:29*, U:2:2*, U:2:1, U:2:36, 0:14:11, 0:14:17*, 0:14:22, 0:14:34, 0:14:35, 0:14:36, 0:14:37, 0:14:38, 0:14:46, 0:14:47, 0:14:48, 0:14:50, 0:14:51
Habitation: Pit houses	Az. U:2:30*, 0:14:8* (?), 0:14:16* (?), 0:14:21* (?), 0:14:34*, 0:14:39*, 0:14:51*
Middens	Az. U:2:31*, U:2:33*, 0:14:21*, 0:14:22*, 0:14:39*, 0:14:41, 0:14:42*, 0:14:44*, 0:14:51*
Sherd and lithic scatters	Az. U:2:24*, U:2:30*, U:2:31*, U:2:33*, 0:14:8*, 0:14:9, 0:14:16*, 0:14:40*, 0:14:26*, 0:14:27*, 0:14:28, 0:14:29, 0:14:30, 0:14:31, 0:14:32, 0:14:49
Unknown	Az. U:2:26*, U:2:32, 0:14:10, 0:14:52
Historic	No sites

*indicates sites that are listed in more than one category.

1. Check Dams. These are also known as trincheras (Sauer and Brand 1931) and terraces (Woodbury 1961). They consist of cobble walls built across intermittent drainages to retard ephemeral flow as well as to retain fine, silty soil. The resulting silt-filled plot provides a potential garden plot in an otherwise non-agricultural area. As many as 18 of these check dams were found in a single agricultural area (Az. O:14:33).

2. Contour Terraces. These features are long, curving alignments of cobbles or boulders that are built across hillslopes rather than within intermittent drainages. Such alignments apparently function to retard sheetwash and to conserve soil for small scale agricultural activities. Several contour terrace systems at Horseshoe are quite expansive. One site (Az. U:2:2), consisting of an extensive series, has one terrace over 360 m long. Another site (Az. O:14:12) consists of a large series of massive terraces almost 1 m high and over 100 m long.

3. Canals. These are defined as artificial cuts in the earth over 1 m in depth and width and used for the diversion of permanent streamflow. Only one canal was recorded (Az. V:5:28), and it remains problematical as to whether the site is prehistoric, historic, or both.

4. Rock Alignments. Several rock alignments were recorded throughout the Horseshoe Reservoir area that did not follow contours and therefore should be differentiated from contour terraces as described above. These alignments were generally part of larger agricultural systems and probably served as water diversion alignments. Az. U:2:22 is a good example of this agricultural feature.

5. Rock Piles. These piles of rock are less than 1 m high and 2 m in diameter and are particularly well illustrated at Az. U:2:29 and O:14:24. The function of such features is not clearly understood, although they probably represent some effort at clearing the surrounding field of cobbles or possibly some sort of field marking system.

Only one agricultural system (Az. V:5:28) was recorded at Roosevelt Lake. This should not, however, be taken as evidence against the practice of agriculture in the area. First, most of the floodplain agricultural systems, such as canals, are presently inundated by Roosevelt Lake, and second, most of the rainfall farming systems appear to be located at the toes of the pediment-terraces which are generally too elevated to be included in the survey contour. While in transit to several sample units, the survey team made observations of several such systems, some of which rival the Horseshoe systems in size and complexity. However, these were not recorded due to time constraints and project requirements. At Horseshoe Reservoir, 24 agricultural systems (Table 6) were recorded as sites. It should be noted, however, that 20 of these sites also included field houses or habitation units.

Habitation Sites (Pueblos)

The bulk of the archaeological material recorded at both of the
project areas consists of pueblos or pueblo-compound units. At Roosevelt,
13 pueblo sites (Table 5) were recorded which included 15 identifiable
pueblos or pueblo-compounds. The smallest of these was a three-room
structure (Az. U:8:73), and the largest was either Az. U:4:9 or U:4:10.
Both are estimated as having well over 100 rooms. Four of these sites
(Az. U:4:8, U:4:17, U:4:18, U:8:73) do not appear to have compound walls.
At Horseshoe, 17 pueblo or pueblo-compound sites were recorded ranging in
size from two rooms (Az. 0:14:11) to over 50 rooms (Az. U:2:1). Seven of
the sites have at least some evidence of compound walls, although rooms
within these compounds are generally hard to distinguish.

Habitation Sites (Pit Houses)

The problem of identifying pit houses on the basis of surface inspection confronted this survey as it has undoubtedly affected past surveys in southern Arizona. It should be stated that no definite pit house
villages were recorded. However, inferential data suggest that one may
have been recorded at Roosevelt (Az. U:8:67) and possibly seven at Horseshoe (Tables 5 and 6). Additionally, it is entirely possible that many
of the pueblos recorded at both areas could be underlain by substantial
pit house occupations. A similar situation occurred near Globe illustrating
that excavations are often needed to reveal all of the components present
at a site (Doyel n.d.). Generally, the presence of Hohokam red-on-buff
sherds found in lieu of surface structures was one of the primary criteria
for tentatively labeling a site as containing pit houses. However, the
recent work at Globe suggests that the local culture-history may be more
complex than equating pit houses with red-on-buff sherds and pueblos with
Salado redwares (Doyel n.d.). Certainly, exploration of such problems is
beyond the scope of these preliminary survey investigations and would,
most profitably, be included in a data recovery phase research orientation
(see Chapter 10).

Middens

This category of site refers to accumulations of organically stained
soil and burnt cobbles. The two middens recorded at Roosevelt (Az. U:8:69,
U:8:71) and one of the nine (Az. 0:14:41) recorded at Horseshoe are isolated features which comprise the entire recorded site. The other eight
recorded at Horseshoe (Table 6) were found in association with other site
features such as sherd scatters or field houses. The size of the middens
range from under 10 m in diameter (Az. U:8:69) to over 30 m in diameter
(Az. 0:14:21). Few or no sherds or other artifactual materials were found
on these features. Commonly called mescal pits, these may have been used
for mescal roasting or some similar function.

Sherd and Lithic Scatters

The category sherd and lithic scatter has been used as a catch-all for those sites that contain no visible features, yet are covered to some extent with sherds and lithics. Only one such scatter was recorded at Roosevelt (Az. V:5:27) and its presence may be due to the downslope movement of trash from a series of five large pueblos that are slightly outside of the project area. Outlying features or activity areas may be indicated by these clusters of sherds, though only subsurface testing would be conclusive. At Horseshoe, the 16 sherd and lithic scatters (Table 6) covered a broad range of manifestations. In three cases these scatters could represent small pit house clusters. In the rest of the sites, the sherds and lithics are probably a residue of some limited activity. Such activities probably relate to the procurement and processing of vegetal resources.

Historic Sites

Relatively few historic sites were found. Five historic Anglo sites were found and recorded at Roosevelt, while none were found at Horseshoe. No historic aboriginal materials have been positively identified. Of the five sites at Roosevelt, one (Az. V:5:27) may be a historic camp, Az. V:5:28 may be a historically utilized or re-utilized canal, Az. U:4:19 is an old highway maintenance camp dating from the 1920s or 1930s, Az.U:8:77 is the Arizona Power Canal that powered the construction of Roosevelt Dam, and the fifth (Az. U:3:26) is an unknown type of historic settlement.

Unknown Sites

Comparatively few sites were placed in this category. Az. U:4:20 at Roosevelt has been so extensively disturbed that its original form is unidentifiable. Az. U:2:26 has been partially destroyed by a road cut. Az. U:2:32 has been eroded and could either represent a habitation feature or an agricultural feature. Az. O:14:10 appears to be the remains of a collapsed rockshelter, and Az. O:14:52 is a boulder-cleared area on top of a butte rising out of the floodplain of the Verde River.

Multi-category Sites

Sites that have been placed in more than one category in this framework are marked with an asterisk. Designating these sites as multi-category should not be confused with the term multi-component. Many of these sites perhaps exhibit both field houses and agricultural features or sherd scatters and middens. This should not necessarily imply that two (or more) separate occupations of the site are represented as is indicated by the term "multi-component" (Willey and Phillips 1958: 21-22).

Summary of Site Data

Tables 7 and 8, which complete this chapter, are inventories of the archaeological sites recorded at both Roosevelt Lake and Horseshoe Reservoir. Included in this tabular listing of sites are rather generalized site attributes including ASM site number, sampling stratum, sample unit, cultural affiliation, dates of use, site type and brief description, site size, site condition, and elevation. The detailed descriptions of these 93 sites are provided in Appendices IIIA and IIIB.

TABLE 7

A Tabular Listing of Site Data: Roosevelt Lake

ASM Site Number *	Stratum	Sample Unit	Culture	Period of Occupation	Description of the Site	Size (sq. m)	Elevation (feet)
AZ. U:8:78	4	5	Salado	Prehistoric	A pueblo compound structure with about 13 rooms.	1,800	2145
AZ. U:8:72	4	6	Salado	Prehistoric	A moderate-size pueblo com-pound.	600	2136
AZ. U:8:73	4	6	Salado	Prehistoric	A three-room structure with associated trash.	875	2145
AZ. U:4:17	1	19	Salado	Prehistoric	A series of disturbed walls and possible rooms.	9,900	2130
AZ. U:4:18	1	19	Salado	Prehistoric	A five-room structure with associated trash.	800	2130
AZ. U:4:19	1	19	Anglo	Historic	Highway maintenance station.	3,125	2160
AZ. U:4:20	1	19	Unknown	Prehistoric	Badly disturbed trash scatter.	500	2136
AZ. U:3:26	1	32b	Anglo	Historic	Unknown type of settlement.	14,000	2150
AZ. U:4:7	3	35b	Salado	Prehistoric	A large pueblo compound with associated structures and trash.	32,500	2140
AZ. U:4:8	3	35b	Salado	Prehistoric	A small pueblo compound with several associated features.	36,000	2140
AZ. U:4:9	3	35b	Salado	Prehistoric	A series of three pueblo com-pounds with a series of trash mounds.	30,800	2140

* Sites are listed in the order as presented in Appendix IIIA.

TABLE 7. (cont.)

ASM Site Number	Stratum	Sample Unit	Culture	Period of Occupation	Description of the Site	Size (sq. m)	Elevation (feet)
AZ. U:4:10	3	35b	Salado	Prehistoric	A large pueblo compound.	24,000	2140
AZ. U:4:11	3	35b	Salado	Prehistoric	A small pueblo compound with about 9 rooms.	1,350	2140
AZ. U:4:12	3	35b	Salado	Prehistoric	A small, amorphous compound with several rooms and associated features.	3,360	2145
AZ. U:4:13	3	35b	Salado	Prehistoric	A trash scatter and several cobble alignments.	14,400	2140
AZ. U:4:14	3	35b	Unknown	Unknown	A cobble cluster.	10	2145
AZ. U:4:15	3	35b	Unknown	Prehistoric	A cobble cluster.	91	2145
AZ. U:4:16	4	38	Unknown	Prehistoric	A one-room structure.	60	2140
AZ. U:8:74	3	50	Unknown	Unknown	A cobble cluster, possibly representing a one-room structure.	70	2140
AZ. U:8:75	3	50	Unknown	Unknown	A one-room structure.	48	2111
AZ. U:8:76	3	54	Unknown	Unknown	A cobble cluster.	16	2136
AZ. U:8:67	4	75	Unknown	Prehistoric	Possibly a small village of pit houses.	600	2140
AZ. U:8:68	4	75	Unknown	Prehistoric	Possibly a partially buried pueblo compound.	2,400	2150
AZ. U:8:69	4	75	Unknown	Unknown	A burnt rock midden.	80	2160
AZ. V:5:27	2	84c	Salado Anglo	Prehistoric Historic	A sherd and lithic scatter and a small historic campsite.	18,750	2150

TABLE 7 (cont.)

ASM Site Number	Stratum	Sample Unit	Culture	Period of Occupation	Description of the Site	Size (sq. m)	Elevation (feet)
AZ. V:5:28	2	84c	Unknown	Unknown	A portion of an irrigation canal.	75,000	2150
AZ. U:8:71	4	96	Unknown	Unknown	A burnt rock midden.	294	2111
AZ. U:8:70	3	101	Unknown	Prehistoric	Three cobble outlined rooms and several possible agricultural features.	80	2150
AZ. U:8:77	2,3,4	84-115	Anglo	Historic	A power generating canal built in order to provide power for the construction of Roosevelt Dam.	----	---

Table 8

A Tabular Listing of Site Data: Horseshoe Reservoir

ASM Site Number *	Stratum	Sample Unit	Culture	Period of Occupation	Description of the Site	Size (sq. m)	Elevation (feet)
AZ. U:2:22	2	1	Unknown	Prehistoric	A small room and an extensive agricultural system of rock piles and diversionary alignments.	11,700	2050
AZ. U:2:23	2	1	Unknown	Prehistoric	Three cobble rooms and a series of agricultural features.	1,300	2080
AZ. U:2:24	2	1	Unknown	Prehistoric	A single room structure with an associated rock alignment and an extensive lithic scatter.	45,000	2050
AZ. U:2:25	2	1	Unknown	Unknown	An agricultural system consisting of rock piles and terraces.	4,000	2100
AZ. U:2:1	2	5	Unknown	Prehistoric A.D. 1200-1300	A large pueblo with an outlying roomblock.	4,900	2050
AZ. U:2:2	2	5	Unknown	Prehistoric	An extensive agricultural system with a small roomblock.	150,000	2040
AZ. U:2:33	2	5	Unknown	Prehistoric	A sherd and lithic scatter with a burnt rock midden.	700	2040
AZ. U:2:34	2	5	Unknown	Prehistoric	A cobble cluster with a sherd and lithic scatter.	900	2100
AZ. U:2:35	2	5	Unknown	Prehistoric	A series of check dams.	150	2040
AZ. U:2:36	2	5	Unknown	Prehistoric	Possibly a boulder outlined structure.	2,500	2040

* Sites are listed in the same order as presented in Appendix IIIB.

Table 8 (cont.)

ASM Site Number	Stratum	Sample Unit	Culture	Period of Occupation	Description of the Site	Size (sq. m)	Elevation (feet)
AZ. U:2:37	2	5	Unknown	Unknown	A series of check dams.	450	2050
AZ. 0:14:46	3	10	Unknown	Prehistoric	A series of three-four non-contiguous rooms.	1,500	2120
AZ. 0:14:47	3	10	Unknown	Prehistoric	Multiple habitation and agricultural features	10,800	2120
AZ. 0:14:48	3	10	Unknown	Prehistoric	A four-five room cobble structure.	225	2080
AZ. 0:14:7	2	17	Unknown	Prehistoric	A one-room structure and three check dams.	225	2100
AZ. 0:14:8	2	17	Unknown	Prehistoric	A sherd and lithic scatter.	2,400	2040
AZ. 0:14:9	2	17	Unknown	Prehistoric	A sherd and lithic scatter.	6,075	2030
AZ. 0:14:10	2	17	Unknown	Prehistoric	An eroded rock shelter.	600	2100
AZ. 0:14:11	3	21	Unknown	Prehistoric	A two-room structure.	675	2100
AZ. 0:14:12	3	21	Unknown	Prehistoric	An extensive series of agricultural features with two single room structures.	43,200	2100
AZ. 0:14:49	1	31 & 32	Unknown	Prehistoric	Possibly a pit house village.	1,000	2120
AZ. 0:14:50	1	31	Unknown	Prehistoric	A masonry pueblo.	1,000	2140
AZ. 0:14:51	1	34	Unknown	Prehistoric	A very large and extensive site consisting of a pueblo compound, several middens, several trash mounds, possible pit houses and a possible ball court.	43,750	2140

Table 8 (cont.)

ASM Site Number	Stratum	Sample Unit	Culture	Period of Occupation	Description of the Site	Size (sq. m)	Elevation (feet)
AZ. 0:14:52	1	34	Unknown	Prehistoric	A boulder outlined site on top of a small butte.	128	2080
AZ. 0:14:13	2	40	Unknown	Prehistoric	A single room structure and two check dams.	56	2040
AZ. 0:14:14	2	40	Unknown	Prehistoric	A one-room structure.	208	2030
AZ. 0:14:15	2	40	Unknown	Prehistoric	A one-room structure.	6	2030
AZ. 0:14:16	2	40	Unknown	Prehistoric	A sherd and lithic scatter and four check dams. The scatter possibly overlies a small pit house village.	4,000	2030
AZ. 0:14:17	2	40	Unknown	Prehistoric	An extensive agricultural site with several distinct activity areas and several structures.	41,125	2050
AZ. 0:14:18	2	40	Unknown	Prehistoric	A small, cobble roomblock.	1,000	2060
AZ. 0:14:19	2	40	Unknown	Prehistoric	A cobble cluster and a series of rock piles.	840	2060
AZ. 0:14:20	2	40	Unknown	Prehistoric	A small rectangular structure and one check dam.	1,200	2060
AZ. 0:14:21	2	40	Unknown	Hohokam (?)	A large midden deposit and a small trash mound	4,608	2060
AZ. 0:14:22	2	40	Unknown	Prehistoric	A very large site with three occupational areas.	54,000	2060
AZ. 0:14:23	2	40	Unknown	Prehistoric	A one-room structure with associated features.	10,800	2100

Table 8 (cont.)

ASM Site Number	Stratum	Sample Unit	Culture	Period of Occupation	Description of the Site	Size (sq. m)	Elevation (feet)
AZ. O:14:24	2	40	Unknown	Prehistoric	An extensive agricultural system.	20,000	2100
AZ. O:14:25	2	40	Unknown	Prehistoric	A one-room cobble structure.	16	2100
AZ. O:14:26	2	40	Unknown	Prehistoric	A one-room structure and associated features.	2,400	2100
AZ. O:14:27	2	40	Unknown	Prehistoric	An extensive agricultural system.	13,500	2080
AZ. O:14:28	2	40	Unknown	Prehistoric	A small sherd and lithic scatter.	266	2080
AZ. O:14:29	2	40	Unknown	Prehistoric	A grinding station and a sherd and lithic scatter.	360	2100
AZ. O:14:30	2	40	Unknown	Prehistoric	A small sherd and lithic scatter.	100	2100
AZ. O:14:31	2	40	Unknown	Prehistoric	A sherd and lithic scatter.	304	2100
AZ. O:14:32	2	40	Unknown	Prehistoric	A sherd and lithic scatter.	36	2080
AZ. O:14:33	2	40	Unknown	Prehistoric	An extensive agricultural system with an associated one-room structure.	7,500	2060
AZ. O:14:34	2	42	Unknown	Prehistoric	A rubble mound, several trash mounds and agricultural features.	14,000	2050
AZ. O:14:35	2	42	Unknown	Prehistoric	A compound structure and associated agricultural features.	6,300	2040
AZ. O:14:36	2	42	Unknown	Prehistoric	A compound structure with associated features.	5,600	2030

Table 8 (cont.)

ASM Site Number	Stratum	Sample Unit	Culture	Period of Occupation	Description of the Site	Size (sq. m)	Elevation (feet)
AZ. O:14:37	2	42	Unknown	Prehistoric	A compound structure with associated features.	16,800	2040
AZ. O:14:38	2	42	Unknown	Prehistoric	Two large compound structures joined by a dense sherd scatter.	16,000	2040
AZ. O:14:39	2	42	Unknown	Prehistoric	Two one-room structures, a midden, and a sherd and lithic scatter.	7,200	2040
AZ. O:14:40	2	42	Unknown	Prehistoric	Two cobble rooms, an extensive sherd scatter, and agricultural rock piles.	6,400	2040
AZ. O:14:41	2	42	Unknown	Unknown	A burnt rock midden.	169	2080
AZ. O:14:42	2	42	Unknown	Prehistoric	A one-room structure and an extensive agricultural system.	10,725	2060
AZ. O:14:43	2	42	Unknown	Prehistoric	A one-room structure.	1,000	2100
AZ. O:14:44	2	42	Unknown	Unknown	A cobble room and three areas of agricultural activity.	19,600	2080
AZ. O:14:45	2	42	Unknown	Prehistoric	A cluster of three-four contiguous rooms	675	2120
AZ. U:2:26	3	49	Unknown	Prehistoric	Two room outlines, a midden, and several alignments.	3,000	2050
AZ. U:2:27	3	49	Unknown	Unknown	A cluster of cobbles and a lithic scatter.	600	2100
AZ. U:2:28	3	49	Unknown	Prehistoric	A two-room structure and a sherd and lithic scatter.	32	2130
AZ. U:2:29	3	49	Unknown	Prehistoric	A small pueblo compound and an agricultural system.	8,000	2130

Table 8 (con.)

ASM Site Number	Stratum	Sample Unit	Culture	Period of Occupation	Description of the Site	Size (sq. m)	Elevation (feet)
AZ. U:2:30	3	49	Hohokam(?)- Anglo	Prehistoric- Historic	Possibly a small pit house village and a historic camp and mining claim.	11,000	2100
AZ. U:2:31	3	49	Unknown	Prehistoric	A large midden and a sherd and lithic scatter.	2,450	2100
AZ. U:2:32	3	49	Unknown	Prehistoric	A series of cobble alignments and a sherd and lithic scatter.	900	2060

Chapter 6

THE EVALUATION OF THE SAMPLE

This chapter critically evaluates the sampling design used for this project in light of the results produced by the sample survey. The sample survey data are presented, and the formulas used to calculate estimates of population parameters are explained. The major statistical problem encountered stemmed from the relative impreciseness of these estimates. The source of this problem is identified as the highly skewed nature of the distribution of archaeological survey data. Several ways of alleviating this problem are discussed.

The Sample Data

The four weeks spent surveying the Roosevelt Lake sample resulted in the discovery and recording of 29 sites. One of these sites, Az. U:8:77, is a historic power canal built for use during the construction of Roosevelt Dam. It was omitted from the statistical calculations because of its specialized nature and because it is located in more than one sample unit, and thus violates the sample design requirement that all sites be associated exclusively with only one sample unit. Exactly one-half of the 24 surveyed sample units contained no sites. The other 12 units contained from one to nine sites. The number of man-days required for total data recovery from each site was also estimated using procedures developed for the survey of the impact zone of the proposed Orme Reservoir (Canouts 1975). These estimates range from a low of 5 man-days per site to a maximum of 4000. Data recovery man-day totals per sample unit ranged from 0 to 8725. See Table 9 for a compilation of the sample data.

At Horseshoe Reservoir three weeks were spent surveying the 12 sample units that had been selected. Only two of these units contained no sites. The number of sites discovered in the other sample units ranged from 2 to 21. A total of 64 sites were recorded. Estimates of the number of man-days required for total data recovery of these sites ranged from 1 to 2000 per site. Data recovery man-day totals per sample unit ranged from 0 to 3745. See Table 10 for the Horseshoe Reservoir sample data.

In general, the sample units were characterized by a relatively wide range of values for the number of sites and the number of man-days required for data recovery. Ideally, the stratification scheme should have grouped together sample units that were similar with respect to the number of sites and data recovery man-days. The sample data indicate that

Table 9

Sample Data for Roosevelt Lake Survey*

Stratum	Sample Unit Number	Site Number	Data Recovery Man-days per Site	Sites per Sample Unit	Data Recovery Man-days per Sample Unit	Site Type
1	19	Az. U:4:17	100			habitation
		Az. U:4:18	125			habitation
		Az. U:4:19	10			non-habitation
		Az. U:4:20	40	4	275	non-habitation
	26	none	0	0	0	
	32b	Az. U:3:26	100	1	100	non-habitation
2	80	none	0	0	0	
	82b	none	0	0	0	
	84c	Az. V:5:27	20			non-habitation
		Az. V:5:28	10	2	30	non-habitation
3	11	none	0	0	0	
	35b	Az. U:4:7	1300			habitation
		Az. U:4:8	200			habitation
		Az. U:4:9	4000			habitation
		Az. U:4:10	2500			habitation
		Az. U:4:11	350			habitation
		Az. U:4:12	300			habitation
		Az. U:4:13	60			habitation
		Az. U:4:14	5			non-habitation
		Az. U:4:15	10	9	8725	non-habitation

*Site Az. U:8:77, a historic power canal built for use during the construction of Roosevelt Dam, was omitted from the calculations because of its specialized nature and its location in more than one sample unit.

Table 9 (cont.)

Sample Data for Roosevelt Lake Survey

Stratum	Sample Unit Number	Site Number	Data Recovery Man-days per Site	Site per Sample Unit	Data Recovery Man-days per Sample Unit	Site Type
	40	none	0	0	0	
	49	none	0	0	0	
	50	Az. U:8:74 Az. U:8:75	10 10	2	20	non-habitation non-habitation
	54	Az. U:8:76	5	1	5	non-habitation
	67	none	0	0	0	
	101	Az. U:8:70	30	1	30	non-habitation
4	2	none	0	0	0	
	5	Az. U:8:78	700	1	700	habitation
	6	Az. U:8:72 Az. U:8:73	350 100	2	450	habitation habitation
	8	none	0	0	0	
	38	Az. U:4:16	5	1	5	non-habitation
	75	Az. U:8:67 Az. U:8:68 Az. U:8:69	50 400 15	3	465	habitation habitation non-habitation

Table 9 (cont.)

Sample Data for Roosevelt Lake Survey

Stratum	Sample Unit Number	Site Number	Data Recover Man-days per Site	Sites per Sample Unit	Data Recovery Man-days per Sample Unit	Site Type
	88	none	0	0	0	
	89	none	0	0	0	
	96	Az. U:8:71	15	1	15	non-habitation
	115	non	0	0	0	

Table 10

Sample Data for Horseshoe Reservoir Survey

Stratum	Sample Unit Number	Site Number	Data Recovery Man-days per Site	Sites per Sample Unit	Data Recovery Man-days per Sample Unit	Site Type
1	31	Az. 0:14:49	200	2	500	habitation
		Az. 0:14:50	300			habitation
	32	none	0	0	0	
	34	Az. 0:14:51	2000	2	2025	habitation
		Az. 0:14:52	25			non-habitation
2	1	Az. U:2:22	25	4	125	non-habitation
		Az. U:2:23	60			non-habitation
		Az. U:2:24	20			non-habitation
		Az. U:2:25	20			non-habitation
	5	Az. U:2:1	2000	7	2440	habitation
		Az. U:2:2	200			habitation
		Az. U:2:33	50			non-habitation
		Az. U:2:34	75			non-habitation
		Az. U:2:35	5			non-habitation
		Az. U:2:36	100			habitation
		Az. U:2:37	10			non-habitation
	8	none	0	0	0	
	17	Az. 0:14:7	15	4	516	non-habitation
		Az. 0:14:8	200			habitation
		Az. 0:14:9	300			non-habitation
		Az. 0:14:10	1			non-habitation

Table 10 (cont.)

Sample Data for Horseshoe Reservoir Sample

Stratum	Sample Unit Number	Site Number	Data Recovery Man-days per Site	Sites per Sample Unit	Data Recovery Man-days per Sample Unit	Site Type
	40	Az. 0:14:13	15			non-habitation
		Az. 0:14:14	10			non-habitation
		Az. 0:14:15	10			non-habitation
		Az. 0:14:16	200			habitation
		Az. 0:14:17	400			habitation
		Az. 0:14:18	60			non-habitation
		Az. 0:14:19	30			non-habitation
		Az. 0:14:20	10			non-habitation
		Az. 0:14:21	750			habitation
		Az. 0:14:22	2000			habitation
		Az. 0:14:23	25			non-habitation
		Az. 0:14:24	20			non-habitation
		Az. 0:14:25	15			non-habitation
		Az. 0:14:26	50			non-habitation
		Az. 0:14:27	50			non-habitation
		Az. 0:14:28	20			non-habitation
		Az. 0:14:29	15			non-habitation
		Az. 0:14:30	5			non-habitation
		Az. 0:14:31	10			non-habitation
		Az. 0:14:32	5			non-habitation
		Az. 0:14:33	35	21	3745	non-habitation
	42	Az. 0:14:34	400			habitation
		Az. 0:14:35	500			habitation
		Az. 0:14:36	400			habitation
		Az. 0:14:37	400			habitation
		Az. 0:14:38	800			habitation

Table 10 (cont.)

Sample Data for Horseshoe Reservoir Survey

Stratum	Sample Unit Number	Site Number	Data Recovery Man-days per Site	Site per Sample Unit	Data Recovery Man-days per Sample Unit	Site Type
		Az. 0:14:39	125			habitation
		Az. 0:14:40	90			non-habitation
		Az. 0:14:41	10			non-habitation
		Az. 0:14:42	60			non-habitation
		Az. 0:14:43	15			non-habitation
		Az. 0:14:44	30			non-habitation
		Az. 0:14:45	30	12	2860	non-habitation
3	10	Az. 0:14:46	140			habitation
		Az. 0:14:47	500			habitation
		Az. 0:14:48	125	3	765	habitation
	21	Az. 0:14:11	50			habitation
		Az. 0:14:12	50	2	100	non-habitation
	49	Az. U:2:26	150			non-habitation
		Az. U:2:27	10			non-habitation
		Az. U:2:28	20			non-habitation
		Az. U:2:29	140			habitation
		Az. U:2:30	200			habitation
		Az. U:2:31	70			non-habitation
		Az. U:2:32	70	7	660	non-habitation

this goal was only partially achieved. For example, virtually every stratum contained at least one empty sample unit. If we had been able to accurately predict which sample units would contain no sites as well as those that would contain many large sites, then we could have isolated them into separate strata. This would have increased the precision of our population parameter estimates.

Formulas Used to Estimate Population Parameters

The goals of our research called for estimating two different population parameters for each survey area. One parameter was an estimate of the total number of sites in the direct impact zone and the other was an estimate of the total number of man-days required for complete data recovery. The same formula was used to estimate both of these totals. In addition, we decided to assess the reliability of these estimates.

The formula used in simple random sampling for estimating a total from sample data is:

$$\hat{t} = N \bar{x} = N \frac{\sum\limits^{n} x_i}{n}$$

where:

N = the number of sample units in the population
n = the number of sample units in the sample
x_i = measured value of sample unit i
$\bar{x}$ = mean of the measured values of all sample units in the sample

The formula simply indicates that the total of the value of the variable being investigated is estimated by multiplying the average value of that variable per sample unit by the total number of sample units in the population. This formula has to be modified for our disproportionate stratified random sample with unequal sample units, but the basic logic remains the same.

The modified formula used also incorporates a combined ratio estimation procedure. Ratio estimation is a method that is inherent in all cluster sampling techniques but can also be used with element sampling techniques in combination with simple random, systematic, or stratified random schemes of selecting sample units (Yamane 1967: 328; Lazerwitz 1968). In order to use the ratio estimation method, measurements must be made for two different variables of each sample unit in the sample. An attempt should be made to select variables that are positively correlated because this results in population parameter estimates that are more efficient, that is, more precise, than non-ratio estimates (Yamane 1967: 346-347; Sukhatme and Sukhatme 1970: 153-160). The ratios used were the number of sites per acre and the number of data recovery man-days

per acre. The strength of the correlation between the sizes of sample
units and the number of sites and mitigation man-days they contained varied
considerably from stratum to stratum in our survey data. The sites per
acre and man-days per acre ratios also compensated for the unequal sizes
of our sample units because they yielded density measures independent of
the size of these units.

The formula used to estimate the total number of sites and total
number of data recovery man-days is:

$$\hat{X}_c = r_c \, Y = \frac{\hat{X}_{st}}{\hat{Y}_{st}} \, Y = \frac{\sum_h^L N_h / n_h \sum^{n_h} x_{hi}}{\sum_h^L N_h / n_h \sum y_{hi}} \, Y$$

where:

Y = total number of acres

x_{hi} = the number of sites or data recovery man-days in sample unit i in
stratum h

y_{hi} = the number of acres in sample unit i in stratum h

n_h = the number of sample units surveyed in stratum h

N_h = the number of sample units in stratum h

N_h/n_h = the reciprocal of the sampling fraction

L = the number of strata

$\hat{X}_{st}$ = total number of sites or data recovery man-days as estimated by
stratified random sampling

$\hat{Y}_{st}$ = total number of acres as estimated by stratified random sampling

r_c = the combined ratio estimate of the number of sites or data recovery
man-days per acre

$\hat{X}_c$ = estimated total number of sites by the combined ratio estimate
(Yamane 1967: 350-353).

According to this formula, the ratio of sites or data recovery man-days
per acre (r_c) is multiplied by the total acreage (Y) as measured with a
compensating polar planimeter. The ratio is calculated by summing the
number of sites or data recovery man-days for all sample units within the
first stratum ($\sum^{n_h} x_{hi}$) and then multiplying this value by the quotient of
the total number of sample units in the stratum (N_h) divided by the number
of sample units actually surveyed from that stratum (n_h). This same
quotient (N_h/n_h) is multiplied by the total number of acres in all sample
units surveyed in stratum one ($\sum^{n_h} x_{hi}$). These calculations were made for
all strata and the results summed. The summation of the number of sites

or data recovery man-days across all strata ($\Sigma N_h / n_h \overset{n_h}{\Sigma} x_{hi}$) was divided

by the acreage values summed across all strata ($\Sigma N_h / n_h \overset{n_h}{\Sigma} y_{hi}$) in order to produce the combined ratio.

When using the ratio estimation procedure with a stratified sampling scheme, it is possible to calculate a separate ratio for each stratum. If the ratios vary much from stratum to stratum, this results in more precise estimates than the combined ratio. However, the combined ratio method was chosen because when the number of sample units per stratum (n_h) is small, as in both the survey areas, the separate ratio method tends to be more biased. The calculation of the precision of the separate ratio is also not valid unless the number of sample units within each stratum is large (Hansen and others 1953: 194-196; Cochran 1963: 171; Kish 1965: 206; Yamane 1967: 359-360).

In addition to an estimate of the total number of sites and data recovery man-days for each survey area, formulas were required for determining the reliability of these estimates. To evaluate the quality of an estimate two factors must be considered--precision and accuracy (cf. Cochran 1963: 12-16; Lazerwitz 1968). Precision refers to the nature of the sampling distribution of an estimating method. For example, an estimating method is more precise than another if its distribution of estimates of the total, based upon all possible samples of a given population, deviates less from the mean.

A common measure of the precision of an estimate is its variance. The variance of an estimate of a population total as calculated by simple random sampling without replacement is estimated by this formula:

$$\hat{V}(\hat{X}) = N^2 \, V(\bar{x}) = N^2 \, \frac{s^2}{n} \, \frac{N-n}{N}$$

where:

s^2 = variance of the sample units = $\dfrac{\overset{n}{\Sigma} (x_i - \bar{x})^2}{n-1}$

x_i = value of sample unit i

$\bar{x}$ = mean of the sample units in the sample = $\dfrac{\overset{n}{\Sigma} x_{hi}}{n}$

n = number of sample units in the sample

N = number of sample units in the population

N-n/N = finite population correction factor

$\hat{V}(\bar{x})$ = estimated variance of $\bar{x}$ = $\dfrac{s^2}{n}$.

This formula calculates the average of the square of the deviations of the measurements about their mean (s^2), divides this by the number of sample units (n), and multiplies this by the square of the number of sample units in the population (N^2). The finite population correction factor (N-n/N) is used to compensate for the percentage of the population sampled when the sample units are selected without replacement. This term is equal to one minus the sampling fraction (1 - n/N). When the sampling fraction is 5 percent or less, this term is equal to or greater than .95 and therefore is usually ignored because its effect is negligibly small.

The square root of the variance of an estimate of a population total is known as the standard error. The standard error can be used to calculate confidence intervals for an estimate. For example, carbon 14 dates are usually given as an estimated date plus or minus a given number of years. This plus or minus factor is the confidence interval. The interval given is usually plus or minus the standard error. By the Empirical Rule the confidence coefficient of this interval is 68 percent (Mendenhall and others 1971: 7). This means that if the same sampling design had been used to draw 100 samples from a given charcoal specimen and used to calculate 100 estimates of its date, the actual date of the specimen would lie within this confidence interval at least 68 out of the 100 times. If the confidence interval is increased to plus or minus 1.96 standard errors, the confidence coefficient increases to 95 percent. The value 1.96 is known as the z score. If Z is increased to 2.58, the confidence coefficient increases to 99 percent. The coefficients are based upon the assumption that the estimating statistic is distributed normally in a bell-shaped curve and that the sample size is large. If the sample is small (less than 30 sample units), t values can be substituted for z scores to compensate for the non-normal distribution of small sample estimates (Parl 1967: 150-153). If the population being sampled is highly skewed, the distribution of estimating statistics also tends to be skewed when the sample size is small. The sampling distribution of most statistics approaches normality as the sample size becomes large regardless of the distribution of the elements being sampled. The problem of estimating confidence intervals with small samples from highly skewed populations, which is increasingly being recognized as a common archaeological problem, will be discussed in more detail below.

The formula used to estimate the size of the standard error of our estimates of the total number of sites and data recovery man-days is:

$$SE(\hat{X}_c) = \sqrt{\hat{V}(\hat{X}_c)} = \sqrt{Y^2 \, \hat{V}(r_c)} = \sqrt{Y^2 \frac{1}{\hat{Y}_{st}^2} \sum_h^L N_h^2 \, \frac{N_h - n_h}{N_h} \, \frac{1}{n_h} \, s_{ch}^2}$$

where:

s_{ch}^2 = variance of the sample ratio of sites or data recovery man-days per acre

$$= s_{xh}^2 + r_c^2 \, s_{yh}^2 - 2r_c \, \rho_h \, s_{xh} \, s_{yh}$$

$s_{xh}{}^2$ = variance of sample sites or data recovery man-days

$$= \frac{\overset{n_h}{\Sigma}}{} (x_{hi} - \bar{x}_h)^2 / n_h - 1$$

$s_{yh}{}^2$ = variance of sample acres = $\frac{\overset{n_h}{\Sigma}}{} (y_{hi} - \bar{y}_h)^2 / n_h - 1$

r_c = ratio of sites or data recovery man-days per acre = $\hat{X}_{st} / \hat{Y}_{st}$

ρ_h = coefficient of correlation between the number of sites or data recovery man-days and the number of acres in stratum h

$$= \frac{s_{xyh}}{s_{xh}s_{yh}} = \frac{\overset{n_h}{\Sigma} (x_{hi} - \bar{x}_h)(y_{hi} - \bar{y}_h) / n_h - 1}{\sqrt{\Sigma (x_{hi} - \bar{x}_h)^2 / n_h - 1} \sqrt{\Sigma(y_{hi} - \bar{y}_h)^2 / n_h - 1}}$$

n_h = number of sample units surveyed in stratum h

N_h = number of sample units in stratum h

x_{hi} = number of sites or data recovery man-days in sample unit i in stratum h

$\bar{x}_h$ = average number of sites or data recovery man-days per sample unit in stratum h $= \dfrac{\overset{n_h}{\Sigma} x_{hi}}{n_h}$

y_{hi} = number of acres in sample unit i in stratum h

$\bar{y}_h$ = average number of acres per sample unit i in stratum h $= \dfrac{\overset{n_h}{\Sigma} y_{hi}}{n_h}$

L = number of strata

$\hat{Y}_{st}$ = estimated total number of acres by stratified random sampling

Y = actual total number of acres

(Yamane 1967: 351-353).

In this formula, $s_{ch}{}^2/n$ is substituted for s^2/n of the simple random formula. It represents the average squared deviations of the measurements about the value predicted when the combined ratio is multiplied by the number of acres in each sample unit. The calculation of $s_{ch}{}^2$ involves the variance $(s_{xh}{}^2)$ and standard error (s_{xh}) of the sample sites or data recovery man-days, the variance $(s_{yh}{}^2)$ and standard error (s_{yh}) of the sample acres, and the coefficient of correlation between sites or man-days and the number of acres (ρ_h). The coefficient of correlation can take values between -1 and +1. A value of 0 represents no correlation between the variables; a value of -1 represents a perfect negative correlation; and a value of +1 represents a perfect positive correlation. The term $(N^2)(N-n/N)$ of the simple random sample variance formula is modified only for stratification. The resulting values $(N_h^2)(N_h-n_h/N_h)(s_{ch}^2)$ are summed across all strata. This sum is multiplied by the term $Y^2/\hat{Y}_{st}^2$ which becomes 1 when the estimate of the acres equals the actual number of acres. The square root of this product is the standard error which can be used to estimate confidence intervals.

As mentioned above, the other factor that must be considered in evaluating an estimate is its accuracy. Precision refers to the spread of the sampling distribution of an estimate around the mean estimate. Accuracy refers to the relationship between this mean and the actual population value of the variable being estimated. If the mean of the sampling distribution of the estimate does not equal the real population value, the estimating procedure is said to be biased. Even if the estimating procedure is unbiased, bias can enter into sample survey data because of measurement or data collection errors. This second type of bias is difficult to estimate quantitatively, but the magnitude of the bias of estimating methods can usually be calculated. Unbiased and precise estimating procedures are ideal. Often in practice, unbiased estimates are imprecise. If a more precise but biased estimating procedure is available, it is often used if the bias is relatively small. Ratio estimation usually falls into this category.

Determining the sampling distribution of ratio estimates remains a difficult theoretical problem (Cochran 1963: 157). It is known that ratio estimation is a biased procedure unless the linear correlation between the variables being used to construct the ratio passes through the origin when graphed. Actual sample survey data seldom satisfies this requirement exactly, but nevertheless, empirical results indicate that even when the sample size is moderately large, the bias is usually small compared to the standard error and therefore negligible (Cochran 1963: 157, 160; Kish 1965: 209; Yamane 1967: 343).

Visual inspection of the survey data plotted on a graph is often sufficient for determining the magnitude of the possible bias of ratio estimation, but the plots of our survey data are ambiguous (Fig. 14). Cochran (1963: 169) shows that when the coefficient of variation of the mean of the denominator of the ratio ($C(\bar{y}_{st})$) is less than 0.10, the bias of the combined ratio estimating procedure is negligible relative to the standard error of the ratio (r_c) or the estimated total ($\hat{X}_c$). $C(\bar{y}_{st})$ for the Roosevelt Lake survey data was 0.11, and for the Horseshoe Reservoir survey data it was 0.15. Because these values exceeded Cochran's criterion for negligible bias, it was necessary to estimate the magnitude of the bias of the combined ratio estimating procedure for our survey data. The formula used to predict the extent of the bias of our total estimate is:

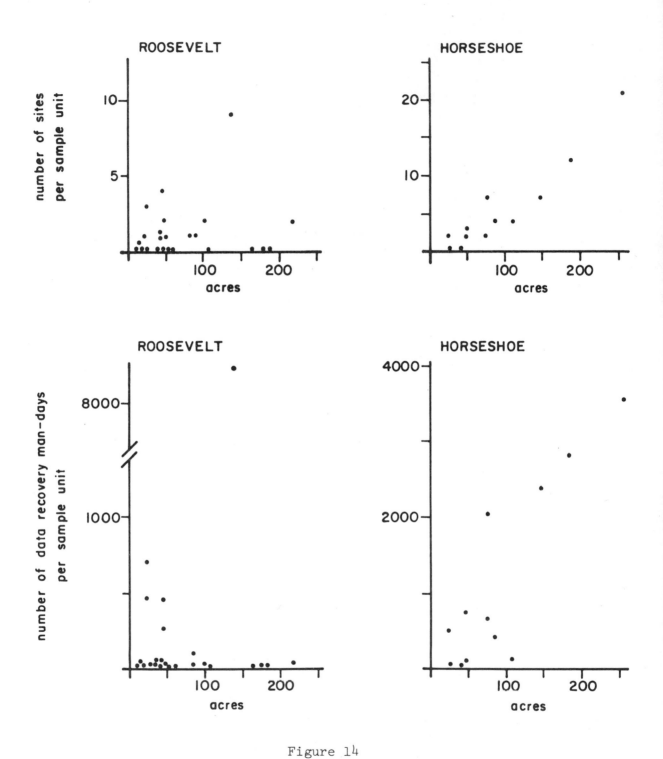

Figure 14

Ratio of Sites and Data Recovery Man-days per Acre
for Roosevelt Lake and Horseshoe Reservoir Surveys

$$\text{Bias} = Y \times E(r_c - R_c) = Y \sum^{L} \frac{N_h - n_h}{N_h n_h} \; \frac{1}{\bar{y}_h^2} \; (r_c \, s_{yh}^2 - \rho_h \, s_{xh} \, s_{xh})$$

where:

Y   = total number of acres in the survey area

$E(r_c - R_c)$ = expected difference between r_c and R_c

r_c = combined ratio estimate of the number of sites or data
            recovery man-days per acre based upon the sample data

R_c = estimated actual ratio of the number of sites of data
            recovery man-days per acre in the entire survey area,

and all other symbols are the same as those used in the formula in the
standard error of the total (Yamane 1967: 336).

Calculations and Results

The estimate of the density of sites for the Roosevelt Lake survey
area is .0154 sites per acre (9.86 sites per square mile). This yields an
estimate of 125 sites for the total number of sites in the area (Table 11).
However, the calculation of the bias indicates that this estimate is about
34 sites too high (Table 12). Therefore, a better estimate of the total
number of sites is 91. The relatively large bias is in part due to the
high negative correlation coefficient (ρ_h) of stratum 1. The standard
error as calculated in Table 13 is large. It is estimated to be 45 sites,
which is 11 greater than the bias and equal to about 50 percent of the
total estimated number of sites.

The estimate of the density of sites for the Horseshoe Reservoir
survey area is .0575 sites per acre (36.80 sites per square mile). This
yields an estimate of a total of 289 sites (Table 14). The bias of this
estimate appears to be only six sites too high (Table 15). The adjusted
ration indicates that the density of sites in the Horseshoe area is more
than five times greater than in the Roosevelt area. The standard error
of the estimated total number of sites is estimated as 36 sites (Table 16).
This is only about 13 percent of the estimated total. The reduction in
the magnitude of the standard error is due in part to the higher correlation coefficients (ρ_h).

The estimated density of data recovery man-days for the Roosevelt
Lake survey area is 6.31 per acre (Table 17). When adjusted for bias, this
density drops to 5.42 (Table 18). This yields an adjusted estimate of a
total of 44,200 man-days required for total data recovery. The estimated
standard error of this total estimate is very large. It is 39,000 data
recovery man-days which is 88 percent of the estimated total of data recovery man-days (Table 19).

*Tables 11-22 follow the text of Chapter 6 on pages 118 to 149.

The density of data recovery man-days for the Horseshoe Reservoir survey area is estimated as 12.51 per acre (Table 20), but when adjusted for bias this increases significantly to 15.89 per acre (Table 21). The total number of data recovery man-days for the direct impact zone at Horseshoe Reservoir is estimated to be 79,700 man-days. The standard error of this estimate is 9900 which is only 12 percent of the estimated total number of man-days (Table 22).

All the calculated estimates and their standard errors are summarized in Table 23. The 70 percent confidence interval is also calculated for the combined total number of sites and man-days. This is done by multiplying the standard error by the appropriate t value (cf. Fisher and Yates 1957). One conclusion that is readily apparent is that the estimates are relatively imprecise, especially for the Roosevelt Lake survey. The magnitude of this impreciseness takes on added significance when it is realized that each data recovery man-day is equivalent to approximately $600 in terms of a total budget as calculated by methods developed for the Orme Reservoir survey (Canouts 1975).

The Problem of Large Standard Errors

Despite increasing concern with probabilistic sampling among archaeologists during the past 10 to 15 years, few have been explicitly concerned with estimating the quality of population parameters. Much attention has been devoted toward developing elaborate probabilistic sample designs, but in many cases the resulting data have been assumed to be an exact or, at least, a very good representation of the population from which it was drawn. As more and more archaeologists are beginning to evaluate parameter estimates by such statistics as the standard error, it is becoming apparent that large standard errors are not uncommon. The source of this problem seems to lie in the fact that the distribution of archaeological data is often highly skewed and archaeological samples are often small (cf. Thomas 1975). See Figure 15 for the plotted distributions of sites and data recovery man-days per sample unit for the Roosevelt Lake and Horseshoe Reservoir survey areas. The raw sample data were adjusted because the sample units were not of equal size, and the distribution of sample unit size in terms of acreage was itself somewhat positively skewed. The adjustment was made by multiplying the actual number of sites and data recovery man-days by a weighting factor which compensated for deviations from the average acreage per sample unit. The weighting factor was the quotient of the average sample unit size of each sample divided by the actual acreage of each sample unit surveyed. Therefore, if a sample unit twice the average size contained four sites, its weighted number of sites would be two. If it contained half the average number of acres, the weighted number of sites would be eight. This assumes that the ratio of sites per acre would remain constant if the sample unit were adjusted to the average size. Since in reality this ratio would change, the totals of the weighted number of sites and data recovery man-days are only an approximation of the totals actually recorded. It can be seen from the graphs of the distributions

103

Table 23

Summary of Parameter Estimates for Roosevelt Lake and Horseshoe Reservoir

	Combined Ratio Adjusted for Bias (r_c)	Estimate of the Total Adjusted for Bias ($\hat{X}_c$)	Estimated Standard Error of the Total ($SE(\hat{X}_c)$)	70 Percent Confidence Interval
Roosevelt Lake Survey				
Sites	.0112/acre (7.17/mile^2)	91	45	t = 1.059 ±48 43 to 139
Data Recovery man-days	5.42/acre (3469/mile^2)	42,200	39,000	±41,300 10,800* to 85,500
Horseshoe Reservoir Survey				
Sites	.0564/acre (36.10/mile^2)	283	36	t = 1.088 ±39 244 to 322
Data Recovery man-days	15.89/acre (10,170/mile^2)	79,500	9,600	±10,400 69,100 to 89,900
Totals				
Sites		374		±87 287 to 461
Data Recovery man-days		121,700		±51,700 79,900 to 175,400

*Minimum value equals actual number recorded for the survey

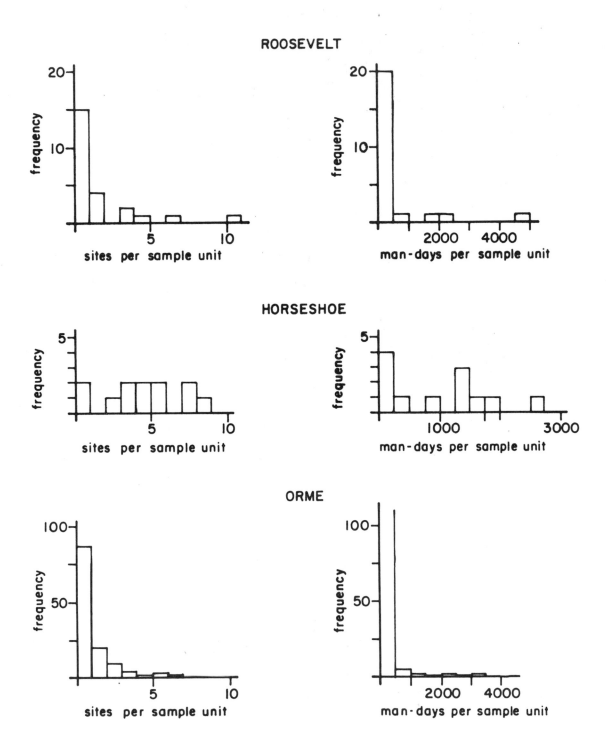

Figure 15

Adjusted Distribution of Sites and Data Recovery Man-days per
Sample Unit for Roosevelt Lake, Horseshoe Reservoir, and the
Orme Reservoir Simulation Survey

that a few of the sample units contained many sites and data recovery man-days, and many sample units contained few or no sites and data recovery man-days. The data from the Horseshoe Reservoir survey are much less skewed than the data from the Roosevelt Lake survey. Some degree of skewness is inherent in areal sampling of relatively rare elements. Even randomly distributed elements produce highly skewed Poisson distributions if the average number of elements per sample unit is small. See Chapter 7 for a fuller discussion of this problem.

Sampling distributions based on highly skewed data tend to be normally distributed as long as sample sizes are large, but when sample sizes are small the distribution of the statistics are also skewed. Despite the fact that estimates of standard errors based on the normal formulas will be large, they may also be unreliable (Cochran 1963: 38-43; Kish 1965: 410-412). Statistics have suggested a variety of methods for sampling skewed populations, but it has been said that "the choice of methods to use when normality is not assured is something of an art at present" (Dixon and Massey 1969: 322).

One method of attempting to reduce the standard error is the ratio estimation procedure we used. The calculations of the efficiency of this procedure as shown in Table 24 indicate that at Horseshoe Reservoir ratio estimation was successful in reducing the variance by three to almost four times as compared with stratified sampling without ratio estimation. For Roosevelt Lake, ratio estimation resulted in no decrease of the variance. These differences are due to the strengths of the correlation between the size of sampling units and the number of sites and data recovery man-days they contained. In the Horseshoe Reservoir survey area, sample unit size was a fairly accurate predictor of the number of sites and data recovery man-days a sample unit contained. In the Roosevelt Lake survey area, this was not the case. This is simply another reflection of the fact that the sample data were not nearly as positively skewed in the Horseshoe Reservoir area as in the Roosevelt Lake area.

Another approach that has been suggested for reducing the skewness of a distribution is the transformation of one or both of the variables used in constructing the ratio. This is often done by using the logarithm or square root of the variable values. In some cases this does allow the use of statistics based upon the assumption of normality, but in order to given meaning to such statistics as the standard error, they must be transformed back into the form in which they were originally measured. This usually results in standard errors that are still large.

A third approach to decreasing the size of the standard error would be to improve the efficiency of the stratification by separating all large sample units into one stratum and small units into another. This is a common technique used by sociologists when they encounter a set of highly skewed data (Hansen and others 1953: 140-148). This approach is practical when complete lists of individual sampling elements and their sizes are known. In the case of this project, as in most archaeological surveys, the

Table 24

Relative Efficiency of
Combined Ratio Estimating Method

$$E_f = \frac{V(\hat{X}_{st})}{\hat{V}(\hat{X}_c)} \qquad \frac{\overset{L}{\Sigma} \, s_{xh}^2}{\Sigma \, s_{ch}^2}$$

where:

E_f = relative efficiency of estimate of total by combined ratio estimating method compared with stratified random sampling procedure

$V(\hat{X}_{st})$ = variance of total as estimated by stratified random procedure
= s_{xh}^2, see Tables 13, 16, 19, and 22

$\hat{V}(\hat{X}_c)$ = estimated variance of total as calculated by combined ratio method
= s_{ch}^2, see Tables 13, 16, 19, and 22

Roosevelt Lake Survey: Sites

	s_{xh}^2	s_{ch}^2	$\overset{L}{\Sigma} \, s_{xh}^2 \, / \, \overset{L}{\Sigma} \, s_{ch}^2 = E_f$
Stratum 1	4.34	6.56	
Stratum 2	1.34	.77	
Stratum 3	9.41	8.87	
Stratum 4	1.07	.98	
$\overset{L}{\Sigma} = 16.16$		$\overset{L}{\Sigma} = 17.18$	.94

Roosevelt Lake Survey: Data Recovery Man-days

Stratum 1	19,375.00	115,492.17	
Stratum 2	300.00	286,124.80	
Stratum 3	9,498,700.00	9,057,250.31	
Stratum 4	71,294.70	78,990.72	
$\overset{L}{\Sigma} = 9,589,669.70$		$\overset{L}{\Sigma} = 9,537,858.00$	1.01

Table 24 (cont.)

Relative Efficiency of
Combined Ratio Estimating Method

Horseshoe Reservoir Survey: Sites

Stratum 1	1.34		2.14	
Stratum 2	56.40		11.23	
Stratum 3	7.00		3.28	

$$\overset{L}{\Sigma} = 64.74 \qquad \overset{L}{\Sigma} = 16.65 \qquad\qquad 3.89$$

Horseshoe Reservoir Survey:

Stratum 1	1,112,708.34	518,408.89
Stratum 2	2,560,734.67	608,230.62
Stratum 3	127,808.34	109,073.42

$$\overset{L}{\Sigma} = 3,801,251.35 \quad \overset{L}{\Sigma} = 1,235,712.93 \qquad\qquad 3.08$$

size of the sample units in terms of acreage is known before the sample design is developed, but the size in terms of the number of sites and the number of man-days is not known. Our stratification based upon microenvironments was an attempt to predict where large and small sites would occur, but as the sample data indicate, this prediction was not particularly successful (Tables 9 and 10). Our definition of microenvironments was crude because it had to be based upon data available before going into the field. During fieldwork, more detailed environmental data were gathered which, when analyzed, may reveal useful variables for predicting the location of sites. Trying to explain why prehistoric people lived where they did has been the research focus of the Southwestern Anthropological Research Group for the past several years (Gumerman 1971). As more of this work is done, archaeologists may achieve greater success in predicting where sites will be found. Almost all of this research is attempting to use environmental variables as site location predictors. Environmental variables are obviously important, but the distribution of sites may also reflect, in part, prehistoric organizational variables that will be much more difficult to measure. Even if good predictive environmental variables are discovered for the various regions of the Southwest, determining the distribution of these variables themselves may require specialized aerial photography, other remote sensing techniques, or preliminary field studies. This would, of course, increase survey costs. Gathering environmental data for all sample units at a level comparable to that gathered during our fieldwork would have increased the amount of field time by at least 50 percent.

Yet another approach to reducing the size of the standard error involves changing the size of the sample units. Several factors must be considered when selecting the size of sample units. If a given amount of area is to be surveyed, dividing it into small units will increase the number of sample units in the survey. In terms of statistical theory, the more units that are in the sample, the more the standard error will be reduced. However, the economics of collecting the data must also be considered. The expenses of gathering data increase as the number of sample units increases. In addition, field time spent locating and getting to the sample survey units increases. Another factor to consider is that the units must be large enough to yield sufficient data for statistical analysis. The sample size used must represent a compromise of all these considerations.

Archaeologists have recognized that the nature of the distribution of the variables being studies will vary from sample to sample, but in general they have recommended keeping sample unit size as small as economically feasible (Judge and others 1975: 86-88; Matson and Lipe 1975: 132; Read 1975: 56; Plog n.d.) In contrast, Mueller (1974: 55) has argued on the basis of a simulated sampling study that large sample units (one square mile) are more satisfactory than smaller ones. However, the index he used to draw this conclusion is apparently invalid because it favorably rates sample designs that yield high variances (Mueller 1974: 45). The size of the sample units commonly used in probabilistic archaeological sample surveys ranges from about 25 to 160 acres (Mueller 1975b). The average size of our sample units for the Roosevelt Lake survey was 67 acres; for the Horseshoe Reservoir survey it was 93 acres. In light of our small sample sizes (n = 24 for the Roosevelt survey and n = 12 for the Horseshoe Reservoir survey), any increase would seem to be warranted, but when all factors are considered, it becomes inappropriate to do this by decreasing the size of our sample units. Given the density of sites in the Roosevelt Lake survey area, there were only about 0.75 sites per average size sample unit. Therefore, the sample units were already near the minimum feasible size. At Horseshoe Reservoir, 5.24 sites could be expected in the average size sample unit. Somewhat smaller sample units could have been used if smaller, naturally bounded units could have been defined. If a smaller sample unit size had required arbitrarily defined units, field time would have increased significantly. Since the standard errors for the Horseshoe Reservoir survey data were already relatively small compared to those for the Roosevelt Lake survey, the increased costs would probably not have been justified.

The unequal size and irregular shape of the sample units created no problems, and the savings in field time that resulted from easily recognizable, naturally bounded sample units was an advantage. It is suggested that, when using this method of defining sample units, the sizes of the sample units be kept as similar as possible and that extremely large and small units be avoided.

If sample unit size cannot be decreased appreciably, a fifth approach to reducing the size of the standard error can be considered. This approach involves increasing the sampling fraction. This would, of course, involve an increase in survey costs. Evaluating whether the increased costs are justified by the decrease of the size of the standard error will be a project-specific decision. We can estimate how much the size of the standard error will decrease with increasing sampling fractions by assuming that the variance of the sample ratio (s_{ch}^2) of the standard error formula given above will remain approximately the same and then substituting increasing values for the number of sample units surveyed (n_h). The graphs of the decline of the standard error of the estimate of the total number of sites and data recovery man-days are shown in Figure 16. It can be seen that the size of the standard error decreases rapidly at first, but then the rate of decline slows. Increasing the sample size of both surveys by 100 percent would have reduced the standard error of the data recovery man-days at Roosevelt Lake by approximately 45 percent and at Horseshoe Reservoir by about 35 percent. In terms of a total data recovery budget, this would have reduced the size of the standard error by approximately 12.25 million dollars. Survey costs would have increased on the order of 50 or 60 percent.

ROOSEVELT LAKE SURVEY

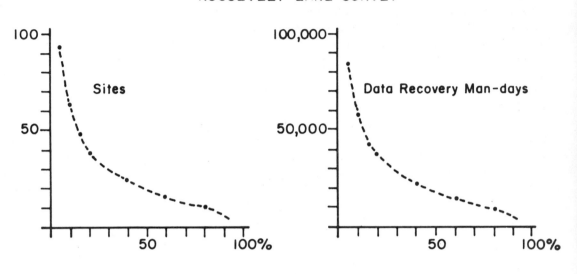

HORSESHOE RESERVOIR SURVEY

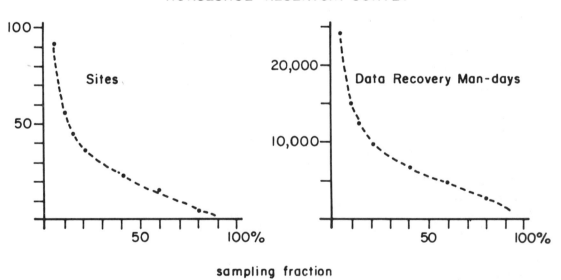

sampling fraction

Figure 16

Estimated Increase in Sampling Precision with Increasing
Sample Size for Roosevelt Lake and Horseshoe Reservoir Surveys

Simulated Sampling of Orme Reservoir Data

In order to independently evaluate our sampling designs, simulated samples were drawn from the 100 percent survey data collected from the proposed Orme Reservoir project area at the junction of the Salt and Verde rivers (Canouts 1975). Here, simulations also provided empirical data about the distribution of the combined ratio estimate of the total when calculated from small samples of highly skewed data.

In order to duplicate the Roosevelt Lake and Horseshoe Reservoir sampling problem as much as possible in the simulation, we hypothetically imposed the prior existence of a reservoir at the junction of the Salt and Verde rivers with a high water elevation of 1440 feet. Furthermore, we assumed that it had been proposed to raise the high water level 80 feet (to 1520 feet above sea level) and that the archaeological resources between these contours were to be evaluated. The amount of area to be sampled as measured with a compensating polar planimeter was 15,397 acres (24.06 square miles). This was about 2200 acres more than in the Roosevelt Lake and Horseshoe Reservoir survey areas combined. A total of 124 naturally bounded sample units were defined and assigned to microenvironmentally defined strata following the procedures used in designing the Roosevelt Lake and Horseshoe Reservoir surveys. The sites recorded by the Orme survey crew and the estimated data recovery man-days for each site were totaled for each of the sample units defined. Because some of the sites recorded were very extensive, they were located in more than one sample unit. Where the overlap was minimal the site was assigned to the sample unit in which the bulk of the site was located. When the overlap was extensive, one site was designated for each sample unit overlapped, and the data recovery man-days were divided proportionately. This tended to inflate the number of sites, but the site density was increased less than one site per square mile. A total of 95 sites were found in the area we had designated as the area to be sampled. This produced a density of .0062 sites per acre (3.9 per square mile) which was low compared to the Roosevelt Lake and Horseshoe Reservoir surveys. The data recovery man-day density was also relatively low. It was about 1.95 man-days per acre (1246 per square mile). In light of this fact, the larger size of the average sample unit for the Orme simulation, which was 124 acres, is an appropriate compensation for the low site density. The distribution of sites and data recovery man-days for the Orme simulation is even more skewed than that in the Roosevelt Lake survey area (Fig. 15). Therefore, the simulation provided a severe test of the estimation formula used.

An interactive FORTRAN IV program was written to select stratified random samples just as they had been slected for the Roosevelt Lake and Horseshoe Reservoir surveys. The program also computed an estimate of the total number of sites and data recovery man-days by the combined ratio method, and plotted the distribution of these estimates. The program was designed so that any designated number of samples could be drawn at any designated sampling fraction. This program is on file at the Data Processing Section of the Arizona State Museum.

Figure 17 shows the distributions of the estimated total number of sites for various sampling fractions as based on 300 different samples of the Orme data. For low sampling fractions the range of the estimated total number of sites is quite large and tends to be positively skewed. As the sampling fraction increases, the range of the estimates of the total number of sites narrows and the distribution becomes more normal. Similar distributions for the estimates of the total number of data recovery man-days are shown in Figure 18. Because the data recovery man-day distribution is more skewed, the ranges of the estimates are larger and the distribution of the estimates are more skewed.

In addition to plotting the distribution of estimates of the total number of sites and data recovery man-days at any given sampling fraction, the simulation program also calculated the mean and standard error of these distributions. Figure 19 shows the manner in which the size of the standard error decreases with increasing sample size. These curves of increasing precision are similar to those estimated on the basis of the Roosevelt Lake and Horseshoe Reservoir survey data (Figure 16). The curves indicate, for example, that an increase of sample size from 20 percent to 40 percent would have reduced the size of the standard error of the estimated total number of sites and data recovery man-days by about 35 percent. This increase in sample size would probably have increased survey costs by approximately 50 percent. In terms of estimating total mitigation costs, this would have meant a decline of 3½ to 4 million dollars in the size of the standard error for a total mitigation budget of approximately 18 million dollars. It should be noted that even at the 80 percent sampling fraction the size of the standard error is approximately 2½ to 3 million dollars. In general, the simulation has shown that the precision of the combined ratio estimate increases regularly with sample size but the absolute size of the standard error may never become very small if the data are highly skewed.

The bias of the combined ratio estimate of the total number of sites was estimated as follows: The number of sites and data recovery man-days was computed. Then, the mean of the distribution of 300 estimates of the total number of sites was calculated. The mean was also calculated for data recovery man-days based upon simulated samples. Finally, the difference between the number and the mean was calculated. The bias at the various sampling fractions is plotted in Figure 19. The magnitude of the bias decreases with increases in sample size but not nearly as regularly as the decrease of the size of the standard error. Repeated drawing of 300 samples at various sampling fractions indicates that the direction and magnitude of the estimated bias may vary considerably, especially at lower sampling fractions. In general, the simulation study indicates that the combined ratio estimate is not an unduly biased statistic even when calculated on small samples from highly skewed data.

The simulation program was also designed to draw simple random samples and systematic samples. The precision and bias of these sampling schemes as estimated on the basis of 300 simulated samples of the Orme

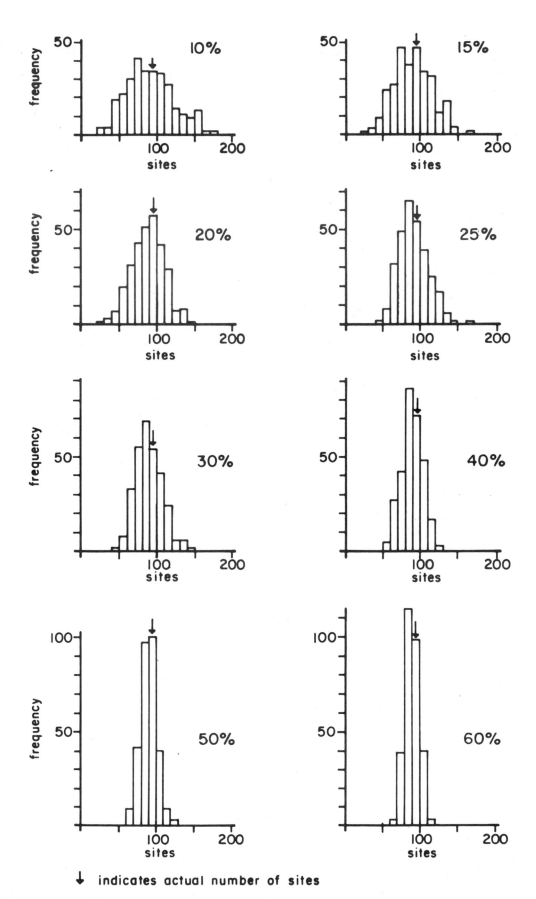

↓ indicates actual number of sites

Figure 17. ORME RESERVOIR SIMULATION: SITE PREDICTIONS. Graphs show the distributions of total site predictions at eight sampling fractions. These are based on 300 combined ratio estimates per sampling fraction. Y-axis represents frequencies of simulation estimates. X-axis represents total number of sites.

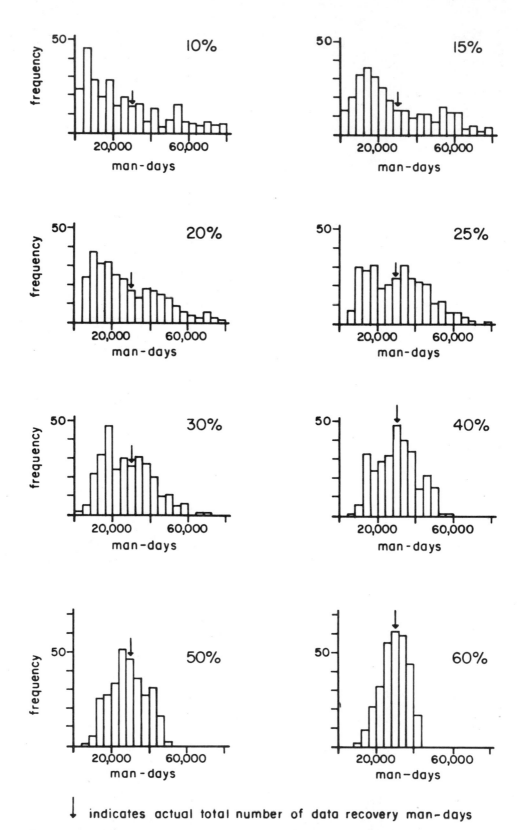

↓ indicates actual total number of data recovery man-days

Figure 18. ORME RESERVOIR SIMULATION: MAN-DAY PREDICTIONS. Graphs show the distributions of data recovery man-day predictions at eight sampling fractions. These are based on 300 combined ratio estimates per sampling fraction. Y-axis represents frequencies of simulation estimates. X-axis represents total number of data recovery man-days.

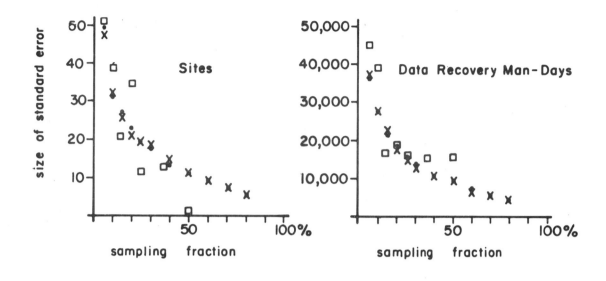

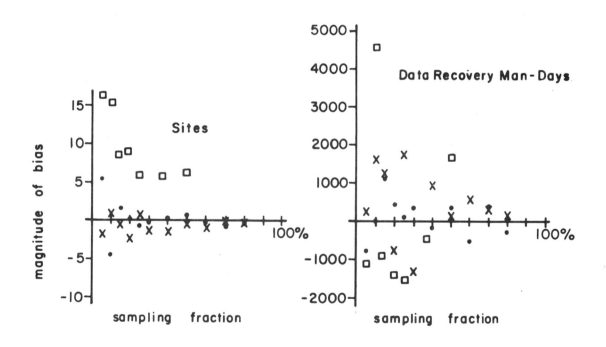

Figure 19. ORME RESERVOIR SIMULATION: PRECISION AND BIAS. Upper graphs show the relationship between the sampling fraction (X-axis) and precision of the combined ratio estimate. The Y-axis shows the standard error as sites or data recovery man-days. The lower graphs show the relationship between the sampling fraction (X-axis) and the bias of the combined ratio estimate. The Y-axis shows the bias as the number of sites or data recovery man-days. Graphs are based on 300 Simple Random, Stratified Random, or Systematic simulated samples of the Orme Reservoir data.

Reservoir data are also depicted in Figure 19. The results indicate that systematic sampling is considerably more biased than simple random or stratified random sampling. In addition, precision increases in a much less regular manner with systematic sampling than with the two other sampling schemes. These difficulties with systematic sampling may be due to periodicities of the distribution of sites in the survey area. Using intermittent drainages as natural boundaries for the sample units may have exaggerated this problem. Systematic sampling should be avoided when surveying in situations similar to those that characterize the simulation data.

A comparison of the precision and bias of the simple random and stratified random sampling schemes indicates that they are virtually identical. This indicates that either the criteria used to stratify the sample units are essentially irrelevant for predicting site densities or that these criteria were used inappropriately. For the most part, degree of slope was the primary stratification measure in the Orme Alternatives survey and the Orme Reservoir simulation project. Intuitively, it would seem that degree of slope is an important variable and does show a relationship to prehistoric settlement (cf. Gumerman 1971). However, the use of slope as a measure for placing sample units in one of the various strata has probably contributed to our problem. When actually conducting the on-the-ground survey of Roosevelt Lake and Horseshoe Reservoir, it became apparent that a few sample units were basically flat, a few were basically steep-sloped, but that most had distinct subdivisions that were either steep or flat. Thus, it seems that it was inappropriate to force the sample units into any one particular stratum. In the future, the combination of using slope as a stratifying criteria with irregular sample units which crosscut physiographic features should be avoided in stratified random sampling designs.

Summary

It is clear that in designing an appropriate sampling plan for any given project, many factors must be considered. Two special factors commonly associated with archaeological surveys are small sample sizes and skewed distributions of the data being sampled. Because of these two factors, the population parameters estimated on the basis of archaeological surveys are often very imprecise. Several methods that can be used to decrease the size of the standard errors of estimates of the total sites and data recovery man-days have been discussed. These include ratio estimation, variable transformation, improved stratification of the sample, changing sample unit size, and increasing the sampling fraction.

Ratio estimation decreased the size of the standard error for the Horseshoe Reservoir survey but not for the Roosevelt Lake survey. This is because the number of sites and data recovery man-days was highly correlated with sample unit size in the Horseshoe Reservoir sample but not in the Roosevelt Lake sample. The variable nature of this relationship is unexplained and should prove to be an interesting subject for future archaeological research. Variable transformation was not really investigated and probably should be, but major limitations of this method were mentioned. The stratification of our sample design certainly could have been improved, but improving stratification depends upon improving the prediction of site location. Understanding site location is the subject of continuing research. But if predictive variables are discovered, gathering information about the distribution of these variables will increase survey costs. After evaluating the size of our sample units, it was concluded that they were of essentially appropriate size, and the fact that they were naturally bounded resulted in a substantial reduction of field time. The increase in precision that would have resulted from increasing the sampling fraction was also investigated. The level of imprecision that will be tolerable will, of course, vary with the goals of any given project. A 20 percent sampling fraction that resulted in a standard error on the order of 28 million dollars is very large. For this project it was tolerable because the estimated cost for the mitigation of the archaeological resources of the Orme alternatives was so much greater than the mitigation budget for the Orme Reservoir project itself. Increasing the sampling fraction would have been the surest way of reducing the size of the standard error if this had been necessary.

Finally, simulated samples from the Orme Reservoir project provided empirical data about the distribution of the combined ratio estimate of the total when based upon stratified random samples from highly skewed data. Estimates of the total number of sites and data recovery man-days based upon small samples of skewed data were shown to be wide ranging. The size of the standard error did decrease rapidly with initial increases of sample size but subsequent increases of sample size resulted in relatively less increase in precision. In general, the bias of the estimated totals also decreased with increasing sample size and was always small compared to the size of the standard error. The simulation study also indicated that systematic sampling should be avoided in circumstances similar to those in which this study was done. In addition the simulation study indicated that the criteria used to stratify the sample units were either irrelevant for predicting site location or inappropriately used. This aspect of designing efficient sampling strategies certainly deserves more attention.

It should be clear that the adoption of probabilistic sampling procedures has not solved all the problems of archaeological surveyors. We now know that it is particularly important to consider the distribution of the archaeological data being sampled. As the variability of these distributions comes to be understood better, more efficient sampling strategies can be designed.

Table 11

Estimated Number of Sites
in the Roosevelt Lake Survey

$$\hat{X}_c = r_c \, Y = \frac{\hat{X}_{st}}{\hat{Y}_{st}} \, Y = \frac{\Sigma N_h \big/ n_h \overset{n_h}{\underset{}{\Sigma}} x_{hi}}{\Sigma N_h \big/ n_h \, \Sigma \, y_{hi}} \, Y$$

where:

n_h = number of sample units surveyed in stratum h

N_h = number of sample units in stratum h

N_h/n_h = reciprocal of the sampling fraction

x_{hi} = number of sites in sample unit i in stratum h

y_{hi} = number of acres in sample unit i in stratum h

Y = total number of acres

$\hat{Y}_{st}$ = estimated total number of acres by stratified random sampling

r_c = estimated number of sites per acre by combined ratio estimate

$\hat{X}_{st}$ = estimated total number of sites by stratified random sampling

$\hat{X}_c$ = estimated total number of sites by combined ratio estimate

	N_h	n_h	N_h/n_h	x_{hi}	$\overset{n_h}{\Sigma} x_{hi}$
Stratum 1	18	3	6.00	4,0,1	5
Stratum 2	15	3	5.00	0,0,2	2
Stratum 3	48	8	6.00	0,9,0,0,2,1,0,1	13
Stratum 4	41	10	4.10	0,1,2,0,1,3,0,0,1,0	8

	y_{hi}	$\overset{n_h}{\Sigma} y_{hi}$
Stratum 1	45, 108, 84	237
Stratum 2	53, 181, 218	452
Stratum 3	54, 138, 164, 179, 101, 49, 49, 85	819
Stratum 4	17,22,46,16,46,22,39,29,43,13	293

Table 11 (cont.)

Estimated Number of Sites
in the Roosevelt Lake Survey

$$r_c = \frac{(6 \times 5) + (5 \times 2) + (6 \times 13) + (4.1 \times 8)}{(6 \times 237) + (5 \times 452) + (6 \times 819) + (4.1 \times 293)} = \frac{150.8}{9797.3}$$

$$= .0154 \text{ sites/acre } (9.86 \text{ sites/mile}^2)$$

$$\hat{X}_c = .0154 \text{ sites/acre} \times 8148 \text{ acres}$$

$$\approx 125 \text{ sites}$$

Table 12

Bias of the Combined Ratio of Estimated
Sites in the Roosevelt Lake Survey

$$\text{bias} = Y \times E(r_c - R_c) = Y \sum_{}^{L} \frac{N_h - n_h}{N_h \, n_h} \frac{1}{\bar{y}_h^2} (r_c \, s_{yh}^2 - \rho_h \, s_{xh} \, s_{yh})$$

where:

Y = total number of acres in the survey area

$E(r_c - R_c)$ = expected difference between r_c and R_c

r_c = combined ratio estimate of the number of sites per acre based upon the sample data

R_c = estimated actual ratio of the number of sites per acre in the entire survey area

See Table 13 for explanation and values of all other symbols.

	N_h	n_h	$\dfrac{N_h - n_h}{N_h \, n_h}$	$\bar{y}_h$	$\bar{y}_h^2$	r_c
Stratum 1	18	3	.28	79.00	6,241.00	
Stratum 2	15	3	.27	150.67	22,701.45	
Stratum 3	48	8	.10	102.38	10,481.66	
Stratum 4	41	10	.08	29.30	858.49	
						.0154

	s_{yh}^2	ρ_h	$s_{xh} \, s_{yh}$	$r_c \, s_{yh}^2 - \rho_h \, s_{xh} \, s_{yh}$
Stratum 1	1011.00	-.99	66.14	81.05
Stratum 2	7496.34	.67	100.43	48.16
Stratum 3	2754.26	.22	161.11	6.97
Stratum 4	171.12	.29	13.47	-1.27

	$\dfrac{N_h - n_h}{N_h \, n_h} \dfrac{1}{y_h^2} (r_c \, s_{yh}^2 - \rho_h \, s_{xh} \, s_{yh})$
Stratum 1	.00364
Stratum 2	.00057
Stratum 3	.00007
Stratum 4	-.00012

$$\sum^{L} = .00416$$

Table 12 (cont.)

Bias of the Combined Ratio of Estimated
Sites in the Roosevelt Lake Survey Area

bias = 8148 acres x .00416 sites/acre

$\approx$ 34 sites

125 sites - 34 sites $\approx$ 91 sites = estimated total number of sites
adjusted for bias

Table 13

Standard Error of the Estimated Sites
in the Roosevelt Lake Survey

$$SE(\hat{X}_c) = \sqrt{\hat{V}(\hat{X}_c)} = \sqrt{Y^2\,\hat{V}(r_c)} = \sqrt{Y^2\,\frac{1}{\hat{Y}_{st}^{\;2}}\,\sum_h^L N_h^2\,\frac{N_h - n_h}{N_h}\,\frac{1}{n_h}\,s_{ch}^2}$$

where:

s_{ch}^2 = variance of the sample ratio of sites per acre

$= s_{xh}^2 + r_c^2\,s_{yh}^2 - 2r_c\rho_h\,s_{xh}\,s_{yh}$

s_{xh}^2 = variance of sample sites = $\sum^{n_h} (x_{hi} - \bar{x}_h)^2/n_h - 1$

s_{yh}^2 = variance of sample acres = $\sum^{n_h} (y_{hi} - \bar{y}_h)^2/n_h - 1$

r_c = ratio of sites per acre = $\hat{X}_{st}/\hat{Y}_{st}$ = .0154 from Table 11

ρ_h = coefficient of correlation between the number of sites and number of acres in stratum h

$= \dfrac{s_{xyh}}{s_{xh}\,s_{yh}} = \dfrac{\sum^{n_h} (x_{hi} - \bar{x}_h)\,(y_{hi} - \bar{y}_h)\,/\,n_h - 1}{\sqrt{\sum (x_{hi} - \bar{x}_h)^2/n_h - 1}\;\sqrt{\sum(y_{hi} - \bar{y}_h)^2/n_h - 1}}$

x_{hi} = number of sites in sample unit i in stratum h

n_h = number of sample units surveyed in stratum h

N_h = number of sample units in stratum h

$\bar{x}_h$ = average number of sites per sample unit in stratum h = $\dfrac{\sum^{n_h} x_{hi}}{n_h}$

y_{hi} = number of acres in sample unit i in stratum h

$\bar{y}_h$ = average number of acres per sample unit in stratum h = $\dfrac{\sum^{n_h} y_{hi}}{n_h}$

L = number of strata

Y_{st} = estimated total number of acres = 9797.3 from Table 11 by stratified random sampling

Y = actual number of acres = 8148

Table 13 (cont.)

Standard Error of the Estimated Sites
in the Roosevelt Lake Survey

	x_{hi}	$\sum_{h}^{n_h} x_h$	$\bar{x}_h$
Stratum 1	4, 0, 1	5	1.67
Stratum 2	0, 0, 2	2	.67
Stratum 3	0,9,0,0,2,1,0,1	13	1.63
Stratum 4	0,1,2,0,1,3,0,0,1,0	8	.80

	$(x_{hi} - \bar{x}_h)$	$(x_{hi} - \bar{x}_h)^2$
Stratum 1	2.33, -1.67, -.67	5.43, 2.79, .45
Stratum 2	-.67, -.67, 1.33	.45, .45, 1.77
Stratum 3	-1.63, 7.37, -1.63, -1.63, .37, -.63, -1.63, -.63	2.66, 54.32, 2.66, 2.66, .14, .40, 2.66, .40
Stratum 4	-.80, .20, 1.20, -.80, .20, 2.20, -.80, -.80, .20, -.80	.64, .04, 1.44, .64, .04, 4.84, .64, .64, .04, .64

	y_{hi}	$\sum_{h}^{n_h} y_{hi}$	$\bar{y}_h$
Stratum 1	45, 108, 84	237	79.00
Stratum 2	53, 181, 218	452	150.67
Stratum 3	54, 138, 164, 179, 101, 49, 49, 85	819	102.38
Stratum 4	17, 22, 46, 16, 46, 22, 39, 29, 43, 13	293	29.30

	$(y_{hi} - \bar{y}_h)$	$(y_{hi} - \bar{y}_h)^2$
Stratum 1	-34, 29, 5	1156, 841, 25
Stratum 2	-97.67, 30.33, 67.33	9539.43, 919.91, 4533.33
Stratum 3	-48.38, 35.62, 61.62, 76.62, -1.38, -53.38, -53.38, -17.38	2340.62, 1268.78, 3797.02, 5870.62, 1.90, 2849.42, 2849.42, 302.06
Stratum 4	-12.30, -7.30, 16.70, -13.30, 16.70, -7.30, 9.70, -0.30, 13.70, -16.30	151.29, 53.29, 278.89, 176.89, 278.89, 53.29, 94.09, .09, 187.69, 265.69

Table 13 (cont.)

Standard Error of the Estimated Sites
in the Roosevelt Lake Survey

	$(x_{hi} - \bar{x}_h)(y_{hi} - \bar{y}_h)$	$\sum\limits^{n_h} (x_{hi} - \bar{x}_h)(y_{hi} - \bar{y}_h)$
Stratum 1	-79.22, -48.43, -3.35	-131.00
Stratum 2	65.44, -20.32, 89.55	134.67
Stratum 3	78.86, 262.52, -100.44, -124.89, -.51, 33.63, 87.01, 10.95	247.13
Stratum 4	9.84, -1.46, 20.04, 10.64, 3.34, -16.06, -7.76, .24, 2.74, 13.04	34.60

	$\sum\limits^{n_h} (x_{hi} - \bar{x}_h)^2$	$\sum\limits^{n_h} (y_{hi} - \bar{y}_h)^2$	n_h	$n_h - 1$
Stratum 1	8.67	2,022.00	3	2
Stratum 2	2.67	14,992.67	3	2
Stratum 3	65.90	19,279.84	8	7
Stratum 4	9.60	1,540.10	10	9

	s_{xyh}	s_{xh}^2	s_{xh}	s_{yh}^2	s_{yh}
Stratum 1	-65.50	4.34	2.08	1011.00	31.80
Stratum 2	67.34	1.34	1.16	7496.34	86.58
Stratum 3	35.30	9.41	3.07	2754.26	52.48
Stratum 4	3.84	1.07	1.03	171.12	13.08

	$s_{xh}s_{yh}$	ρ_h	$2r_c$	r_c^2	$2r_c\rho_h \, s_{xh} \, s_{yh}$
Stratum 1	66.14	-.99			-2.02
Stratum 2	100.43	.67			2.07
Stratum 3	161.11	.22			1.09
Stratum 4	13.47	.29			.12
			.0308	.0002	

	$s_{xh}^2 + r_c^2 \, s_{yh}^2$	s_{ch}^2	N_h	$N_h - n_h$
Stratum 1	4.54	6.56	18	15
Stratum 2	2.84	.77	15	12
Stratum 3	9.96	8.87	48	40
Stratum 4	1.10	.98	41	31

Table 13 (cont.)

Standard Error of the Estimated Sites
in the Roosevelt Lake Survey

	$N_h{}^2 \dfrac{N_h - n_h}{N_h} \dfrac{1}{n_h}$	$N_h{}^2 \dfrac{N_h - n_h}{N_h} \dfrac{1}{n_h} s_{ch}{}^2$
Stratum 1	89.64	588.04
Stratum 2	60.00	46.20
Stratum 3	239.04	2120.28
Stratum 4	127.76	125.20

$$\overset{L}{\underset{}{\Sigma}} = 2879.72$$

$$SE(\hat{X}_c) = \sqrt{66{,}389{,}904 \quad \frac{1}{95{,}987{,}087} \quad 2879.72}$$

$$= \sqrt{1991.77}$$

$$\approx 45 \text{ sites}$$

Table 14

Estimated Number of Sites
in the Horseshoe Reservoir Survey

$$\hat{X}_c = r_c \, Y = \frac{\hat{X}_{st}}{\hat{Y}_{st}} \, Y = \frac{\sum^{L} N_h \, / \, n_h \sum^{n_h} x_{hi}}{\sum N_h \, / \, n_h \sum y_{hi}} \, Y$$

where:

n_h = number of sample units surveyed in stratum h

N_h = number of sample units in stratum h

N_h/n_h = reciprocal of the sampling fraction

x_{hi} = number of sites in sample unit i in stratum h

y_{hi} = number of acres in sample unit i in stratum h

Y = total number of acres

$\hat{Y}_{st}$ = estimated total number of acres by stratified random sampling

r_c = combined ratio estimate of number of sites per acre

$\hat{X}_{st}$ = estimated total number of sites by stratified random sampling

$\hat{X}_c$ = estimated total number of sites by combined ratio estimate

	N_h	n_h	N_h/n_h	x_{hi}	$\sum^{n_h} x_{hi}$
Stratum 1	15	3	5.00	2,0,2	4
Stratum 2	25	6	4.16	4,7,0,4,21,12	48
Stratum 3	14	3	4.67	3,2,7	12

	y_{hi}	$\sum^{n_h} y_{hi}$
Stratum 1	24, 25, 73	122
Stratum 2	109, 143, 40, 85, 253, 185	815
Stratum 3	49, 48, 74	171

Table 14 (cont.)

Estimated Number of Sites
in the Horseshoe Reservoir Survey

$$r_c = \frac{(5 \times 4) + (4.16 \times 48) + (4.67 \times 12)}{(5 \times 122) + (4.16 \times 815) + (4.67 \times 171)} = \frac{275.72}{4798.97}$$

$$= .0575 \text{ sites/acre } (36.80 \text{ sites/mile}^2)$$

$$\hat{X}_c = .0575 \text{ sites/acre} \times 5018 \text{ acres}$$

$$\approx 289 \text{ sites}$$

Table 15

Bias of the Combined Ratio of Estimated
Sites in the Horseshoe Reservoir Survey

$$\text{bias} = Y \times E(r_c - R_c) = Y \sum_{}^{L} \frac{N_h - n_h}{N_h \, n_h} \frac{1}{\bar{y}_h^2} (r_c \, s_{yh}^2 - \rho_h \, s_{xh} \, s_{yh})$$

where:

Y = total number of acres in the survey area

$E(r_c - R_c)$ = expected difference between r_c and R_c

r_c = combined ratio estimate of the number of sites per acre based upon the sample data

R_c = estimated actual ratio of the number of sites per acre in the entire survey area

See Table 16 for explanation and values of all other symbols.

	N_h	n_h	$\dfrac{N_h - n_h}{N_h \, n_h}$	$\bar{y}_h$	$\bar{y}_h^2$	r_c
Stratum 1	15	3	.27	40.67	1,654.05	
Stratum 2	25	6	.13	135.83	18,449.79	
Stratum 3	14	3	.26	57.00	3,249.00	
						.0575

	s_{yh}^2	ρ_h	$s_{xh} \, s_{yh}$	$r_c \, s_{yh}^2 - \rho_h \, s_{xh} \, s_{yh}$
Stratum 1	784.34	.48	32.49	29.50
Stratum 2	5,736.97	.98	568.81	-227.56
Stratum 3	217.00	.99	39.03	-26.16

	$\dfrac{N_h - n_h}{N_h \, n_h} \dfrac{1}{\bar{y}_h^2} (r_c \, s_{yh}^2 - \rho_h \, s_{xh} \, s_{yh})$
Stratum 1	.00482
Stratum 2	-.00160
Stratum 3	-.00209
$\sum^{L}$ =	.00113

Table 15 (cont.)

Bias of the Combined Ratio of Estimated
Sites in the Horseshoe Reservoir Survey

bias = 5018 acres x .00113 sites/acre

$\approx$ 6 sites

289 sites − 6 sites $\approx$ 283 sites = estimated total number of sites
adjusted for bias.

Table 16

Standard Error of the Estimated Sites
in the Horseshoe Reservoir Survey

$$SE(\hat{X}_c) = \sqrt{\hat{V}(\hat{X}_c)} = \sqrt{Y^2\,\hat{V}(r_c)} = \sqrt{Y^2\,\frac{1}{\hat{Y}_{st}^2}\,\sum_{}^{L} N_h^2\,\frac{N_h - n_h}{N_h}\,\frac{1}{n_h}\,s_{ch}^2}$$

where:

s_{ch}^2 = variance of the sample ratio of sites per acre

$\quad = s_{xh}^2 + r_c^2\,s_{yh}^2 - 2r_c\rho_h\,s_{xh}\,s_{yh}$

s_{xh}^2 = variance of sample sites = $\displaystyle\sum_{}^{n_h} (x_{hi} - \bar{x}_h)^2/n_h - 1$

s_{yh}^2 = variance of sample acres = $\displaystyle\sum_{}^{n_h} (y_{hi} - \bar{y}_h)^2/n_h - 1$

r_c = ratio of sites per acre = $\hat{X}_{st}/\hat{Y}_{st}$ = .0575 from Table 14

ρ_h = coefficient of correlation between number of sites and number of acres in stratum h

$$= \frac{s_{xyh}}{s_{xh}s_{yh}} = \frac{\sum^{n_h} (x_{hi} - \bar{x}_h)(y_{hi} - \bar{y}_h)/n_h - 1}{\sqrt{\sum (x_{hi} - \bar{x}_h)^2/n_h - 1}\,\sqrt{\sum (y_{hi} - \bar{y}_h)^2/n_h - 1}}$$

x_{hi} = number of sites in sample unit i in stratum h

n_h = number of sample units surveyed in stratum h

N_h = number of sample units in stratum h

$\bar{x}_h$ = average number of sites per sample unit in stratum h = $\dfrac{\sum^{n_h} x_{hi}}{n_h}$

y_{hi} = number of acres in sample unit i in stratum h

$\bar{y}_h$ = average number of acres per sample unit in stratum h = $\dfrac{\sum^{n_h} y_{hi}}{n_h}$

L = number of strata

$\hat{Y}_{st}$ = estimated total number of acres = 4798.97 from Table 14 by stratified random sampling

Y = actual total number of acres = 5018

Table 16 (cont.)

Standard Error of the Estimated Sites
in the Horseshoe Reservoir Survey

	x_{hi}	$\overset{n_h}{\underset{\Sigma}{}}\ x_h$	$\bar{x}_h$	$(x_{hi} - \bar{x}_h)$
Stratum 1	2, 0, 2	4	1.33	.67, -1.33, .67
Stratum 2	4, 7, 0, 4, 21, 12	48	8.00	-4.00, -1.00, -8.00, -4.00, 13.00, 4.00
Stratum 3	3, 2, 7	12	4.00	-1.00, -2.00, 3.00

	$(x_{hi} - \bar{x}_h)^2$	y_{hi}
Stratum 1	.45, 1.77, .45	24, 25, 73
Stratum 2	16.00,1.00,64.00,16.00,169.00,16.00	109,143,40,85,253,185
Stratum 3	1.00, 4.00, 9.00	49, 48, 74

	$\overset{n_h}{\underset{\Sigma}{}}\ y_{hi}$	$\bar{y}_h$	$(y_{hi} - \bar{y}_h)$
Stratum 1	122	40.67	-16.67,-15.67,32.33
Stratum 2	815	135.83	-26.83,7.17,-95.83,-50.83,117.17,49.17
Stratum 3	171	57.00	-8.00,-9.00,17.00

	$(y_{hi} - \bar{y}_h)^2$
Stratum 1	277.89, 245.55, 1045.23
Stratum 2	719.85, 51.41, 9183.39, 2583.69, 13,728.81, 2417.69
Stratum 3	64.00, 81.00, 289.00

	$(x_{hi} - \bar{x}_h)\ (y_{hi} - \bar{y}_h)$	$\overset{n_h}{\underset{\Sigma}{}}\ (x_{hi} - \bar{x}_h)\ (y_{hi} - \bar{y}_h)$
Stratum 1	-11.17, 20.84, 21.66	31.33
Stratum 2	107.32, -7.17, 766.64, 203.32, 1523.21, 196.68	2790.00
Stratum 3	8.00, 18.00, 51.00	77.00

Table 16 (cont.)

Standard Error of the Estimated Sites
in the Horseshoe Reservoir Survey

	$\sum\limits^{n_h} (x_{hi} - \bar{x}_h)^2$	$\sum\limits^{n_h} (y_{hi} - \bar{y}_h)^2$	n_h	$n_h - 1$
Stratum 1	2.67	1,568.67	3	2
Stratum 2	282.00	28,684.84	6	5
Stratum 3	14.00	434.00	3	2

	s_{xyh}	s_{xh}^2	s_{xh}
Stratum 1	15.67	1.34	1.16
Stratum 2	558.00	56.40	7.51
Stratum 3	38.50	7.00	2.65

	s_{yh}^2	s_{yh}	$s_{xh} s_{yh}$	ρ_h	$2r_c$	r_c^2
Stratum 1	784.34	28.01	32.49	.48		
Stratum 2	5736.97	75.74	568.81	.98		
Stratum 3	217.00	14.73	39.03	.99		
					.1150	.0033

	$2r_c \rho_h s_{xh} s_{yh}$	$s_{xh}^2 + r_c^2 s_{yh}^2$	s_{ch}^2
Stratum 1	1.79	3.93	2.14
Stratum 2	64.10	75.33	11.23
Stratum 3	4.44	7.72	3.28

	N_h	$N_h - n_h$	$N_h^2 \dfrac{N_h - n_h}{N_h} \dfrac{1}{n_h}$	$N_h^2 \dfrac{N_h - n_h}{N_h} \dfrac{1}{n_h} s_{ch}^2$
Stratum 1	15	12	60.00	128.40
Stratum 2	25	19	79.17	889.08
Stratum 3	14	11	51.61	169.28

$$\sum^{L} = 1186.76$$

Table 16 (cont.)

Standard Error of the Estimated Sites
in the Horseshoe Reservoir Survey

$$SE(\hat{X}_c) = \sqrt{25,180,324 \quad \frac{1}{23,030,113} \quad 1186.76}$$

$$= \sqrt{1297.56}$$

$$\approx \quad 36 \text{ sites}$$

Table 17

Estimated Number of Man-days
for Roosevelt Lake Data Recovery

$$\hat{X}_c = r_c\, Y = \frac{\hat{X}_{st}}{\hat{Y}_{st}}\, Y = \frac{\sum\limits^{L} N_h \,/\, n_h \sum\limits^{n_h} x_{hi}}{\sum N_h \,/\, n_h \sum y_{hi}}\, Y$$

where:

n_h = number of sample units surveyed in stratum h

N_h = number of sample units in stratum h

N_h/n_h = reciprocal of the sampling fraction

x_{hi} = number of man-days in sample unit i in stratum h

y_{hi} = number of acres in sample unit i in stratum h

Y = total number of acres

$\hat{Y}_{st}$ = estimated total number of acres by stratified random sampling

r_c = estimated number of man-days per acre by combined ratio estimate

$\hat{X}_{st}$ = estimated total number of man-days by stratified random sampling

$\hat{X}_c$ = estimated total number of man-days by combined ratio estimate

	N_h	n_h	N_h/n_h	x_{hi}
Stratum 1	18	3	6.00	275, 0, 100
Stratum 2	15	3	5.00	0, 0, 30
Stratum 3	48	3	6.00	0, 8725, 0, 0, 20, 5, 0, 30
Stratum 4	41	10	4.10	0,700,450,0,5,465,0,0,15,0

	$\sum^{n_h} x_{hi}$	y_{hi}	$\sum^{n_h} y_{hi}$
Stratum 1	375	45, 108, 84	237
Stratum 2	30	53, 181, 218	452
Stratum 3	8780	54,138,164,179,101,49,49,85	819
Stratum 4	1635	17,22,46,16,46,22,39,29,43,13	293

Table 17 (cont.)

Estimated Number of Man-days
for Roosevelt Lake Data Recovery

$$r_c = \frac{(6 \times 375) + (5 \times 30) + (6 \times 8780) + (4.1 \times 1635)}{(6 \times 237) + (5 \times 452) + (6 \times 819) + (4.1 \times 293)} = \frac{61,783.5}{9,797.3}$$

$= 6.31$ man-days/acre (4038 man-days/mile^2)

$\hat{X}_c = 6.31$ man-days/acre $\times$ 8148 acres

$\approx 51,400$ man-days

Table 18

Bias of the Combined Ratio of Estimated Data
Recovery Man-days in the Roosevelt Lake Survey

$$\text{bias} = Y \times E(r_c - R_c) = Y \sum_{}^{L} \frac{N_h - n_h}{N_h\, n_h} \frac{1}{\bar{y}_h^2} (r_c\, s_{yh}^2 - \rho_h\, s_{xh}\, s_{yh})$$

where:

Y	= total number of acres in the survey area
$E(r_c - R_c)$	= expected difference between r_c and R_c
r_c	= combined ratio estimate of the number of data recovery man-days per acre based upon the sample data
R_c	= estimated actual ratio of the number of data recovery man-days per acre in the entire survey area

See Table 19 for explanation and values of all other symbols.

	N_h	n_h	$\dfrac{N_h - n_h}{N_h\, n_h}$	$\bar{y}_h$	$\bar{y}_h^2$	r_c
Stratum 1	18	3	.28	79.00	6,241.00	
Stratum 2	15	3	.27	150.67	22,701.45	
Stratum 3	48	8	.10	102.38	10,481.66	
Stratum 4	41	10	.08	29.30	858.49	
						6.31

	s_{yh}^2	ρ_h	$s_{xh}\, s_{yh}$	$r_c\, s_{yh}^2 - \rho_h\, s_{xh}\, s_{yh}$
Stratum 1	1011.00	−1.00	4,426.24	10,805.65
Stratum 2	7496.34	.67	1,499.57	46,297.19
Stratum 3	2754.26	.27	161,743.36	−26,291.32
Stratum 4	171.12	−.02	3,492.49	1,149.62

	$\dfrac{N_h - n_h}{N_h\, n_h} \dfrac{1}{\bar{y}_h^2} (r_c\, s_{yh}^2 - \rho_h\, s_{xh}\, s_{yh})$
Stratum 1	.48
Stratum 2	.55
Stratum 3	−.25
Stratum 4	.11
	$\sum^{L} = .89$

Table 18 (cont.)

Bias of the Combined Ratio of Estimated Data
Recovery Man-days in the Roosevelt Lake Survey

bias = 8148 acres x .89 man-days/acre

$\approx$ 7200 man-days

51,400 man-days – 7200 man-days $\approx$ 44,200 man-days = estimated total number
of man-days adjusted
for bias

Table 19

Standard Error of the Estimated Number
of Man-days for Roosevelt Lake Data Recovery

$$SE(\hat{X}_c) = \sqrt{\hat{V}(\hat{X}_c)} = \sqrt{Y^2\, V(r_c)} = \sqrt{Y^2\, \frac{1}{\hat{Y}_{st}^2}\, \sum_h^L N_h^2\, \frac{N_h - n_h}{N_h}\, \frac{1}{n_h}\, s_{ch}^2}$$

where:

s_{ch}^2 = variance of the sample ratio of man-days per acre

$\quad = s_{xh}^2 + r_c^2\, s_{yh}^2 - 2r_c \rho_h\, s_{xh}\, s_{yh}$

s_{xh}^2 = variance of sample man-days = $\sum_h^{n_h} (x_{hi} - \bar{x}_h)^2 / n_h - 1$

s_{yh}^2 = variance of sample acres = $\sum_h^{n_h} (y_{hi} - \bar{y}_h)^2 / n_h - 1$

r_c = ratio of man-days per acre = $\hat{X}_{st} / \hat{Y}_{st}$ = 6.31 from Table 17

ρ_h = coefficient of correlation between the number of man-days and number of acres in stratum h

$$= \frac{s_{xyh}}{s_{xh}\, s_{yh}} = \frac{\sum^{n_h} (x_{hi} - \bar{x}_h)\,(y_{hi} - \bar{y}_h) / n_h - 1}{\sqrt{\sum (x_{hi} - \bar{x}_h)^2 / n_h - 1}\, \sqrt{\sum (y_{hi} - \bar{y}_h)^2 / n_h - 1}}$$

x_{hi} = number of man-days in sample unit i in stratum h

n_h = number of sample units surveyed in stratum h

N_h = number of sample units in stratum h

$\bar{x}_h$ = average number of man-days per sample unit in stratum h = $\dfrac{\sum^{n_h} x_{hi}}{n_h}$

y_{hi} = number of acres in sample unit i in stratum h

$\bar{y}_h$ = average number of acres per sample unit in stratum h = $\dfrac{\sum^{n_h} y_{hi}}{n_h}$

L = number of strata

$\hat{Y}_{st}$ = estimated total number of acres = 9797.3 from Table 17 by stratified random sampling

Y = actual total number of acres = 8148

Table 19 (cont.)

Standard Error of the Estimated Number
of Man-days for Roosevelt Lake Data Recovery

	x_{hi}	$\overset{n_h}{\underset{}{\Sigma}} \, x_h$	$\bar{x}_h$
Stratum 1	275, 0, 100	375	125.00
Stratum 2	0, 0, 30	30	10.00
Stratum 3	0, 8725, 0, 0, 20, 5, 0, 30	8780	1097.50
Stratum 4	0, 700, 450, 0, 5, 465, 0, 0, 15, 0	1635	163.50

	$(x_{hi} - \bar{x}_h)$	$(x_{hi} - \bar{x}_h)^2$
Stratum 1	150, -125, -25	22,500; 15,625; 625
Stratum 2	-10, -10, 20	100, 100, 400
Stratum 3	-1097.5, 7627.5, -1097.5 -1097.5, -1077.5, -1092.5, -1097.5, -1067.5	1,204,506.25; 58,178,756.25; 1,204,506.25; 1,204,506.25; 1,161,006.25; 1,193,556.25; 1,204,506.25; 1,139,556.25
Stratum 4	-163.5, 536.5, 286.5, -163.5, -158.5, 301.5, -163.5, -163.5, -148.5, -163.5	26,732.25; 287,832.25; 82,082.25; 26,732.25; 25,122.25; 90,902.25; 26,732.25; 26,732.25; 22,052.25; 26,732.25

	y_{hi}	$\overset{n_h}{\underset{}{\Sigma}} \, y_{hi}$	$\bar{y}_h$
Stratum 1	45, 108, 84	237	79.00
Stratum 2	53, 181, 218	452	150.67
Stratum 3	54, 138, 164, 179, 101, 49, 49, 85	819	102.38
Stratum 4	17, 22, 46, 16, 46, 22, 39, 29, 43, 13	293	29.30

	$(y_{hi} - \bar{y}_h)$	$(y_{hi} - \bar{y}_h)^2$
Stratum 1	-34, 29, 5	1156, 841, 25
Stratum 2	-97.67, 30.33, 67.33	9539.43, 919.91, 4533.33
Stratum 3	-48.38, 35.62, 61.62, 76.62, -1.38, -53.38, -53.38, -17.38	2340.62, 1268.78, 3797.02, 5870.62, 1.90, 2849.42, 2849.42, 302.06
Stratum 4	-12.30, -7.30, 16.70, -13.30, 16.70, -7.30, 9.70, -0.30, 13.70, -16.30	151.29, 53.29, 278.89, 176.89, 278.89, 53.29, 94.09, .09, .09, 187.69, 265.69

Table 19 (cont.)

Standard Error of the Estimated Number
of Man-days for Roosevelt Lake Data Recovery

	$(x_{hi} - \bar{x}_h)(y_{hi} - \bar{y}_h)$	$\sum\limits^{n_h} (x_{hi} - \bar{x}_h)(y_{hi} - \bar{y}_h)$
Stratum 1	−5100, −3625, −125	−8,850.00
Stratum 2	976.7, −303.3, 1346.6	2,020.00
Stratum 3	53,097.05; 271,691.55; −67,627.95; −84,090.45; 1486.95; 58,317.65; 58,584.55; 18,553.15	310,012.50
Stratum 4	2011.05; −3916.45; 4784.55; 2174.55; −2646.95; −2200.95; −1585.95; 49.05; −2034.45; 2665.05	−700.50

	$\sum\limits^{n_h} (x_{hi} - \bar{x}_h)^2$	$\sum\limits^{n_h} (y_{hi} - \bar{y}_h)^2$	n_h	$n_h - 1$
Stratum 1	38,750.00	2,022.00	3	2
Stratum 2	600.00	14,992.67	3	2
Stratum 3	66,490,900.00	19,279.84	8	7
Stratum 4	641,652.50	1,540.10	10	9

	s_{xyh}	s_{xh}^2	s_{xh}	s_{yh}^2	s_{yh}
Stratum 1	−4,425.00	19,375.00	139.19	1011.00	31.80
Stratum 2	1,010.00	300.00	17.32	7496.34	86.58
Stratum 3	44,287.50	9,498,700.00	3082.00	2754.26	52.48
Stratum 4	−77.83	71,294.72	267.01	171.12	13.08

	$s_{xh} s_{yh}$	ρ_h	$2r_c$	r_c^2	$2r_c \rho_h s_{xh} s_{yh}$
Stratum 1	4,426.24	−1.00			−55,859.15
Stratum 2	1,499.57	.67			12,679.46
Stratum 3	161,743.36	.27			551,124.32
Stratum 4	3,492.49	−.02			−881.50
			12.62	39.82	

Table 19 (cont.)

Standard Error of the Estimated Number
of Man-days for Roosevelt Lake Data Recovery

	$s_{xh}^2 + r_c^2\, s_{yh}^2$	s_{ch}^2	N_h	$N_h - n_h$
Stratum 1	59,633.02	115,492.17	18	15
Stratum 2	298,804.26	286,124.80	15	12
Stratum 3	9,608,374.63	9,057,250.31	48	40
Stratum 4	78,108.72	78,990.72	41	31

	$N_h^2\, \dfrac{N_h - n_h}{N_h}\, \dfrac{1}{n_h}$	$N_h^2\, \dfrac{N_h - n_h}{N_h}\, \dfrac{1}{n_h}\, s_{ch}^2$
Stratum 1	89.64	10,352,718
Stratum 2	60.00	17,167,488
Stratum 3	239.04	2,165,045,114
Stratum 4	127.76	10,091,854

$$\overset{L}{\Sigma} = 2,202,657,174$$

$$SE(\hat{X}_c) = \sqrt{66,389,904\ \frac{1}{95,987,087}\ 2,202,657,174}$$

$$= \sqrt{1,523,477,823}$$

$$\approx 39,000 \text{ man-days}$$

Table 20

Estimated Number of Man-days
for Horseshoe Reservoir Data Recovery

$$\hat{X}_c = r_c \ Y = \frac{\hat{X}_{st}}{\hat{Y}_{st}} \ Y \ = \frac{\overset{L}{\Sigma} N_h \ / \ n_h \ \overset{n_h}{\underset{}{\Sigma}} x_{hi}}{\Sigma N_h \ / \ n_h \ \Sigma \ y_{hi}} \ Y$$

where:

n_h = number of sample units surveyed in stratum h

N_h = number of sample units in stratum h

N_h/n_h = reciprocal of the sampling fraction

x_{hi} = number of man-days in sample unit i in stratum h

y_{hi} = number of acres in sample unit i in stratum h

Y = total number of acres

$\hat{Y}_{st}$ = estimated total number of acres by stratified random sampling

r_c = estimated number of man-days per acre by combined ratio estimate

$\hat{X}_{st}$ = estimated total number of man-days by stratified random sampling

$\hat{X}_c$ = estimated total number of man-days by combined ratio estimate

	N_h	n_h	N_h/n_h	x_{hi}
Stratum 1	15	3	5.00	500, 0, 2025
Stratum 2	25	6	4.16	125,2440,0,516,3745,2860
Stratum 3	14	3	4.67	765, 100, 660

	$\overset{n_h}{\Sigma} x_{hi}$	y_{hi}	$\overset{n_h}{\Sigma} y_{hi}$
Stratum 1	2525	24, 25, 73	122
Stratum 2	9686	109,143,40,85,253,185	815
Stratum 3	1525	49, 48, 74	171

Table 20 (cont.)

Estimated Number of Man-days
for Horseshoe Reservoir Data Recovery

$$r_c = \frac{(5 \times 2525) + (4.16 \times 9686) + (4.67 \times 1525)}{(5 \times 122) + (4.16 \times 815) + (4.67 \times 171)} = \frac{60,040.51}{4,798.97}$$

= 12.51 man-days/acre (8006 man-days/mile^2)

$\hat{X}_c$ = 12.51 man-days/acre x 5018 acres

$\approx$ 62,800 man-days

Table 21

Bias of the Combined Ratio of Estimated Data
Recovery Man-days in the Horseshoe Reservoir Survey

$$\text{bias} = Y \times E(r_c - R_c) = Y \sum_{}^{L} \frac{N_h - n_h}{N_h \, n_h} \frac{1}{\bar{y}_h^{2}} \left(r_c \, s_{yh}^{2} - \rho_h \, s_{xh} \, s_{yh} \right)$$

where:

Y	= total number of acres in the survey area
$E(r_c - R_c)$	= expected difference between r_c and R_c
r_c	= combined ratio estimate of the number of data recovery man-days per acre based upon the sample data
R_c	= estimated actual ratio of the number of data recovery man-days per acre in the entire survey area

See Table 22 for explanation and value of all other symbols.

	N_h	n_h	$\dfrac{N_h - n_h}{N_h \, n_h}$	$\bar{y}_h$	$\bar{y}_h^{2}$	r_c
Stratum 1	15	3	.27	40.67	1,654.05	
Stratum 2	25	6	.13	135.83	18,449.79	
Stratum 3	14	3	.26	57.00	3,249.00	
						12.51

	s_{yh}^{2}	ρ_h	$s_{xh} \, s_{yh}$	$r_c \, s_{yh}^{2} - \rho_h \, s_{xh} \, s_{yh}$
Stratum 1	784.34	.97	29,546.35	−18,847.87
Stratum 2	5736.97	.94	121,201.42	−42,159.84
Stratum 3	217.00	.40	5,265.98	608.28

	$\dfrac{N_h - n_h}{N_h \, n_h} \dfrac{1}{\bar{y}_h^{2}} \left(r_c \, s_{yh}^{2} - \rho_h \, s_{xh} \, s_{yh} \right)$
Stratum 1	−3.08
Stratum 2	− .30
Stratum 3	.05
$\sum^{L}$	= −3.33

Table 21 (cont.)

Bias of the Combined Ratio of Estimated Data
Recovery Man-days in the Horseshoe Reservoir Survey

bias = 5018 acres x -3.33 man-days/acre

$\approx$ 16,700 man-days

62,800 man-days - (16,700 man-days) $\approx$ 79,500 man-days = estimated total
number of man-days
adjusted for bias

Table 22

Standard Error of the Estimated Man-days
for Horseshoe Reservoir Data Recovery

$$SE(\hat{X}_c) = \sqrt{\hat{V}(\hat{X}_c)} = \sqrt{Y^2 \, \hat{V}(r_c)} = \sqrt{Y^2 \, \frac{1}{\hat{Y}_{st}^2} \, \sum_{h}^{L} N_h^2 \, \frac{N_h - n_h}{N_h} \, \frac{1}{n_h} \, s_{ch}^2}$$

where:

s_{ch}^2 = variance of the sample ratio of man-days per acre

$\quad = s_{xh}^2 + r_c^2 \, s_{yh}^2 - 2r_c \rho_h \, s_{xh} \, s_{yh}$

s_{xh}^2 = variance of sample man-days = $\sum^{n_h} (x_{hi} - \bar{x}_h)^2 / n_h - 1$

s_{yh}^2 = variance of sample acres $\quad = \sum^{n_h} (y_{hi} - \bar{y}_h)^2 / n_h - 1$

r_c = ratio of man-days per acre = X_{st} / Y_{st} = 12.51 from Table 20

ρ_h = coefficient of correlation between number of man-days and number of acres in stratum h

$$= \frac{s_{xyh}}{s_{xh} s_{yh}} = \frac{\sum^{n_h} (x_{hi} - \bar{x}_h)(y_{hi} - \bar{y}_h) / n_h - 1}{\sqrt{\sum (x_{hi} - \bar{x}_h)^2 / n_h - 1} \sqrt{\sum (y_{hi} - \bar{y}_h)^2 / n_h - 1}}$$

x_{hi} = number of man-days in sample unit i in stratum h

n_h = number of sample units surveyed in stratum h

N_h = number of sample units in stratum h

$\bar{x}_h$ = average number of man-days per sample unit in stratum h = $\dfrac{\sum^{n_h} x_{hi}}{n_h}$

y_{hi} = number of acres in sample unit i in stratum h

$\bar{y}_h$ = average number of acres per sample unit in stratum h = $\dfrac{\sum^{n_h} y_{hi}}{n_h}$

L = number of strata

Table 22 (cont.)

Standard Error of the Estimated Man-days
for Horseshoe Reservoir Data Recovery

$\hat{Y}_{st}$ = estimated total number of acres by stratified random sampling

= 4798.97 from Table 20

Y = actual total number of acres = 5018

	x_{hi}	$\sum^{n_h} x_{hi}$	$\bar{x}_h$
Stratum 1	500, 0, 2025	2525	841.67
Stratum 2	125,2440,0,516,3745,2860	9686	1614.33
Stratum 3	765, 100, 660	1525	508.33

$(x_{hi} - \bar{x}_h)$

Stratum 1	-341.67, -841.67, 1183.33
Stratum 2	-1489.33; 825.67; -1614.33; -1098.33; 2130.67; 1245.67
Stratum 3	256.67; -408.33; 151.67

$(x_{hi} - \bar{x}_h)^2$

Stratum 1	116, 738.39; 708,408.39; 1,400,269.89
Stratum 2	2,218,103.85;681,730.95;2,606,061.35;1,206,328.79; 4,539,754.65;1,551,693.75
Stratum 3	65,879.49; 166,733.39; 23,003.79

	y_{hi}	$\sum^{n_h} y_{hi}$	$\bar{y}_h$
Stratum 1	24, 25, 73	122	40.67
Stratum 2	109, 143, 40, 85, 253, 185	815	135.83
Stratum 3	49, 48, 74	171	57.00

	$(y_{hi} - \bar{y}_h)$	$(x_{hi} - \bar{x}_h)(y_{hi} - \bar{y}_h)$
Stratum 1	-16.67, -15.67, 32.33	5695.64; 13,188.97; 38,257.06
Stratum 2	-26.83, 7.17, -95.83, -50.83, 117.17, 49.17	39,958.72; 5920.05; 154,701.24; 55,828.11; 249,650.60; 61,249.59
Stratum 3	-8.00, -9.00, 17.00	-2053.36; 3674.97; 2578.39

Table 22 (cont.)

Standard Error of the Estimated Man-days
for Horseshoe Reservoir Data Recovery

	$\sum\limits^{n_h} (x_{hi} - \bar{x}_h)(y_{hi} - \bar{y}_h)$	$\sum\limits^{n_h} (x_{hi} - \bar{x}_h)^2$	$\sum\limits^{n_h} (y_{hi} - \bar{y}_h)^2$
Stratum 1	57,141.67	2,225,416.67	1,568.67
Stratum 2	567,308.31	12,803,673.34	28,684.84
Stratum 3	4,200.00	255,616.67	434.00

	n_h	$n_h - 1$	s_{xyh}	s_{xh}^2	s_{xh}
Stratum 1	3	2	28,570.84	1,112,708.34	1054.85
Stratum 2	6	5	113,461.66	2,560.734.67	1600.23
Stratum 3	3	2	2,100.00	127,808.34	357.50

	s_{yh}^2	s_{yh}	$s_{xh} s_{yh}$	ρ_h	$2r_c$	r_c^2
Stratum 1	784.34	28.01	29,546.35	.97		
Stratum 2	5736.97	75.74	121,201.42	.94		
Stratum 3	217.00	14.73	5,265.98	.40		
					25.02	156.53

	$2r_c \rho_h s_{xh} s_{yh}$	$s_{xh}^2 + r_c^2 s_{yh}^2$	s_{ch}^2
Stratum 1	717,072.19	1,235,481.08	518,408.89
Stratum 2	2,850,511.96	3,458,742.58	608,230.62
Stratum 3	52,701.93	161,775.35	109,073.42

	N_h	$N_h - n_h$	$N_h^2 \dfrac{N_h - n_h}{N_h} \dfrac{1}{n_h}$	$N_h^2 \dfrac{N_h - n_h}{N_h} \dfrac{1}{n_h} s_{ch}^2$
Stratum 1	15	12	60.00	31,104,533.40
Stratum 2	25	19	79.17	48,153,618.19
Stratum 3	14	11	51.61	5,629,279.21

$$\sum^L = 84,887,430.80$$

Table 22 (cont.)

Standard Error of the Estimated Man-days
for Horseshoe Reservoir Data Recovery

$$SE(\hat{X}_c) = \quad 25{,}180{,}324 \quad \frac{1}{23{,}030{,}113} \quad 84{,}887{,}430.80$$

$$= \quad 92{,}812{,}962.36$$

$$\approx \quad 9600 \text{ man-days}$$

Chapter 7

A SETTLEMENT PATTERN ANALYSIS

This chapter presents an analysis of the prehistoric patterns of occupation in the Roosevelt Lake and Horseshoe Reservoir survey areas. Because evidence recoverable by archaeological survey methods often misrepresents subsurface evidence, it should be remembered that the classification and synthesis of the sample survey data presented in this chapter are tentative. The major part of this chapter consists of an attempt to simply quantify the variability of settlement patterns between the two survey areas. The chapter also discusses possible explanations of this variability and includes comparisons with two other surveys that have been made in central Arizona.

The Archaeological Analysis of Settlement Patterns

The archaeological analysis of settlement patterns began about a quarter of a century ago with Willey's (1953) work in the Viru Valley of Peru. (See Plog (1974) for a brief history of settlement pattern studies.) Since then the analysis of settlement patterns has come to be applied at three levels (Trigger 1968). The finest level of analysis involves the study of single structures. The next level investigates the ways in which individual structures are assembled to form sites, and at the broadest level the patterns of the location of sites across a landscape are analyzed. Because of the limitations of our survey data, this analysis will be limited to the broadest level.

The standard settlement pattern analysis of the location of sites involves two steps. The first is to functionally classify each site according to the activities that were carried on within it. Some examples of the functional types often used include habitation sites, ceremonial centers, field houses, and gathering stations. The second step consists of attempting to describe the pattern of distribution of these various functional site types and how these patterns changed through time. A logical third step would be to explain these patterns but this has seldom been achieved. As Plog (1974) suggests, this failure may be due, in part, to the inadequacy of the standard methodology. The required inferences of site function are often too subjective, especially when based only upon surface evidence. In addition, comparison of settlement patterns is difficult because formal quantitative techniques are seldom used to describe settlement patterns. Plog also notes that while the current methodology is most easily applied to stable patterns, archaeologists could use the great time depth of archaeological data to study how and why settlement patterns change.

152

Plog recommends that archaeologists adopt the more quantitative approach that has been developed by locational geographers. He suggests that archaeologists should attempt to measure attributes of the distribution of human populations such as density, degree of aggregation, range and distribution of site sizes, and symmetry of spatial patterns. The use of quantitative indexes to describe settlement patterns would facilitate comparison of survey data from different regions, but it should be kept in mind that the quantified values may often be subject to substantial measurement error. Problems such as varying definitions of "site," differential site visibility, and different intensities of surveying will continue to hamper comparisons of survey data. In order to measure what Plog calls differentiation of settlement patterns, it is still necessary to classify each site as a habitation or non-habitation site and this is often a subjective decision, especially when only survey data are available. This problem is complicated by the fact that site functions may very well have changed through time. For example, in the Southwest, many habitation sites may have been originally established as temporarily occupied field houses. To measure the degree of interaction among sites in the manner Plog suggests is an even more difficult task because it requires a comparison of the range of artifact stylistic variability among sites. Archaeologists will have to investigate the processes that create surface evidence of archaeological sites in order to be able to select representative samples on which to base such analyses (cf. Schiffer 1975b). On the whole, Plog's recommendations do indicate promising new directions for settlement pattern analyses. In the following section we present an attempt to carry out such an analysis.

Settlement Pattern Attributes of the Roosevelt Lake
and Horseshoe Reservoir Sample Survey Data

We began the analysis by converting the list of sites found in each survey area into a list of "site components." According to standard archaeological usage, a site component is the manifestation of a "phase" or "focus" at any given site (Willey and Phillips 1958: 21-22). Because the definition of phases is poorly defined in both survey areas and because the dating of the sites we recorded is so ambiguous, the definition of components was often subjective and arbitrary. Our goal in defining a list of components, even if it was extremely tentative, was to compensate for the fact that some sites in both survey areas appeared to have been occupied more than once, or for very long periods of time.

Our definition of a list of site components was based upon the list of site types or categories given at the end of Chapter 5. These categories were defined on the basis of surface manifestations at the sites recorded and in some cases incorporated standard but subjective functional interpretations. Components were defined by considering the temporal dimension in addition to the morphological criteria that were used to define site categories. When two or more site categories were present in any one given site they were often listed as separate components even if we only assumed they might not be contemporaneous. The multi-component sites we

defined are not the typical vertically stratified sites which the term
multi-component is often used to designate. A typical multi-component
site in our survey areas might include the following "horizontally stratified" components: (1) a room block surrounded by a compound wall, (2) an
agricultural system, and (3) a spatially separate one-room cobble structure
and associated midden. In some ways the list of site components could be
thought of as a maximal list except for the possibility that many buried
components may not have been recognized.

Each of the units identified as a site category was classified as
habitation or non-habitation on the basis of two criteria. The first was
a subjective appraisal of how substantial the architecture at a site had been.
Large compounds and pueblos were easy to classify, but small masonry or
partial masonry structures and suspected pit house sites posed some difficulty. The criterion used in these cases was a subjective evaluation of
the quantity of cultural debris at any given site. The assumption made was
that habitation sites would have larger amounts of prehistoric refuse than
non-habitation sites. The analysis of the sherd collections from pit house
habitation sites in the Horseshoe Reservoir survey area, as defined by these
criteria, revealed that they typically and uniquely contained both red-on-
buff and black-on-white sherds.

The explicit, but somewhat arbitrary, rules used to combine the site
categories into site components are:

(1) All agricultural systems associated with other non-habitation
     components were designated as one component unless distinctly
     subdivided spatially or temporally as indicated by the analysis
     of the sherd collections.

(2) All non-habitation categories associated with, but spatially
     distinct from, one or more habitation categories within the
     same site were designated as separate components unless the
     analysis of the sherd collections specifically indicated that
     they were contemporaneous.

(3) Structurally and spatially distinct habitation categories within
     a single site were designated as separate components.

Only prehistoric components were used in this analysis. At Roosevelt
Lake the 29 sites discovered were divided into 30 components (Table 25);
74 components were defined for the Horseshoe Reservoir survey area where
64 sites had been recorded (Table 26).

Because the dating of the non-habitation components was so vague,
no attempt was made to order them chronologically. The dating of the habitation components was not much better, but the results of the analysis of
the sherd collections were used in conjunction with an architectural classification to assign habitation components to one of three time periods. Pit
house sites were assigned to a period dating from about A.D. 700 to 1100.

Table 25

Prehistoric Site Components for the Roosevelt Lake Survey

Stratum	Sample Unit	Habitation	Non-habitation
1	19	AZ U:4:17 (T2)* AZ U:4:18 (T2)	AZ U:4:20
	26	none	none
	32b	none	none
2	80	none	none
	82b	none	none
	84c	none	AZ V:5:27 AZ V:5:28
3	11	none	none
	35b	AZ U:4:7a (T2) AZ U:4:7c (T2) AZ U:4:8 (T2) AZ U:4:9a (T3) AZ U:4:9b (T2) AZ U:4:9c (T2) AZ U:4:10 (T3) AZ U:4:11 (T2) AZ U:4:12 (T2) AZ U:4:13 (T2)	AZ U:4:7b AZ U:4:14 AZ U:4:15
	40	none	none
	49	none	none
	50	none	AZ U:8:74 AZ U:8:75
	54	none	AZ U:8:76
	67	none	none
	101	none	AZ U:8:70
4	2	none	none
	5	AZ U:8:78 (T2)	none
	6	AZ U:8:72 (T2) AZ U:8:73 (T2)	none
	8	none	none
	38	none	AZ U:4:16
	75	AZ U:8:67 (T1) AZ U:8:68 (T2)	AZ U:8:69
	88	none	none
	89	none	none
	96	none	AZ U:8:71
	115	none	none

*T1 = time period 1, A.D. 700 to 1100
 T2 = time period 2, A.D. 1000 to 1300
 T3 = time period 3, A.D. 1200 to 1450

Table 26

Prehistoric Site Components for the Horseshoe Reservoir Survey

Stratum	Sample Unit	Habitation		Non-habitation
1	31	AZ 0:14:49	(T1)*	none
		AZ 0:14:50	(T3)	
	32	none		none
	34	AZ 0:14:51a	(T1)	AZ 0:14:52
		AZ 0:14:51b	(T2)	
2	1	none		AZ U:2:22
				AZ U:2:23
				AZ U:2:24
				AZ U:2:25
	5	AZ U:2:1	(T3)	AZ U:2:2b
		AZ U:2:2a	(T2)	AZ U:2:33
		AZ U:2:36	(T2)	AZ U:2:34
				AZ U:2:35
				AZ U:2:37
	8	none		none
	17	AZ 0:14:8	(T1)	AZ 0:14:7
				AZ 0:14:9
				AZ 0:14:10
	40	AZ 0:14:16	(T1)	AZ 0:14:13
		AZ 0:14:17a	(T1)	AZ 0:14:14
		AZ 0:14:21	(T1)	AZ 0:14:15
		AZ 0:14:22a	(T2)	AZ 0:14:17b
				AZ 0:14:17c
				AZ 0:14:17d
				AZ 0:14:18
				AZ 0:14:19
				AZ 0:14:20
				AZ 0:14:22b
				AZ 0:14:22c
				AZ 0:14:23
				AZ 0:14:24
				AZ 0:14:25 and 27
				AZ 0:14:26
				AZ 0:14:28
				AZ 0:14:29
				AZ 0:14:30
				AZ 0:14:31
				AZ 0:14:32
				AZ 0:14:33

*T1 = time period 1, A.D. 700 to 1100
 T2 = time period 2, A.D. 1000 to 1300
 T3 = time period 3, A.D. 1200 to 1450

Table 26 (continued)

Stratum	Sample Unit	Habitation	Non-habitation
2	42	AZ O:14:34 (T3)	AZ O:14:39b
		AZ O:14:35 (T2)	AZ O:14:40
		AZ O:14:36 (T2)	AZ O:14:41
		AZ O:14:37 (T2)	AZ O:14:42
		AZ O:14:38a(T2)	AZ O:14:43
		AZ O:14:38b(T2)	AZ O:14:44
		AZ O:14:39a(T1)	AZ O:14:45
3	3	AZ O:14:46 (T2)	AZ O:14:47b
		AZ O:14:47a(T2)	
		AZ O:14:48 (T2)	
	21	AZ O:14:11 (T2)	AZ O:14:12
	49	AZ U:2:29 (T2)	AZ U:2:26
		AZ U:2:30 (T1)	AZ U:2:27
			AZ U:2:28
			AZ U:2:29b
			AZ U:2:31
			AZ U:2:32

Small cobble masonry habitation components and small compounds were estimated to have been occupied from about A.D. 1000 to A.D. 1300. Large compounds and large masonry structures without compound walls were assigned to
the period from about A.D. 1200 to 1450.

Because of the tentative nature of the definition of site components,
the results of the subsequent analysis should also be considered tentative.
The quantified indexes based upon these lists were calculated at three levels
of analysis comparable to those used by Green (1974) in his analysis of
settlement patterns in two canyons of southeastern Utah. Level 1 included
all site components. For Level 2, habitation and non-habitation components
were separated, and for Level 3, habitation components were separated into
time periods. It should be noted that the validity of our measured indexes
decreases with each increase in the level of analysis because the size of
the sample of each category becomes smaller as we subdivide the original
sample.

Density of Site Components

The first variable measured was density. This attribute should
provide an index of how intensively each area was occupied prehistorically.
Site component density was estimated for both survey areas on the basis of
our samples by using a formula for the combined ratio estimate discussed
in Chapter 6. The results are presented in Table 27 and graphically
depicted in Figure 20. The estimated densities are relatively imprecise,
but they indicate that the density of all components in the Horseshoe Reservoir area was about 43 components per square mile which is on the order of
5 times as dense as in the Roosevelt Lake survey area. Habitation components
were about three times as dense and non-habitation components about seven
times as dense in the Horseshoe Reservoir area as in the Roosevelt Lake
survey area. During Period 1 there were less than 0.5 habitation components
per square mile in the Roosevelt Lake area while in the Horseshoe Reservoir
area, the density was about 4 per square mile. During Period 2, density of
habitation components increased to similar magnitude in both areas. Density
in the Roosevelt Lake area was about 6 per square mile and 8 per square mile
in the Horseshoe Resevoir area. During Period 3, both survey areas averaged
only about 0.7 habitation components per square mile.

Degree of Aggregation

The second attribute measured was the degree of aggregation of site
components or, in other words, the evenness of the densities recorded.
Variations in the patterns of density within a region may provide clues in
identifying relevant variables that can be used to explain regional settlement pattern differences. The locational pattern of sites across a landscape can vary from uniform to random to clustered (Greig-Smith 1964: 11-12;
Southwood 1966: 24; Odum 1971: 205). A uniform arrangement is one in which
the sites would be located so as to form a regular grid pattern. A clustered

Table 27

Prehistoric Site Component Density per Square Mile for the
Roosevelt Lake and Horseshoe Reservoir Surveys

		Roosevelt	Horseshoe
Level 1:	All prehistoric components	8.4 $^{+8.0}_{-6.0}$ *	43.2 $\pm$10.1
Level 2:	Habitation components	4.4 $^{+6.3}_{-3.1}$	14.7 $\pm$4.5
	Non-habitation components	3.8 $\pm$2.4	27.5 $\pm$5.0
Level 3:	Period 1 (A.D. 700 to 1100) habitation components	0.2 $^{+0.4}_{-0.1}$	4.0 $\pm$2.2
	Period 2 (A.D. 1000 to 1300) habitation components	5.5 $^{+5.0}_{-4.4}$	8.3 $\pm$4.5
	Period 3 (A.D. 1200 to 1450) habitation components	0.7 $^{+1.2}_{-0.5}$	0.7 $^{+1.6}_{-0.3}$

*The confidence intervals were calculated by multiplying the standard
errors by the appropriate t value. Asymmetrical intervals are due to
the fact that the actual survey results sometimes exceeded minimum
estimates.

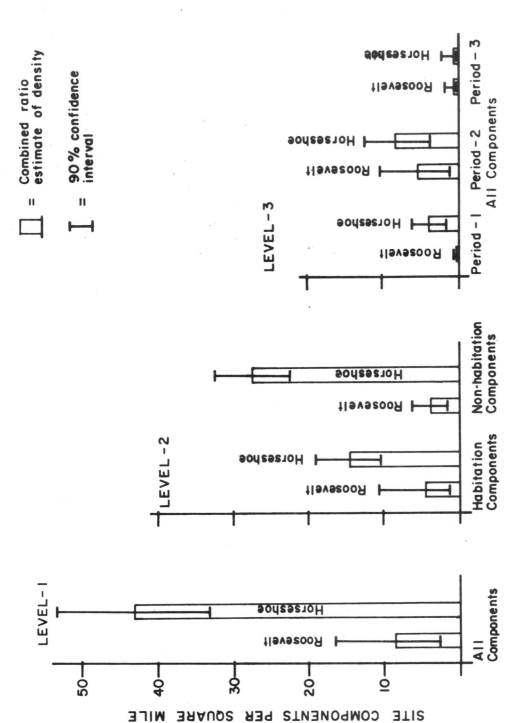

Figure 20. Prehistoric site component density for the Roosevelt Lake and Horseshoe Reservoir surveys.

pattern, which is also sometimes called a "contagious" pattern, would be one in which the sites occurred in discrete clumps. These clumps, in turn, can be arranged in a uniform, random, or clustered pattern. A random arrangement is one in which there is equal probability that a site is located on any point in the landscape. It is characterized by a lack of patterns.

Plog (1974) suggests that the nearest neighbor statistic be used to measure the degree of aggregation. This statistic is useful when applied properly, but it has often been used inappropriately (Pinder and Witherick 1972). It would be inappropriate for the Roosevelt Lake and Horseshoe Reservoir survey data because the sample units are not spatially contiguous and the number of points involved is relatively small. We adopted the method used in Chapter 6 of adjusting the raw number of components per sample unit in order to compensate for the unequal acreages of the sample units. The adjustment was made by calculating the density of components per acre per sample unit and then multiplying this by the average number of acres per sample unit for each of the survey areas. This adjustment technique rests on the assumption that the site component densities recorded in each sample unit would have remained constant if the size of each of the sample units had been expanded or contracted to the mean size. Because this assumption is probably incorrect to some degree, the adjusted values should be considered to be no more than estimates and the resulting analysis is no more than a first approximation of the actual degree of site component aggregation.

The adjusted numbers of prehistoric site components per sample unit for the Roosevelt Lake and Horseshoe Reservoir survey areas are listed in Tables 28 and 29 and graphically displayed in the frequency histograms of Figure 21. These histograms are difficult to evaluate visually but they can be reduced to composite indexes. If the probability of finding a site on any given point is relatively low and the sites are arranged randomly, then the frequency distribution of the number of sites per sample unit can be described by a Poisson series (Greig-Smith 1964: 12-14; Kershaw 1964: 96-106; Southwood 1966: 23-43; Pielou 1969: 79-110; Odum 1971: 206; Collier and others 1973: 167-168). The formula for a Poisson distribution indicates that the probability (p) of finding a certain number of sites (x) per sample unit in a population with a mean number of sites ($\bar{x}$) per sample unit is:

$$p_x = e^{-\bar{x}} \frac{\bar{x}^x}{x!}$$

where e is the base of the natural logarithms.

Poisson distributions are highly skewed when the mean ($\bar{x}$) is low but they approach symmetrical normal distributions as the size of the mean increases.

Table 28

Adjusted Number of Prehistoric Site Components per Sample Unit for the Roosevelt Lake Survey

Sample Unit	Level 1	Level 2		Level 3		
	All Components	Habitation Components	Non-habitation Components	Period 1 Habitation Components	Period 2 Habitation Components	Period 3 Habitation Components
19	5.0	3.3	1.7	0	3.3	0
26	0	0	0	0	0	0
32b	0	0	0	0	0	0
80	0	0	0	0	0	0
82b	0	0	0	0	0	0
84c	0.7	0	0.7	0	0	0
11	0	0	0	0	0	0
35b	7.0	5.4	1.6	0	4.1	0.5
40	0	0	0	0	0	0
49	0	0	0	0	0	0
50	1.5	0	1.5	0	0	0
54	1.5	0	1.5	0	0	0
67	0	0	0	0	0	0
101	0.9	0	0.9	0	0	0
2	0	0	0	0	0	0
5	3.4	3.4	0	0	3.4	0
6	3.3	3.3	0	0	3.3	0
8	0	0	0	0	0	0
38	1.6	0	1.6	0	0	0
75	10.2	6.8	3.4	3.4	3.4	0
88	0	0	0	0	0	0
89	0	0	0	0	0	0
96	1.7	0	1.7	0	0	0
115	0	0	0	0	0	0

Table 29

Adjusted Number of Prehistoric Site Components per Sample Unit for the Horseshoe Reservoir Survey

Sample Unit	Level 1 All Components	Level 2 Habitation Components	Non-habitation Components	Level 3 Period 1 Habitation Components	Period 2 Habitation Components	Period 3 Habitation Components
31	7.7	7.7	0	3.8	0	3.8
32	0	0	0	0	0	0
34	3.8	2.5	1.3	1.3	1.3	0
1	3.4	0	3.4	0	0	0
5	5.1	1.9	3.2	0	1.3	0.6
8	0	0	0	0	0	0
17	4.3	1.1	3.2	1.1	0	0
40	9.0	1.4	7.6	1.1	0.4	0
42	7.0	3.5	3.5	0.5	2.5	0.5
10	7.5	5.6	1.9	0	5.6	0
21	3.8	1.9	1.9	0	1.9	0
49	9.9	2.5	7.4	1.2	1.2	0

dotted lines depict Poisson (random) distribution

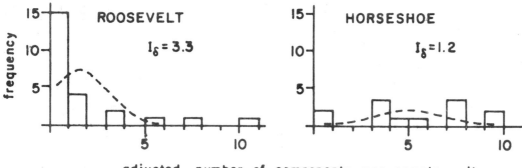

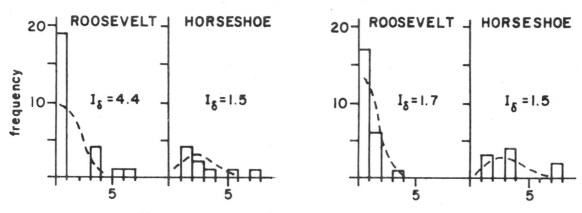

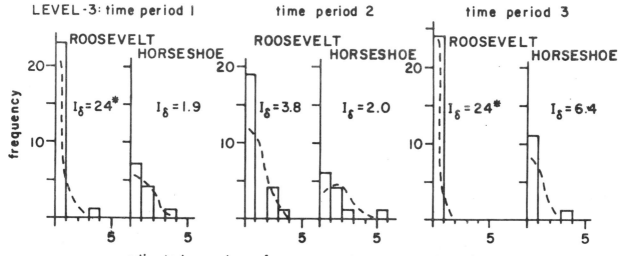

*When only one sample unit contains components, I_δ is equal to the number of sample units. This implies complete clustering.

Figure 21.   Degree of Prehistoric Site Component Aggregation for the Roosevelt Lake and Horseshoe Reservoir Surveys.

Population ecologists recognized the correspondence between the random arrangement of elements across a landscape and the Poisson frequency distribution of elements per sample unit more than a half century ago. In the intervening years they have developed several statistics for testing the randomness of distributions. These statistics involve comparing actual frequency distributions of elements per sample unit with the predicted Poisson distribution. Unfortunately many of these statistics are affected by sample unit size and shape as well as the type and density of the distribution of elements. In addition, many are biased when only samples of a population are available for study. (This is one reason the nearest-neighbor statistic and other "plotless" sampling approaches were developed.) We decided to calculate Morisita's index of dispersion (Southwood 1966: 37; Pielou 1969: 102-114) to measure the degree of aggregation in the two survey areas. If it can be assumed that site components in a region form a mosaic of large (relative to sample unit size) "patches" of different densities within which components are randomly arranged, this index is relatively independent of the type and density of distribution and the number of samples. Whether this assumption is justified in archaeological contexts is open to question but a limited test that we made, which is discussed below, indicates that the index is relatively stable over a range of sample unit sizes from about 25 to 100 acres. The formula for Morisita's index of dispersion is:

$$I_\delta = N \ \frac{\sum\limits_{i}^{N} x_i \ (x_i - 1)}{\sum\limits_{i} x_i \ (\sum\limits_{i} x_i - 1)} = N \ \frac{\sum\limits_{i}^{N} x_i^2 - \sum\limits_{i}^{N} x_i}{(\sum\limits_{i} s_i)^2 - \sum\limits_{i} x_i}$$

where:

N = total number of sample units

x_i = number of components in the ith sample unit

If the arrangement of site components is random, the distribution of the frequency of components per sample unit will fit a Poisson series and the index will equal 1. When the arrangement of components is uniform, the value of the index will be less than 1. Values greater than 1 indicate a clustered arrangement of components.

The calculated indexes of dispersion (Figure 21) indicate that the arrangement of all components in the Horseshoe Reservoir survey area approaches randomness in contrast to the clustered pattern at Roosevelt Lake. The Level 2 analysis indicates that, in the Roosevelt Lake survey area, habitation components are considerably more clustered than non-habitation components. The habitation and non-habitation components at Horseshoe Reservoir were equally aggregated and relatively more random than at Roosevelt Lake. Because so few habitation components were dated to Periods 1 and 2 at Roosevelt Lake, little confidence can be placed in the calculated trend. At Horseshoe Reservoir, the Level 3 analysis indicated a trend toward increasingly more clustered arrangements.

Size of Site Components

The next dimension of settlement pattern variability that was measured was that of site size. Plog (1974) suggests that two aspects of this dimension be measured. One is the range of site size categories. The other is the distribution of sites across these categories. Plog refers to this as a measure of agglomeration. These measurements add more detail to the distributional patterns revealed by the measures of density and the evenness of density. In order to be able to understand the social and economic systems of any given society it is useful to know how its population was distributed among habitation sites and how the intensity of activity at non-habitation sites varied. Archaeologists are not able to make census counts nor measure the amount of time spent at non-habitation sites but these variables can be estimated by measuring other indexes. Room counts, such as Plog made, are perhaps the most accurate index of site populations developed to date, but often rooms are not visible on the surface, as was the case for the vast majority of sites in the Roosevelt Lake and Horseshoe Reservoir survey areas. Site size as measured in square meters was the best index we were able to use.

Two weaknesses of this measure are readily apparent. First, the measurement of the area of a site is subject to substantial error because of the subjective definition of site boundaries. Secondly, the relationship between the area of any given site and the number of people that lived at the site or the intensity of activities performed at the site probably is not constant.

One way of minimizing the measurement errors for interpretive purposes is to plot the area measurements on a logarithmic scale. More importantly, this interpretive device has been used for more than 60 years by geographers investigating what has come to be known as the rank-size rule (Zipf 1949; Simon 1955, 1972; Berry and Garrison 1958; Berry 1961, 1964; Dziewonski 1972, 1975). The rule as originally formulated stated that if the populations of the cities of a region are plotted in order of decreasing size on a log-log graph, they will form a straight line. This would imply that there are relatively few large cities, more medium-sized ones, and many small ones. Some geographers have argued that if any given plot did not conform to this rule it is because the cities plotted do not form a naturally-bounded economic system. Others have argued that systems of cities go through developmental stages and a linear plot is not typical of all stages. Geographers are still debating the merits of the several explanations that have been developed for the rank-size regularities that have been observed.

This geographical research deals with large modern, urban centers of nation states. How the results of this research can or should be applied

to the archaeological analysis of settlement patterns, which is usually
done on a much smaller scale, is unclear at present. We plotted our survey
data on rank-size log-log graphs because we found it to be a useful heuristic
device for documenting variability between the Roosevelt Lake and Horseshoe
Reservoir survey areas. These plots were constructed by ranking the components from largest to smallest along the horizontal logarithimic scale and
then plotting their size as measured in square meters along the vertical
logarithimic scale. From Figure 22 it is apparent that the rank-size
relationship for the Level 1 analysis was not particularly linear and this
proved to be the case for all levels of analysis. The graph does show that
the range of the size of site components in the Horseshoe area is somewhat
larger than at Roosevelt Lake, but on the whole they are similar. The
Horseshoe Reservoir survey area did contain more "medium-sized" site components than the Roosevelt Lake survey area. The graph also indicates that
the lower density of components in the Roosevelt Lake area is not compensated for by larger components.

The Level 2 analysis (Figure 23) revealed that the habitation site
size heirarchies of both survey areas are very similar but that the non-
habitation site size hierarchies differ considerably. The Horseshoe Reservoir survey area had more and bigger non-habitation sites than did the
Roosevelt Lake survey area.

The Level 3 analysis shown in Figure 24 indicates that the hierarchies
of habitation site size are similar in both areas for time Periods 2 and 3.
During Period 1, the Horseshoe Reservoir survey area was characterized by
a relatively complete hierarchy of site sizes in contrast to the Roosevelt Lake survey area, which contained only one small habitation site.
Although the site size hierarchies of Period 2 are somewhat expanded in
comparison to Periods 1 and 3, the Level 3 analysis indicates relatively
little change over time with regard to site size except for the anomalous
Period 1 at Roosevelt Lake.

For most of the habitation sites dating to Period 2, a measurement
of the size of the actual roomblocks could be made. The measurements are
also plotted in Figure 24. These curves are similar in shape to those based
on the areas of entire sites. Although the rank of many of the components
changed, this correspondence adds some confidence to the use of site area
as an index of population size. But the conclusion that there was relatively
little change in the distribution of population between the time periods is
still open to doubt because of changes in architectural styles. Period 1
habitation sites are pit house sites, Period 2 habitation sites are clusters
of cobble rooms or "early" compound sites, and Period 3 habitation sites are
masonry pueblos without compound walls or "late" compound sites which are
larger and appear to have a higher density of rooms within the compound
than "early" compound sites. Because living space was probably used differ-
ently in each of these types of sites, site area may be a poor index of population size across the boundaries of the three time periods.

Because of the probable error inherent in using site area as an index
of the distribution of habitation and non-habitation activities, drawing

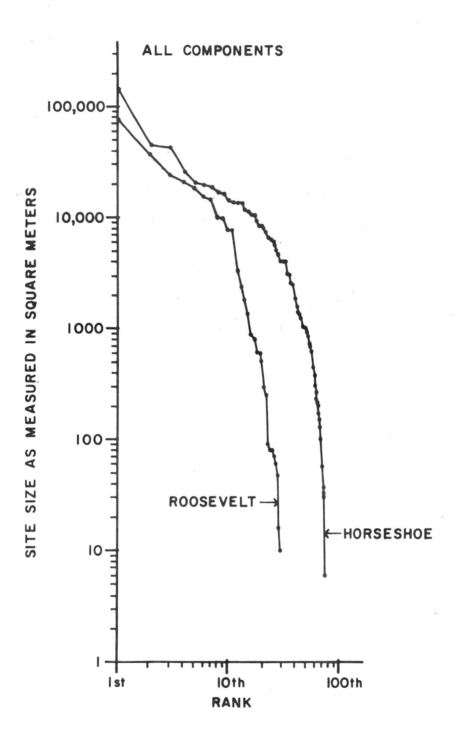

Figure 22. Rank-size Relationships for the Level 1 Analysis of the
Roosevelt Lake and Horseshoe Reservoir Surveys.

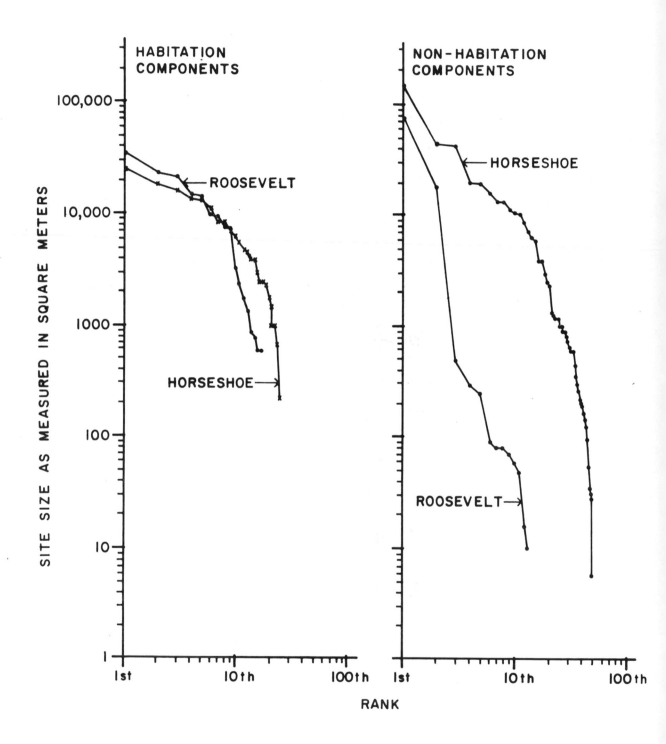

Figure 23.   Rank-size Relationships for the Level 2 Analysis of
the Roosevelt Lake and Horseshoe Reservoir Surveys.

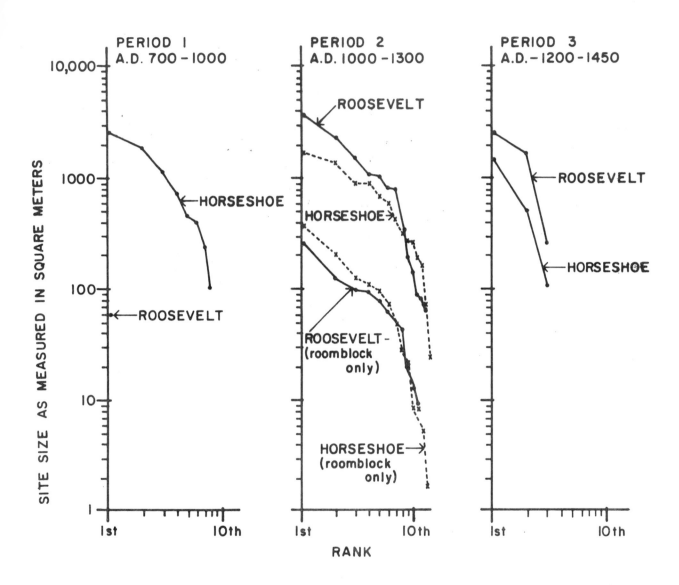

Figure 24.   Rank-size Relationships for the Level 3 Analysis of the
Roosevelt Lake and Horseshoe Reservoir Surveys.

further inferences on the basis of the slopes of the curves and the differences between the curves is probably unwarranted. Developing theoretical explanations for the rank-size relationships of archaeological sites will have to wait until more comparative data make clear exactly what the relationships are.

Spatial Patterns

After making these measurements, it should be possible to more objectively define spatial clusters of sites that reflect prehistoric territorial organization. But because our sample survey units are not contiguous the identification of regional clusters is impossible. The survey at Roosevelt Lake did indicate that, prehistorically, the area along Tonto Creek, at what is now the northwest end of the lake, was a major habitation center. All large habitation sites that we recorded were located here. Because of the discontinuous nature of our survey, the location of other comparable habitation centers remains unknown.

During Period 1 in the Horseshoe Reservoir area, a large habitation site was located in each of the lower, middle, and upper sections of the survey area. If future research in the area indicates that there are no other major habitation centers in the intervening non-surveyed areas, the territorial frontage along the Verde River of each of these sites may have been about three to four miles. During Period 2, all of the largest habitation sites were located in the middle region. This may represent an actual shift in territorial patterns or very possibly limitations of our survey knowledge. During Period 3, major habitations were again located in each of the three areas as they had been during Period 1.

This attempt to quantitatively describe the settlement patterns in the Roosevelt Lake and Horseshoe Reservoir survey areas has shown that the higher site component density in the Horseshoe area is due to the presence of more Period 1 habitation sites and more and larger non-habitation sites. In addition, the site components at Roosevelt Lake are distributed in a more clustered pattern than at Horseshoe Reservoir. By quantifying the description of settlement patterns in both survey areas we have more explicitly defined the nature of the variability that must be explained.

Seeking an Explanation

Why does the Horseshoe Reservoir survey area contain a higher density of Period 1 habitation sites representing a full range of site sizes, as well as more and larger non-habitation sites than the Roosevelt Lake survey area? The descriptions of the non-habitation sites suggest that there are not only more habitation sites in the Horseshoe Reservoir area but that they also represent a wider diversity of activities. However, the bulk of the increase seems to be due to the presence of more agricultural systems (defined in Chapter 5) and wild plant gathering and processing stations. Obvious variables to consider in attempting to explain the differences between the Roosevelt Lake and Horseshoe Reservoir survey areas are environmental factors. Both areas are located in the Arizona Upland division of the Sonoran Desert-scrub vegetative community and within 10 to 15 miles of both areas, chaparral, juniper-pinyon woodland, and montane conifer communities can be reached (Brown 1973). Although both survey areas are located in the same Sonoran Desertscrub community, certain environmental conditions may vary considerably between the two regions. Two possible variables that might account for the different settlement patterns in the two survey areas are annual rainfall and soil types.

A map of normal annual precipitation (University of Arizona, Hydrology Program 1965) shows that both survey areas currently receive about 16 inches of rain annually with about 6 inches falling during the summer months. This suggests that precipitation does not differ enough between the two regions to account for the differences in settlement patterns. Hydrological charac-teristics of Tonto Creek, the Salt River, and the Verde River vary consider-ably as discussed in Chapter 2, but the agricultural systems recorded in the Horseshoe Reservoir area were based on conservation of rainfall rather than irrigation. How the prehistoric practice of irrigation varied between the Verde Valley and the Tonto Basin is poorly documented.

General soil maps of Gila, Maricopa, and Yavapai counties provide some information about the types of soils found in the two regions. Two warm semi-arid soil associations have been defined in the Roosevelt Lake survey area (Vogt and Richardson 1974). The Glendale-Gila-Anthony associa-tion consists of deep soils formed on floodplains. These soils are more than 60 inches deep, have high to moderate available water capacity, and the topsoil is characterized as fair to good. The Continental-Eba-Nickel association consists of deep soils on dissected uplands formed in mixed, old alluvium. The soils of this association are also deeper than 60 inches, but available water capacity is rated as only low to moderate and the top-soil is characterized as poor because of its gravelly texture. Some soils in the Horseshoe Reservoir area have been identified as the hot dry soils of the Cellar-Lehman Rock Outcrop association (Hartman 1973). These are shallow soils 5 to 14 inches deep formed over granite, gneiss, or andesite. Available water capacity is very low and topsoil is rated poor. Other soils found in the area are formed over limestone and sandstone but these are also characterized as poor because of their shallowness, the limited rainfall, and the high evapo-transpiration rates that characterize the area (Wendt 1969). The available evidence indicates that the distribution of soils is opposite to that expected if soil types were the cause of the variability of settlement patterns between the two survey areas.

The Scale of Settlement Pattern Variability

Up to this point in our search for an explanation we have been looking for environmental differences between areal units on the scale of

the lower Tonto Basin and the middle portion of the lower Verde Valley.
However, it is quite possible that settlement patterns vary on a much
smaller scale and that because of the relatively narrow arbitrary ele-
vational boundaries of our sample units our survey results are not characteristic of regions any larger than our survey areas. If this is the
case, the relevant environmental factors would have to vary on a much
smaller scale than we have been investigating. For example, it is possible
that annual rainfall and soil types vary significantly with respect to
settlement patterns on a much finer scale than is currently recorded.
Another possibility is that the differences between the Horseshoe Reservoir and Roosevelt Lake surveys are relatively insignificant when compared
with the differences in settlement patterns that occur on a larger regional
scale. To make our search for an explanation more efficient it would be
useful to know on what scale settlement patterns do vary.

Variation Within the Horseshoe Reservoir Survey Area

In order to investigate how rapidly settlement pattern attributes
can vary in short distances, the sample units surveyed at Horseshoe Reservoir were subdivided. Each unit was initially divided in half. The lower
unit included the area between 2000 and 2070 feet above sea level and the
upper level included the next 70 feet of vertical elevation. Since we
made no effort to measure the areas of the two divisions, changes in site
densities cannot be evaluated, but a simple calculation of the relative
percentages of habitation and non-habitation components shows that they
are essentially the same as those of the total surveyed area (Table 30).
The site component size-rank relationships of non-habitation sites are
fairly similar except for the fact that the lower level lacked any sites
of the biggest category (Figure 25). The habitation site component size-
rank curves diverged considerably.

The Horseshoe Reservoir sample units were next divided into four
units each spanning 30 vertical feet of elevation. With this division the
ratios of habitation to non-habitation site components varied considerably
among the divisions and all differed from that of the ratio for the total
area. The size-rank relationships of habitation components again were
more diverse than those of non-habitation components (Figure 26). This
may indicate that the factors determining habitation component location
and size are more complex than those determining the location and size of
non-habitation components. This is fully expectable because a greater
diversity of activities are performed in habitation sites.

This brief analysis seems to indicate that size-rank relationships
may vary considerably over very short distances, but this is probably
because the samples include only portions of networks of interacting sites.
It should also be noted that we know relatively little about sampling size-
rank relationships. The abrupt change in the ratio of habitation to non-
habitation components when the sample units were divided into four parts
may indicate that these ratios may change very rapidly in only 30 vertical

Table 30

Settlement Pattern Variability within the Horseshoe Reservoir Sample

	Number of Habitation Components	Percent	Number of Non-habitation Components	Percent
Total sample	25	34%	49	66%
Sample divided into two parts				
2000–2070 feet	16	36%	29	64%
2070–2140 feet	9	31%	20	69%
Sample divided into four parts				
2020–2050 feet	13	45%	16	55%
2050–2080 feet	3	18%	14	82%
2080–2110 feet	2	12%	15	88%
2110–2140 feet	7	64%	4	36%

174

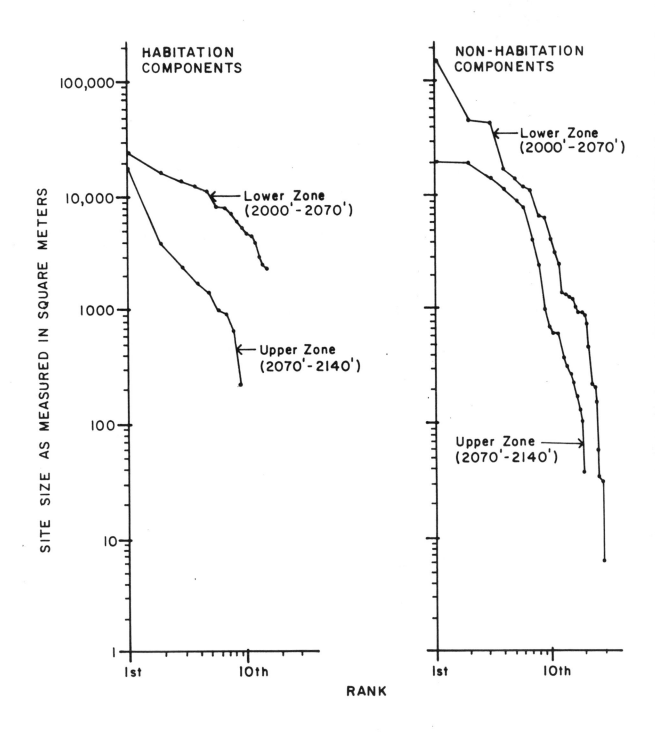

Figure 25.   Rank-size Relationships for the Level 2 Analysis of the
Horseshoe Reservoir Survey Subdivided into Two Zones.

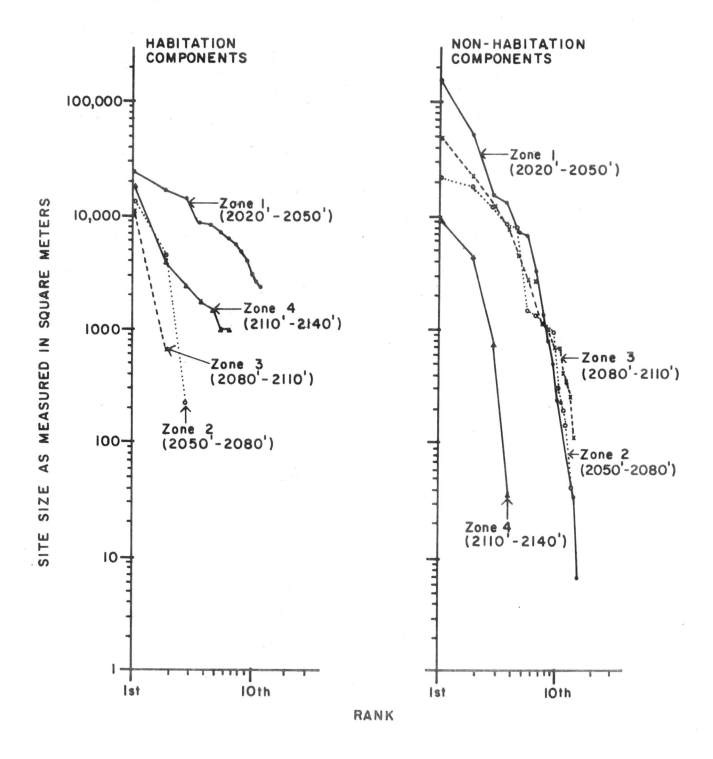

Figure 26.   Rank-size Relationships for the Level 2 Analysis of the
Horseshoe Reservoir Survey Subdivided into Four Zones.

feet of elevation. However, one complicating factor casts considerable doubt upon the reality of this pattern. This is the imprecision associated with small sample sizes. When the area surveyed at Horseshoe Reservoir is divided into four parts, each division covers an average of only 0.4 square miles and contains only 18 site components. Much of the variation noted may be due simply to the small size of the samples. Because each half of the Horseshoe Reservoir sample is a fairly accurate predictor of at least some of the attributes of settlement patterns in the other half, samples of this size are apparently large enough to avoid much of the imprecision associated with very small samples. The area surveyed at Roosevelt Lake covers only 30 vertical feet of elevation but it covers 2.8 square miles and contains 30 prehistoric site components. The analysis of the Horseshoe Reservoir survey data indicates that this should be large enough to avoid much of the imprecision of very small samples. However, at present we are not able to predict how the settlement pattern attributes would change if the survey areas were made twice as large or simply moved 100 vertical feet higher or lower than they were. Therefore it would seem prudent to urge caution in trying to extend the characterization of settlement patterns within our survey areas to the larger regions in which they are located.

Comparison With Other Surveys

As pointed out above, both the Tonto Basin and lower Verde Valley are located in the vegetative community known as the Arizona Upland division of the Sonoran Desertscrub. This vegetative community also occurs in portions of the Agua Fria River drainage to the west of the Verde Valley. Gumerman, who has carried out archaeological work in this area, has described the region as environmentally transitional between the deserts to the south and the high plateau to the north (Gumerman and Johnson 1971). His archaeological research was designed to test the hypothesis that the archaeological resources of the area were also transitional. Doyel (1972) has described the Tonto Basin and portions of the Verde Valley as also being environmentally and culturally transitional. This research indicates that if we wanted to compare the larger region which includes both the Tonto Basin and lower Verde Valley with other major regions, the greatest potential variability in settlement patterns would occur along a north-south transect. Two sets of survey data were selected for comparison. One was the survey of the Vosberg district located about 30 miles northeast of Roosevelt Lake (Figure 27). The other was the survey of the proposed Orme Reservoir area located about 20 to 30 miles south of Horseshoe Reservoir (Figure 27).

Settlement Patterns in the Vosberg District. The Arizona State University archaeological field school conducted research in the Vosberg district from 1967 to 1970 (Chenhall 1972). The district is located on the headwaters of Walnut Creek and is separated from the Tonto Basin by the Sierra Ancha Mountains. The district is situated more than 3000 feet higher than the Roosevelt Lake and Horseshoe Reservoir survey areas. As a result the

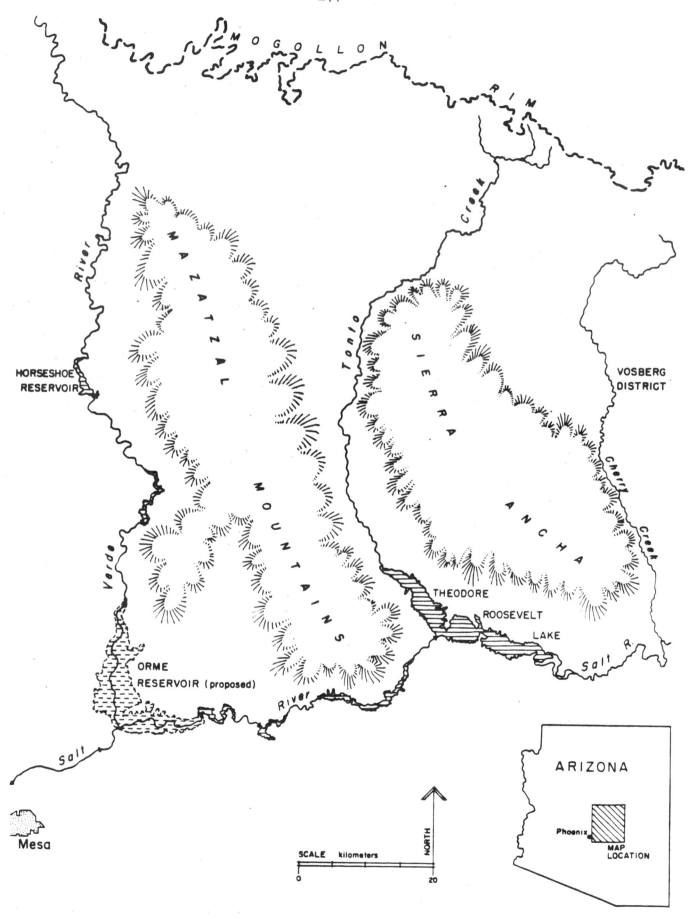

Figure 27. Map of Orme Reservoir, Horseshoe Reservoir, Roosevelt Lake, and the Vosberg District.

natural vegetation is considerably different. Major vegetative communities include pine and juniper forests, manzanita and oak chaparral, and high grasslands.

Chenhall (1972: 40) estimates that about 90 percent of the sites within a 4 square mile area were recorded, but does not clearly indicate which areas were completely surveyed. For this analysis, a grid of 97 "two-inch square sample units" was superimposed on Chenhalls's maps. Chenhall had used this size of sample units in his sampling study but never reported the area of these units. According to our calculations each unit contains just over 24 acres and the total area used in our analysis is approximately 3.7 square miles. Because the areas apparently surveyed, but excluded from our analysis, contain very few sites, our estimates of site density may be somewhat too high.

Chenhall described the sites in terms of units roughly comparable to the units we tentatively labeled site components, and it was possible to classify them as habitation or non-habitation components. Dating by ceramic groups was much better in the Vosberg district than in the Roosevelt Lake and Horseshoe Reservoir areas. In order to compare temporal trends, seven time periods were collapsed into three which are approximately the same as those used to describe the Roosevelt Lake and Horseshoe Reservoir survey data. In the Vosberg district pit house architecture characterized the period from A.D. 700 to 1000. Because of a distinct break in the ceramic types, Chenhall postulates that the area was abandoned from A.D. 1000 to 1050. Several small masonry pueblos were occupied from A.D. 1050 to 1250 or 1275. Chenhall hypothesized that the Vosberg district was again unoccupied for another 25 to 50 years and dates the next occupation from A.D. 1300 to 1400. One large pueblo, estimated to have more than 40 rooms, was the only habitation site occupied within the Vosberg district during this third period. After A.D. 1400 the area was abandoned until the Apaches entered the area at some unknown date.

The densities of site components in the Vosberg district for all three levels of analysis are given in Table 31. The density of all components, all habitation components, and all non-habitation components are intermediate between the densities recorded in the Roosevelt Lake and Horseshoe Reservoir surveys. The habitation component density in the Vosberg district is higher than both Roosevelt Lake and Horseshoe Reservoir densities during Period 1 but lower than both during Periods 2 and 3. The trend of habitation component density in the Vosberg district from Period 1 to Period 3 is a steady decline, if the two hypothesized periods of complete abandonment are ignored. This contrasts to both the Roosevelt Lake and Horseshoe Reservoir surveys where density increased from Period 1 to 2 and then decreased from Period 2 to 3.

The degree of clustering of all components as well as all habitation components was intermediate between that of the Roosevelt Lake and Horseshoe Reservoir surveys (Figure 28). Non-habitation components at Vosberg

Table 31

Density of Tentatively Defined Site Components in the Vosberg District
and the Orme Reservoir Area*

		Vosberg	Orme
Level 1:	All prehistoric components	$18.9/mile^2$	$4.3/mile^2$
Level 2:	Habitation components	$8.1/mile^2$	$1.3/mile^2$
	Non-habitation components	$10.8/mile^2$	$3.0/mile^2$
Level 3:	Period 1 habitation components	$5.1/mile^2$ (A.D. 700-1000)	?
	Period 2 habitation components	$2.7/mile^2$ (A.D. 1050-1250)	?
	Period 3 habitation components	$0.3/mile^2$ (A.D. 1300-1400)	?

*based on data in Chenhall (1972) and Canouts (1975)

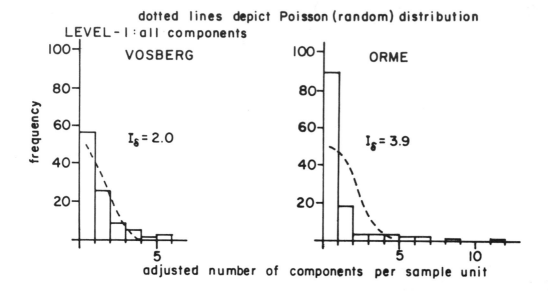

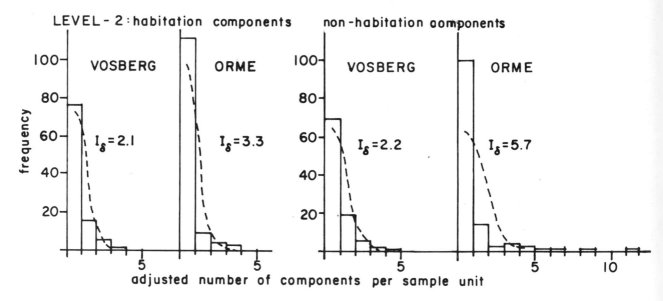

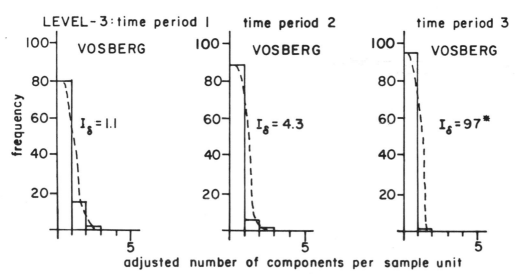

*When only one sample unit contains components, I_δ is equal to the number of sample units. This implies complete clustering.

Figure 28.   Degree of Prehistoric Site Component Aggregation for the Vosberg District and Orme Reservoir Area.

were slightly more clustered than in both the Roosevelt Lake and Horseshoe
Reservoir survey areas. The Level 3 analysis revealed a trend toward
increasingly more clustered habitation components from Period 1 to Period 3.
This was similar to that documented in the Horseshoe Reservoir area during
Period 1 except that the distribution was more random in the Vosberg dis-
trict during Period 1 and became more completely clustered than in the
Horseshoe Reservoir area.

The Vosberg survey data were also used to cursorily check the
stability of Morisita's index of dispersion with changing sample unit
size. We did this by combining the original sample units into groups of
4 and then recalculating the index for all components. This yielded a
value of 1.8 compared to the original value of 2.0. This relatively small
difference indicates that if sample units had been about 100 acres in size
rather than approximately 25, the index would have indicated only a slightly
less clustered distribution. Given the range of sizes for the sample units
used in the various surveys compared in this chapter, we can expect Morisita's
index of dispersion to be comparable within values of 0.2 to 0.3 between the
different surveys.

Insufficient data are available concerning site size for investigating size-rank relationships of the Vosberg district. The limited
information that is available indicates that during Period 1 no habitation
sites contained many more than 5 pit houses. During Period 2 habitation
sites contained from about 5 to 30 surface masonry rooms and during Period 3
only one masonry pueblo was occupied and it contained more than 40 rooms.
This may have represented a 50 to 75 percent decline in the total number
of rooms from Period 2, but because room counts could not be made on many
sites it is impossible to characterize demographic trends with any significant degree of confidence.

Settlement Patterns in the Orme Area. Rainfall in the Orme area is only
10 to 12 inches per year or even less, but the vegetative cover is essentially the same type of Sonoran Desertscrub that is found in the Tonto
Basin and lower Verde Valley. Perhaps the most significant environmental
differences between the two regions is that access to woodland and chaparral
species would be much more difficult from the Orme area.

The proposed Orme dam would inundate 38 square miles. Much more
area than this was actually surveyed but this settlement pattern analysis
is based only upon those areas used in the sampling simulation study described in Chapter 6. This involves approximately 24 square miles. Dating
problems in the Orme area were as difficult as in the Roosevelt Lake and
Horseshoe Reservoir areas. Even defining site boundaries was difficult
and often arbitrary (Canouts 1975: 7). Therefore defining site components
is even more arbitrary. All of the sites recorded during the Orme survey

were classified on the basis of activities inferred to have taken place
at them. The classification included: (1) limited activity sites related
to manipulation of biotic resources, (2) limited activity sites related to
manipulation of abiotic resources, (3) secondary habitation sites and (4)
primary habitation sites. Only those sites classified as primary habitation sites in the Orme survey report (Canouts 1975: 17-38) were considered as habitation sites for this analysis. Sites classified as secondary
habitation and all limited activity sites were considered to be comparable
to the sites we have labeled as non-habitation sites. All sites listed as
multi-activity were considered to be multi-component and each site that
was dated to more than one Hohokam period (Pioneer, Colonial, Sedentary, or
Classic) was also considered to be multi-component. In addition, some sites
were so large that they overlapped some of the sample units we had defined
for our sampling simulation study. Each part of a site that was in a discrete sample unit was counted as an extra component. Using these very
arbitrary procedures, 104 components were defined. Despite the fact that
this represents a 65 percent increase over the number of sites it is still
probably an underestimate of the actual number of components present.

Because of the problems discussed above, the density values given in
Table 31 may embody considerable error. The density values for all prehistoric components are amazingly low compared to the other surveys that
have been considered here. A survey of more than 80 square miles on the
Gila River Indian Reservation, south of the Orme area, resulted in the
discovery of only 2 to 3 sites per square mile (Wood 1972). This may indicate that low densities are typical of the southern deserts of Arizona.
The ratio of non-habitation to habitation components is also higher than
in any of the other survey areas. Because of the poor dating no attempt
was made to calculate the changing density of habitation components through
time. The available data do suggest a trend more like the Roosevelt Lake
and Horseshoe Reservoir areas than the Vosberg district. The prehistoric
occupation of the Orme area seems to have been most dense during the late
Colonial and Sedentary periods.

The evenness of the site component density is shown in Figure 28.
The distribution of all components as well as non-habitation components
are more clustered than in any of the other surveys discussed. In the
Orme area habitation components were less clustered than in the Roosevelt
Lake survey but more clustered than in the Vosberg district and Horseshoe
Reservoir area.

Because of the problems encountered in defining components it was
impossible to investigate the size-rank relationship between them, but
in order to provide some basis of comparison, the size-rank relation for
all sites included in the analysis is shown in Figure 29. This curve indicates that the size of sites is several magnitudes larger than in the other
areas and would tend to indicate that relatively large populations were
residing in relatively few sites. How the actual population size compares
with that of the other areas is impossible to determine until more research
is done.

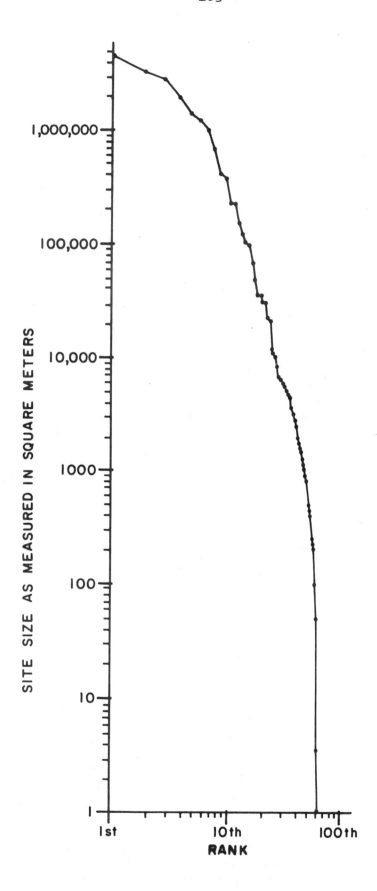

Figure 29. Rank-size Relationships of Sites in the Orme Area.

Summary

In this chapter we described the settlement patterns in the Roosevelt Lake and Horseshoe Reservoir survey areas by calculating density, degree of aggregation, and size-rank relationships of site components. These indexes were calculated at three levels of analysis. The first included all components. For the second level habitation and non-habitation components were analyzed separately. Habitation components were divided into three time periods for the third level of analysis.

This analysis revealed that the prehistoric site component density was approximately five times as dense in the Horseshoe Reservoir survey area as in the Roosevelt Lake survey area. Most of this higher density was due to the presence of more non-habitation and Period 1 habitation components. The overall degree of aggregation of site components was clustered in both survey areas for all levels of analysis but often approached randomness in the Horseshoe Reservoir survey area. When the habitation components were broken down by time period, trends were different in the two survey areas; however, because so few components were recorded for Periods 1 and 3 in the Roosevelt Lake survey area little confidence can be placed in the changes shown there. The trend in the Horseshoe Reservoir area is one towards increasingly more clustered distributions. The analysis of the rank-size relationships indicated that the major variability occurred between non-habitation and Period 1 habitation sites. The range of the sizes of non-habitation components was somewhat larger in the Horseshoe Reservoir area, but the major difference was the presence of many more "medium-sized" non-habitation components. During Period 1 a relatively complete size hierarchy was present in the Horseshoe Reservoir survey area whereas only a single small Period 1 habitation component was located in the Roosevelt Lake survey area.

We began a search for an explanation of this variability by looking for environmental factors that varied between regions the size of the lower Tonto Basin and the central region of the lower Verde Valley. An examination of the hypothesis that the distribution of annual rainfall and soil types could be the cause of this variability was rejected.

Suspecting that our survey data did not accurately represent settlement patterns of the entire lower Tonto Basin and all of the central region of the lower Verde Valley we next attempted to determine on what scale the settlement pattern attributes we measured do vary. This was done by examining variability on both a smaller and larger scale than the regions initially selected. We investigated how rapidly settlement pattern attributes can vary over small spatial distances by subdividing the Horseshoe Reservoir sample on the basis of elevation above sea level. If only the lower half of each of the sampled units had originally been surveyed, we could have fairly accurately predicted the proportion of habitation and non-habitation sites in tne upper half of the sample units. Site component size-rank relationships varied somewhat between the two divisions.

When each sample unit was subdivided four times each division was a poor
indicator of the proportion of habitation and non-habitation components
in the other divisions. This could indicate that the sizes of our survey
areas were large enough to avoid most of the problems of very small sample
size, but it is still not known how settlement pattern attributes may vary
in other areas in the immediate vicinity of our survey areas. This information can be gained only by a sample survey of the larger region.

In order to determine how significant the magnitude of settlement
pattern variability between the Roosevelt Lake and Horseshoe Reservoir
surveys was we compared them with two other surveyed areas. The two areas
were selected to form a sample along a transect from the southern deserts
through the interior basins and valleys in which the Roosevelt and Horseshoe surveys were located and into the mountainous zone beyond. This was
done in an attempt to provide maximum contrast. If our analysis of these
two other surveys is not in error and they are representative of the maximum differences that might be expected in central Arizona, then the variability we recorded between the Roosevelt Lake and Horseshoe Reservoir
surveys is quite substantial. The quantified settlement pattern attributes
from all four areas are summarized in Table 32. Because the precision of
the values given in this table are generally low, they should be considered
to be only approximate estimates.

Density of all site components was lowest in the Orme area at about
4 per square mile. At Roosevelt the density was about twice that. In the
Vosberg district density was about twice that of the Roosevelt Lake survey
and in the Horseshoe survey it was about twice the density of the Vosberg
area. Habitation component density varied from approximately 1 to 15 per
square mile increasing from Orme to Roosevelt to Vosberg and to Horseshoe
rather than along the transect. Density of non-habitation components
varied from about 3 to 28 per square mile again in the same sequence. The
range of densities of habitation components by time period was from less than
1 to about 8 per square mile. The trend of density changes in the Vosberg
district was toward increasingly low densities. In the Roosevelt Lake and
Horseshoe Reservoir areas the density of habitation components was highest
during Period 2. The trends in the Orme area could not be defined with the
available data.

The analysis of the evenness of site component densities indicated
that the typical pattern at all levels of analysis was a clustered distribution. Index of dispersion values greater than one indicate the degree of
clustering. The degree of clustering was in many cases inversely related
to density. This implies that as the density of components increases they
tend to be distributed in a more random and less clustered pattern. These
patterns are similar to those noted by population ecologists who have discovered that the typical distribution of many species is highly clustered
but increased competition is one force that can create uniform distributions.

Size hierarchies of site components as measured in square meters
vary considerably among the survey areas. These hierarchies are ranked in

Table 32

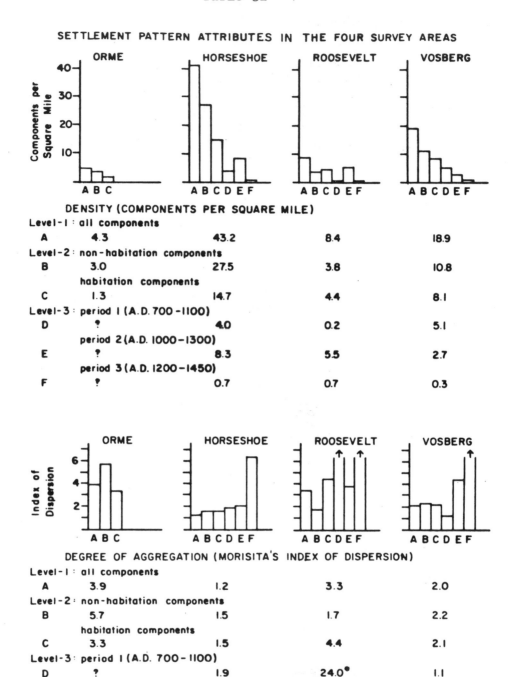

SETTLEMENT PATTERN ATTRIBUTES IN THE FOUR SURVEY AREAS

DENSITY (COMPONENTS PER SQUARE MILE)

		ORME	HORSESHOE	ROOSEVELT	VOSBERG
Level-1: all components					
A		4.3	43.2	8.4	18.9
Level-2: non-habitation components					
B		3.0	27.5	3.8	10.8
	habitation components				
C		1.3	14.7	4.4	8.1
Level-3: period 1 (A.D. 700-1100)					
D		?	4.0	0.2	5.1
	period 2 (A.D. 1000-1300)				
E		?	8.3	5.5	2.7
	period 3 (A.D. 1200-1450)				
F		?	0.7	0.7	0.3

DEGREE OF AGGREGATION (MORISITA'S INDEX OF DISPERSION)

		ORME	HORSESHOE	ROOSEVELT	VOSBERG
Level-1: all components					
A		3.9	1.2	3.3	2.0
Level-2: non-habitation components					
B		5.7	1.5	1.7	2.2
	habitation components				
C		3.3	1.5	4.4	2.1
Level-3: period 1 (A.D. 700-1100)					
D		?	1.9	24.0*	1.1
	period 2 (A.D 1000-1300)				
E		?	2.0	3.8	4.3
	period 3 (A.D. 1200-1450)				
F		?	6.4	24.0*	97.0*

*When only one sample unit contains components the I_δ is equal to the number of sample units. This implies complete clustering.

SITE COMPONENT SIZE (RANGE OF SQUARE METERS PER SITE IN LOGARITHMIC CYCLES

6 to 7*	5	5	3 to 4
(1,000,000 to 10,000,000)	(100,000)	(100,000)	(1000 to 10,000)

*Sites not broken down into components.

Table 32 on the basis of the number of logarithmic cycles they span. All components at Roosevelt Lake and Horseshoe Reservoir span about 5, that is from 1 to 100,000 square meters. Size hierarchies at Vosberg are poorly defined, but if the largest habitation site (estimated to have at lease 40 rooms) is comparable to AZ U:2:1 at Horseshoe Reservoir, (estimated to have about 40 ground floor rooms) the Vosberg size hierarchy may span only 3 to 4 cycles. This means that the largest site in the area would contain no more than 1000 to 10,000 square meters. The size hierarchy for site components in the Orme area is also not well documented but preliminary estimates indicate it may span 6 to 7 cycles and is therefore significantly larger than in any of the other surveys considered.

The size-rank relationships were grossly similar in the Roosevelt Lake and Horseshoe Reservoir areas. Since these relationships could not be examined with available data for the Vosberg district and the Orme area, no conclusions can be reached about the significance of the variability that does exist. We can only suggest that it may be worthwhile for future archaeological surveyors to look for generalizable size-rank relationships.

We must conclude that the search for an explanation of settlement pattern variability between the Roosevelt Lake and Horseshoe Reservoir surveys has just begun. This search would be much easier if we knew the scale on which these settlement pattern attributes varied. This would facilitate the search for environmental variables that vary at the same scale. Some techniques developed by population ecologists may be useful in orienting future research of this problem (for example, Kershaw 1964: 106-113; Greig-Smith 1964: 85-93), but are by are by no means completely adequate (Pielou 1969: 105-106).

Although the cultural ecological paradigm of anthropological research posits strong causal relations between regional environments and settlement patterns, such intervening factors as political organization and trade networks may also be important in explaining variability of settlement patterns. We have not discussed these at all, but trade between the Colorado Plateau and southern deserts of Arizona probably influenced intermediate areas differentially.

Another factor relating to settlement pattern is the relatively late occupation in both the Roosevelt Lake and Horseshoe Reservoir areas. The earliest habitation sites recorded were dated no earlier than A.D. 700 and very probably not before A.D. 900. Is this simply because density was so low during earlier periods and our sample so small that early sites were missed, or are there other reasons? Could it be that farming was not practiced until relatively late in these areas because of the abundance of wild foods in this transitional zone? Because the sedentary villages of farmers are more easily recognized than camp sites of hunter and gatherers, we tend to emphasize this period of the prehistoric occupation. But since the prehistoric period of intensive farming in both areas was preceded and followed by periods of complete or substantial reliance upon hunting and gathering, it would be extremely useful to develop archaeological methods for recognizing this type of occupation as easily as that of the sedentary farmers. This could allow us to discuss major shifts in the prehistoric settlement-subsistence systems of central Arizona.

Chapter 8

THE SIGNIFICANCE OF THE ORME ALTERNATIVES RESOURCES

In order to facilitate an understanding of the relative values of
the resources located by the Orme Alternatives survey, this chapter discusses the problem from several different points of view. First, the
general concept of archaeological significance is presented and the categories of historical, scientific, social, and monetary significance are
defined and developed. Second, each of these categories is perceived
through consideration of specific Orme Alternative resources and their
relationship to actual research, social, or monetary problems. And third,
the significance of the Orme Alternative archaeological resources is compared with the significance that has been assessed for the Orme Reservoir
resources (Canouts 1975). Those sites that appear to qualify for the
National Register of Historic Places are listed at the end of the chapter.

The Concept of Archaeological Significance

In order to fully evaluate the potential environmental impact upon
the archaeological resources caused by the enlarging of Roosevelt Lake and
Horseshoe Reservoir, it is necessary to demonstrate how those resources
are significant, if at all. Archaeological resources attain significance
to different members of society through different means. Archaeological
resources are naturally significant to archaeologists, both for their
scientific potential as well as providing substance and sustenance to the
profession. However, this chapter attempts to further ideas of archaeology's
significance by applying them to a wider spectrum of interests and needs--
those of the American public. It should be noted that this discussion of
archaeological significance is based on the premise that the significance
of something is primarily dependent upon the context in which it is viewed
(Schiffer and House 1975). Thus, the significance of the archaeological
resources at Roosevelt Lake and Horseshoe Reservoir is variable and, in
order to demonstrate this significance, several viewpoints will be explored.
In order to cover as broad a range as possible, the archaeological values
of these two reservoir areas will be viewed in terms of historical significance, scientific significance, social significance, and finally monetary
significance, as recommended by Scovill and others (1972: 12-14) of the
National Park Service.

The term historical significance should be understood as the potential
of archaeological resources to provide substantive information on specific

cultures, periods, lifeways, events, or personages in history or prehistory (Scovill and others 1972: 13). It could be further defined as the ability of certain resources to provide various factual information for the sake of a better knowledge of man's general history or prehistory.

Scientific significance, as discussed in this report, relates to the potential of the archaeological resources in contributing to social scientific theory. More specifically, scientific significance refers to the capabilities of the resources in contributing to nomothetic, or generalizing, studies of past cultural development, change, stability, or behavior. Theoretically, resources that are scientifically significant can be productive in the formulation and testing of hypotheses capable of explaining the differences and similarities in the archaeological record (Scovill and others 1972: 13). Beyond scientific significance to general and specific archaeological problems, archaeological resources should also be considered as relevant to general anthropological problems-- problems that are not addressed to any specific cultures, times, or places. Such general anthropological problems might concern the adaptive changes involved in a shift from a hunting and gathering life of transhumance to one characterized by a sedentary horticultural lifestyle, or perhaps the relationships between growth and stress in certain societies (cf. Reid 1973). A promising application of archaeology to general anthropology has been recently conducted by Thomas (1973). He has tested and confirmed Steward's ethnographically postulated theory of patrilineal band society (1938) while utilizing the archaeological resources of the Great Basin for empirical evidence. A third area of scientific significance is the general applicability of archaeological resources toward the solving of methodological or technical problems within the discipline.

Social significance consists of the various ways in which archaeological resources can directly or indirectly benefit society at large, or its various segments. Scovill and others (1972: 14) suggest that these benefits are fivefold: (1) the acquisition of knowledge concerning man's past; (2) indirect benefits received by educational and research institutions and their communities, from salaries and funds supporting archaeological studies; (3) the acquisition and preservation of objects and structures for public benefit and enjoyment; (4) educational and economic benefits from tourism attracted by archaeological exhibits; and (5) practical applications of scientific findings acquired in archaeological research. Of course, social significance of archaeological resources goes beyond the educational and financial values to include the recreational needs of an increasingly mobile American public as well as the social needs of emerging Native American ethnic groups. A more specific example of archaeological usefulness to society is its capacity to be relevant to certain non-related "hard" sciences.

Scovill and others (1972: 14) suggest that archaeological resources also should be evaluated with regard to their monetary significance, or the cost of total data recovery from the resources to be affected. While this aspect will be examined later in the chapter in comparison to the original Orme Reservoir data (Canouts 1975), we feel inclined to point out an alternate view of monetary significance as presented by Schiffer and House (1975). They point out that archaeological resources are simply not convertible into dollars and cents indices, as their significance or potential depends entirely upon the research questions to which they relate. Since research questions and orientations are open-ended and are variable over time, any dollar value on archaeological resources and their relevant research problems is probably meaningless. A second point that Schiffer and House (1975) make is that the concept of recovering all significant archaeological data is an unrealistic possibility. What data may be considered relevant to today's research problems may not be sufficient to meet next year's research goals, let alone the data requirements of the more distant future.

The following section is by no means an attempt to list all of the specific aspects of archaeological significance related to the Orme Alternatives resources. Rather, several generalized examples are given for each of the four categories (historical, scientific, social, and monetary) that relate the actual, recorded resources to the research, social, and financial aspects of significance.

Historical Significance

The prehistory of the Roosevelt Lake and Horseshoe Reservoir study areas could conceivably cover 10 to 12 thousand years, though direct evidence for only about 1500 years was obtained from the Orme Alternatives survey. Additionally, over 100 years of history is represented. The purpose of this section of the chapter is to discuss this prehistory and history on a stage-by-stage basis with respect to the potential of the Orme Alternative resources in solving relevant historical problems of who lived there, and for what periods of time. It is hoped that this discussion will not only demonstrate one aspect of the archaeological significance of these resources, but will also isolate important, historically-oriented research problems in order to provide the groundwork for a mitigation research design.

Paleo-Indian

No sites that could be ascribed to a general Paleo-Indian, big-game hunting tradition have been found in the two reservoir areas. This generalized stage, dating to about 11 thousand years ago, has been documented and examined in many portions of the Southwest, especially in southeast Arizona (cf. Haury and others 1953, 1959; Haynes 1969). Contemporaneous sites of a more limited nature have been found on the Colorado Plateau (Wilmsen 1970), but Paleo-Indian material is rare in central Arizona. It would seem that two alternatives explain this absence: (1) Paleo-Indian bands did not utilize this portion of the state due to a lack of preferred resources, especially Pleistocene megafauna; or (2) the sites of such an occupation have not been preserved or, more likely, are not presently visible using traditional survey methods. If this latter alternative can be accepted as a possibility, then the presence or absence of such a culture should be determined only after a planned, concentrated effort is made to search out the possible locations of Paleo-Indian sites. In the meantime, the potential of the Orme Alternatives resources for increasing our understanding of a terminal Pleistocene occupation in central Arizona is somewhat limited, though it should not be dismissed entirely.

Archaic

No pre-pottery sites were recorded within the two reservoir areas, though the existence of such seasonally-mobile hunters and gatherers is certainly suspected to be represented in the local archaeological record. In the middle Tonto Basin, some 20 air miles northwest of Roosevelt Lake, Huckell (1973b) excavated a lithic site that he ascribed to the Chiricahua stage of the Cochise culture on the basis of projectile point stylistic attributes. On the basis of these points a date between 5000 and 1000 B.C. was assigned to the site. The only other possible Archaic site that has been documented for the Tonto Basin is a large base camp or village near Huckell's excavation which he feels is contemporaneous with his excavated camp site (Huckell 1973b: 195-196), and thus, affiliated with the Chiricahua stage of the Cochise culture. In the Verde Valley, Archaic sites are also fairly rare. Shutler (1950) excavated a pre-ceramic site in the middle Verde Valley near Camp Verde, which he tentatively dates between 2000 B.C. and A.D. 1. Breternitz (1960) discusses this site and other similar sites in the Verde Valley as part of the Dry Creek phase, a phase associated with either the Chiricahua Cochise culture or possibly with the Amargosa culture of the Colorado River basin. Thus, the presence of such an Archaic occupation in the Roosevelt and Horseshoe areas is certainly a possibility. Furthermore, many scatters of lithic debris, mainly primary flakes and cores, were noted during the survey. While these scatters were not recorded as sites because of a lack of certain site criteria, there is a possibility that they represent the presence of a pre-ceramic, non-sedentary occupation. In this sense, the resources associated with Orme Alternatives have a potential for identifying whether these valleys were extensively occupied before A.D. 700, whether such people are more closely associated with the Cochise of southeastern Arizona, the Amargosa culture of the Colorado River basin, or some, as yet unidentified, cultural group. Additionally, it would be of value to determine the date of the initial utilization of these valleys, if, indeed, such archaic people were the first inhabitants. It would also be important to know if such hunters and gatherers permanently occupied these valleys and for how long. For a better understanding of the initial Hohokam occupation of this region, it would also be necessary to know when this Archaic occupation terminated, or whether it blended into the later Hohokam manifestation around A.D. 700. Although the presently recorded sites are probably incapable of answering these questions, a complete survey of the project areas in addition to a more rigorous study of the extensive lithic scatters may provide data necessary for understanding such a cultural stage.

Colonial Period Hohokam

The Colonial period of the Hohokam represents one of the more dynamic
phases of that culture, while it also remains poorly understood. As its
name implies, the Colonial period, dating roughly between A.D. 500 and 900,
represents a general expansion of these people, previously confined to the
general area of the Salt and Gila basins. During this period, Hohokam settlements are found on all of the major tributaries leading into the Salt
River and Gila River. Documentation of such Colonial period outposts has
been furnished at the Henderson site (Weed and Ward 1970) and the Beardsley
Canal site (Huckell 1973a; Weed 1972) on the Agua Fria River; in the
middle Verde Valley at the Calkins Ranch site (Breternitz 1960); in the
upper Cherry Creek region (Morris 1970); in the Tonto Basin at the Ushklish
Ruin (Haas 1971) and at Roosevelt 9:6 (Haury 1932); in the Globe-Miami area
(Doyel n.d.; Windmiller 1972a); in the San Pedro River at the First Canyon
Ruin (Hammack 1970); and in the Santa Cruz River, Santa Rosa Wash, and
Vekol Wash (Grebinger and Adam 1974). Colonial Hohokam sites have also
been found as far west as Bouse, Arizona (Haury 1932). While all of these
sites illustrate the colonial or expansionist nature of the Hohokam at
that time, very little historical information is available on such a manifestation in the Roosevelt Lake or Horseshoe Reservoir areas. It is true
that Roosevelt 9:6 (Haury 1932) was excavated within one of the Orme Alternative project areas. It should be pointed out, however, that this excavation was conducted over 45 years ago and many modern technical dating
methods were not available. Furthermore, the site was submerged for almost
20 years before the excavation, and silting and water disturbance had disturbed certain features of the site. Nevertheless, the report (Haury 1932)
does provide valuable comparative information which is not, at this time,
duplicated in the immediate locale. No Colonial period Hohokam sites have
been excavated in the vicinity of Horseshoe Reservoir, and any information
on such an occupation is entirely based on survey evidence. Due to this
lack of information on this period of occupation, several problems remain
unsolved, all of which are crucial to a further understanding of the dynamic
aspects, or scientific aspects, of the Colonial period. First of all, sites
in the two reservoir areas should be of use in determining the date of the
initial Hohokam colonization as well as the date of their exit, if, in fact
they did leave these tributary valleys after A.D. 900. Not only are the
dates of occupation of importance, but also the character of the occupation
is not at all well understood. For instance, it is not definitely known
whether the Colonial period occupation actually does represent an expansion
of Hohokam people or whether it is merely a convincing adoption of Hohokam
traits by an indigenous, previously non-sedentary, non-agricultural society.
Three recorded sites at Roosevelt Lake have a potential for answering these
questions: Az. U:8:67, Az. U:4:17, and Az. U:5:28. At Horseshoe, seven
recorded sites indicate some potential for answering these questions: Az.
U:14:8, Az. U:14:16, Az. U:14:21, Az. U:14:22, Az. U:14:39, and Az. O:14:51.
It should be pointed out, however, that Colonial components could be buried
beneath later sites and, therefore, would not be readily visible on the
surface.

Hohokam-Pueblo Transition

One of the dim spots in the prehistoric record for the Roosevelt and Horseshoe sequences is a clear understanding of the span between the Colonial period Hohokam and the later appearance of Salado people in the Roosevelt area and Sinagua people in the Horseshoe area. Perhaps part of this problem dates back to the Gladwins' (1935) original statement that the Tonto Basin was abandoned by the Hohokam colonists around A.D. 900 and was deserted until the arrival of the Salado around A.D. 1100. Recent evidence suggests that this historical reconstruction is misleading, if not totally inaccurate. Beginning in the 1950s (Brandes 1957), more systematic survey efforts revealed evidence of an occupation during this 200 year span. Brandes' (1957) survey in Gila County determined that the presence of a substantial Sacaton phase Hohokam occupation of this area was, indeed, contradictory to Gladwin's idea concerning a Hohokam withdrawl or contraction into their core area in the Salt-Gila basins. In the middle Verde Valley, Breternitz (1960) discussed this period between A.D. 900 and A.D. 1100 as one of the prominent occupations of the area. His Camp Verde phase is characterized by a blend of Hohokam and puebloid traits, with an emphasis on the former.

More recent investigations in these two areas have confirmed these general interpretations of Brandes (1957) and Breternitz (1960) and have amplified an understanding of this period. Doyel's (n.d.) recent excavations in the Miami Wash area, near Globe, have contributed the most to knowledge of the period. There, three Sacaton phase Hohokam components (A.D. 900-1150) were excavated in addition to one component that was truly transitional between Sacaton phase Hohokam and the Salado culture. To this later manifestation, Doyel (n.d.) has ascribed a new, tentative phase designation: the Miami phase (ca. A.D. 1150-1200). Also indicative of this phase is a site excavated near Globe prior to recent mine construction (Windmiller 1974a). In the Verde Valley, a recent excavation (Shaffer 1972) has indicated a similar manifestation at this time horizon. There, the excavation of a Honanki phase site (A.D. 1100-1300) is suggested as the logical conclusion to an indigenous and continuous cultural development from a prior Hohokam occupation.

As a result of these more recent investigations, the earlier sequence of Hohokam colonization, an abandonment of the region, and a subsequent infusion of Salado and Sinagua groups as proposed by the Gladwins (1935) is certainly not substantiated. Unfortunately, the more recent investigations have not been large enough in scope to do more than suggest a revised historical interpretation of the prehistoric sequence of central Arizona. In order to fully understand the nature of culture change and development as outlined in the next section of the chapter, a better grasp on the archaeology of a Hohokam-Pueblo transition is desperately needed. First of all, it is necessary to confirm whether this whole region was or was not occupied during the interval between the Colonial Hohokam and the Salado or Sinagua occupation. Second, if such an occupation is documented, as it has been in portions of the Verde Valley and the Globe area, then a better understanding should be developed concerning whether these people were permanent residents of the region throughout the period or whether such sites represent tentative forays into this region by the Hohokam of the Salt-Gila Basin. If a substantial occupation is evidenced through the period between A.D. 900 and 1100, then it should be determined whether this development represents a continuation of the Colonial Hohokam, a predecessor to the later puebloid development, or both.

The Orme Alternatives study should be partially capable of solving most of the historical questions outlined above. At Roosevelt Lake, four sites are suggested as tentatively capable of producing data relevant to this time period: Az. U:8:68, Az. U:4:12, Az. U:4:13, and Az. U:4:17. It should be noted, though, that many of the later Salado pueblos in the Roosevelt Lake vicinity could be masking earlier, transitional components. Such a situation was experienced during the recent excavations in the Globe-Miami transitional components, both ceramically and architecturally, as well as in the village plan layout (David E. Doyel, personal communication). These six sites at Horseshoe are Az. O:14:34, Az. O:14:35, Az. O:14:36, Az. O:14:37, Az. O:14:38, and Az. O:14:39. Az. U:2:29 could also be capable of contributing to the culture history of this time period.

Early Pueblo (Salado and Sinagua)

The early pueblo period (ca. A.D. 1100-1300) is the one that has received the most attention from archaeologists working this area and, in fact, has fostered the most disagreement among them. In the Roosevelt area, this puebloid manifestation is termed Salado (Gladwin and Gladwin 1935), while in the Verde Valley, a somewhat similar manifestation is known as the Southern Sinagua (Colton 1946). The Gladwins (1935) were the first to name and describe this period as the Roosevelt phase in the Tonto Basin. They characterized it as the initial occupation of the basin by a group of people newly arrived from the Little Colorado River drainage in northeastern Arizona (Gladwin and Gladwin 1935: 27). A more recent interpretation of the Salado sees this occupation as essentially the same, except for their origin. Steen (Steen and others 1962: 4) feels that the Salado migrated into the Tonto Basin from the Gila Valley, near Safford, Arizona, and maintained a trade relationship with pueblo peoples to the northeast. McGregor (1965) in a synthesis of Southwestern archaeology sees the Salado as a blending of Anasazi, Mogollon, and Hohokam traits. The most recent work in the area (Doyel 1972, n.d.) has, perhaps, cleared up some of this problem. In his earlier work, Doyel (1972) tended to see this occupation as the result of an indigenous, evolutionary development out of a Hohokam cultural base, but after conducting more work in the area and examining more data, Doyel (n.d.) now feels that the Salado is a modification on an existing, Hohokam-derived culture by an influx of puebloid people from the northeast. Whether any of these hypotheses actually represent the historical record of Salado origins is unclear, and it will remain unclear until more systematic work is conducted in the region. The sites recorded in the Roosevelt Lake project area could probably be of great benefit in any definition of the Roosevelt phase, including its origin, its dates of occupation, the culture responsible for its presence, as well as other aspects of the phase. As the Tonto Basin, which includes Roosevelt Lake, has always been considered the "heartland of the Salado," perhaps answers to all of these problems will be visible in this archaeological record. It is interesting to note that, as the "heartland of the Salado," the Tonto Basin has been the object of only peripheral archaeological investigations. The Tonto Cliff Dwellings were excavated in 1940 (Steen and others 1962), but these represent an anamalous type of site for the area. The Orme Alternatives survey represents the first systematic survey in the basin since the Gladwins' early work (1935). With these problems in mind, the Roosevelt phase components recorded at Roosevelt Lake take on added historical significance. Such sites include Az. U:8:68, Az. U:8:72, Az. U:8:73, Az. U:8:78, Az. U:4:7, Az. U:4:8, Az. U:4:11, Az. U:4:12, Az. U:4:13, Az. U:4:17, and Az. U:4:18.

The Verde Valley may be characterized by less controversy, but many of the same ideas are bandied about by archaeologists and, as yet, a minimal amount of information exists on which to base any firm conclusions. Nevertheless, Schroeder (1960) has presented a synthetic model of Verde Valley prehistory. After an initial Hakataya occupation of the valley, a Hohokam colonization, and an indigenous development out of this colonization, Schroeder sees a Sinagua migration or expansion south through the Verde Valley all the way to the Salt-Gila Basin. It is this movement that explains the appearance of puebloid traits in the middle and lower Verde Valley after A.D. 1100, approximately the same time that similar traits appear in the Tonto Basin. Also like the Tonto Basin area, the cultural remains in the Verde Valley at this time are far too complex to be easily "explained away" as resulting solely from a Sinagua population intrusion. It would appear from limited, recent evidence that the lower portion of the valley cannot be characterized as receiving a Sinagua migration at this time, but rather that the Honanki phase (ca. A.D. 1100-1300) represents a blending of Hohokam, Anasazi, and Sinagua traits overlaid upon an indigenous cultural pattern (Shaffer 1972). Howerver convincing, or unconvincing this may sound, we are still faced with a historical model that has been developed upon an insufficient data base. Like the Salado problem, the Verde Valley cultural sequence is still beset with important questions of who occupied these early masonry pueblos, where were these people or ideas derived from, how long did this occupation last, and how, if at all, did it differ from the Roosevelt phase Salado of the Tonto Basin? In short, various sites representative of this phase are present in the Horseshoe Reservoir project area which should be of use in sorting out some of this confusing cultural-historical record: Az. U:2:2, Az. U:2:36, Az. O:14:11, Az. O:14:17, Az. O:14:18, Az. O:14:16, Az. O:14:47, Az. O:14:48, Az. O:14:50, and possibly Az. U:2:29, Az. O:14:34, and Az. O:14:38.

Late Pueblo (Salado and Sinagua)

Unlike the confusion noted for the preceding period, the nature of this final prehistoric phase is fairly clear, with dating problems comprising the most disagreement. Regardless of the origin of the early pueblo peoples in this region of central Arizona, it is fairly certain that the people of the Tuzigoot phase of the Verde Valley and the Gila phase of the Tonto Basin developed from the preceding early Pueblo people with relatively little out- side influence. The major characteristic of this phase is a population aggregation into large pueblos, many of which are well over 200 rooms. However, one of the problems with the historic record concerns the dating of the phase, including the beginning of large pueblo construction as well as the date of abandonment of these pueblos. Of course, an important related question concerns where these people went around A.D. 1400. At Roosevelt Lake, two recorded sites were probably occupied during this phase and could contribute relevant data to the culture-history of this terminal prehistoric occupation: Az. U:4:9 and Az. U:4:10. At Horseshoe Reservoir, Az. U:2:1 and Az. O:14:51 should be extremely valuable in any such reconstruction of the prehistory of this region.

Protohistoric

For at least part of the time between the abandonment of the region by puebloid people (ca. A.D. 1400-1450) and the initial Anglo penetration, nomadic and semi-nomadic groups of Yavapai and Apache Indians made use of the areas for hunting and gathering, as well as for occasional agricultural activities. In the Tonto Basin, ethnographic sources indicate that the area was occasionally occupied by Athabaskan Western Apache Indians inclu- ding Southern Tonto bands and the Pinal band of the San Carlos Apache group (Goodwin 1942). Also present were the Yuman-speaking Yavapai Indians who intermarried with the Tonto Apache. Very little is known about the nature of this population, especially concerning the date of their initial occupation of the basin. Although no sites that could be definitely as- cribed to these groups were recorded in the Roosevelt Lake project area, it is possible that some of the burnt rock middens, such as Az. U:8:69 and U:8:71, could be either Apache or Yavapai in affiliation. Other sites that could be expected to be found in the area would consist of agricultural systems, dwelling unit outlines, trash scatters, and campsite remains.

The Horseshoe Reservoir area is in what was once the range of the Yavapai Indians, although almost nothing is known considering the nature of this occupation. Burnt rock middens, similar to those found at Roose- velt Lake, are possibly indicative of mescal roasting pits and may indicate the presence of the Yavapai between the end of the Sinagua occupation and the time of Anglo contact. Sites such as Az. U:2:31, Az. U:2:33, Az. O:14:39, Az. O:14:41, Az. O:14:42, and Az. O:14:44 could be of use in demonstrating the initial dates of Yavapai occupation as well as other important aspects of that culture's presence.

Historic Anglo

The Roosevelt and Horseshoe areas are not particularly distinguished by their historic period resources. At Roosevelt, the area was inhabited by Anglos from around 1870 to the present. Before construction of Roosevelt Dam, the basin was utilized for wheat, vegetable, and fruit farming as well as for ranching. Since construction of the dam, the main activities in the area have been recreational, although grazing is still permitted throughout the area. Three historic Anglo sites were recorded in addition to one canal that could have been utilized during the historic period (Az. V:5:28). Az. U:4:19 (a highway maintenance station), Az. U:8:77 (the Roosevelt Dam Power Canal), and Az. U:3:26 (a late historic settlement of unknown function) can all add an extended perspective on the Anglo occupation in the Tonto Basin, though no sites were recorded that seem to be directly tied to the more central subsistence activities in the area such as ranching or farming.

At Horseshoe Reservoir, no historic period sites were recorded and the historic occupation of the immediate area appears to have been minimal. A few ranches exist today in the vicinity and apparently existed as far back as the 1870s, but these resources are not within the 20 percent sample area surveyed.

Scientific Significance

The following section of this chapter describes the significance of the Orme Alternatives resources with regard to general archaeological or anthropological problem areas, as well as to pertinent methodological problems within the discipline. Whereas the preceding section on historical significance pertained to those contributions to Southwestern history and prehistory that the Orme Alternatives resources are potentially capable of, this section will try to build on how such resources can contribute to the general questions of "how" and "why" as well as the historical questions of "who," "when," and "where." In order to demonstrate this potential, the archaeological record of the Roosevelt and Horseshoe areas will be reviewed with an emphasis on such "how" and "why" questions, particularly those related to studies of long term culture change and cultural adaptation to a transitional environment. While the following may represent particularly fertile aspects of such research, it should be understood that these questions are presented only as examples of such research goals and are not especially inclusive in their scope. In reality, the archaeological research to which any one set of resources may contribute is primarily limited by available time, money, or the investigator's initiative.

Archaeological and Anthropological Problems

Paleo-Indian. As indicated earlier, no Paleo-Indian sites were recorded during this investigation. Nevertheless, their presence should still be considered a possibility, either in those unsurveyed portions of the project areas or beneath recent sedimentation. If future prospecting for such sites fails, then the ecological factors extant during the end of

the Pleistocene epoch in this area should be examined in order to understand the absence of such big-game hunters. Whether this absence was due
to a lack of critical resources necessary to support Pleistocene megafauna,
and therefore their hunters, or if the absence of Paleo-Indian populations
was due to the lack of some other resource critical to their adaptation
is entirely unknown. Only through controlled paleo-ecological studies
could a reconstruction of the environment at that time be accomplished.
Unfortunately, such paleo-ecological research is often dependent upon
archaeological data as extraneous controls. If Paleo-Indian sites are
found in the two project areas during more intensive surveys, then studies
of such sites would be valuable for understanding the environment and ecology of such big-game hunters. Additionally, it would provide valuable
comparative data for evaluating differences in the adaptation of such
hunters to that picture that is rapidly emerging from studies conducted
in Clovis sites in southeast Arizona (cf. Haury and others 1953, 1959;
Haynes 1969).

If such a Paleo-Indian occupation is documented for this area of
central Arizona, and if a succeeding Archaic occupation is similarly documented, it may then be possible to understand the dynamics of the transition from a primary dependence on big-game animals to a dependence on small
game and collecting wild plant food. Although a sequence of sites representing a transition between Paleo-Indian hunters and Archaic hunters and
gatherers may not be found, such a transition could provide the data to
study important changes in adaptation to what has been characterized a
rapidly shifting environment immediately after the Pleistocene epoch.
Besides a documentation of a change in the environment's energy potential,
attenuating shifts in social systems, settlement patterns, and technological industries may also be indicated in the archaeological record.

Archaic. Even though no sites that could be attributed to an Archaic
period occupation have been documented in either reservoir area, their
presence is, at least, strongly suspected. When such sites surface, so
to speak, it would be particularly beneficial to understand their inhabitants' adaptation to this environment of central Arizona. Because such
Archaic hunters and gatherers are so closely related to and dependent upon
their physical environment, such groups are most traditionally considered
in cultural-ecological terms (Netting 1971: 4), especially by cultural
anthropologists. It is possibly the identification and examination of
these Archaic groups that could be most directly beneficial to the general
discipline of anthropology. Because so few hunting and gathering societies
now exist in a pristine state, and fewer are expected to remain in such a
state for very long, the potentialities for initiating cultural-ecological
studies on these living populations is quickly diminishing. It is for this
reason that the significance of Archaic period cultural resources may be
thought of as especially relevant. Since so many questions are left unanswered concerning a hunting and gathering adaptation, anthropologists
will, by necessity, have to rely more and more on archaeological data.
One general anthropological question concerning hunters and gatherers is

the nature of their subsistence pattern or general economy. For years, anthropologists have depicted such societies as adapted to a harse, unforgiving environment, and a pathetically limited technology (Netting 1971: 4.) However, recent ethnological research on the near-extinct !kung bushman society in Africa has demonstrated that such assumptions are unfounded and, quite to the contrary, that hunting and gathering societies live an effective and efficient mode of life (Lee and Devore 1968). Other current problems with regard to hunters and gatherers relate to their social organization and characterization of territoriality. None of these problem areas is clearly resolved, and it is unlikely that enough crosscultural information will be assembled prior to the extinction of such societies to warrant any firm conclusions. Such a situation makes it incumbent upon the archaeologist to realize the importance of the resources that he manages. In this specific case, any Archaic sites found in the Orme Alternatives project areas should be viewed as processing the potential to contribute to a wider range of problems than just the reconstruction of central Arizona's prehistory.

Another aspect of Archaic site studies in these two areas would center on the identification of changes within this general, broad horizon. In southeastern Arizona, three distinct stages have been identified in the Archaic Cochise culture (Sayles and Antevs 1941). A similar threefold division also appears in other Archaic sequences in North America, and it would appear that similar evolutionary forces were affecting such populations (Jennings 1968). That such a sequential development is present in central Arizona is likely, though it can only be speculated upon at this time. If such a sequence is found, either through vertical or horizontal stratigraphy, then understanding the nature of the changes throughout the span as well as the mechanisms of change from one stage to another is warranted. Whether this change is a response to a changing environment or whether it is a response to social or demographic factors is unknown at this time and can only be speculated on. If such a sequence is found in the Orme Alternatives project areas, the proper study of such sites may provide a developmental understanding or Archaic manifestations that could have positive implications for all North American archaeologists.

If future studies in these areas demonstrate that no Archaic populations were present, then this absence should be explained. Particularly confusing at this time is the absence of recorded Archaic sites when the past environment of central Arizona apparently provided a lush, almost unlimited biomass potential to a hunting and gathering population. Was this environment different during the Archaic times horizon or were such Arizona Archaic populations adapted to environments offering a different set of resources? At this time the answers to such questions are beyond our understanding, but perhaps more intensive cultural and ecological studies will provide an explanation of this phenomenon.

Hunting and gathering-agricultural transition. The transition between a hunting and gathering Archaic adaptation and a sedentary, agricultural adaptation is one of those processes that generally proves elusive

to archaeologists. This shift in southern and central Arizona has generally
been ascribed to three different processes: (1) a migration of sedentary
agriculturalists north from Mexico and into the Gila Basin (Haury 1967, 1976);
(2) a diffusion of sedentary and agricultural traits north from Mexico
(Schroeder 1965); and (3) the evolutionary development of indigenous hunters
and gatherers into sedentary agriculturalists (Martin and Plog 1973). With
the evidence now available, it would appear that this shift in the Roosevelt
and Horseshoe areas is really a secondary response, or chain-reaction, to
such a shift in the Salt-Gila Basin area. According to Haury (1967), the
Salt-Gila Basin was colonized around 300 B.C. by Mesoamerican immigrants.
As this population adapted to the Sonoran Desert and its resources, and
increased their numbers, they apparently expanded up all of the major tributaries leading into central Arizona. According to the traditional interpretation (Gladwin and Gladwin 1935; Haury 1932), this Hohokam colonization
reached the Tonto Basin around A.D. 700 as demonstrated at Roosevelt 9:6,
a Hohokam pit house village that Haury excavated within Roosevelt Lake.
While no objection is presently aimed at this model, it is only fair to
suggest that alternate processes could also account for these phenomena.
Perhaps most obvious would be that this Hohokam occupation in the Tonto
Basin was not a result of a population expansion but rather an expansion
(or diffusion) of Hohokam traits into this area. Another possibility is
that these sites, such as Roosevelt 9:6, represent the amalgamation of
Hohokam colonists with an indigenous Archaic population. In any case,
we little understand the actual means for this shift in the archaeological record. Furthermore, aspects of why an indigenous population would
accept foreign, and radically different traits, or physically blend with
an intrusive population is unknown. Perhaps the abrupt presence of Hohokam-like settlements actually does argue for a small to non-existent
Archaic population in this region. Surely, we have few of the answers
to the above questions and only by treating the relevant archaeological
resources as significant will such problems be solved.

Hohokam. Concerning a Colonial period Hohokam occupation between
A.D. 500 and 900 in this region, we really know very little about the subsistence, the settlement pattern, or any other aspect of the cultural
ecology. It is usually postulated that such a colonist occupation of the
Tonto Basin and the Verde Valley was based on the same economy as that
characteristic of the heartland Hohokam--irrigation agriculture supple-
mented by gathering and some hunting. This, in combination with early
reports of irrigation canals in the Verde Valley and Tonto Basin in the
19th century (Bandelier 1892; Mindeleff 1896), has for too long served
as implicit proof that such a typical Hohokam subsistence pattern was
characteristic of the Horseshoe and Roosevelt populations. In reality,
the excavation of one site in the Tonto Basin (Haury 1932) has provided
little in the way of information on the Colonial Hohokam culutral ecology.
In fact, the recent documentation of a substantial Colonial Hohokam presence in the Globe-Miami area (Doyel n.d.) mitigates against such an
irrigation agricultural subsistence model for this time period. Rather,
as Doyel (n.d.) points out, the Globe-Miami Hohokam were, in all likelihood,
floodwater farming in Miami Wash while also utilizing the rich natural

biota of the surrounding area. In light of this, it is important that a
fresher understanding of the Colonial Hohokam's way of life be provided
for the Roosevelt and Horseshoe areas so that speculations can be tested
for their accuracy rather than becoming accepted as fact on the basis of
their persistence.

Additionally, it would be interesting, once an understanding is
reached concerning the Colonial Hohokam adaptation to this area, to compare that adaptation to the "heartland Hohokam" adaptation of the Salt-
Gila Basin, as well as other Hohokam manifestations around southern and
central Arizona. In this sense, it would be interesting to see specifically how an adaptation to a new, different environmental situation affects
the subsistence activities or pattern of a culture, and what, if any,
chain reaction effects are felt by the settlement patterns and social
organization of such a group. Sites that can specifically relate to such
problems have been noted in the previous section on the historical significance of Colonial period Hohokam resources.

The period between the Colonial period Hohokam occupation and a
later puebloid occupation is not only poorly understood from a historical
point of view (see section on historical significance) but also in terms
of the processes of this transition. Traditional history of the Tonto Basin
(cf. Steen and others 1962) sees this period as one of abandonment of the
region by the Hohokam prior to an immigration by the Salado around A.D.
1100. If this history proves to be accurate, then it should be understood
what factors forced or encouraged the Hohokam to retreat to their core area,
and what factors attracted or forced the Salado to move into the basin. In
the Verde Valley, the traditional interpretation is somewhat similar; after
a Hohokam colonization of an indeterminate length of time, they moved back
to the Salt River Basin either on their own accord or as a result of pressures from the Sinagua to the north. If this history survives the application of additional data, then it should be understood exactly what
processes encouraged a Hohokam abandonment. Was this due to environmental
factors or to competition with an expanding Sinagua population? If the
latter proves to be true, then an understanding of what forces caused the
Sinagua expansion southward would be important. The historical models
noted above are not based on a substantial amount of data. The picture
that is slowly emerging is one of a Hohokam-Salado (or Sinagua) transition,
rather than a Hohokam abandonment-Salado (or Sinagua) replacement. Doyel's
recent work in the Globe-Miami area (n.d.) has documented such a transition
and recent work in the Horseshoe area (Shaffer 1972) has suggested similarities. Indeed, the present Orme Alternatives site information is consistent with such a model. If future work confirms such a transition, then it
will be necessary to understand the processes of this change. At the present
time, it appears that the transition is based partially upon an evolutionary
tendancy of the culture with a liberal influence of puebloid traits, if not
an actual population influx of puebloid people (Doyel n.d.). Understanding
whether this transition represents a fundamental change in the adaptation
of these people to the social and physical environment is also important.

If such an adaptational change is documented, it should be ascertained
whether this was stimulated by an environmental change or by other causes.
At the present time, our understanding of this period is so poor that it
is almost impossible to know the significance in the Orme Alternatives
resources.   On one hand, further examination of the sites in these reservoir areas might determine that the area was, indeed, abandoned between
A.D. 900 and A.D. 1100.   On the other hand, examination of a major cluster
of sites in Sample Unit 42 at Horseshoe Reservoir may reveal extensive
data on a transition between the Colonial Hohokam and the later puebloid
occupation of this region of central Arizona.

Salado-Southern Sinagua.   The Roosevelt phase in the Tonto Basin and
the Honanki phase in the Verde Valley are both characterized as puebloid
occupations resulting from an immigration of puebloid people--in the
Roosevelt area these are the Salado, while in the Horseshoe area, these
puebloid people are the Southern Sinagua.   Whether this immigration model or
a transitional, evolutionary model from Colonial Hohokam to Salado or
Sinagua is the correct historical model, an impressive array of potential
archaeological problems remain.   The first is an understanding of the dem-
ography or population dynamics of this region.   Based on less than systematic survey data, it appears that this period is characterized by a dramatic
population increase.   Whether or not this is more apparent than real and
whether such an increase can be documented is one problem.   If such an
increase is real, then determining if it is due to an indigenous population
expansion or an actual immigration of people would be important.   If the
former proves to be the case, then isolation of those factors encouraging
this growth should be undertaken.   If the latter proves to be true, then
aspects of the integration of these two populations could be studied.   Also
characteristic of this group period is the appearance of mud and cobble
masonry pueblos.   Whether this innovation in architectural style was a
result of an adoption of a pueblo style of architecture by indigenous
people or whether the building of such pueblos represents the skills of
pueblo peoples is as yet undetermined.   Perhaps most important in regard
to this early pueblo period is how, in more specific terms, these people
regardless of their origins, adapted to this particular environment of
central Arizona.   Additionally, the comparisons of this adaptation to that
characterized by earlier Hohokam (or Hohokam-like) populations would possibly
illuminate the similarities (or differences) in the ways different cultures
adapt to similar environments.   The fact that irrigation canals in the
Verde Valley and the lower Tonto Basin have been documented has been
variously used to substantiate the idea that the Hohokam were irrigation
farming, that the Salado were irrigation farming, or that one and not the
other was using these canals.   In reality, we do not know who was using
these canals and exactly what kind of subsistence activities characterized
the Salado or the Hohokam in these areas.

The change from the early pueblo period (Roosevelt and Honanki
phases) to the late Pueblo period (Gila phase in the Tonto Basin and
Tuzigoot phase in the Verde Valley) is characterized by an aggregation of

the population into very large pueblos. Other changes probably occurred during this transition, but stylistic traits in ceramics comprise our only good data at this time. However, this change in settlement pattern from small pueblos to very large pueblos is probably a response to unknown ecological or social factors. Concomitant to such studies would be the necessity of understanding how these late pueblo people subsisted in the Verde Valley and Tonto Basin areas. Was this different from the earlier pueblo period in crucial ways, and if so, are there any correlates between the shift in settlement pattern and a possible shift in subsistence activities? Were these shifts caused by changing environmental conditions, and if so, were the changing environmental conditions a result of natural factors or were these man-induced through some sort of maladaptation?

Another potential research topic of the late pueblo period and its many large pueblos (such as Az. U:2:1, Az. U:4:9, and Az. U:4:10) would be sophisticated and innovative studies into the social organization of these people. Over the past 10 years, such studies have been conducted within large pueblo sites (cf. Hill 1970; Longacre 1970a; Longacre and Reid 1975) and are considered by some to be the most anthropologically relevant of current archaeological investigations.

And finally, the ultimate problem concerning the prehistoric occupations of the Horseshoe and Roosevelt areas is why these people abandoned an area that had previously proved its ability to sustain large populations. Various hypotheses have been put forth concerning this phenomenon. Two long-standing explanations involve either an increasingly dessicated environment or attacking Athabaskan raiders. Although the former still enjoys a fair degree of popularity, the latter has generally been discarded due to the lack of any substantial evidence that Athabaskan populations were in the Southwest in the 15th century. However, the pressures from Yavapai Indians from the southwest and west could have contributed a similar pressure and, therefore, could be considered as a possible causal factor at this time. Whether other Indians were involved in encouraging this abandonment or not, a stressful ecological situation was probably at the root of the problem.

Protohistoric. As in the Archaic period, no protohistoric sites have been found in the two reservoir areas, at least none that can be definitely ascribed to the period between the abandonment of the area by puebloid people and the advent of Anglo explorers and settlers. As noted earlier, several sites (Az. U:8:67, Az. U:8:71, Az. U:2:31, Az. U:2:33, Az. O:14:39, Az. O:14:41, Az. O:14:42, and Az. O:14:44) recorded in both reservoir areas could possibly be identified as either Apache or Yavapai. If these sites prove to be protohistoric, and if others are found in the remaining 80 percent of the sample areas, then it would be appropriate to try to understand the cultural ecology of such nomadic and semi-nomadic hunters and gatherers. Primarily, such knowledge would provide not only a strong contrast to the prior pueblo adaptation in this area, but this protohistoric information could provide interesting comparisons with the suspected Archaic adaptation. Such information could also be compared to sparse ethnographic accounts of the lifeways of Yavapai and Apache

Indians. In this sense, such resources would be significant because the ethnographic accounts are either very old and not well documented, or they are recent, well documented, but descriptive of a post-contact culture. By comparing early ethnographic models of Yavapai and Apache subsistence to the sites in the archaeological record, such models could be tested for accuracy. In this sense, data obscured from the modern ethnographer by the process of acculturation, could be retrieved through archaeological investigations.

Historic. The utilization of the two reservoir areas by Anglo groups was apparently never widespread or concentrated in any one locale. However, the remains of this utilization could provide the basis for archaeological tests, the results of which could be compared to the historical record. Not only would such studies enhance archaeologists' ability to make sound inferences, but the historical perspectives on this important period of Arizona's past would be broadened.

While each of the problem areas listed above are considered of scientific significance in their own right, perhaps they would be even more important in a comparative framework. As mentioned in Chapter 2 (The Environment), both Roosevelt Lake and Horseshoe Reservoir occupy qualitatively similar environments. The preceding discussion of the prehistoric occupations in these areas has stressed a fair degree of similarity in the archaeological sequences of the two reservoirs. Also stressed were the adaptational aspects of these cultures and how these adaptations are assumed to have changed through time. For these reasons, a diachronic comparison of the cultural adaptations in each reservoir would be essential for a further understanding of the processes of such adaptations. On the surface, it appears that there were parallel developments in the two areas, but whether this indicates that similar people adapted to similar environments in like fashion, or if there are no basic similarities in the adaptation of the populations of these two areas is not known.

Methodological Problems

Any large scale archaeological project should be considered for its potential to contribute to general archaeological methods and techniques. In fact, any large scale archaeological project that fails to "spin off" methodological information should be considered negligent. Like anthropological and archaeological problems, the potential of any set of resources to contribute to methodological problems depends upon the time and money available, as well as the initiative of the investigators.

One of the foremost archaeological problems to which the Orme Alternatives project can contribute is that of probability sampling—an area that could be considered a current "issue." Amply demonstrated in this report (Chapters 5, 6, 7, and 9) are the needs that archaeologists have for experimentation with general sampling designs, sampling frequencies, and other aspects of survey sampling. Perhaps our poorest understanding of probability sampling with regard to the methodology of archaeology is in excavation (or mitigation) sampling. While several research papers have recently been published on the techniques of intra-site sampling (Mueller 1975b), these designs are usually concerned with how to excavate one large site that happens to be the focus of long-term research interests. What is not well understood, nor even addressed by sampling experts, is how to sample a large number of sites that may be facing destruction. How many sites of the total should be completely excavated, what percentage of each of the sites should be tested, what combination of these two techniques should be utilized? Furthermore, questions exist as to how many sites must be excavated to avoid loss of data, on one hand, or how few to avoid duplication of data on the other hand. Is this figure 40 to 50 percent, as suggested in the Orme Reservoir report (Canouts 1975), or is it as much as 100 percent or as low as 5 or 10 percent? As Read stresses (1975: 51), "there is no magic figure. In one case a 10 percent sample may be sufficiently large and in another an 80 percent sample too small." This impression concurs with one of the major premises of this chapter, that significance of archaeological resources cannot be evaluated in a research vacuum. Just as archaeological significance has to be evaluated within the parameters of accepted research problems, the frequency of any sample problem has to be determined in a similar framework. On one hand, generalized research problems may be solved with a minimal sample of one percent (Read 1975), while more specific problem areas may need data from up to 100 percent of the resources. What all this suggests is that archaeologists really do not know the "right" technique for sampling a set of resources such as those recorded in the Roosevelt Lake and Horseshoe Reservoir project areas. Therefore, investigations into the resources of these project areas should permit the experimentation necessary to contribute substantitive answers to some of these pertinent questions.

Other methodological problems that could be better understood by mitigation of the Orme Alternatives resources concerns aspects of excavation techniques, such as the most efficient, least injurious, use of heavy equipment; the selective merits of screening deposits; the size of screen mesh to use in order to strike a balance between adequate data removal and efficiency of excavation; and the relative efficiency of student labor as compared to general labor or possibly Indian labor. A further methodological problem that a large excavation project could study is the relationship between surface and subsurface materials at a site. Additionally, general refinements of the archaeologist's use of the ecological approach should result from such extensive experimentation as well as refinements in various analytic techniques.

Conclusion

In conclusion, the archaeological resources within the Orme Alternatives project areas have potential for contributing to scientific aspects of archaeology, anthropology, and archaeological methodology. Many of the statements presented in this section of the chapter can be scoffed at as being unrealistic, or at least improbable. This may be so, but these aspects of scientific significance can only be discredited as useless speculation if the significance of these resources is entirely tied down to the here and now. Rather, as cultural resource management specialists, archaeologists should realize (and most do) that these resources are non-renewable, very finite, and therefore have to serve as our data base for as long as archaeology continues to function. For this reason, the scientific significance has been stretched in order to include not only those problem areas that all archaeologists recognize as important, but also to include research interests held by the anthropological community. In this way, perhaps the resources can be judged for their significance today, as well as evaluated for their possible importance in the not so distant future. Furthermore, what has been presented here should not be considered as representative of all aspects of scientific significance. Rather, these examples have been presented to cover the major topics in order to justify the protection, planning, or mitigation that should be afforded these resources.

Social Significance

In order to demonstrate that the archaeological resources in the Orme Alternatives project areas are significant to a broader spectrum of our society, the following discussion assesses their potential in regard to education, recreation, relevance to Native American ethnic groups, application in solving modern social problems, and application in solving modern technical problems in the physical and biological sciences.

One of the more apparent aspects of archaeological significance is its potential for providing the foci of recreational activies. During the past 10 years, Americans have become increasingly mobile and as a result, the numbers of people visiting America's national parks and monuments has increased dramatically. In 1974, over 200 million Americans visited these recreational features; a large number of these parks and monuments are archaeological or historical in nature. It would seem, therefore, that Americans are becoming increasingly interested in such phenomena.

While cultural resources, such as archaeological sites, are interesting to the American public purely for recreational purposes, they should also be thought of as educational resources in that they provide the general public with an important, albeit low-key lesson in American history and prehistory. As Grahame Clark says:

By its power to engage attention, archaeology has also the opportunity to educate and to educate in the sense of drawing out latent interests, enhancing a sense of aware-ness, and stimulating the job of living that many occupations of modern life have done so much to atrophy (1960: 252).

Some of the educational benefits that Clark envisions (1960: 253-254) include: (1) as a historical discipline, archaeology helps lift people out of the limitations of their own time and place and to make them free to the whole experience of mankind; (2) archaeology appeals to the imagination and bids us to look into the unknown, and shows how, by deploying the resources of modern science, technology, and scholarship, progressively larger areas can be brought within the sphere of exact knowledge; (3) archaeology stimulates an interest in geography, both in terms of other peoples and places; and (4) archaeology's emphasis on artifacts and styles, in a time when our own utilitarian artifacts are generally made of plastic and mass-produced, engenders a sense of aesthetic appreciation in the objects designed and made by primitive societies.

More specifically at Roosevelt Lake, despite the presence of Tonto National Monument, there seems to be a potential for additional public interpretative displays due to the high frequency of tourists and outdoor enthusiasts who utilize the area. Several recorded sites such as Az. U:4:9 and Az. U:4:10, in addition to many observed, though unrecorded sites such as the Horse Pasture Ruin, the Schoolhouse Point Ruin, and the Meddler Point Ruin, all possess the potential to exist as stabilized pueblos for public display. An additional, as well as attractive, factor that should be considered is that all of these ruins would constitute the least impact upon the cultural resource base. Although some fine-grained data have already been destroyed at these sites by pothunting activities, the architectural features appear to be relatively intact and ammenable to reconstruction and stabilization. Additionally, public displays could be designed so as to emphasize the deleterious effects of such activities as pothunting so as to gain public support of our federal and state antiquities laws. Another type of archaeological exhibit that could be designed at Roosevelt Lake would be the reconstruction of a community settlement system rather than just the reconstruction of isolated, and out-of-context pueblos. Such a settlement system might consist of 5, 10, or 20 sites, all representing the occurrence of different sets of activities, by different members of the community. A variation upon such an interpretive display of sites would be the depiction of a diachronic system, or one that represents a significant change in pattern through time. In such an interpretive exhibit would be types of sites representing different time horizons, cultures, and types of activities that took place throughout the sequence. Sample Unit 35b at Roosevelt Lake represents a major cluster of sites that could possibly provide a display of at least a good portion of a settlement system.

A similar potential exists at Horseshoe Reservoir for such public displays of cultural resources. Two sites, Az. U:2:1 and an unrecorded site just north of Sample Unit 40, are representative of the larger pueblos in the area. As these sites are both moderately vandalized, it is recommended that they eventually be considered for excavation and stabilization for the same reasons noted for the Roosevelt pueblos. Of course, such large pueblos are not entirely representative of the area, though they may be more of an attraction for the public. As at Roosevelt, a cluster of sites might make a more unusual interpretive exhibit. An example of such a cluster of sites would be those contained in Sample Unit 5 where a range from an isolated, simple agricultural system (Az. U:2:37) to a large pueblo (Az. U:2:1) exists. Other clusters, such as those found in Sample Units 40 and 42 would also be of significant interpretive and educational value.

Besides their significance as general educational and recreational devices, the resources being considered in this report should also be considered as potentially important to American Indians, in general, and to the Pima, Yavapai, Apache, and Pueblo Indians in particular. A resurgence of Indian nationalism has caused an increased concern with group identity and pride. Clark (1960), Ford (1973), and Lipe (1974) all stress archaeology's importance in establishing such identity and pride in past accomplishments among emerging nations or such newly self-conscious ethnic groups. Examples of what Ford calls "nationalistic archaeology" includes Mexico's fervent interest and investment in its Indian heritage, African countries' stress in an idyllic past in contrast to today's ethnic rivalries, and Israel's employment of archaeology to justify her existence as well as to integrate immigrants of diverse backgrounds (Ford 1973: 85). In such a sense, the contribution to general Indian history and prehistory should be considered a significant potential of the archaeological resources at Roosevelt Lake and Horseshoe Reservoir.

On a more specific level, these resources should be considered for their potential significance to specific Indian groups that may be related to the past inhabitants of these two reservoir areas. Numerous Hohokam sites have been tentatively identified in both areas, and the likely possibility that the Pima Indians are directly descended from the Hohokam (Gladwin and others 1937; Haury 1945) suggests several kinds of significance. First, such sites add to the historical richness of the Pima's past as well as providing valuable information on the spatial range of their ancestors, an important point in Indian land claims cases. Any Yavapai or Apache sites within the two reservoir areas should also be considered as being significant to present-day Apache and Yavapai Indians. Additionally, the abandonment of the region by the Salado has always created a problem in interpretation of where this sizable population went, and what Indians, if any, are their living descendents. Wendorf and Reed (1955) have suggested that the modern Zuni Indians are, at least partially, derived from Salado immigrations to that area around the 15th century. If archaeological investigations in central Arizona could help prove this hypothesis, then the resulting significance to the Zuni would be substantial. In short, the many and varied archaeological resources recorded in the two project areas should be considered significant to the possible descendents of such inhabitants as well as to American Indians in general for the sense of "brotherhood" that a knowledge of American Indian prehistory engenders.

As William Lipe (1974: 218-219) has pointed out, archaeologists do not emphasize the contribution that archaeology has made and can make to socio-cultural anthropology, and by extension to modern social problems, through the testing of general hypotheses and theories relevant to the social sciences. Through such methods, patterns of human behavior are explained by "laws" that are theoretically valid regardless of time, space, or culture. Such laws are then capable of not only explaining all similar behavior, but are also capable of predicting future behavioral patterns. Perhaps the most fruitful aspect of archaeology's significance to general anthropology and modern social problems results from archaeology's inherent time depth. While anthropologists are somewhat limited to synchronic studies of the present cultural conditions, archaeology's time depth enables studies to be conducted into the general behavioral laws of cultural change. In this respect, the resources around Roosevelt Lake and Horseshoe Reservoir, with up to a 12 thousand year time depth, should provide ample opportunity to test theories of culture change.

Archaeological resources can be related to more than just modern social problems; they also possess the capability of contributing to the solution of modern technological problems. What we may learn about human adaptation from investigating the sites discussed here concievably could be of use in planning man's future in the Southwest. An example is provided for the general central Arizona region (Grady n.d.):

> For example, adequate study of water control methods in southern Arizona could provide urban planners with a number of solutions to current water resource problems. The Hohokam were masters at exploiting the energy and agricultural potential of available water resources, given their level of technology, through a variety of diversion and conservation techniques. Contemporary consideration of these techniques could allow for more economic use of, for example, surface runoff, thus permitting conservation of the natural water supply.

Another example of modern man making use of prehistoric technical knowledge to aid in present-day adaptation to an arid environment is related by Evenari and others (1971) concerning the development of the Negev Desert in Israel, an area once heavily occupied in ancient times. Their prehistoric investigations led to the formulation of a deductive model capable of testing hypotheses related to water control and agricultural production. As related by Ford (1973: 90), they demonstrated that utilization of rainfall runoff from large sections of land could produce a bountiful harvest. Through knowledge derived from archaeological data, desert communities are now designed to preserve ample land for comparable runoff control. Thus, in some cases we may be able to benefit from understanding man's past adaptation to and experience with the environment. The resources of Roosevelt and Horseshoe seem particularly amenable to such studies, as noted in the preceding section of this chapter. In regard to Arizona's present need for additional knowledge of water control and conservation techniques, the varied agricultural systems recorded at Roosevelt Lake and Horseshoe Reservoir may be of some utility.

At Roosevelt Lake, two canals were recorded (Az. U:5:28 and Az. U:8:77) although several extensive conservation systems were noted just beyond the maximum pool limits and in what could be considered as the indirect impact area. At Horseshoe, such water control systems made up the largest class of sites. Within the 24 agricultural components, water control systems ranged from small, isolated check dams, to complex contour terraces, and other unidentified features such as those recorded at Az. U:2:2.

In other cases, however, we must learn to avoid prehistoric peoples' mistakes with the environment. A southwestern example consideres the example of the extinction of many late Pleistocene megafauna. Although the exact causes of these extinctions are unknown, some believe (cf. Martin 1963) that their demise was due to the direct and indirect effects of prehistoric man. Such a maladaptative practice as destroying their own food supply may have forced big-game hunters to reorganize their adaptative strategies in order to survive. As inhabitants of the modern world, we too have to learn to live within the balance of nature in order not to destroy our own critical resources as may have happened in southern Arizona some 11 thousand years ago.

Aside from contributing to the general technological problems facing our society, archaeological resources are of some significance to certain "hard" sciences--the physical and biological sciences. Archaeological sites are often rich storehouses of geological, biological, and climatological data that, by their association with cultural material, can be precisely dated. This application is especially apparent in the study of past climatic shifts, the evolution of plant and animal species, and in following the past wanderings of the magnetic pole (Lipe 1974: 218). Cultural material is also found useful, if not essential, in geological studies of the late Quaternary period. With these applications in mind, the archaeological resources we are considering should be thought of as capable of providing micro- and macro-fossil evidence pertaining to past climates of central Arizona, the past changes in the plant and animal populations of this area, as well as historical perspectives on the geology of these basins.

And finally, one general point concerning archaeology's social significance that can apply to any and all cultural resources has been described by Clark (1970) and reiterated by Lipe (1974: 291). They both feel that possibly archaeology's greatest benefit to society is the perspective it provides man on his rather humble place in cultural evolution and within the world ecosystem. If man is going to weather many of the crises he faces, then he must be able to perceive his socio-political, demographic, and adaptive situation as something very unusual on the scale of human history (Lipe 1974: 219).

Monetary Significance

As discussed earlier in this chapter, the monetary significance of the resources potentially to be affected by the Orme Alternatives project is that cost estimated for recovering the total data potential of all of the sites (Scovill and others 1972). Based on the statistical projection of the Orme Alternatives sample data (see Chapter 6 for a fuller discussion of this projection), a total of 91 sites is expected to exist in the Roosevelt Lake direct impact zone with a potential range between 43 and 139 sites*. The number of sites expected to exist in the Horseshoe Reservoir direct impact zone is 283, with a possible range of 244 to 322*. The total cost of data recovery from these sites (as fully explained in Chapter 9) is presented in tabular form.

	Total Costs	Possible Range in Costs*
Roosevelt Lake	$28,400,600	$7,268,126 to 57,541,500
Horseshoe Reservoir	$53,503,500	$46,504,300 to 60,502,700
TOTAL	$81,904,100	$53,772,700 to 118,044,200

A Comparison of Orme Reservoir and
Orme Alternatives Significance

As requested by the Bureau of Reclamation, this section of the chapter attempts to compare the relative significance of those resources found in the Orme reservoir project area with those recorded in the two Orme Alternatives project areas. Like the preceding discussion of the significance of the Orme Alternatives resources, this discussion is segmented into aspects of historic, scientific, social, and monetary significance.

Historical Significance

The archaeological resources that may be impacted by the construction of Orme Reservoir or the Orme Alternatives Reservoirs are all of historical significance as illustrated earlier in this chapter and in the original Orme Reservoir report (Canouts 1975). To say that one set of resources is more significant in a historical sense than the other will have to be qualitative in nature and ultimately reduced to relative values of research applicabilities.

At the Paleo-Indian and Archaic time horizons, or what could be called the pre-ceramic period, both the Orme Reservoir and Orme Alternatives resources are minimally significant, at least at this time. No Paleo-Indian sites have been recorded yet, and few Archaic sites have definitely been identified, though many are expected to turn up after a more rigorous analysis of lithic materials. In comparison, it would appear that both reservoir projects have a similar potential for contributing to the pre-ceramic sequences of central Arizona.

*This range is based on a 70 percent confidence coefficient.

The sedentary agricultural period is the phase of Arizona prehistory in which these archaeological sites attain their greatest historical significance. At Orme Reservoir, the survey documented an intensive occupation and utilization of the area between approximately A.D. 1 and A.D. 1400 by the Hohokam culture and later in this sequence by the Hohokam-Salado (Classic period Hohokam?). As that survey indicated, this represents one of the heaviest occupations in southern Arizona and is potentially capable of contributing to the prehistory of an area that is not, as yet, fully understood. At the Orme Alternatives project areas, the resources represent not one, but three prehistoric cultural sequences throughout this time horizon. First, a Colonial period Hohokam occupation is documented at both Roosevelt Lake and Horseshoe Reservoir. Following this is a major puebloid sequence at both reservoirs: a Salado occupation at Roosevelt and a Sinagua sequence at Horseshoe. Additionally, there appears to be transitional material at both of these areas that spans the Hohokam and later puebloid occupations.

To say that Salado resources are historically more significant than Hohokam resources, or that Hohokam resources are more significant than Sinagua resources is, of course, conjectural and based entirely on certain research biases. What can be said, however, is that our relative lack of knowledge about certain of these cultural sequences suggests that their manifestations are of slightly greater historical significance. Whereas the Hohokam sites of the Orme Reservoir project area are important for refining and exacting the historical development of that culture, previous work in the Hohokam area (the Salt-Gila Basin) nevertheless has provided an adequate historical sequence with which to work. Beginning in the 19th century with the excavation of Los Muertos (Haury 1945) and proceeding through this century with the excavation of Snaketown in the 1930s (Gladwin and others 1937), the excavations at Painted Rocks Reservoir (Wasley and Johnson 1965), the re-excavation of Snaketown in 1964-1965 (Haury 1967, 1976), and the recent excavation of the Escalante Ruin (Doyel 1974a), the Hohokam have been relatively well studied and a historical sequence is reasonably well known. The central Arizona highlands, however, have never received the attention that this area has deserved. In the Tonto Basin, including the Roosevelt Lake area, there has been relatively little work completed. Our basis for understanding the sequence for the "heartland Salado" is a Gila Pueblo survey conducted in the 1930s (Gladwin and Gladwin 1935), a salvage excavation of a Colonial Hohokam site in the 1920s (Haury 1932), and the excavations in the Tonto Cliff Dwelling in 1940 (Steen and others 1962). Unfortunately, most other archaeological work accomplished in the Tonto Basin has been by vandals. In the Horseshoe area, the situation is similar. The Gladwins evaluated the archaeology of the Verde Valley in the 1930s (Gladwin and Gladwin 1930), and more recently, Jim Shaffer, then an Arizona State University graduate student, excavated a small site near Horseshoe Dam (Shaffer 1972). For the most part, our knowledge of the Horseshoe prehistoric sequence is extrapolated from work conducted some 40 miles north near Camp Verde (Breternitz 1960; Schroeder 1960).

In conclusion, two factors seem to indicate that the Orme Alternatives resources are historically more significant in regard to Arizona's prehistory. First, the resources of the Orme Alternatives project areas are capable of contributing to the sequential record of three separate cultures whereas the Orme Reservoir resources are primarily relevant only to the Hohokam culture. Second, as the prehistoric record of the Hohokam is relatively well understood, and the sequence for the Tonto Basin and middle Verde River is relatively poor, it would seem that the latter resources take on increased historical significance.

Concerning the protohistoric period, neither project is especially significant at this time, as remains of such occupatons are often undiagnostic from surface evidence only. We suspect the presence of Yavapai Indians in the Horseshoe Reservoir area between the abandonment of the region by the Sinagua and the time of Anglo contact. At Roosevelt Lake, the area was reported to have been occupied by Apache and Yavapai Indians during this time. At the proposed Orme Reservoir location, the area was believed to have been occupied by the Pima Indians and the Yavapai Indians. No protohistoric period sites were recorded, though two late historic Yavapai sites were recorded in that project area. It would appear that both Orme Reservoir and Orme Alternatives can contribute equally toward the historical reconstruction of the protohistoric period.

The historic period is particularly well represented at Orme Reservoir due to the presence of Fort McDowell as well as several other Anglo and recent Yavapai remains. As indicated in the Orme Reservoir report (Canouts 1975), the presence of as important a site as Fort McDowell enables those resources to make a significant contribution to the little-known period of early Anglo settlement in central Arizona. In contrast to this significance, the historic sites recorded at Roosevelt and Horseshoe seem to be of less importance, consisting of an irrigation canal, the power canal, a highway maintenance station, and a settlement of unknown function. This apparent lack of historical period manifestations in the Orme Alternatives areas should be tempered somewhat by the fact that additional sites may yet remain in the unsurveyed 80 percent of these two project areas.

Intuitively weighing the preceding arguments of relative significance of these two projects and their archaeological resources, one must conclude that both Orme Reservoir and Orme Alternatives are potentially of significance in understanding culture-history. Both sets of resources can make valuable contributions to certain aspects of Arizona's prehistory and history. At Orme Reservoir, this is especially apparent in regard to the Hohokam occupation between A.D. 1 and A.D. 1400 and the historic Anglo utilization of Fort McDowell. The Orme Alternatives project areas can potentially contribute to aspects of the Hohokam Colonial period expansion throughout central Arizona, to the Salado cultural development, including their origins, and to the Sinagua cultural development and their origins. The fact that so little is known about these occupations in the Roosevelt and Horseshoe areas suggests that the historic significance of these resources is slightly greater than the historical significance of those resources recorded in the Orme Reservoir project.

Scientific Significance

As pointed out earlier in this chapter, the scientific significance
of any set of resources is primarily determined in a research framework.
That is, such significance is best demonstrated in terms of specific
research problems or questions that such resources can help solve. In
this sense then, it becomes rather futile to try to determine if one
major set of resources is more scientifically significant than another
major set of resources. The resources of both Orme Reservoir and Orme
Alternatives have been examined from such a perspective (Canouts 1975;
this volume) and have been evaluated as to their potential to contribute
to modern archaeological research. If this potential can be accepted as
a measure of scientific significance, then both reservoir projects are
of similar value.

Social Significance

Perhaps the most abstract aspect of significance is that of social
significance. As noted earlier, social significance consists of the direct
or indirect value of archaeological resources to society at large.

In regard to social significance, the resources of Orme Reservoir
and Orme Alternatives are probably of equal potential. In terms of
educational-recreational facilities, both the project areas contain the
number and diversity of sites to be of interest to the public--if developed properly. The Yavapai and Pima Indians should be interested in historical connections with prior inhabitants of the Orme Reservoir locality,
and Yavapai, Apache, and possibly Zuni Indians should be historically
concerned with the Orme Alternatives resources. The occupation spans
at both of the projects should be of general significance to all Native
Americans they could contribute a better understanding to American Indian
history and prehistory. The possible relevance of these sites to the
social sciences or the "hard" sciences is impossible to predict with
accuracy. In conclusion, the archaeological resources of Orme Reservoir
and Orme Alternatives are probably of equal social significance.

Monetary Significance

Perhaps the most clear-cut comparison between the significance of
the Orme Alternatives resources and those recorded at Orme Reservoir is
that expressed in monetary terms. At Orme Reservoir, it was estimated
that a cost of $53,875,510 was necessary for a recovery of all of the
data (Canouts 1975). In the earlier section on the monetary significance
of the Orme Alternatives resources, it was estimated that a cost of
$81,904,100 would be necessary to retrieve and study all of the data
within the direct impact zones of these two reservoir areas. Because of
the nature of the sample statistics, a range in these costs is estimated

to run from $53,772,700 to $118,044,200 depending on the accuracy of the sample prediction. Therefore, it is clear that if the cost of data recovery can be considered a measure of significance, as Scovill and other have suggested (1972), then the Orme Alternatives resources are quantitatively more significant than those recorded within the Orme Reservoir project. A further point to be considered is that an indirect impact zone (or developmental zone) was not sampled at Roosevelt or Horseshoe as it was during the original Orme Reservoir study. From superficial field observations, it is felt that inclusion of such a zone at Horseshoe and Roosevelt lakes would substantially increase the cost of total data recovery for the Orme Alternatives project and, therefore, increase its monetary significance. Such an increase would, of course, add to the present disparity between the monetary significance of Orme Reservoir and that projected for the two Orme Alternatives reservoir sites.

Recommendations for Nomination to the
National Register of Historic Places

In response to the contract stipulations between the Bureau of Reclamation and the Arizona State Museum, a listing of sites that qualify for nomination to the National Register of Historic Places is provided. According to federal regulation (36 CFR 800), any site that has in the past added to our knowledge of prehistory or history or is potentially capable of doing so in the future may qualify for nomination to the National Register of Historic Places. For this reason, it is recommended that the 93 sites described in Appendix III A and B be nominated to the register as all 93 sites are capable of adding to our understanding of America's history or prehistory.

Chapter 9

RECOMMENDATIONS

The survey of the direct impact zones at Horseshoe Reservoir and Roosevelt Lake has been the subject of the first eight chapters of this report. The survey produced information on the nature and significance of the cultural resources of these areas. Briefly abstracted, the cultural resources surrounding these existing reservoirs are very numerous, in certain respects unique, in many cases undisturbed, and definitely of significance, as outlined in the previous chapter.

With this in mind, it is the purpose of this chapter to discuss the alternative methods for mitigating the potential adverse effects of the Orme Alternatives project upon these cultural resources. In its archaeological usage, the term mitigation is defined as the "alleviation of adverse impact by taking action to avoid, protect, or scientifically investigate the resources" (Lipe and Lindsay 1974; McGimsey and Davis in press). These recommendations, then, are based on the assumptions originally posed for the Orme Reservoir project (Canouts 1975) that there are three options available to the U.S. Bureau of Reclamation for dealing with cultural resources at Roosevelt Lake and Horseshoe Reservoir. These options include: 1) site protection in the project areas through avoidance of resources; 2) total data preservation (recovery and study) from all impacted sites; and 3) adequate mitigation of impact through partial data recovery, modification of project plans, or some combination of the two (Canouts 1975: 164).

Site Protection

A total of 93 archaeological sites were recorded during the 20 percent sample survey of the two Orme Alternatives direct impact zones. Based on the nature of the sample, it was statistically predicted that a total of 374 sites (with a possible range of 287 to 461) are in these direct impact zones (see Chapter 6). Due to our understanding of the Bureau of Reclamation's project plans for Orme Alternatives, all of these 374 sites will be adversely affected by rising water levels and, therefore, any plan for mitigating the impact will involve all the sites.

The term "adverse effect" upon the resources involves three variables of impact. All are associated with inundation. First, the inundation of sites is purported to have an adverse effect upon the physical integrity of the site. This point is currently being debated by land use agencies and cultural resource managers. One side claims that inundation of sites does little inherent damage to their physical integrity; the other side claims that such action homogenizes the site, leaving little in the way of contextual information. It would appear that such impact is variable and could be a function of the site's relation to the proposed shoreline, the nature of the site, and the prospects of siltation in the reservoir. Hopefully, these premises will be archaeologically tested in the near future. The second type of impact resulting from inundation is that the resources are effectively removed from any future scientific inquiry. For the most part, they are beneath the water line and therefore out of reach from traditional data recovery techniques. Additionally, if the reservoir is drained for some reason, it is also possible that the site will be effectively buried beneath lacustrine deposits formed by the lake. This latter case has been documented at Roosevelt Lake. In the late 1920s, the lake was virtually empty and a Hohokam pit house was excavated that had been six feet beneath the surface of the lake deposits (Haury 1932). It was not determined whether this cover was entirely lacustrine and therefore post-Roosevelt Dam or if part of the deposits were pre-reservoir and alluvial. A third potential adverse impact results from the alteration of the environmental context of the site and the region that could be caused by enlarging the reservoirs. Today, much archaeology is ecologically oriented and even if inundation of sites had little effect upon their physical integrity, the relation of those sites to their environmental surroundings would be partially lost. Therefore, the combination of a large number of archaeological sites within this project area and the vast potential for adversely affecting the sites suggests that the most effective and responsible method for mitigating this impact would be to avoid (and protect) the resources in the Orme Alternatives project area.

Our recommendation for site protection is based on more than just the combination of large numbers of sites and a potentially destructive impact. Both of these reservoirs seem to have large numbers of sites that are not only individually significant (as shown in Chapter 8) but also, as a population of sites, take on an added regional significance. In other words, the archaeological sites surrounding these two existing reservoirs were once a part of larger subsistence-settlement systems. Although certain cultural patterns are repeated over and over again throughout the regions, the behavior that characterized the adaptation to the specific Roosevelt Lake and Horseshoe Reservoir areas is unique and not likely to be duplicated elsewhere. By depleting certain components of this overall system through land modification, the remaining, intact, portions are partially removed from their original context.

In order to amplify this argument, the Horseshoe Reservoir situation is discussed in more detail. The Horseshoe Reservoir region, at the northern edge of the lower Verde Valley (Figure 3), is one that has received little in the way of systematic archaeological inquiry (see Chapter 3). Using Horseshoe Reservoir as a focal point in a hypothetical regional settlement-subsistence system, we can suggest that related components of this system were in operation throughout a region delimited by the Mazatzal Mountains on the east, Fossil Creek on the north, Perry Mesa on the northwest, nearly to the Agua Fria on the west, and the constriction in the

Verde Valley just below Horseshoe Dam on the south. Within this region, the prehistoric (as well as the protohistoric) inhabitants were dispersed throughout the total diversity of the environment. This included areas high up in the chapparal zone in the Mazatzal Mountains (Steen and others 1962), on the grasslands of Perry Mesa (Gumerman and Johnson 1971), in the steep walled canyons of the East Verde (Peck 1956), as well as in the open sections of the Verde Valley (Gladwin and Gladwin 1930; this volume). Possibly all of the sites in these various environmental situations collectively represent a regional adaptation to the Central Arizona Transition Zone. Whether the people occupying these sites lived in certain zones during certain seasons and moved to other zones during other seasons is unknown. It is also possible that each of the zones was permanently occupied and the resources that were extracted from certain zones were then distributed to other zones in a system of exchange. Weed (1974) has developed a model of such a redistributive system for the Perry Mesa area. A third possibility is that the residents of these different zones were economically self-sufficient.

In any case, these alternative hypotheses have not been tested adequately and the chances of doing so would be severely compromised if an entire component or zone of this overall system were removed from consideration. Such a situation would occur if Horseshoe Dam were raised 140 feet and a predicted 283 sites impacted. The particular geomorphological characteristics of this portion of the lower Verde Valley are such that the Horseshoe Reservoir is the only place from the Orme Reservoir in the south nearly to Camp Verde in the north where the valley opens up into a broad floodplain with associated alluvial terraces and pediment-terraces. It is also the only place in this extended stretch of the Verde River where the site density has been documented as unusually high. Therefore, removing this zone from future scientific consideration effectively removes the major component of this Horseshoe Reservoir regional subsistence-settlement system. The importance of this zone, as demonstrated by the site density, is that a large number of micro-environmental zones are found within a rather small amount of horizontal space. At Horseshoe Reservoir, the prehistoric occupants were apparently in a "mini-max" (minimum amount of labor to attain a maximum of resources) relationship with the fluvial resources of the Verde River, the associated floodplain and riparian resources, and the nearby Lower Sonoran desertscrub resources that border the floodplain. It is such an adaptation to this streamside setting that is crucial to a fuller understanding of the general cultural adaptation to the Central Arizona Transition Zone. Conversely, without an understanding of the nonstreamside adaptation characteristic of the other zones in this region, it would be difficult to fully understand the data recovered in the zone immediately surrounding Horseshoe Reservoir. Thus, impacting sites that are in the Horseshoe Reservoir direct impact zone will not only adversely affect that particular set of resources, but it will also deplete the overall research potential of the regional resource base.

While this argument is largely developed for the Horseshoe portion of the Orme Alternatives project, it has partial applicability to the

Roosevelt Lake area. Like the Horseshoe Reservoir region, Roosevelt Lake occupies a major basin bottom and, similarly, relates to a particular component of a hypothesized regional subsistence-settlement system. The argument for site preservation at Roosevelt Lake based on preservation of the regional integrity of the cultural resources is somewhat weaker than in the Horseshoe area due to the larger size of the existing reservoir. While surveying at Horseshoe Reservoir, we noticed very little evidence of damage caused by the construction of Horseshoe Dam. At Roosevelt Lake, however, a large number of sites are currently inundated (these can be seen from the air) and many others around the perimeter of the lake are severely eroded. Therefore, our recommendations for site protection at Roosevelt Lake based on regional integrity are similar to those recommendations for Horseshoe, but are somewhat weaker due to prior disturbances.

Arguments for the preservation of the 374 sites predicted for the Orme Alternatives direct impact zone can also be tied to the general situation that is developing in central and southern Arizona. Due to the current population increase in the Phoenix and Tucson metropolitan areas, and the spread of these urban and suburban centers, many of the identifiable archaeological regions are quickly being paved over or bulldozed out of existence (Canouts 1975: 165). Additionally, very few regional studies have been conducted in the Sonoran Desert and only the Painted Rocks Reservoir Project (Wasley and Johnson 1965) stands out as being a broadly based regional study of the Hohokam. Even that project is considered inadequate by today's standards and the area is currently being restudied under a contract between the Corp of Engineers and the Arizona State Museum. As a result of this previous lack of regional emphasis, it is recommended that the Horseshoe Reservoir and Roosevelt Lake regions be left intact archaeologically so as to form a data bank for future regional studies in central Arizona.

Total Data Study

Another method of mitigating the adverse affects of the Orme Alternatives project upon the cultural resources would be a program of total data recovery and study. Although we strongly recommend against a program of total data recovery, cost figures and guidelines are presented in accord with the suggestions in Scovill and others (1972). The following chapter presents a preliminary research plan for such a total data study.

This section estimates the costs of man-days per excavation unit, the costs per man-day with regard to different site type, and the various logistical support costs. These data-study formulas were prepared for the Orme Reservoir Project (Canouts 1975) and, for comparative purposes, are utilized unaltered in this report. In this sense, the cost estimates for a total data study in the Orme Alternatives resources are based on the same cost parameters as those presented for the Orme Reservoir resources. Following the discussion of general cost units are specific cost estimates for the 93 archaeological sites recorded in the 20 percent sample of the Roosevelt Lake and Horseshoe Reservoir direct impact areas. Based on the average cost per man-day for these 93 sites and the projected total man-days required for the 100 percent sample (Table 23), an estimate of total data study costs is derived. It is this latter cost, when compared to the total data recovery costs of the Orme Reservoir (Canouts 1975), that provides the relative monetary significance of the two projects' resources.

Cost Parameters

The concept of "total data recovery" has been discussed briefly in Chapter 8 of this report and previously by Schiffer and House (1975). Basically, the concept that 100 percent of all data can be retrieved by known methods from any one site or set of sites is ill conceived. Archaeological, anthropological, and ecological problems are open-ended and almost limitless in their range and scope; the data necessary to answer such problems are probably beyond the collecting capabilities of any project's personnel or resources. Furthermore, what we may consider to be 100 percent of the data today may only represent 50 percent of the data of interest to archaeologists 50 years from now. As all sites are non-renewable and very finite in nature, we must constantly be aware that cultural resources are data banks for all future studies (Lipe 1974). In this sense, we must try to think of the resources from the perspective of future needs and future research questions. Such a perspective widens the gap between our ability to collect data and the concept of total data. A third problem with "total data recovery" is that only a fraction of the cultural material laid down or discarded by a site's inhabitants is preserved for recovery (Reid and others 1975). Due to differential preservation of materials, any data recovered are less than a 100 percent sample.

Despite these three problems, the monetary figures produced for this section of the chapter are considered necessary for future mitigation plans, as well as for comparative cost analysis with the Orme Reservoir Project. As far as is presently possible, the figures in this section are for the complete excavation of every recorded site, the recovery of all cultural and ecological data that may be considered relevant, and the necessary analysis, research, and dissemination of results.

The first table (Table 33) is a listing of all anticipated procedures in such a total data study. Included in Table 33 are specialized aspects of data recovery techniques, analyses, and the various tasks of report preparation and publication. By no means is this to imply that all of these procedures are either necessary or sufficient for total data recovery. Rather, these various procedures are incorporated in Table 33 in order to demonstrate the range of possible studies that these cultural resources may require. It would be almost impossible to estimate costs for most of these procedures. Some, such as excavation procedures are marginally quantifiable, while others will be largely dependent upon the nature of the collected data. Because of these limitations in our ability to accurately predict time and cost estimates for many aspects of archaeological study, we have (following the Orme Reservoir study) calculated the specific estimates for one major variable: time/labor necessary for excavation of certain standard site units. These figures are presented in Table 34 and represent averages for the number of man-days required for complete data recovery from certain standardized site units. In other words, based on the collective experiences of many Arizona archaeologists, a single pueblo room would take, on the average, 25 man-days to excavate (Table 34). These figures are presented in Table 34 and form the basis for all of our man-day estimates in Chapter 6 and in this chapter. Although problems certainly exist with these figures in terms of their actual cost predictability, it is felt that, as these estimates are based on the averages of many excavation experiences, and as large number of sites are involves in the Orme Alternatives Project, the results will be reasonably accurate.

Table 35 is a formula for the costs of data recovery from habitation sites. It is based on the average costs per man-day and includes the average professional staff wages, costs for labor, taxes, indirect costs, supplies, subsistence, and transportation. A cost of $200.00 is estimated for each man-day of data recovery from habitation sites. Non-habitation site recovery costs are presented in Table 36 and are slightly lower due to less staff supervision. A cost of $170.00 is estimated for each man-day of data recovery from non-habitation sites.

The second and third stages of data study involve aspects of data analysis, research, report preparation, and publication (Table 33). The analysis and report write-up costs in Table 37 are generally dependent upon the data recovery costs listed above. Based on averages of previous work conducted by the Arizona State Museum, certain general relationships are seen to exist between the number of man-days required for data recovery and the cost of analysis and publication. This cost (Table 37) is calculated at $465.00 per man-day of data recovery, whether for habitation or non-habitation sites. The costs listed in Tables 35 and 37 yield a total cost per man-day for habitation sites of $665.00. A total of Tables 36 and 37 yields a cost of $635.00 for non-habitation sites (Table 38).

Cost Estimates: 20 Percent Sample

The cost of complete study of the 93 sites recorded in the Orme Alternatives 20 percent sample is based on the preceding parameters. Each site is evaluated according to the criteria listed in Table 34, and a man-day figure is derived for data recovery. This man-day figure is then multiplied by the total costs of data recovery, analysis, and write-up as illustrated in Table 38. Heavy equipment cost of $144 per day are included where applicable. Table 39 lists the 29 sites recorded at Roosevelt Lake by ASM site number, man-days, heavy equipment days, and total costs. Table 40 lists the same data for Horseshoe Reservoir sites. Table 41 presents these total costs with additional cost items including the costs of preparing a detailed research design. A figure of $7,233,654.00 is estimated for the costs of total data study for the 29 Roosevelt Lake sites; $9,110,562.00 is estimated for the 64 Horseshoe sites. $16,609,216.00 is the estimated cost for a total data recovery program at the 93 sites recorded at both reservoirs.

Table 33

Procedures in Archaeological Site Study
(after Canouts 1975)

Recovery	Analysis	Write-up/Publication
Research Design	Architectural Studies	Report Composition
Provenience Control Method	Archival Research	Typing
Data Collecting	Artifact Typology	Drafting
Aerial photography	Burial/Cremation	Photography
Copying (rock art)	Studies	Editing/Proofreading
Environmental docu-	Ceramic Studies	Duplication
mentation	X-ray defraction	
Excavation (mechanical/	Petrographic analysis	
manual)	Computer Studies	
Extramural stripping	Dating	
habitation sites)	Alpha recoil	
Remote sensing	Archaeomagnetism	
Specialized sampling	Dendrochronology	
Mapping	Obsidian hydration	
Test excavation	Radiocarbon	
Topographic studies	Geology	
(agricultural	Lithologic studies	
features)	Soil analysis	
Data Recording	Depositional studies	
Photography	Lithic Artifact Studies	
Drafting/illustration	Perishable Studies	
Data Computerization	Macrofossil analysis	
	Microfossil analysis	
	Photogrammetry	
	Pollen Studies	
	Shell Studies	
	Trace Element Studies	

Table 34

Time and Labor Estimates: Data Recovery

Habitation sites

Mounds
  (average for trash or other plus backhoe
    time):   1 man for 25 days
Pit houses
  (one house plus backhoe time):   1 man for 5 days
Ball courts
  (plus backhoe time):   1 man for 100 days
Pueblo rooms
  (includes compound; plus backhoe time):   1 man for 25 days
Additional features
  (includes extramural stripping, specialized
    sampling, other special activity areas,
    plus backhoe time):   1 man for 20 days

Non-habitation sites

Sherd and lithic scatters
  (based on collecting or stripping 10 m^2/day
    to a depth of 20 cm):   1 man for 1 day
Lithic scatters
  (based on collecting or stripping 20 m^2/day
    to a depth of 20 cm):   1 man for 1 day
Fieldhouses: 1 man for 10 days
Agricultural sites
  (based on stripping or trenching; mapping;
    specialized sampling; average of
    5000 m^2/day):   1 man for 1 day

Table 35

Cost Formula: Habitation Site Data Recovery

<u>Habitation Sites</u> (primary prehistoric habitation sites, historic habitations)

Staff:
```
        Direction
            1 Assistant Director          @ $58.00/day
            1 Supervisor III              @ $40.00/day
        Laboratory
            1 Supervisor II               @ $36.00/day
            1 Laboratory Technician III   @ $32.00/day
            1 Laboratory Technician II    @ $29.20/day
        Field Supervision
            1 Supervisor II               @ $36.00/day
        Excavation, Mapping, Recording
            2 Archaeological Assistants II @ $22.80/day
            1 Photographer II             @ $36.00/day
            1 Draftsman II                @ $36.00/day
                                          _____
                        Average           $34.88/day
```

Two Staff Members per Labor Man-day	$ 69.76
Labor: 1 Laborer @ $22.00/day	22.00
Taxes and Insurance: 17% of wages	15.59
Indirect Costs: Off Campus (30% of wages)	27.53
Supplies: $15.00/day	15.00
Subsistence and Lodging: $20.00/day/staff person	40.00
Transportation: Est. 50 mi./day @ 13¢/mi.+ $3.00/day	9.50
Total	$199.38
Rounded to....................	$200.00

Table 36

Cost Formula: Non-Habitation Site Data Recovery

Non-habitation Sites (Fieldhouses, lithic scatters, sherd and lithic
scatters, agricultural features)

Staff:
Direction
　　1 Assistant Director　　　　　　@ $58.00/day
　　1 Supervisor III　　　　　　　　@ $40.00/day
Laboratory
　　1 Laboratory Technician III　　@ $32.00/day
Field Supervision
　　1 Supervisor II　　　　　　　　 @ $36.00/day
Excavation, Mapping, Recording
　　1 Archaeological Assistant II　@ $22.80/day
　　1 Draftsman/Photographer II　　@ $36.00/day

　　　　　　　　　　　　Average　　　$37.47/day

One and one-half Staff Members per Labor Man-day　　　$ 56.20

Labor:
　　1 Laborer @ $22.00/day　　　　　　　　　　　　　　　　22.00

Taxes and Insurance:
　　17% of wages　　　　　　　　　　　　　　　　　　　　 13.29

Indirect Costs:
　　Off Campus (30% of wages)　　　　　　　　　　　　　　23.46

Supplies:
　　$15.00/day　　　　　　　　　　　　　　　　　　　　　 15.00

Subsistence and Lodging:
　　$20.00/day/staff person　　　　　　　　　　　　　　　30.00

Transportation:
　　Est. 50 mi./day @ 13¢/mi.　　　　　　　　　　　　　　 9.50

　　　　　　　　　　　　　Total　　　　　　　　　　　　$169.45

　　　　　　　　　Rounded to...................　　$170.00

Table 37

Cost Formula: Analysis and Write-Up of Recovered Data

Analysis

Average analysis costs:
     Includes travel or shipping costs where necessary.
     Prorated to cost per man-day.   Sub-Total $ 60.00

Write-Up/Publication

Staff:
     Direction
          1 Assistant Director -- ½ time   @ $58.00/day   29.00
          1 Supervisor II   @ $36.00/day   36.00
     Write-Up
          1 Supervisor II   @ $36.00/day   36.00
          2 Assistant Archaeologists   @ $32.00/day   64.00
     Report Preparation
          1 Draftsman II -- 3/4 time   @ $36.00/day   27.00
          1 Editor -- ½ time   @ $54.00/day   27.00
          1 Typist -- 3/4 time   @ $21.32/day   16.00
Taxes and Insurance:
     17% of wages   39.95
Indirect Costs:
     On Campus (46% of wages)   108.10
Supplies and Operations:
     $20.00/day   20.00
Publication:
     Estimated cost per man-day   3.50
                                                                 _____

                                        Sub-Total $406.55

                                        Rounded to... $405.00

                    Total Analysis and Write-Up $465.00

Table 38

Total Site Study Formulas: Total Costs per Man-Day

Habitation Sites

Data Recovery Costs	$200.00
Analysis/Write-Up/Publication Costs	$465.00
Total Costs per Man-Day	$665.00

Non-Habitation Sites

Data Recovery Costs	$170.00
Analysis/Write-Up/Publication	$465.00
Total Costs per Man-Day	$635.00

Heavy Equipment Costs

Backhoe rental (plus operator) when
applicable: $144.00/day

Table 39

Complete Study Costs: Roosevelt Lake (20 Percent Sample)

ASM Number*	Man-days	Heavy Equipment Days	Costs
U:4:17	100	3	$ 66,932
U:4:18	125	1	83,269
U:4:19**	10		6,350
U:4:20**	40	1	25,544
U:3:26**	100	2	63,788
V:5:27**	20	2	12,988
V:5:28**	10	5	7,070
U:4:7	1300	5	865,220
U:4:8	200	2	133,288
U:4:9	4000	30	2,644,320
U:4:10	2500	15	1,664,660
U:4:11	350	1	232,894
U:4:12	300	5	200,220
U:4:13	60	1	40,044
U:4:14**	5		3,175
U:4:15	10		6,650
U:8:74**	10		6,350
U:8:75**	10		6,350
U:8:76**	5		3,175
U:8:70**	30		19,050
U:8:78	700	5	466,220
U:8:72	350	5	233,470
U:8:73	100	2	66,788
U:4:16**	5		3,175
U:8:67	50		33,250
U:8:68	400		266,000
U:8:69**	15		9,525
U:8:71**	15	1	9,669
U:8:77**	100	5	64,220
TOTALS	10,920	91	$7,223,654

*   Sites are listed in same order as Table 9.

** Non-habitation sites (all others are habitation)

Table 40

Complete Study Costs: Horseshoe Reservoir
(20 Percent Sample)

ASM Number*	Man-days	Heavy Equipment Days	Costs
0:14:49**	200	5	$ 127,720
0:14:50	300	5	200,220
0:14:51	2000	20	1,332,880
0:14:52**	25		15,875
U:2:22**	25		15,875
U:2:23**	60		38,100
U:2:24**	20		12,700
U:2:25**	20		12,700
U:2:1	2000	15	1,332,160
U:2:2	200	5	133,720
U:2:33**	50		31,750
U:2:34**	75		47,625
U:2:35**	5		3,175
U:2:36	100	1	66,644
U:2:37**	10		6,350
0:14:7**	15		9,525
0:14:8	200	1	133,144
0:14:9**	300	2	190,500
0:14:10**	1		635
0:14:13**	15		9,525
0:14:14**	10		6,350
0:14:15**	10		6,350
0:14:16	200	1	133,144
0:14:17	400	3	266,432
0:14:18**	60	1	38,244
0:14:19**	30	1	19,194
0:14:20**	10		6,350
0:14:21	750	3	499,182
0:14:22	2000	25	1,333,600
0:14:23**	25		15,875
0:14:24**	20		12,700
0:14:25**	15		9,525
0:14:26**	50		31,750
0:14:27**	50		31,750
0:14:28**	20		12,700

*   Sites are listed in same order as presented in Table 10.

**   Non-habitation sites (all others are habitation)

Table 40 (continued)

ASM Number	Man-days	Heavy Equipment Days	Costs
0:14:29**	15		$ 9,525
0:14:30**	15		9,525
0:14:31**	10		6,350
0:14:32**	5		3,175
0:14:33**	35		22,225
0:14:34	400	5	266,720
0:14:35	500	5	333,220
0:14:36	400	5	266,720
0:14:37	400	5	266,720
0:14:38	800	10	533,440
0:14:39	125	1	83,269
0:14:40**	90	1	57,294
0:14:41**	10		6,350
0:14:42**	60		38,100
0:14:43**	15		9,525
0:14:44**	30		19,050
0:14:45**	30		19,050
0:14:46	140		93,100
0:14:47	500		332,500
0:14:48	125		83,125
0:14:11	50		31,750
0:14:12**	50		31,750
U:2:26**	150	2	95,538
U:2:27**	10		6,350
U:2:28**	20		12,700
U:2:29	140	1	93,244
U:2:30	200	1	133,144
U:2:31**	70		44,450
U:2:32**	70	1	44,594
TOTALS	13,736	125	$9,096,472

** Non-habitation sites (all others are habitation)

Table 41

Total Costs: Sites Recorded in the Orme Alternatives Survey
(20 Percent Sample)

Roosevelt Lake Costs

Total of Table 39 : $ 7,233,654

Horseshoe Reservoir Costs

Total of Table 40 : $ 9,096,472

Miscellaneous Costs

Aerial photographs: 5,000
Research design: 10,000
Pre-project preparation*:   250,000
                             _____

TOTAL COSTS $16,595,126

* Includes testing procedures, data gathering for design of sample
procedures, laboratory construction, etc.

Cost Estimates: Sample Projection

Chapter 6 has discussed the statistical aspects of using the 20 percent sample in order to predict the 100 percent population of sites in the two reservoir direct impact areas. Based on these predictions and a cost per man-day figure derived from the 20 percent sample cost analysis, a range of costs is estimated for the total data study of the 100 percent sample.

An average cost per man-day figure of $673.00 is derived by dividing the total costs for the 20 percent sample (Table 41) by the total number of man-days required for data recovery as listed in Tables 39 and 40. This average cost per man-day figure, when multiplied by the projected number of man-days required for total data study of the 100 percent sample (Table 23) will provide an estimated range in costs.

Based on these figures, the range in costs for total data study of all the Roosevelt sites is from $7,268,126.00 to $57,541,500.00. The range in costs for the total data study of all the Horseshoe sites is $46,504,300.00 to $60,502,700.00. A total figure, therefore, ranges from $53,772,700.00 to $118,044,200.00. These figures are illustrated in Table 42. It should be noted that these figures do not include two items. First, the costs of surveying the remaining 80 percent of the direct impact areas at both of these reservoirs are not included; they are listed in the next chapter. Second, the costs of mitigating the indirect impact zones of this project have not been considered. These costs are expected to be considerable and are only dealt with briefly at the end of this chapter.

Adequate Data Study

Two main points have been presented in the preceding section. First, the cost of total data recovery is great, and second, the specific goals of data recovery cannot be detailed on the basis of a 20 percent sample survey. Only with 100 percent survey data can a responsible research design be created, and only on the basis of this research design can an adequate data study plan be devised. Thus, only the sample needed to solve these research problems would constitute an adequate data study. Of course, such research problems would have to include the full range of potential problems recognized now and those that can be predicted for the near future.

These specific research plans are not formulated due to the lack of survey data, therefore, only some generalizations concerning an adequate data study will be presented. First of all, any "adequate data study" will have to be based on the laws of probability sampling. The actual design of the sample will have to be predicated upon the nature of the sites and the various research problems. The frequency of the data recovery sample will similarly vary with sites and research problems. In some cases, perhaps only 5 percent of the relevant data will have to be studied in order to predict the nature of the population. In other cases, perhaps 100 percent of

Table 42

Total Costs for the Orme Alternatives Projection

Roosevelt Lake

	Projection	Possible Range*
Man-days	42,200	10,800 to 85,500
Cost	$28,400,600	$7,268,126 to $57,541,500

Horseshoe Reservoir

	Projection	Possible Range*
Man-days	79,500	69,100 to 89,900
Cost	$53,503,500	$46,504,300 to $60,502,700

Total

	Projection	Possible Range*
Man-days	121,700	79,900 to 175,400
Cost	$81,904,100	$53,772,700 to $118,044,200

* This range is based on a 70 percent coefficient of confidence.

the relevant data will have to be recovered. Not only are these variable frequencies tied into the research goals, but they are also based on the nature of the surveyed population. For instance, if burnt rock middens were found to be equally distributed throughout a single project area in large numbers (perhaps 200+), it would probably not be necessary to excavate more than 5 percent of them. The combination of a large number of these features in relation to the low complexity of the features would enable fairly accurate predictions to be made on the basis of such a small sample.

Conversely, if only one Pioneer period Hohokam pit house village is located during the survey, the idea of sampling the population of such sites would be inane. Perhaps the site itself could be sampled, but a frequency of 50 percent to almost 100 percent would probably be necessary to begin answering questions about this early period.

As noted earlier in Chapter 8, there is really no single answer to this problem. Sample frequencies and designs must be variable if more than one research problem is to be dealt with in any one project. Cowgill's (1975: 274) discussion of the problem articulates some of this rationale:

> The size and complexity of the sample required depends very strongly on the kinds of questions we ask. For rather simple questions fairly small samples will serve, but for many of the questions we are asking today, especially concerning internal structure and systemic aspects of regions or sites, the samples need to be rather large. The implication is neither that we should forget about probability sampling and rely wholly on intuition, nor that meaningful research is impossible. Rather, it is that statistical expertise can make our research more efficient, but it cannot enable us to work miracles with tiny budgets.

In general, however, a 40 to 50 percent sample seems to represent the most responsible estimate prior to research design formulation. This is based on empirical survey tests (Chenhall 1972; Mueller 1974) and may or may not be entirely applicable to mitigative sampling. The Orme Reservoir study (Canouts 1975) estimated that a 50 percent sample would be considered best at this time, and for comparison, a 50 percent mitigation sample is recommended for Orme Alternatives.

Based on a 50 percent data recovery sample, "adequate data study" costs at the Roosevelt Lake direct impact zone could be $14,200,300.00, with a possible range from $3,634,063.00 to $28,770,750.00. At the Horseshoe Reservoir direct impact zone, an adequate data study cost of $26,751,750 is predicted with a possible range of $23,252,150.00 to $30,351,350.00. The cost for adequately studying both reservoirs, then, is $40,952,050 with a possible range of $26,886,350.00 to $59,022,100.00.

Conclusions

This chapter has discussed three alternative courses of action that could mitigate the effects of enlarging Horseshoe Reservoir and Roosevelt Lake. Below, these three mitigative schemes are summarized with our final recommendations concerning each of these plans. They are presented in an order of least to most desirable from a cultural resource management point of view.

Total Data Recovery

The concept of recovering all of the cultural data from the Roosevelt Lake and the Horseshoe Reservoir project areas is an unrealistic goal, mechanically and monetarily. First, the concept itself is somewhat naive and should be qualified. Only the data that we consider relevant to today's research questions are recoverable. Other types of data would not be recognized and therefore would not be collected. Data necessary to solve tomorrow's research problems or the research problems of the 21st century are not recoverable because they are beyond our immediate research conceptualization.

Even considering today's "total data" in relation to today's research problems, a total data recovery program would cost a tremendous amount of money. In this chapter, the cost was estimated at $81,904,100.00 with a possible range of from $53,772,700.00 to $118,044,200.00. It should be noted, furthermore, that this cost covers total excavation of the sites within the direct impact zone. At Orme Reservoir, a consideration of both direct and indirect impact zones yielded a total data recovery estimate of about $54 million.

Another negative aspect of a total data recovery program at the Orme Alternatives project areas is that the time required to complete such a massive project would probably run past the proposed completion date of this portion of the Central Arizona Project. Additionally, the professional and institutional capabilities necessary for doing quality work in such a massive recovery program would be severely taxed especially if preparation time and planning were not adequate.

Therefore, it is recommended that a total data study plan not receive further consideration as a means for mitigating the potential adverse effects of the Orme Alternatives Project.

Adequate Data Recovery

Many of the problems discussed above concerning total data recovery also pertain to an adequate data recovery program. The foremost problems concern what is an adequate amount of data, what kinds of research questions need to be dealt with, and how to minimize the loss of the remaining data. Compounding these problems is the consideration of future research interests.

Any adequate data recovery program that is too tightly tied to research problems of today and ignores research data needs of the future should be considered short-sighted.

None of these problems can be adequately answered here. However, if 50 percent is considered an adequate sample for data recovery, as was suggested for the Orme Reservoir project (Canouts 1975), then a cost of mitigation for the Orme Alternatives direct impact zones would be approximately $40 million. An additional large sum would also be necessary for mitigation of the indirect effects of reservoir enlargement. These figures, when compared to the projected cost for mitigating the effects of Orme Reservoir, are at least twice as great, making Roosevelt Lake and Horseshoe Reservoir undesirable alternatives to Orme Reservoir.

Therefore, any plan to mitigate the effects of enlarging Roosevelt Lake or Horseshoe Reservoir by recovering an adequate sample of the total data should not be considered as a viable course of action.

Site Protection

Our recommendation that the cultural resources within the Orme Alternatives direct impact zones be protected is based on both positive and negative considerations.

From a positive point of view, the projected 374 sites within these impact zones are of historical, scientific, social, and monetary significance as discussed extensively in the preceding chapter (Chapter 8). In this chapter (Chapter 9), these potentially impacted resources are discussed in terms of their "regional significance," a concept that cross-cuts aspects of historical, scientific, and social significance. In this sense any data recovery program in these two reservoir areas would not only deplete the immediate resource base surrounding Roosevelt Lake and Horseshoe Reservoir, but it would also disturb the systemic integrity of all of the sites within the same regional subsistence-settlement system. For these reasons, it is recommended that the Orme Alternatives archaeological sites be protected as a positive measure.

From a negative point of view, site protection is recommended as a mitigative course of action due to the general unfeasibility of the two alternative mitigative schemes: either total data study or adequate data study. As pointed out above, these schemes are unrealistic in that even a partial data study (and recovery) based on a 50 percent recovery sample would be much too expensive and probably too time consuming.

The Indirect Impact Zone

The Orme Alternatives study that is presented in this report has dealt with the direct impact zone -- that area between the present high water line of Roosevelt Lake and Horseshoe Reservoir and that high water line that would exist if both reservoirs were enlarged. At Roosevelt Lake, this direct impact zone consists of 30 vertical feet around the lake. At Horseshoe Reservoir, this direct impact zone encompasses 140 vertical feet.

Throughout this report, numerous comparisons have been made between these Orme Alternative data and those recorded in the Orme Reservoir project area. What must be considered, however, is that the Orme Reservoir project area includes an indirect impact zone, or a developmental zone. Such a zone was evaluated archaeologically because it was felt that after reservoir construction, sites in this zone would experience a significant though indirect impact. Such impacts would result from increased recreational use and general traffic, from increased access for vandals, and from long-range land development plans. It is even possible that such impact would have a greater effect on the cultural resources than the direct impact of the reservoir. Thus, all comparisons between Orme Alternatives and Orme Reservoir must be qualified as being comparisons of a total project area (Orme Reservoir) with a partial project are (Orme Alternatives).

It is recommended that if the Orme Alternatives options are to be seriously considered by the Bureau of Reclamation, that the indirect impact zones surrounding those reservoirs be evaluated. At Roosevelt Lake, it appeared that the number, density, and size of the sites in the indirect impact area was greater than those in the direct impact area surveyed during this project. At Horseshoe Reservoir, a very limited glimpse at the indirect impact zone indicated that sites are surely present, but it cannot be intuited as to how these compare in density, size, etc., with the sites described in the direct impact zone.

Chapter 10

A PRELIMINARY RESEARCH PLAN

Although the preceding chapter has made a strong recommendation that a data recovery program not be initiated and that the sites associated with the Orme Alternatives direct impact areas be protected, this chapter is presented as a preliminary research design should such a data recovery operation ever become necessary. This plan is also prepared in compliance with the Arizona State Museum's contract obligation to the Bureau of Reclamation.

Since only 20 percent of the direct impact zones have been surveyed, site population parameters are rather generalized. Information on the variability, both temporal and functional, of the total site population is even less exact. Information on all of the sites in these zones is necessary before a workable research design can be formulated. Therefore, formulation of a complete, detailed research design will not be attempted at this time.

Instead, the following research plan is presented. This plan would guide the survey of the remaining 80 percent of the project areas. And the 80 percent survey of the direct impact zones should provide the data necessary for designing a final mitigative design. Additionally such a survey would also provide the chance to conduct research into relevant behavioral and methodological problems. Included in the survey plan is a testing phase designed to elicit information on the sites' research potential, as well as certain behavioral data that may be of use in the testing of hypotheses.

Pre-Excavation Survey (Remaining 80 Percent)

It is recommended that the remaining portions of the Roosevelt and Horseshoe direct impact zones be surveyed in order to provide more complete pre-excavation data. This would involve the same general methodological techniques as discussed in Chapter 5 (The Survey).

The following research plan is oriented toward three general problem domains. First, and most important for this survey, is the " valuation of Site Research Potential." Second is the "Methodological Evaluation;" this would comprise an empirical comparison of the 20 percent sample predictions and the 100 percent population data. Third is the "Behavioral Evaluation," or the actual archaeological studies that could be undertaken.

Evaluation of Site Research Potential

This evaluation is considered a necessary and logically prior step to the final formulations of data recovery mitigation plans. It is recommended that every recorded site by evaluated (during survey) as to its specific research potential. The magnitude and effect of erosional and depositional processes should be noted. The degree and effect of any vandalism should also be recorded along with the size and estimated depth of the site. The 93 sites recorded during the initial 20 percent survey were all evaluated using these criteria. It is suggested, however, that more data are necessary if a truly informed research design is to be formulated for the mitigation of these sites. Therefore, a testing program ought to be included in this pre-excavation survey stage. Small, limited activity sites can probably be evaluated from a surface inspection. However, habitation sites and medium-sized sites of a questionable functional nature should be sub-surface tested in order to better understand their research potential. It is recommended that a series of test pits (1 m by 1 m) be sunk into trash mounds, possible pit house locations, and perhaps into pueblo rooms. Such tests will provide data on the cultural depth of sites, on-site stratification, the occupational phases present, and whether certain sites are primary habitation sites or non-habitation, limited activity sites. Synthesizing these test data with the more traditional research evaluation data should provide substantial input into a final excavation plan and insure that these sites will be studied to the fullest extent of their potential prior to destruction or alteration.

Of the 374 sites (Table 23) that are projected for the total direct impact areas, approximately one-half will probably need sub-surface testing. It is estimated that approximately four man-days will be sufficient to test each of these 187 sites. Therefore, 748 man-days will be necessary for this testing operation (in addition to basic survey costs). Costs are included in the section on "Cost Data (Complete Survey)" at the end of this research plan.

Methodological Evaluation

The primary methodological research goal for the 80 percent sample is a test of the sampling predictions included in this report. With the 80 percent data added to the 20 percent data already presented, the exact population parameters of the survey area will be known. It will, then, be a simple task to evaluate our sample design, its accuracy, its shortcomings, and perhaps determine better methods for conducting future surveys of a similar nature.

Perhaps the most promising prospect is the potential for computer simulations with these data. When the project area is totally surveyed, a computer simulation similar to that conducted on the Orme Reservoir data in Chapter 6 (this volume) can be made. A desirable method would be to employ the same sampling design as that used in this 20 percent survey, and apply it to the total data at varying sample frequencies (percentages). By running thousands of such simulations, sampling distributions of total site estimates could be obtained for various frequencies. It is such information that archaeologists are in need of in order to design future sampling projects. An additional simulation problem would involve imposing different sampling designs on the Orme Alternatives survey data. In addition to the stratified random sample design used for the 20 percent survey, additional simulation tests could be performed using simple random, systematic, or cluster designs. Differing frequencies could also be used in order to evaluate the accuracy and efficiency of all of these combinations. It would then be possible to recommend the best combination of sample design and frequency for future projects of a similar nature.

All of these combinations of designs and frequencies have been considered in reference to one research goal: determining the accuracy of estimates of the total number of sites. However, as research goals vary, sample designs and frequencies must vary. So, in addition to simulating variations upon the population parameter problem, simulations should also be made to test sample designs and sample frequencies for different kinds of research problems. An example might be to try to evaluate sampling procedures necessary to predict the populations of various types of sites, at various time periods, or within various environmental settings. A more complex set of research questions increases the number of site variables and lessens the number of sites in each category. Therefore, a larger sample frequency would be necessary for solving such problems. A general rule, then, would have the sample frequency increase with increased complexity of research goals. Such rules, however, would benefit from future simulation testing.

Another kind of methodological research, one that also involves sampling, would be experimentation with intra-site surface sampling of artifactual material. During the initial 20 percent survey, ceramics were collected from sites in what is called a "grab sample." Generally, these samples consisted of diagnostic sherds, or sherds taken from from vandalized contexts. It is suggested that during the 80 percent survey, experiments be conducted with on-site surface sampling in order to try to determine the advantages and disadvantages of such procedures. Such experimentation could be accomplished in any number of ways. For example, conducting grab samples at one reservoir and systematic surface collection at the other reservoir might produce interesting comparisons. However, it might be more realistic to test this comparison in a limited experiment. Perhaps a sample design could be implemented where every tenth site surveyed would be systematically collected.

Actual on-site sample designs would be dependent on the site being sampled. In complex sites, a stratified random sample procedure might be appropriate, while small sites might be best sampled with a simple random design or a systematic design. In any case, it would be necessary for the field crew to be well trained in such techniques so that on-the-spot field decisions could be made. Probably the most important result to come from such experimentation is some analysis of the relationship of costs to benefits of such procedures.

Behavioral Evaluation

The two problem domains discussed above are the most immediate concerns of the proposed 80 percent survey, however certain behavioral problems could perhaps be solved, or at least examined, during such a survey. Some of these behavioral problems are logical extensions of the archaeological problems raised during the Orme Alternatives 20 percent survey. Other behavioral problems are suggested due to their "research relevance" or because of the general fit between the problems and the data potential of the project areas. The following eight problem domains are suggested to provide some orientation for an initial mitigative stage, if one becomes necessary.

Problem Domain I. One problem orientation that has both short- and long-term implications for studies in these reservoir areas is population study or the paleodemography of the area.

In the short-term sense, the settlement pattern analysis in Chapter 7 amply demonstrated various gaps in our ability to account for differences between the two localities or between two or more time periods. More specifically, the densities of Period I sites (A.D. 700-1100) vary significantly from Horseshoe Reservoir to Roosevelt Lake. Determining whether this results from poorly sampled data or from some unknown environmental-behavioral variables would make a valid research question. Another problem consists of the differences between Period II and Period III site densities at both reservoirs. Offhand, it would appear that differences between sites of these two periods are primarily a result of differing ratios of habitation and non-habitation sites. Additionally, changes in size of sites from Period II to Period III could also explain some of the differences in the site densities. It appears that this shift represents both an aggregation of people into larger sites and a greater concentration of activities in a centrally located pueblo. A third population problem concerns the nature of the pre-Period I population and the post-Period III population of these two basins.

More generalized demographic problems that could be approached during the 80 percent survey revolve around the derivation of approximate population curves for these areas. Involved in such a study would be the accurate measure of site frequencies, site types, site occupation spans, site sizes, number of habitation rooms, and any other variables relevant to the number of people living at any one site or locale. Population studies have proved notoriously difficult for archaeologists due to the impossibility of counting actual heads. Thus, archaeologists are forced to use such indirect indices as those noted above in order to construct a reasonable population curve.

Once such a curve has been, at least tentatively, worked out, the results should have some explanatory potential as an independent variable in other studies. In this sense, the changing demographic aspects of the Horseshoe and Roosevelt areas would be of use in studying causes of changing settlement patterns, subsistence patterns, or social organization.

To turn the population problem around, it would also constitute a valid research orientation to treat the demographic information as a dependent variable. Then a search could be made for the causes of the changing population levels.

Problem Domain II. As much of the archaeological emphasis of this study is related to past subsistence activities, this problem domain is designed to aid in the interpretation of such activities. It is almost embarrassingly clear to archaeologists how little subsistence information is obtainable during surface surveys. This is particularly true of the existing Orme Alternatives site data. The prospects that the completion of the survey would shed valuable new light on the subsistence problem are, furthermore, not very encouraging. For this reason, it is suggested that, in addition to collecting primary data on subsistence activities (such as artifact types, site locations, agricultural systems), an indirect index of subsistence practices be obtained.

Leone (1968a, 1968b) has dealt with this problem, but from another point of view. He conducted a study in northeastern Arizona where subsistence patterns were already understood for most of the prehistoric sequence. The available subsistence information indicated an increased dependence upon agriculture between A.D. 200 and 400. From A.D. 400 to 650, the dependence on agriculture declined. It increased again from A.D. 650 to 900 and declined again from A.D. 950 to 1050, but increased thereafter to an ultimate peak around A.D. 1300.

Using this subsistence scheme, Leone (1968a, 1968b) attempted to test the hypothesis that an increasing dependence upon agriculture leads to increasing social autonomy between the minimal economic units of a settlement system. An indication of the increasing social autonomy would be the presence of more and more village endogamy.

To determine the increasing degree of village endogamy and social autonomy, sherds were collected from a series of datable sites. Based on the variables of color, temper, and design, Leone was able to quantify the variation in ceramics between the village sites. In order to determine the changing degree of social autonomy from this indirect evaluation he made two basic assumptions: women made the pottery, and women passed on pottery-making traditions to their daughters. Therefore, the more variable the ceramics were at a site, the more exogamous the village was. With less internal variation, it could be inferred that a village was more endogamous.

The result of this study demonstrated a covariation between an increase in dependence on agriculture and a decrease in the variability of ceramic attributes (increasing endogamy). At Orme Alternatives, this same methodology could be used but adapted for different purposes. Using Leone's ceramic criteria, it would be possible to chart changes through time in the amount of ceramic variability within village sites. It should then be possible to understand inferred changes in village endogamy and therefore social autonomy through time at Roosevelt Lake and Horseshoe Reservoir. A final step would be to infer changes in subsistence patterns which Leone has been able to correlate to changes in social autonomy. The result would, then, give some indication of changing ecological relationships at Roosevelt Lake and Horseshoe Reservoir.

Problem Domain III. Another research problem that could be investigated during a completion of the survey concerns aspects of locational analysis. As Swedlund has indicated (1975: 22), "Recently there has been a growing interest in applying locational analysis in anthropological studies." Most of these studies are attempts to understand the processes involved in the organization of populations by examining variables within the social, biological, and ecological realms (Swedlund 1975). Swedlund attempted such research while testing a locational model (Hudson 1969) with historic data from New England. It is suggested that site survey data from Orme Alternatives also be utilized to test Hudson's (1969) geographic model of rural settlement patterns. The model developed by Hudson consists of three phases in the initial settlement of an area:

(1) Colonization - Occupation of a frontier area by units of a given population. Density is low and the location of settlement is random.

(2) Spread - Usually the result of population growth or further immigration. The population spreads by diffusion and a corresponding increase in site densities. The pattern most often results from "offspring" communities that develop near the original colonizing communities and move out successively. Locations tend to be clustered.

(3) Competition - Settlement is a density dependent process and eventually the available area becomes filled. At this stage, competition between the units occurs and the eventual effect is an equilibrium state with the settlements approaching optimum size. The theoretical distribution of settlements at this stage should be regular with a maximum spacing between settlements given a density of settlements over the total area (after Swedlund 1975: 22).

This geographic model has already been utilized by three anthropologists. Wood (1971) has suggested that this model can be productive in archaeological research and discusses some of the statistical methodologies involved. Swedlund (1975) has tested this model, at least in preliminary form, using historic data from two counties in northwestern Massachusetts. Population and settlement data for the period between 1650 and 1850 suggest a close fit between the data and Hudson's model. Blouet (1972) also makes use of the model in a theoretical discourse on the evolution of settlement patterns.

It appears that this three-stage development may represent the changing patterns in the Roosevelt Lake and Horseshoe Reservoir project areas. The first stage of colonization in Hudson's model could easily be represented by the Colonial Hohokam at both reservoir areas. The second stage, or spread, could be represented by the early Pueblo period. The third stage, characterized by competition, could be represented by the late Pueblo period. It appears, then, that there is a significant preliminary correlation between the rural settlement model and the settlement sequences in the Orme Alternatives localities. The model can be easily tested once the total survey data are available, and once there is better understanding of site dating and the distinctions between habitation and non-habitation sites.

Problem Domain IV. As indicated during the 20 percent survey, a significant number and variety of agricultural features were observed. These were only recorded briefly and numerous variables important to an understanding of the functioning of these features are needed. Because agricultural sites are generally quite visible on the surface, many of these variables could be recorded during a pre-mitigation survey.

To better understand these features, careful mapping is necessary, especially in regard to topographic variables. The relationship of different types of agricultural systems to either colluvial deposits or alluvial deposits should also provide an agricultural site typology. A third variable would involve detailed recording of the soil type associated with each system. A fourth variable would involve sporadic testing of deposits backed up behind dams in order to determine if pedogenesis (pedological soil formation) has taken place. If so, then perhaps types of soil formation could be temporally correlated with specific systems. Depth of soils should also be recorded. A fifth variable would consist of the spatial relationships of agriculture systems to nearby habitation sites or limited activity sites such as field houses. Such relationships might be of use in inferring temporal variability in agricultural systems. A sixth variable would include an estimation of area suitable for cultivation within each system. Such data on cultivable acreage in combination with fuller population data could provide important information on subsistence practices and adaptation to these environments. It is suggested that a professional soils scientist or agricultural scientist be consulted on these problems, especially the relationships of plant productivity and soil type.

Problem Domain V. Also associated with subsistence practices and general adaptation would be a more precise understanding of the biotic environment and the relationships of certain microenvironments to archaeological resources. In order to quantify such variables, it is recommended that on-site biotic species be quantified and that near-site species be sampled. Sample units that do not have any archaeological resources should also be sampled in order to gain some comparison between site areas and non-site areas. If such a study is properly implemented, certain environmental variables may be found to correlate with certain site types. Such data would be of prime importance in any explanation of the variability in site locations recorded at each reservoir project area.

Problem Domain VI. A problem that arose during the initial survey and one that remains unresolved concerns lithic scatters that were observed but were not recorded. These areas usually consisted of cores and primary flakes widely scattered over extensive areas. Their low density made them "non-sites" according to our site recording criteria (Chapter 5), but it is imperative that we better understand these scatters as they do represent significant cultural behavior. It is recommended that these scatters be recorded during any future survey and that they be minimally sampled and surface collected. Presently, temporal or cultural affiliations are total- ly unknown. It is possible that these represent some Archaic utilization of the area, or possibly some resource procurement activities of Hohokam or puebloid occupants of these valleys, or even some manifestation of proto-historic occupants of these valleys, or even some manifestation of proto-historic Apache or Yavapai people. Additionally, spatial relation- ships of these lithic scatters to the surrounding sites may infer some connection between Hohokam or pueblo habitation sites and lithic resource procurement areas. A relationship between these lithic scatters and cer- tain micro-environments or specific economic plant species may, on the other hand, infer that these lithics are related to the procurement of some biotic resource.

Problem Domain VII. Related to this lithic problem is the meaning and importance of isolated artifacts that have also been considered as "non-sites" during the initial survey. Various studies have been conducted in central Arizona recently (Doelle 1975; Goodyear 1975; Rodgers 1974) in which this problem has comprised the major research interest. Generally, these researchers have demonstrated tentative correlations between isolated artifacts, isolated tool kits, and present-day plant resources. Because these studies have been dependent upon the very intensive ground search of small sample units, logistical factors may prohibit such studies from being truly effective in the Orme Alternatives area. Thus, in addition to the 80 percent sample survey of these Roosevelt and Horseshoe direct impact areas with regard to recording archaeological sites, the areas would also have to be sampled at a much lower frequency in order to record non-site data such as individual, isolated artifacts and related biotic data. It is suggested that such a goal is probably unrealistic within the parameters of this pre-mitigation survey. An alternative would be to delay isolated artifact studies until an actual mitigation phase is implemented. At such a time when a long-term, large-scale mitigation phase is taking place, ancillary studies such as isolated artifact surveys could be accomplished with relative ease.

Problem Domain VIII. Logically derived from the 20 percent initial survey, and in preparation to any actual mitigation plans are problems of dating sites and assigning functions to sites. These problems were inher- ent in the analyses and discussions contained in this report. As a result, our temporal control on sites is very loose and certainly not adequate for fine-grained diachronic studies. Many of the cultural problems listed in the previous problem domains are also dependent upon better dating techniques. In fact, any future mitigation studies will be heavily dependent upon sampling procedures. Offhand, it would appear that a primary stratifying criterion prior to selecting sites for excavation would be temporal phase. It is hard to come up with any bag of tricks that will automatically date these surveyed sites. Perhaps, just the accumulation of more ceramic material will allow tentative dates to be assigned to certain architectural styles. If so, many sites may then be cross-dated. Another possibility is that the testing program proposed earlier will make available more temporal data.

The problem of assigning a function to sites resulted in labeling sites as either habitation or non-habitation. All too often, placement in these categories was based on hunches, especially in regard to small pit house villages. Again, perhaps the testing program will alleviate some of this problem. Hopefully, sites can be assigned to these two major functional categories with a high degree of accuracy and into further sub-categories with at least some degree of accuracy.

Cost Data (Complete Survey)

The costs of completing the survey of the direct impact zones at Roosevelt Lake and Horseshoe Reservoir are tabulated in Tables 43 and 45. The costs of a testing operation recommended in the previous discussion is presented in Tables 44 and 46. Final cost figures for both survey projects and both testing projects are listed in Table 47.

At Roosevelt Lake, there remains 6347 acres of unsurveyed ground within the direct impact area. The 20 percent survey averaged about 25 acres per man-day. As the proposed 80 percent survey will entail more detailed and comprehensive data collecting strategies, it is estimated that 20 acres per man-day will be a more appropriate figure. Thus, 317 man-days will be required for completion of this field work. Using a three-man crew, one supervisor and two assistants, a total of 105 field days will be necessary. A similar number of days will be necessary for an analysis and write-up crew consisting of a Supervisory Research Archaeologist, an Assistant Research Archaeologist, an Archaeological Assistant I, and an Archaeological Assistant II. Costs for these personnel are listed in Table 43 along with standard costs for administration, support personnel, equipment vehicles, etc. Total costs of surveying the Roosevelt Lake project area would be $83,640.00

The costs of the recommended test investigations at Roosevelt Lake are itemized in Table 44. Based on a sample projection of 91 sites (Chapter 6), and an estimation that only 50 percent of the sites would require testing, a total of 45 sites are considered for testing. An average of four man-days is probably sufficient for testing each one. Thus, 180 field man-days would

Table 43

Cost Estimate for 80 Percent Survey of the
Roosevelt Lake Project Area

Supervisory Field Archaeologist
   1 person for 105 days @ $39.20/day $4116.00*
Supervisory Research Archaeologist
   1 person for 105 days @ $39.20/day   4116.00
Assistant Field Archaeologist
   2 persons for 105 days @ $35.04/day   7358.40*
Assistant Research Archaeologist
   1 person for 105 days @ $35.04/day   3679.20
Archaeological Assistant II
   1 person for 105 days @ $29.36/day   3082.80
Archaeological Assistant I
   1 person for 105 days @ $27.04/day   2839.20
Draftsman I
   1 person for 22 days @ $31.92/day   702.24
Editor
   1 person for 22 days @ $31.92/day   702.24
Equipment/Records Control
   1 person for 145 days @ $37.25/day   462.84
Project Direction
   1 person for 103 days @ $41.75/day   4300.25
Section Direction
   1 person for 48 days @ $46.25/day   2220.00
Section Administration
   1 person for 62.5 days @ $57.00/day   3562.50
Clerk-Typist
   1 person for 95.5 days @ $23.84/day   2276.72
Curatorial (Student Technician)
   1 person for 1 hour @ $2.60/hour   2.60

             Wage Sub-Total $40,020.99
Vacation/Sickleave Accrual
   7% of Wage Sub-Total   2801.67

             TOTAL WAGES AND
               ACCRUALS $42,822.46

Wage Extensions
   13% of Total Wages and Accruals   5566.92
Subsistence
   3 persons for 105 days @ $30.00/day   9450.00

*Field Wages

Table 43 (continued)

Vehicles
    10,500 miles @ 18¢/mile (4 x 4 carryall) $ 1890.00
    $3/day dispatch fee (including non-working days)   441.00
Field Equipment and Supplies
    $5/day for total staff field days (including non-
        working days)   2205.00
Report Supplies
    $2/day first 60 days   120.00
    $1/day second 60 days   60.00
    50¢/day beyond 120 days   45.00
Lieu Insurance
    Equipment: $2/day (including non-working days)   294.00
    Vehicle: $2/day (including non-working days)   294.00
Report Production
    Field Notes: Xerox @ 5¢/page   10.00
    Report: 100 copies (300 pp ea.) paperplate   870.00
Consultants
    Agricultural Scientist: 10 days @ $150/day   1500.00
    Plant Ecologist: 10 days @ $150/day   1500.00

                TOTAL DIRECT COSTS $67,068.38

Indirect Costs
    46% of On Campus Wages ($28,546.59)   13,131.43
    30% of Off Campus Wages ($11,474.40)   3442.32

                TOTAL COSTS $83,642.13

                Rounded to......... $83,640.00

Table 44

Cost Estimate for Supplementary Testing
at Roosevelt Lake

Supervisory Field Archaeologist
    1 person for 60 days @ $39.20/day $ 2352.00*
Assistant Field Archaeologist
    2 persons for 60 days @ $35.04/day   4204.80*
Laboratory Archaeologist
    1 person for 60 days @ $35.04/day   2102.40
Laboratory Assistant I
    1 person for 60 days @ $27.04/day   1622.40
Draftsman I
    1 person for 9 days @ $31.92/day   287.28
Equipment/Records Control
    1 person for 6 days @ $31.92/day   191.52
Project Direction
    1 person for 42 days @ $41.75/day   1753.50
Section Direction
    1 person for 26 days @ $46.25/day   1202.50
Section Administration
    1 person for 25.5 days @ $57.00/day   1938.00
Curatorial (Student Technician)
    1 person for 122 hours @ $2.60/hour   317.20
Faunal Analysis
    1 Student Tech. for 1½ hours @ $2.60/hour   3.90
    1 Lab. Tech. I for 10 hours @ $3.38/hour   33.80
    1 Lab. Tech. II for 64 hours @ $3.99/hour   255.36
Osteological Analysis
    1 Lab. Tech. I for 70 hours @ $3.38/hour   236.60
    1 Lab. Tech. II for 80 hours @ $3.99/hour   319.20
    1 Typist for 10 hours @ $2.98/hour   29.80

                   Wage Sub-Total $16,847.26

Vacation/Sickleave Accrual
    7% of Wage Sub-Total   1179.31

                 TOTAL WAGES AND
                     ACCRUALS $18,026.57

*Field Wages

Table 44 (continued)

Wage Extensions	
13% of Total Wages and Accruals	$ 2343.45
Subsistence	
3 persons for 60 days @ $30.00/day	5400.00
Vehicles	
6000 miles @ 18¢/mile (4 x 4 carryall)	1080.00
$3/day dispatch fee (including non-working days)	216.00
Field Equipment and Supplies	
$5/day for total staff field days (including non-working days)	1080.00
$20/day for 60 days of non-field lab	1200.00
Lieu Insurance	
Equipment: $2/day (including non-working days)	144.00
Vehicles: $2/day (including non-working days)	144.00
Report Production	
Field Notes: Xerox @ 5¢/page	10.00
TOTAL DIRECT COSTS	$29,644.02
Indirect Costs	
46% On Campus Wages ($10,290.46)	4733.61
30% Off Campus Wages ($6556.80)	1967.04
TOTAL COSTS	$36,344.67
Rounded to.........	$36,345.00

Table 45

Cost Estimate for 80 Percent Survey
of Horseshoe Reservoir Project Area

Supervisory Field Archaeologist
    1 person for 65 days @ $39.20/day $ 2548.00*
Supervisory Research Archaeologist
    1 person for 65 days @ $39.20/day   2548.00
Assistant Field Archaeologist
    2 persons for 65 days @ $35.04/day   4555.20*
Assistant Research Archaeologist
    1 person for 65 days @ $35.04/day   2277.60
Archaeological Assistant II
    1 person for 65 days @ $29.36/day   1908.40
Archaeological Assistant I
    1 person for 65 days @ $27.04/day   1757.60
Draftsman I
    1 person for 12 days @ $31.92/day   383.04
Editor
    1 person for 12 days @ $31.92/day   383.04
Equipment/Records Control
    1 person for 8 days @ $31.92/day   255.36
Project Direction
    1 person for 54.5 days @ $41.75/day   2575.37
Section Direction
    1 person for 25.5 days @ $46.25/day   1179.37
Section Administration
    1 person for 33 days @ $57.00/day   1881.00
Clerk-Typist
    1 person for 50. 5 days @ $23.84/day   1203.92
Curatorial (Student Technician)
    1 person for 1 hour @ $2.60/hour   2.60

                      Wage Sub-Total $23,458.50

Vacation/Sickleave Accrual
    7% of Wage Sub-Total   1642.10

                   TOTAL WAGES AND
                      ACCRUALS $25,100.60

*Field Wages

Table 45 (continued)

Wage Extensions
    13% of Total Wages and Accruals $ 3263.08
Subsistence
    3 persons for 65 days @ $30.00/day   5850.00
Vehicles
    65 miles @ 18¢/mile (4 x 4 carryall)   1170.00
    $3/day dispatch fee (including non-working days)   273.00
Field Equipment and Supplies
    $5/day for total staff field days (including
        non-working days)   1365.00
Report Supplies
    $2/day for first 60 days   120.00
    $1/day for second 60 days   60.00
    50¢/day for 20 days beyond   5.00
Lieu Insurance
    Equipment: $2/day (including non-working days)   182.00
    Vehicles: $2/day (including non-working days)   182.00
Report Production
    Field Notes: Xerox @ 5¢/page   10.00
    Report: 100 copies (300 pp ea.) paperplate   870.00
Consultants
    Agricultural Scientist: 5 days @ $150/day   750.00
    Plant Ecologist: 5 days @ $150/day   <u>750.00</u>

                    TOTAL DIRECT COSTS $39,950.68

Indirect Costs
    46% of On Campus Wages ($16,355.30)   7523.44
    30% of Off Campus Wages ($7103.20)   <u>2130.96</u>

                    TOTAL COSTS $49,605.08

                    Rounded to......... $49,605.00

Table 46

Cost Estimate for Supplementary Testing
at Horseshoe Reservoir

Supervisory Field Archaeologist	
1 person for 190 days @ $39.20/day	$ 7448.00*
Assistant Field Archaeologist	
2 persons for 190 days @ $35.04/day	13,315.20*
Laboratory Archaeologist	
1 person for 190 days @ $35.04/day	6557.60
Laboratory Assistant I	
1 person for 190 days @ $27.04/day	5137.60
Draftsman I	
1 person for 28.5 days @ $31.92/day	909.72
Equipment/Records Control	
1 person for 19 days @ $31.92/day	606.48
Project Direction	
1 person for 133 days @ $41.75/day	5552.75
Section Direction	
1 person for 62 days @ $46.25/day	2867.50
Section Administration	
1 person for 81 days @ $57.00/day	4613.00
Curatorial (Student Tech.)	
1 person for 122 hours @ $2.60/hour	317.20
Faunal Analysis	
1 Student Tech. for 3 hours @ $2.60/hour	7.80
1 Lab. Tech. I for 20 hours @ $3.38/hour	67.60
1 Lab. Tech. II for 128 hours @ $3.99/hour	510.72
Osteological Analysis	
1 Lab. Tech. I for 140 hours @ $3.38/hour	473.20
1 Lab. Tech. II for 160 hours @ $3.99/hour	638.40
1 Typist for 20 hours @ $2.98/hour	59.60
Wage Sub-Total	$49,082.17
Vacation/Sickleave Accrual	
7% of Wage Sub-Total	3435.75
TOTAL WAGES AND ACCRUALS	$52,517.92

*Field Wages

Table 46 (continued)

Wage Extensions
    13% of Total Wages and Accruals $ 6827.33
Subsistence
    3 persons for 190 days @ $30.00/day   17,100.00
Vehicles
    19,000 miles @ 18¢/mile (4 x 4 carryall)   3420.00
    $3/day dispatch fee (including non-working days)   798.00
Field Equipment and Supplies
    $5/day for total staff field days (including
        non-working days)   2850.00
    $20/day for non-field lab   3800.00
Lieu Insurance
    Equipment: $2/day (including non-working days)   532.00
    Vehicles: $2/day (including non-working days)   532.00
Report Production
    Field Notes: Xerox @ 5¢/copy   20.00

                          TOTAL DIRECT COSTS $88,397.25

Indirect Costs
    46% On Campus Wages ($28,318.97)   13,026.73
    30% Off Campus Wages ($20,763.20)   6228.96

                          TOTAL COSTS $107,652.94

                          Rounded to........ $107,655.00

Table 47

Total Costs for Pre-Mitigation Surveying
and Testing in the Roosevelt Lake
and Horseshoe Reservoir Direct Impact Zones

	80 Percent Survey	Site Testing Program	Survey and Testing
Roosevelt Lake	$ 83,640.00	$ 39,345.00	$122,985.00
Horseshoe Reservoir	$ 49,605.00	$107,655.00	$157,260.00
BOTH RESERVOIRS	$133,245.00	$147,000.00	$280,245.00

be necessary. Using a crew of three persons, 60 field days would be sufficient to accomplish this work. Two laboratory personnel for a similar
number of days would also be necessary to process the excavated artifactual
material. Research and write-up costs are not figured for the testing.
Data from such an operation would be included in the survey research report,
the costs of which are listed in Table 43. Total costs of testing would be
$36,345.00.

The Horseshoe Reservoir project area has 3910 acres of unsurveyed
ground remaining. Based on 20 acres per man-day, a total of 195 man-days
would be required for completion of the survey. A three-person crew would,
then, require 65 field days. Table 45 itemizes these costs as well as the
costs of research and writing a report. A total cost for the completion of
the Horseshoe Reservoir project area is $49,605.00.

Based on a sample projection (Chapter 6) of 283 sites, approximately
142 sites would require testing at Horseshoe Reservoir. Four man-days per
site would require a total of approximately 568 man-days for testing. With
a crew of three, approximately 190 field days would be sufficient for testing these sites. Like Roosevelt Lake, the costs of research analysis and
write-up are not included in this estimate (Table 46) and are considered
as part of the 80 percent survey project (Table 44). A cost for testing
these sites is estimated at $107,655.00.

Table 47 summarizes these survey and testing costs. A total figure
for completing the survey of both reservoirs is $133,245.00. An additional
$147,000.00 would be necessary for testing sites in both reservoir areas.
Thus a total figure for survey, testing, analysis, and report preparation
at Roosevelt Lake and Horseshoe Reservoir is $280,245.00.

Appendix I

CERAMIC ANALYSIS

During the Orme Alternatives survey, a total of 2435 sherds were collected from 73 sites. The sherds were collected in order to compare the Verde and Tonto plainwares and redwares, develop general temporal ranges for sites at both reservoirs, and indicate possible cultural affiliations. Because the ceramics were not collected systematically, or in great numbers, they can only be used to broadly indicate temporal and cultural relationships. Since all the specimens were collected from the surface of the ground, they provide poor data on site chronologies. In addition, at Roosevelt Lake, vandalism has been extensive, resulting in the probable under-representation of decorated sherds in that area. Because of a restricted data base, the information obtained from the ceramic analysis is descriptive and general, but can be used with other information to indicate possible cultural and temporal affiliations.

Ceramic Categories

The sherds have been divided into four groups -- decorated, corrugated, redwares, and plainwares -- then categorized into established types where possible. The type identifications were made after comparison with the Arizona State Museum type collection, and discussions with other archaeologists. Of the 2435 sherds collected, only 96 are decorated. These sherds have been divided into 15 categories and used to indicate general dates for sites. Eight corrugated sherds were collected, but only two have been tentatively identified as to type. The 478 redware sherds, divided into five categories, are used primarily for comparison between the two reservoirs. Plainwares are the most abundant sherd group. The 1853 plainware sherds were divided into seven descriptive categories and then used for comparative purposes. Sherds have been grouped according to site, collection area, and site type (for example, compounds, agricultural sites), and compared in that context.

Table 48 is a list of sherd types, their probable temporal ranges, sources for typing and dating, and the number of each sherd type found at both reservoirs.

Plainwares

Seventy-six percent of the sherds recovered are plainwares; many of the sherds are so similar in appearance that typing has been difficult.

Two plainware groups are recognized; Alameda Brownware, usually dated
between A.D. 1100-1400 (Colton 1958), and including Tonto Plain, Verde
Brown, Tuzigoot Plain, plainwares with calcium carbonate inclusions,
and plainwares with biotite inclusions; and a smaller group, composed
of Wingfield Plain and Gila Plain.

The majority of plainwares recovered from both reservoirs are part
of the Alameda Brownware group. Types included in this group differ
gradationally in terms of temper and paste. The type categorized as Tuzigoot Plain consists of a fine paste with 30 to 50 percent temper made up
of large fragments of rounded quartz sand, angular grayish fragments, and
rare flecks of mica. Surface color of those sherds identified as Tuzigoot
Plain ranges from orange-red to light brown. Sherds with fine paste, abundant fine temper with occasional large pieces of quartz and yellowish
fragments, sparse mica, and having a gritty look and feel on broken edges,
were classified as Verde Brown. Surface color of the Verde Brown sherds
ranges from dark to light brown. A third type of plainware, Tonto Plain,
makes up 83 percent of the Alameda Brownware. This type includes descriptive categories previously classified as Tonto Red and Tonto Brown. It was
first described by Windmiller (1972b: 9). Sherds in this category were compared with the Miami Wash collection (Doyel n.d.). They have temper consisting of abundant angular to subangular quartz sand, with yellow or red
opaque fragments, little or no mica to abundant mica (often phlogopite).
Surface color of Tonto Plain sherds ranges from gray-brown to maroon to
orange-red. A few sherds within the general grouping of Alameda brownwares
were not classed as to type. These sherds contain either biotite or calcium
carbonate temper inclusions. Although some examples of each Alameda
Brownware type fall clearly into one category, the majority of the sherds
lie somewhere between the various categories, and were placed into a category (usually Tonto Plain), on a rather arbitrary basis.

Sherds included in the Alameda Brownware category were recovered
from all types of sites at both reservoirs, including those sites or collection
areas classified as possible pit house villages. Because of the small sherd
sample no firm conclusions as to temporal range can be reached. However,
judging by the types of sites from which Alameda Brownwares were recovered,
the time range of A.D. 1100 to 1400 generally accepted for those plainwares,
and used in this report, may not be extensive enough.

Without petrographic analysis, we were unable to readily distinguish between Tonto Plain sherds from Horseshoe Reservoir and those
from Roosevelt Lake. Tonto Plain is a type usually restricted to the
Salado culture of the Tonto Basin and Globe-Miami areas. Similarly, Verde
Brown and Tuzigoot Plain, usually associated with Sinagua sites, also occur
at both reservoirs. If these Alameda Brownware are gradational types
reflecting, perhaps, locally available tempering agents, cultural associations
implied by one plainware type as opposed to another are not meaningful.
Therefore, the names assigned the above groupings of plainwares are intended to represent observational similarities and not cultural affiliations.

Table 48

Ceramic Information from the Orme
Alternatives Survey

Sherd Type	Dates (all A.D.)	Sources	No. from Horseshoe	No. from Roosevelt	Total No. Sherds
DECORATED					
Santa Cruz/ Sacaton Red-on-buff	700-1100	Gladwin and others 1937: 216	11	1	12
Buffwares	no date	---	11	0	11
Pinedale Polychrome	1275-1325	Carlson 1970: 53	0	4	4
Pinedale Black-on-red	1275-1325	Carlson 1970: 57	0	4	4
Undetermined White Mtn. Redware	1175-1400	Carlson 1970: 103	2	6	8
Salado polychromes	1250-1400	Breterniz 1966: 88; Colton & Hargrave 1937: 86-87	1	4	5
Tonto Polychrome	1250-1400	Colton & Hargrave 1937: 90	2	0	2
Gila Polychrome	1250-1400	Breternitz 1966: 77; Colton & Hargrave 1937: 88	1	3	4
Tularosa/ Roosevelt Black-on white	1100-1350	Breternitz 1966: 92; Steen and others 1962: 28	0	3	3
P-III/P-IV polychromes	1100-1500	---	1	1	2
Kayenta Polychrome*	1250-1300	Breternitz 1966: 79; Colton & Hargrave 1937: 90	1	0	1
Citadel Polychrome*	1100-1150	Breternitz 1966: 72; Colton & Hargrave 1937: 75; Colton 1956	1	0	1
Jeddito Black-on-yellow	1300-1500+	Breternitz 1966: 78; Colton & Hargrave 1937: 161	4	0	4

*Tentative Identification

Table 48 (continued)

Sherd Type	Dates (all A.D.)	Sources	No. from Horseshoe	No. from Roosevelt	Total No. Sherds
DECORATED (cont)					
P-II/P-III Little Colo. Whiteware	900-1300	Colton & Hargrave 1937: 235; L. Hammack, personal communication.	24	5	29
Unidentified whitewares	no date	---	4	5	9
CORRUGATED					
Undetermined corrugated	no date	---	0	6	6
Jeddito Corrugated*	1300-1500+	Colton 1956	2	0	2
REDWARES					
Salt Red	1300-1400	Haury 1945: 81; Schroeder 1952b: 332	95	3	15
Gila Red, White-on-red	1200-1400	Colton & Hargrave 1937: 176	12	3	15
Salado Red	1250-1400	Colton & Hargrave 1937: 65; Steen and others 1962: 16-17	0	36	36
Inspiration Red	1200-1450	Doyel n.d.	61	61	122
Indeterminate	no date	---	169	41	210
PLAINWARES					
Gila Plain	300-1300	Breternitz 1966: 76; Colton & Hargrave 1937: 174	4	11	15
Wingfield Plain (redwares)	700-1250	Rodgers 1974: 25; Colton 1941: 46	197	5	202
Tonto Plain	1100-1400	Doyel n.d. McGuire n.d. Windmiller 1972b	993	369	1362
Verde Brown	1100-1300	Colton 1958	108	28	136
Tuzigoot Plain	1150-1400	Colton 1958	65	5	70
Plainwares with $CaCO_3$ inclusions	no date	---	10	0	10
Plainwares with biotite inclusions	no date	---	39	19	58
		TOTALS	1819	616	2435

*Tentative Identification

The second plainware grouping consists of two categories, often affiliated with Hohokam sites: Gila Plain and Wingfield Plain. The few Gila Plain sherds collected have been identified as such because of the abundance of muscovite mica and lack of phlogopite mica in the temper. Wingfield Plain, a type also affiliated with Sinagua sites, is characterized by coarse to medium-coarse mica-schist temper. The sherds of Wingfield Plain collected during the Orme Alternatives survey closely resemble those recovered from Miami Wash by Doyel (n.d.). Both Wingfield Plain and Gila Plain enjoy extensive time ranges in central Arizona, with Wingfield Plain probably dating from A.D. 700-1250 (Rodgers 1974: 25), and Gila Plain dating from A.D. 300-1300 (Breternitz 1966: 76). Wingfield Plain has been described as a gradational variety of Gila Plain (Rodgers 1974: 25; Doyel n.d.).

Eleven out of the 15 sherds classified as Gila Plain came from sites or collection areas at Roosevelt Lake. Conversely, out of 202 Wingfield Plain sherds, all but five were collected at Horseshoe Reservoir. As in the case of the Alameda Brownware category, Wingfield Plain and Gila Plain sherds were collected from a variety of site types. The cultural affiliation of Wingfield Plain has not been firmly established, as it has been found with both Hohokam and Sinagua ceramics (Rodgers 1974: 25). At Horseshoe Reservoir and Roosevelt Lake, Wingfield Plain occurs in association with Alameda Brownware, and occasionally with Gila Plain and other Hohokam ceramics, as well as with Salado and Sinagua decorated types.

Redwares

Of the five categories established for redwares, only sherds classified as Salado Red are consistent with accepted typology, time range, and geographical distribution (Lindsay and Jennings 1968: 10). Salado Red sherds were collected only from Roosevelt Lake sites from compounds, cobble masonry structures, and non-habitation cobble components.

Three redware types may represent gradations or local variations of each other. Gila Red, dated from A.D. 1200 to 1400 (Colton and Hargrave 1937: 176) is a possible base for the derivation of both Salt Red (Schroeder 1952b: 322) and Inspiration Red (Doyel n.d.). Salt Red and Gila Red are adequately described elsewhere (Table 48). Although Gila Red sherds were collected from both reservoirs, Salt Red occurred only at Horseshoe Reservoir.

Doyel, in his Miami Wash report (n.d.), named and described Inspiration Red as a local redware, probably derived from Gila Red, and previously classified in part as Tonto Red. Although Inspiration Red may not be a full-fledged type (David E. Doyel, personal communication), but only a local variant, the category occurs as a distinguishable entity at both Horseshoe Reservoir and Roosevelt Lake. Probably dating from A.D. 1200-1450, Inspiration Red had an exterior slip similar in color and texture to Salado Red and the Salado polychromes. Surface texture is generally rough or bumpy, and the striations found on Gila Red ceramics are lacking. The texture of the core is medium. Abundant temper consists of large grains of white sand, opaque quartz, and phlogopite mica (Doyel n.d.). Inspiration Red sherds were collected primarily from compound and pueblo sites at both reservoirs, which are believed to date from A.D. 1200-1400.

Those redwares that could not be definitely placed in one redware category were placed in an indeterminate category (Table 48).

Corrugated Sherds

Out of eight corrugated sherds, two have been tentatively identified as Jeddito Corrugated. According to Colton (1956), this late northern Arizona type has not been identified from sites outside of the Tusayan region. It is, however, apparent that the two sherds classified as Jeddito Corrugated are not of local manufacture; they were found at a site (AZ O:14:51) with other later northern Arizona types.

Decorated Sherds

Because relatively few decorated sherds were collected, typing of those sherds was often tentative. Only a few pieces could be positively identified as a specific type, and larger categories, such as Pueblo II-Pueblo III Little Colorado Whiteware, were often used. The decorated sherd types are discussed adequately in the sources listed in Table 48.

Ceramic Dating

Table 49 lists possible time ranges for each collection area, based on all categories of sherds. In most instances, a broad span of dates is given because of the scarcity of diagnostic sherds. Dates obtained from decorated sherds were used to support, rather than define temporal ranges for given sites and site types. Generally accepted dates for plainwares and redwares were also used in establishing time ranges. Those sites and collection areas from which plainwares only were recovered are the least reliably dated, as most of the plainwares identified have long time spans, and occur at all types of sites at both reservoirs. The time ranges given in Table 49 should be considered tenuous, because of problems in establishing dates for plainware sherds.

The time ranges indicated by sherd samples do not correspond exactly with probable dating ranges established in this report for habitation types. However, the ranges of ceramic dates tend to indicate that possible pit house sites are earliest, followed by small cobble masonry structures. The latest dated ceramic types occur on habitation sites that have been classified as compounds and pueblos.

Table 49

Temporal Ranges for Sites

Site number/ collection area	Site/component type	Possible dates (all A.D.)	Plain wares	Red- wares	Deco- rated	Corru- gated	Total
ROOSEVELT							
Habitation							
U:4:7A	compound	1100-1400	21	14	3	0	38
U:4:8A	compound	1200-1400	28	3	0	1	32
U:4:8B	compound	1200-1400	13	4	0	0	17
U:4:9A	compound	1200-1400	9	6	0	0	15
U:4:9B	compound	1200-1400	13	4	0	0	17
U:4:10	compound	1200-1400	35	25	6	0	66
U:4:11	compound	1200-1400	16	6	1	0	23
U:4:12A	compound	1200-1400	33	5	5	1	44
U:4:12B	compound	1100-1400	12	5	2	0	19
U:8:72	compound	1100-1400	21	5	1	1	28
U:8:78	compound	1200-1400	26	15	1	1	43
U:4:7C	cobble structure	1100-1400	14	2	0	0	16
U:4:13A	cobble structure	1200-1400	4	6	1	0	11
U:4:13B	cobble structure	1100-1400	11	2	0	0	13
U:4:17	cobble structure	1200-1400	52	16	2	2	72
U:4:18	cobble structure	1200-1400	24	15	0	0	39
U:8:73	cobble structure	1100-1400	11	0	0	0	11
U:8:68	pueblo	1100-1400	15	1	1	0	17
U:8:67	pit house	900-1100?	13	0	0	0	13
Non-Habitation							
U:4:7B	cobble/non-agriculture	1200-1400	22	5	3	0	30
U:4:14	cobble/non-agriculture	1250-1400	0	1	0	0	1
U:4:15	cobble/non-agriculture	1250-1400	9	2	0	0	11
U:4:16	cobble/non-agriculture	1200-1400	1	0	1	0	2
U:4:20	sherd/lithic scatter	1100-1400	13	0	0	0	13
V:5:27	sherd/lithic scatter	1100-1400	15	1	5	0	21
U:8:71	sherd/lithic scatter	1100-1400	4	0	0	0	4
HORSESHOE							
Habitation							
0:14:8	pit house	900-1100	22	1	0	0	23
0:14:16	pit house	about 1100	20	1	2	0	23
0:14:17-3	pit house	about 1100	13	0	0	0	13
0:14:21	pit house	900-1100	32	0	4	0	36
0:14:30	pit house	about 1100	2	2	1	0	5
0:14:39	pit house	900-1100	23	3	4	0	30

Table 49 (cont.)

Site number/ collection area	Site/component type	Possible dates (all A.D.)	Plain wares	Red-wares	Deco-rated	Corru-gated	Total
Horseshoe Habitation (cont.)							
0:14:49-1	pit house	900-1100	22	1	1	0	24
0:14:49-2	pit house	900-1100	19	1	4	0	24
0:14:51-2	pit house	900-1100	11	1	4	0	16
0:14:51-6	pit house	900-1100	4	0	0	0	4
0:14:51-9	pit house	900-1100	17	0	3	0	20
U:2:30A	pit house	900-1100	27	6	4	0	37
U:2:30B	pit house	900-1100	2	0	0	0	2
0:14:22-B1	compound	1200-1400	54	13	0	0	67
o:14:22-B2	compound	1200-1400	19	8	1	0	28
0:14:22-B3	compound	1200-1400	35	5	0	0	40
0:14:22-B4	compound	1200-1400	26	13	0	0	39
0:14:35-1	compound	1200-1400	24	11	1	0	36
0:14:35-2	compound	1200-1400	23	9	0	0	32
0:14:35-3	compound	1100-1400	38	3	0	0	41
0:14:36-1	compound	1100-1300	33	7	1	0	41
0:14:36-2	compound	1200-1400	16	6	0	0	22
0:14:37-1	compound	1100-1400	36	11	0	0	47
0:14:37-2	compound	1100-1400	17	5	0	0	22
0:14:37-3	compound	1100-1400	19	6	0	0	25
0:14:38-1	compound	1100-1400	36	0	1	0	37
0:14:38-2	compound	1200-1400	12	5	0	0	17
0:14:38-3	compound	1200-1400	9	7	0	0	16
0:14:51-1	compound	1200-1400	11	3	6	0	20
0:14:51-4	compound	1300-1400	14	8	1	1	24
0:14:51-5	compound	1200-1400	15	4	2	0	21
0:14:51-3	compound	1200-1400	10	4	0	0	14
0:14:51-7	compound	1300-1400	13	5	0	1	19
0:14:51-8	compound	1200-1400	4	5	2	0	11
0:14:51-10	compound	1100-1400	18	11	1	0	30
U:2:29	compound	1200-1400	10	1	0	0	11
U:2:36	compound	1200-1400	23	15	0	0	38
0:14:11	cobble structure	1100-1400	8	0	0	0	8
0:14:46-1	cobble structure	1100-1400	17	0	0	0	17
0:14:46-2	cobble structure	1100-1400	5	0	0	0	5
0:14:47-2	cobble structure	1100-1400	13	1	1	0	15
0:14:48	cobble structure	1100-1400	17	2	0	0	19
U:2:2-1	cobble structure	1100-1400	20	4	0	0	24
U:2:2-2	cobble structure	1200-1400	11	7	0	0	18
0:14:34-1	pueblo	1100-1400	8	1	2	0	11
0:14:34-2	pueblo	1200-1400	18	2	0	0	20
0:14:34-3	pueblo	1100-1400	15	2	1	0	18
0:14:50	pueblo	1200-1400	8	9	0	0	17
U:2:1-1	pueblo	1250-1400	35	17	1	0	53

Table 49 (continued)

Site number/ collection area	Site/component type	Possible dates (all A.D.)	Plain wares	Red- wares	Deco- rated	Corru- gated	Total
Horseshoe Habitation (cont.)							
U:2:1-2	pueblo	1250-1400	12	11	1	0	24
U:2:1-3	pueblo	1200-1400	8	12	0	0	20
U:2:1-4	pueblo	1100-1400	32	3	0	0	35
Non-Habitation							
O:14:7	Agricultural system	1200-1400	6	1	0	0	7
O:14:12	Agricultural system	1100-1400	3	0	0	0	3
O:14:13	Agricultural system	1100-1400?	1	0	0	0	1
O:14:20	Agricultural system	1100-1400?	1	0	0	0	1
O:14:22-A1	Agricultural system	1100-1400	21	0	0	0	21
O:14:22-A2	Agricultural system	1200-1400	61	5	0	0	66
O:14:23	Agricultural system	1100-1400?	3	0	0	0	3
O:14:27	Agriculutral system	1100-1400	19	1	2	0	22
O:14:40	Agricultural system	1100-1400	17	0	0	0	17
O:14:42	Agricultural system	1100-1400	6	0	0	0	0
U:2:22	Agricultural system	1100-1400	5	0	0	0	5
U:2:23-1	Agricultural system	1100-1400	5	1	0	0	6
U:2:23-2	Agricultural system	1100-1400	9	4	0	0	13
U:2:23-3	Agricultural system	1100-1400	8	0	0	0	8
O:14:47-1	Agricultural system	1100-1400	22	0	2	0	24
U:2:29	Agricultural system	1200-1400	10	4	0	0	14
O:14:14	cobble--non-agricul.	1100-1400	3	0	1	0	4
O:14:17-1	cobble--non-agricul.	1100-1400	23	1	0	0	24
O:14:17-2	cobble--non-agricul.	1100-1400	37	0	3	0	40
O:14:18	cobble--non-agricul.	1100-1400	16	0	0	0	16
O:14:22-C1	cobble--non-agricul.	1100-1400	6	3	0	0	9
O:14:26	cobble--non-agricul.	1100-1400	21	7	0	0	28
O:14:39	cobble--non-agricul.	900-1100	23	3	4	0	30
O:14:43	cobble--non-agricul.	1100-1400?	3	0	0	0	3
O:14:52	cobble--non-agricul.	1100-1400	6	1	0	0	7
U:2:24	cobble--non-agricul.	1100-1400	2	0	0	0	2
U:2:26	cobble--non-agricul.	1200-1400	19	2	0	0	21
U:2:28	cobble--non-agricul.	1100-1400	8	0	0	0	8
O:14:45	cobble--non-agricul.	1100-1400	6	0	0	0	6
U:2:34	cobble--non-agricul.	1100-1400	19	2	0	0	21
O:14:10	rockshelter	1200-1400	11	10	0	0	21
O:14:9	sherd/lithic scatter	1100-1400	8	1	0	0	9
O:14:29	sherd/lithic scatter	1100-1400	8	0	0	0	8
O:14:30	sherd/lithic scatter	1200-1400	1	3	1	0	5
O:14:31	sherd/lithic scatter	1200-1400	6	7	1	0	14
O:14:32	sherd/lithic scatter	1100-1400	5	0	0	0	5
O:14:41	sherd/lithic scatter	1100-1400	4	0	0	0	4
O:14:28	sherd/lithic scatter	1200-1400	7	4	1	0	12
U:2:32	sherd/lithic scatter	1200-1400	16	6	0	0	22
U:2:33	sherd/lithic scatter	1200-1400	17	7	0	0	24

Phase I: Pit House Sites

Three of 14 pit house sites or collection areas (AZ O:14:39, AZ U:2:30A, AZ O:14:49-2) which probably date between A.D. 700-1100 (see Chapter 7), contained a few sherds of both Pueblo II-Pueblo III Little Colorado Whiteware, and Santa Cruz or Sacaton Red-on-buff. From three other sites or collection areas, sherds of Santa Cruz or Sacaton Red-on-buff (AZ O:14:21 and AZ O:14:51-9) and one Little Colorado Whiteware sherd (AZ O:14:49-1) were recovered. Also associated with those six sites, and with the remainder of the possible pit house sites are plainwares, such as Tonto Plain, Verde Brown, and Tuzigoot Plain, that are generally associated with the A.D. 1100-1400 period (Colton 1958; Doyel n.d., McGuire n.d.). A few sherds of Wingfield Plain with a possible temporal range of A.D. 700-1250 (Rodgers 1974: 25) were recovered from ten of the pit house site or collection areas. The only indicative ceramic dates for pit house sites are from those few sites with identifiable decorated sherds. Of those, the three with both Sacaton or Santa Cruz Red-on-buff and Pueblo II-Pueblo III Little Colorado Whiteware (AZ O:14:39, AZ U:2:30A, and AZ O:14:49-2) have been dated at A.D. 900-1100. Other pit house site or collection areas were dated either from A.D. 900 to 1100, if they included Wingfield Plain, or, as in the case of AZ U:4:67, Gila Plain sherds; or at about A.D. 1100, if they included only plainwares, exclusive of Wingfield Plain.

Phase II: Cobble Structures

Sherd collections from the 13 sites or collection areas that make up the category of small cobble masonry structures, did not include any identifiable decorated sherds. Three of the Roosevelt Lake sites, AZ U:14:13A, AZ U:4:17, and AZ U:4:18, were dated from A.D. 1200-1400, on the basis of the presence of Salado Red sherds. At Horseshoe Reservoir, one collection area, AZ U:2:2-2, has been assigned dates of A.D. 1200-1400, because of redwares recovered from the collection area. The remaining cobble structure sites were assigned A.D. 1100-1400 dates on the basis of plainwares present.

Phase III: Pueblos and Compounds

The large compound and pueblo sites correspond most directly with the dates assigned them in Chapter 7. Sherds recovered from compound and pueblo sites generally include redwares and plainwares associated with the later time periods, and/or small numbers of diagnostic decorated sherds.

Two collection areas at one Horseshoe Reservoir compound/pit house site (AZ O:14:51) have been dated from A.D. 1300-1400 on the basis of several diagnostic sherds. From these two collection areas, AZ O:14:51-4 and AZ O:14:51-7, are sherds of Salt Red, Jeddito Black-on-yellow, and the two possible Jeddito Corrugated sherds, all of which postdate A.D. 1300 (Schroeder 1952b: 332; Colton 1956; Breternitz 1966: 78). Other components and collection

areas at this site (which includes a possible pit house village), have
yielded sherds ranging in time from about A.D. 900 (Santa Cruz/Sacaton
Red-on-buffs) through 1500 (Jeddito Black-on-yellow). Az O:14:51 is the
only site in which multiple time components could be detected through the
types of sherds present.

From two collection areas at a pueblo site (AZ U:2:1) at Horseshoe
Reservoir, collected sherds indicate an A.D. 1250-1400 date. From those
two areas (AZ U:2:1-1 and AZ U:2:1-2), sherds of Salt Red, Gila Polychrome,
and Tonto Polychrome were recovered. The two Salado polychromes have been
dated from A.D. 1250-1400 (Breternitz 1966: 77), and the time range usually
accepted for Salt Red is A.D. 1300-1400 (Schroeder 1952b: 332).

At AZ O:14:34, a pueblo site, the few decorated sherds recovered
indicate a possible temporal range of A.D. 1100-1400. One sherd of Pueblo II-
Pueblo III Little Colorado Whiteware (A.D. 900-1300), a possible Citadel
Polychrome sherd (A.D. 1100-1250) (Colton and Hargrave 1937: 75), and one
sherd of Jeddito Black-on-yellow were collected, along with redwares and
plainwares.

The remaining compound and pueblo sites at Horseshoe Reservoir have
been tentatively dated on the basis of redwares and plainwares.

At Roosevelt Lake, the majority of compounds were dated from A.D.
1200-1400 based on the presence of Salado Red (A.D. 1250-1400) and Inspiration
Red sherds (A.D. 1200-1450). Several sites, including AZ U:4:7A, AZ U:4:12B,
and AZ U:8:72, may date from A.D. 1100 to 1400, as each of those sites contains one or two sherds of either Tularosa or Roosevelt Black-on-white
(A.D. 1100-1300) or Pueblo II-Pueblo III Little Colorado Whiteware (A.D. 900-
1300). One sherd of Pinedale Red-on-black (A.D. 1175-1325) was collected
from U:4:10, along with sherds of Salado polychromes, indicating a temporal
range for the site of A.D. 1200-1400.

Other compound sites at Roosevelt were dated from A.D. 1200-1400 on the
basis of plainwares and redwares. The pueblo site (AZ U:8:68), was dated from
A.D. 1100-1400 because Wingfield Plain and Gila Plain sherds were collected
at that site.

Non-habitation Sites

Non-habitation sites generally are the least reliably dated because
of a scarcity of diagnostic decorated sherds and a general lack of knowledge concerning the association of specific non-habitational features
with established time periods. AZ V:5:27, at Roosevelt Lake, a sherd and
lithic scatter near a series of large pueblo compounds, can be dated reliably,
from A.D. 1100-1400, because sherds collected from the site include Pinedale
Black-on-red, Pueblo II-Pueblo III Little Colorado Whiteware, and Tularosa or
Roosevelt Black-on-white sherds.

Cultural Affiliations

Although nothing definite can be said about cultural affiliations based on the small number of diagnostic sherds collected from each site, a number of observations can be made. The ceramic assemblages from Roosevelt Lake generally follow a pattern similar to other areas with Salado sites. All of the Salado Red sherds come from the Roosevelt Lake sites. Also present in greater numbers at Roosevelt Lake than at Horseshoe Reservoir are White Mountain Redware, Salado polychromes, and Tularosa or Roosevelt Black-on-white sherds. Inspiration Red sherds outnumber Gila Red sherds 61 to 3 (there were no Salt Red sherds collected from Roosevelt), and 60 percent of the plainwares collected are Tonto Plain. Possible Hohokam contacts are perhaps indicated by the persence of Gila Red sherds, Gila Plain sherds at eight sites, Wingfield Plain sherds at three sites, and one red-on-buff sherd. The ceramic evidence from Roosevelt Lake indicates a typical Salado pattern, with some ceramic contact with the White Mountain area, and some with the Hohokam.

At Horseshoe Reservoir, the combined cultural influences of Sinagua and Hohokam groups are demonstrated ceramically. All but one of the 22 Hohokam red-on-buff and buffware sherds come from Horseshoe Reservoir sites. Later sites (A.D. 1200-1400) include a greater number of Salt Red sherds than Inspiration Red, and eight site collections include Gila Red or White-on-red sherds. Wingfield Plain was collected in comparatively greater numbers at Horseshoe Reservoir, and Tuzigoot Plain occurs more frequently at Horseshoe Reservoir than at Roosevelt Lake. Only a few Salado or White Mountain Redware sherds were collected from Horseshoe sites. The majority of northern Arizona decorated sherds recovered came from collection areas at Horseshoe Reservoir. These include Pueblo III-Pueblo IV polychromes, possible Kayenta and Citadel Polychromes, Jeddito Black-on-yellow, and examples of Pueblo II- Pueblo III Little Colorado Whiteware. The presence of these sherds indicates ceramic contact with northern Arizona, possibly from A.D. 1100 (Little Colorado Whiteware, Citadel Polychrome) to at least A.D. 1400 (Jeddito Black-on-yellow and possibly Jeddito Corrugated).

Similarities between the ceramic assemblages of the two reservoir areas may be indicated by the presence at both reservoirs of Salado polychromes Inspiration Red, and Alameda Brownware. Of these, the plainwares show the greatest similarity. This similarity does not necessarily reflect cultural affiliation, but instead may be a result of locally available tempering agents and corresponding technologies. At both reservoirs, plainwares make up by far the greatest percentage of sherd types collected. Seventy-eight percent of the sherds at Horseshoe, and 71 percent at Roosevelt Lake are plainwares. Redwares are the next highest category, making up 23 percent of the total sherd count at Roosevelt, and 18.5 percent at Horseshoe. Decorated types make up only 5.2 percent of the total number of sherds at Roosevelt and 3.5 percent at Horseshoe. Corrugated sherds make up less than one percent of the total sherd count from both reservoirs.

Summary

Because of the small number of sherds per site, and the comparatively high numbers of plainware sherds, only general observations could be made in the course of this ceramic analysis. While such observations can be used with other types of data to indicate possible cultural and temporal associations at each reservoir, the data presented are not conclusive. Similarities between sherds collected at both reservoir areas made typing of plainwares and redwares difficult, and decorated sherds were so few in number that some types could only be tentatively identified. Temporal ranges are especially tenuous because of the great numbers of non-diagnostic sherds and the small number of sherds per site.

Appendix II

PEER REVIEWS

Included in this appendix are three reviews of the Orme Alternatives report which have been prepared by independent reviewers. This represents a continuation of an experiment initiated by the Arkansas Archeological Survey (McGimsey 1975: 325-326). As discussed by McGimsey, the traditional review process in archaeology has virtually broken down due to the mass of published reports and articles, as well as the lengthy lag between publication of reports and publication of relevant reviews. Another problem more germane to cultural resource management studies involves the need to provide the sponsoring agency with a more visible index of quality control. One response to these concerns is to include reviews within the report being reviewed. Although there are potential problems, this method seems to have been productively utilized by the Arkansas Archeological Survey (cf. Schiffer and House 1975) and by the professional journal, Current Anthropology. In order to further experiment with this procedure, reviews were solicited for this report from three professional anthropologists who were not affiliated with either the authors or the Arizona State Museum. Furthermore, each of the reviewers was solicited because their research interests indicated that they were particularly qualified to review the subject matter covered by the Orme Alternatives report. We feel that the information contained in the following reviews and the quality of the comments is indicative of the potential benefits of the peer review process. Unfortunately, time did not allow revisions to be made which would incorporate many of the suggestions made in the reviews.

Review I

by

Robert C. Euler
Grand Canyon National Park

It has been pleasurable and profitable to have had the opportunity to read a manuscript relating to contract archaeological survey that is not purely descriptive of the culture-history of the areas under consideration. This lengthy report, stemming from generally well designed field work (with one possible exception to be discussed below), while addressing itself to a primary goal of determining impact upon archaeological resources should inundation occur, goes well beyond that in contributing something positive to archaeological techniques and theory.

273

Its rather detailed history of past research in the Tonto Basin and the Verde Valley as well as the section on culture-history of this poorly understood area of Arizona, will not only be of value to professional archaeologists, but should put the data and problems stemming from them in good perspective for U. S. Forest Service and Bureau of Reclamation personnel (as well as lay readers) who may ultimately make management decisions affecting the cultural resources. The report clearly enunciates the scientific import of these resources so that there should be no possibility of their being dismissed as just another group of ruins.

It is obvious that much serious and dynamic thought have gone into the planning, the actual field surveys, and especially the statistical and theoretical analysis as well as recommendations presented in this study. While this reviewer is greatly impressed by these aspects, so intellectually refreshing after reading many other "contract" reports, he is still left with some nagging questions. Was all this elaboration really necessary for effective managerial decision making? Was the cost of the entire analysis, including the computer simulation, (and this must have been considerable) worth the results? Could some of the cost of analysis have been better devoted to additional field sampling? Perhaps these questions will ultimately be answered to everyone's satisfaction but, at the present, they remain in one's mind.

I shall try to elaborate upon my reservations as well as my enthusiasm for the study in the following brief comments.

First of all, I have concerns about how the field sample percentage was selected. At one point it is noted that the 20 percent figure was determined jointly by the Bureau of Reclamation, the Forest Service, and the Arizona State Museum. My question is not with the adequacy or inadequacy of this sample, but rather, how did the archaeologists perceive this in terms of adequacy related to their problems and/or research design? What was their reaction to learn that this sample missed all Anglo-American sites in the Horseshoe Reservoir area?

Early in the report it is noted that deductive testing of hypotheses was ruled out because of limited previous knowledge of the area. This may be justifiable, but it might have been better if regional hypotheses could have been formulated. Although admittedly the two areas are not well known archaeologically, a number of postulates could have been based upon statements of earlier workers as set forth in the chapter on the history of anthropological research there. For example, a deductive hypothesis could have been developed in terms of such matters as "inter-region influence . . . /which/ . . . remain as problems today."

In chapter 2, that describing environmental conditions, certain of the plants listed in Table 1 as lacking in economic uses might very well have been utilized prehistorically. A comparison with ethnobotanical sources might have been helpful. I am puzzled, too, by the authors' statement that "no major climatic or biotic changes have been documented for the Southwest for the past 8,000 years." Perhaps their use of the word "major" is misunderstood, but certainly the literature abounds with examples of prehistoric climatic and environmental variation in the Southwest during the times the Verde and Tonto basins were occupied.

At the end of chapter 3, the authors state that ". . . the archaeology of the historic period in the Tonto Basin and Verde Valley has never been intensively pursued." Quite true, and just as an aside, with certainly no criticism intended, the use of the direct historical approach might resolve the problem of "mixture" between Yavapai and Apache that was fostered by intermarriage and other forms of contact between the two groups.

I would question the validity of the statement that opens chapter 4, to the effect that approaching the project area in terms of current water management planning "constitutes a coherent program of research in terms of the prehistory of the region." While archaeologists obviously must be eclectic in their attitudes, there is danger here that contract restrictions, as with the arbitrary 20 percent sample selected, may not provide enough areal flexibility for a coherent program. The archaeologist must be in a position to have that flexible freedom of choice.

The actual survey and the sampling design as described in chapter 5 seem to have been well planned and carried out, given the 20 percent restriction. Further, the general discussion of sampling strategy should prove of value not only to archaeologists for future testing, but should be important to managers in their further understanding of archaeological survey procedures. The evaluation of this sample, however, is complex and, lacking expertise in much of these statistical manipulations, I do not feel qualified to comment further.

To me, the most confusing part of the report is chapter 7, the settlement pattern analysis. Certainly, a discussion of the settlement pattern in any archaeological zone is important. But, unless I completely misunderstand the authors, they have established rules to combine site categories into site components in an all too arbitrary fashion, using the term component as I would describe a feature, and not in the sense that Willey and Phillips (1958: 21-22), whom they cite, would have it. Further, some of the hypotheses, based upon incomplete data, may not be statistically valid; and sampling limitations become apparent in the inability of the techniques to permit the use of "nearest neighbor" and other spatial determinants to assist in the establishment of regional patterns. I am left with the distinct impression, rightly or wrongly, that much of this section appears much too belabored. Their summary of the chapter is much clearer even though it concludes that the "search for an explanation of settlement pattern variability between the Roosevelt Lake and Horseshoe Reservoir surveys has just begun." Perhaps more socially oriented hypotheses rather than only environmental ones could be formulated to explain this variability.

Chapter 8, which discussed the significance of the resources, is well done although in some spots is somewhat redundant to the data presented in the culture-history portion. Nonetheless, the section relating the scientific significance is especially thoughtful. I would only suggest that more research into the surficial geology would be advantageous.

My only comment regarding the cost of the proposed mitigation is rather subjective. While the estimated expenses seem exceedingly large, the wage rates per individual seem low. One wonders about the validity of the indirect costs now charged by institutions engaged in contract archaeology and whether or not detailed cost accounting would justify these amounts.

A preliminary research plan has been presented in chapter 10, even though it is recommended that the sites be protected rather than excavated. In this plan the authors indicate that they need data on all the sites "before a workable research design can be formulated." This sounds a bit naïve and a different type of or more initial sampling could well have provided sufficient information for this.

Additional computer simulation is projected after every site has been evaluated as to its research potential. Over the past few years all sorts of sampling designs have been put forth in American archaeology. Is it really necessary to simulate more? What is wrong with all the other sampling concepts if now we discover that every site must be surveyed to permit a realistic design for mitigation (a word that somehow sticks in my research and problem oriented craw). Long before this phase of the projected additional study, research goals should have been set on regional grounds. In addition, the authors suggest the need to sample collect each site. Think of the time and money involved in this. Is this really necessary in this instance or is it but an excercise that is the "in" thing to do. Mind you, I am not opposing this on theoretical grounds; I am merely concerned about costs, responsibility to the funding agency, and the economic principle of diminishing returns. On the whole, however, some very worthwhile problems have been presented in this chapter. At the same time, one paramount question may be raised. Suppose archaeologists never are enabled to do any more research in these two areas. Can we test these problems on the basis of the 20 percent sample now available? For example, the field party did not record, for reasons that also seem too arbitrary, the lithic scatters in the initial survey. They were considered "non-sites," whatever that means. This, in my opinion, was a mistake that may not be rectifiable unless additional field work is to be undertaken.

Finally, I was pleased to see the specific site locations placed in a separate volume. Hopefully, this will not be generally available to the hordes of vandals who are a scourge upon the finite cultural resources of Arizona.

As I re-read the foregoing remarks, they sound like harse notes of criticism. They are not so meant. The report is a good one. Rather than a mere "romanticized" view of prehistory, it underscores the importance and complexity of current archaeological resources and research. The geographic

areas considered <u>are</u> important to these ends. Furthermore, the authors
have set an example in processual oriented contract archaeology that could
well be emulated by others now flocking to this field of so-called cultural
resource management --- CRM if one wishes to speak in bureaucratese. Most
such reports are not so oriented; they rarely even address themselves to
scholarly cultural anthropology. Hopefully, the type of analyses presented
here will narrow the ever widening schism that is undeniably growing
between "contract" and "professional" archaeology.

Review II

by

Stephen Plog
Southern Illinois University

    The Orme Alternatives project report has adequately assessed the
impact on cultural resources of the proposed changes in Roosevelt and
Horseshoe Lakes. The historical, scientific, social, and monetary significance of the resources which would be impacted has been demonstrated.
In addition, the project has made valuable contributions to anthropological
knowledge. Important information on the culture history of the area and
on archaeological sampling techniques is presented. Contractual obligations
have been met by comparing the significance of cultural resources in the
Orme Alternatives area and in the proposed Orme Reservoir area. However,
this comparison is weakened by the failure to fully consider the effects
that vandalism and water damage have had and will have on cultural resource
in the Orme Alternatives area. Additional weaknesses of the project are:
(1) the decision of the contracting institutions to employ a single-stage
sampling method and the arbitrary selection of the sampling fraction by
the Bureau of Reclamation and (2) the surface collection method selected.
In the following sections, I will discuss each of these weaknesses.

Vandalism and water damage

    The Orme Alternatives report clearly indicates that many of the
archaeological sites in the Horseshoe and Roosevelt Lakes direct impact
zones have been vandalized or damaged by wave action. However, I do not
feel that this damage was fully considered in estimating the monetary significance of the resources. The site notes indicate that the damage to
some sites has been extensive, particularly in the Roosevelt Lake area.
Yet it has been estimated that large amounts of money would be needed to
mitigate the impact of the lake expansion on these sites. For example,
it was estimated that $1,664,660 would be needed to mitigate the inundation
of U:4;11. However, in the site notes it is stated that "The site has
been about 90 percent disturbed by pothunting. Few rooms are still intact."
I think it is reasonable to question the value of budgeting over one and
one-half million dollars to mitigate the impact of flooding on a site that
has been so completely disturbed. Most of the information potential of the

site has already been lost and as a result any remaining information that is salvaged will be less meaningful. While U:4:11 is the most obvious example, a similar criticism can be made of other estimates. Thus, I would argue that the monetary significance of the cultural resources of the Orme Alternatives area has been overestimated.

The damage which has already occurred to sites was also not fully considered in the section comparing the significance of the cultural resources in the Orme Alternatives area to the significance of the resources in the Orme Reservoir area. More importantly, the damage that may occur in the future was not considered. While it would be unfortunate for the estimated 374 sites to be inundated, it may also be the case that in twenty years many of these sites will be completely destroyed by vandalism or wave action. For example, it is estimated that $226,600 would be required to mitigate the inundation of U:8:68. Yet the site notes indicate that "The site is being destroyed by erosional processes of the lake."

Assuming that the U.S. Bureau of Reclamation would not fund a 50 percent sample or even a 25 percent sample of the cultural resources in the Orme Alternatives area (and I would guess this assumption is correct), we are faced with an important question. Would it be better to accept a mitigation budget that the Bureau of Land Reclamation could afford in order to obtain some information on the cultural resources in the areas or would it be better to suggest that the sites not be inundated and hope that by the time money is available to do research in the area the sites have not been completely destroyed by vandalism or by wave action? There is no clear answer to this question. There are also many factors that should be considered in attempting to answer the question, such as the exact amount of funding that the bureau could supply. However, this question should have been considered in making recommendations for the Orme Alternatives area. We cannot allow continued large-scale destruction of cultural resources for the sake of economic progress, but we should also not ignore the fact that cultural resources can be destroyed in many ways.

Sampling fractions and multi-stage sampling

The sampling experiments discussed in Chapter 6 have important implications for archaeological research and contract archaeology in particular. One of the topics considered was sampling fractions. The data presented in this study and the results of previous studies indicate that no particular sampling fraction can be considered to be the best for every situation. As the authors note, "an adequate sample may vary from 1 percent to 50 percent or more." To determine the size of the sampling fraction, the questions being asked and the variability in the population being sampled must be considered. Thus, in the future the final sampling fraction for impact assessments should not be set prior to the beginning of fieldwork, as it was in this study. The authors note that the 20 percent sampling fraction was chosen and that this figure was accepted by the National Forest Service

"as a minimally adequate level of sampling at this stage of the project."
For the Horseshoe Lake impact zone, the 20 percent sample provided reasonably
precise estimates of the number of sites and mitigation man-days. However,
for the Roosevelt Lake impact zone the standard errors of these estimates
were high. The estimates derived from the survey of this area were not precise. It is clear from these results that due to the greater amount of
variability in the Roosevelt Lake population, more reliable information
for the Orme Alternatives project, as a whole, could have been obtained by
surveying less than 20 percent of the Horseshoe Lake impact zone and more
than 20 percent of the Roosevelt Lake impact zone. The same amount of
effort could have resulted in more precise information.

Instead of arbitrarily choosing the final sampling fraction prior to
the beginning of fieldwork, the sampling should be done in stages. For
example, the contracting agencies could initially agree to do a small test
survey for the sole purpose of estimating the variability in the population
to be sampled. These estimates of the variability could then be used in
standard equations to estimate the necessary sample size, given the desired
estimation precision. Once this is determined, the agencies could contract
to do a survey of the required size. Multistage sampling will help insure
that the necessary data for decision-making is obtained and may in some
cases save money.

Surface collection

The question of whether or not collections should be made during surveys has been frequently discussed recently. The authors note that one of
the primary reasons for not making collections is that there may be a significant spatial relationship between surface and subsurface remains. The
distribution of different artifact types on the surface of a site may provide important indications of activity areas or indications of multiple
occupations at a site. If artifacts are collected from the surface without
recording their provenience this information is lost. A second reason for
not making surface collections is that "a large percentage of cultural
remains in Southern Arizona actually consist of surface sites."

This problem can be solved in several ways. First, no artifacts can
be collected and no information on artifacts recorded. While no provenience
information is lost with this method, one also gains no information on the
types of artifacts on the site. Temporal or functional classifications of
sites are thus not possible. Second, information on various artifact attributes can be recorded in the field and the artifacts can be left where they
are found. This type of "no collection" survey is the alternative that many
institutions seem to be adopting. The primary problem with this approach is
that only limited types of information can be recorded in the field and the
information that is collected will usually be recorded in terms of extant
categories (Schiffer 1975a: 6). The authors of this report, for example,
note that the ceramic information desired for the sites in the Orme Alternatives area "could not be accurately perceived in the field." Schiffer

notes that the "no collection" method "tacitly assumes that nothing new can be learned from site survey data" (Schiffer 1975a: 6). In addition, if provenience information for the artifacts is not recorded, the data cannot be used to study intra-site variability in artifact distributions. I would argue that knowledge of these distributions is necessary for assessing the significance of sites. For example, it has been my experience that artifact distributions indicating multiple occupations of sites often are not discovered until data gathered through systematic surface collections are analyzed. The knowledge that multiple occupations occurred at a site or that distinct activity areas are indicated by surface distributions will affect mitigation man-day estimates and decisions as to whether or not sites should be excavated during the mitigation phase. If intra-site provenience information is recorded on surveys, then artifacts might as well be collected, for the primary problem with collected artifacts, loss of provenience information, would be avoided. Thus, I suggest that: (1) collections should be made from sites in order that a wide variety of artifact attributes may be recorded and (2) provenience information should also be collected for the artifacts in order to analyze intra-site variability in artifact distributions.

For the Orme Alternatives project, collections were made from previously disturbed areas when possible or small collections were made from areas where potential disturbance was felt to be minimal. This is not a satisfactory solution for two reasons. First, it does not insure that a representative sample of the artifacts on a site is collected. In fact, the collection is likely to be very biased. It seems unreasonable to argue that we need to obtain a representative sample of sites in an area but that we do not need to obtain a representative sample of the artifacts on the surface of those sites. Second, the collection method does not allow intra-site variability in artifact distributions to be studied.

The authors argue that a random sample of site surfaces was not possible because of time constraints. They estimate that it would take one man-day per site to carry out such a procedure. I believe the authors have overestimated the length of time such a collection requires. For a survey during 1975 on the northern portion of Black Mesa in northeastern Arizona carried out by the Black Mesa Archaeological Project a systematic unaligned sample of at least 10 percent of the site surface was collected using a grid system with 4 x 4 m squares as the basic unit. Collection units of this size reduce the loss of provenience information while providing enough collection units for analysis of intra-site variability. We found that a team of five individuals could collect a site in this manner and record additional information on the site in 30 to 60 minutes. Thus, an average of less than one-half a man-day was needed to obtain a large, representative sample. Representative samples of site surfaces with adequate provenience information are therefore very feasible. For the reasons outlined above they are also necessary.

Conclusions

The relative amounts of space that I have devoted to the strengths and weaknesses of the Orme Alternatives report should not be considered indicative of the overall quality of the report. While weaknesses do exist, they are overshadowed by the strengths listed at the beginning of this review. The most significant aspect of the report is that in addition to meeting contractual obligations, valuable research was also carried out. This report thus continues a promising trend, also exemplified by Schiffer and House (1975), in cultural resource management studies.

Review III

by

Dwight W. Read
University of California, Los Angeles

Probabilistic sampling in archaeology is now generally accepted as a basic part of archaeological methodology. Previous arguments against its use were motivated more by a misunderstanding of the nature of probabilistic sampling than by valid statements that the peculiarities of archaeological data make probablistic sampling inappropriate in archaeology. The Orme Alternatives Survey can well serve as an example of the principles of probability sampling applied to regional surveys. It is carefully constructed and utilizes the whole gamut of ideas that have been suggested for such surveys. If anything, the range of analyses done on the collected data indicates that definition of the data to be collected from sites is now the issue needing resolution in probabilistic sampling of regions, not the utility or the specifics of constructing a probabilistic sample.

It quickly becomes evident upon reading the investigators' analysis that the limiting factor for obtaining answers to the questions raised about the historical development of Tonto Basin and Verde Valley is not the sample size (20 percent of the region), but being able only to give general characteristics of sites. Sites are classified as habitation or non-habitation, and broken down into but three time periods. Cultural affinities are equally broad. Yet detailed delineation of the development of a region via the framework of settlement studies, for instance, requires being able to stipulate the political, social, and economic affinities that existed among the social groups occupying the sites, along with the time of founding of a site and its development through time, since settlement systems involve relationships among aggregates of individuals both synchronically and diachronically. The end product of such systems, the archaeological sites, must be partitioned spatially and temporally in a fashion paralleling the relationships among the aggregations of individuals before the material remains can be claimed to reflect the properties of the settlement system.

The solution to obtaining these data will not be found by simply increasing the amount of data collected, but rather by more refined interpretation. In turn, the question is raised whether there is a need for extensive excavation of a particular site, or less extensive excavation of a larger number of sites. The latter strategy places greater demand for well-constructed sampling schemes to ensure that the sample obtained is representative of the total set of information obtainable.

The demand for environmental impact reports will also accelerate the need for well designed probabilistic sampling designs. In many instances archaeological sites will be destroyed by development, regardless of any sentiment about the intrinsic value of archaeological sites and data derived therefrom in comparison to alternative land uses. We must be able to extract as much information as is possible given the severe constraints on time and money available for mitigating the loss of archaeological resources. That the Orme Reservoir would require some $53 million and the Orme Alternatives from $54 to $118 million (as well as from 80,000 to 175,000 man days) for mitigation of the loss of archaeological resources, indicates the difficulty in attempting to do anything approaching a complete recovery of all the archaeological material.

Consequently, the procedure most acceptable to the archaeologist—as complete recovery of archaeological material as is possible—will often not be feasible. Instead, the total area surveyed and the percentage of sites excavated will be determined by time and money available.

The survey of the Orme Alternatives illustrates well the kinds of data that can be effectively obtained via survey work, as well as some of the limitations of sampling schemes that are presently practiced in archaeology. Given the goals of the project—the impact of the proposed reservoirs on the archaeological resources, description of the local cultural historical sequence, relationship of environmental variability to archaeological manifestations, and methodological study of sampling procedures—its successes and failures are indicative of areas in which improvement can be made in increasing the quantity of data obtained for the number of hours invested.

The aim of probabilistic sampling is to obtain precise and accurate information with the least amount of redundancy. A primary aspect of probability sampling which meets these aims is stratification of the universe of sample transects to minimize heterogeneity of the variables of interest within the chosen strata. If a stratum is relatively homogeneous with respect to the variable of interest, comparatively few sample units are needed for estimating population parameters with accuracy in comparison to strata which are heterogeneous.

While the fact that the values of the variables of interest about a site may have different spatial distributions and so one stratification scheme may be more effective for, say, site size than proportion of bowls to jars, a common goal of surveys is maximization of the number of sites found. We can use this as a basic criterion for measuring the effectiveness of stratification. Sampling units with no sites only provide evidence of where sites are not located. Hence the return for the time and money invested is low. This is not a criticism of probability sampling, but rather a statement indicating our lack of knowledge about the factors affecting location of sites by prehistoric groups. Consequently, one of the areas where probability sampling can be improved is through better understanding of the relationship of site location to environmental factors. The deficiency of our crude intuitions about the relationship is illustrated well by the two surveys. In both cases one of the strata has a large variance associated with the estimated number of sites, indicating that the stratum in question includes more than one environmental characteristic important for the location of sites.

Rather interestingly, the sample units with an excessively large number of sites in comparison to other sample units in that stratum are on gently sloping pediment terraces bordering the confluence of Tonto Creek with Roosevelt Lake (unit 35B) in one case, and the confluence of Verde River and Lime Creek with Horseshoe Reservoir (units 40 and 42) in the other case. A more refined stratification which included both landform and location of landform with respect to drainages would, at least in this instance, have provided a more accurate stratification and hence a decreased standard error for the total number of sites.

Specifically, the value of s^2_{xh} of 56.4 for Stratum 2 in the Horseshoe survey would be changed to values of 5.78 and 3.79 (corrected for unequal acreage per sample unit) if Stratum 2 had been subdivided as indicated above and the present sample units in Stratum 2 were also the random sample from these two new strata. A change this great in the magnitude of s^2_{xh} will have a correspondingly large change in the standard error of the estimated total number of sites in the Horseshoe Reservoir area.

This observation is not meant as a criticism of the survey since it uses information from the survey to improve on their stratification. Rather, the intent is to point out that good stratification of a region is probably the single best way to increase the accuracy of estimation of regional parameters using the same total sample size. In addition, finer stratification permits more precise testing of the association of site attributes and features with environmental factors that have less than a regional distribution.

Since good stratification of a region is important in designing an efficient sampling strategy, and much of the needed information may not be available a priori, one solution not discussed by the investigators for reducing the standard error of estimates is to use multistage sampling, with the results of an initial survey used to redesign a second survey. For example, the present author designed a 1 percent survey of the Chevelon drainage in Arizona to determine criteria useful for predicting the location of sites. The second survey used the information of the first. In some localities a 100 percent survey was then used to obtain detailed information on settlement patterns, while other localities were left with the original survey.

As the Orme Alternatives Survey indicates, it is possible in some instances to increase the accuracy and precision of parameter estimates through proper choice of statistical procedures. The ratio estimate technique reduces by a factor of 4, at least for Horseshoe Reservoir, the standard error of the estimate of the total number of sites.

The discovery of the location of sites and their description using surface features and artifacts can be considered phase 1 in a regional survey. Phase 2 consists of the measurement of a series of variables over those sites whole values are not obtainable without excavation. What is measured is primarily a function of our present conception of the factors of interest about archaeological sites. The space-time and function-environment paradigms have been widely used as frameworks for classification of sites and description of regional development. But regardless of the particular paradigm, information about a site consists primarily of artifacts and features, along with their spatial and temporal coordinates. If we view a site as a population of artifacts and a population of features, then site sampling is analogous to regional sampling, though on a drastically reduced scale. Thus the same factors affecting efficiency of a sampling scheme for a region also apply to sites.

The investigators of the Orme Alternatives Survey rightly see the question of the number of sites to be excavated and the amount of excavation per site as a major current methodological issue. In addition, the data to be obtained also need to be taken into consideration. It is the experience of this author with the Chevelon Archaeological Research Project that in many instances complete site excavation yields comparatively little increase in information over what can be obtained by partial site excavation aimed solely at delineating the features of a site and obtaining a representative sample of artifactual material.

In sum, the Orme Alternative Survey is a well designed project which certainly succeeds in giving an accurate general description of the archaeological resources that would be affected by increasing the size of the two reservoirs. It is exemplary in its use of statistics and in the settlement pattern analysis. Any lack of success in answering the questions posed reflects more on the present limitations in obtaining detailed information from archaeological sites than on the survey itself.

REFERENCES

Allen, Agnes M.
    1937   Sequence of Human Occupancy in the Middle Rio Verde Valley,
                Arizona. MS, Master's thesis, Clark University, Worcester,
                Massachusetts.

Arizona State Museum
    1974   Preliminary Manual for Use with ASM Site Survey Record. MS,
                Cultural Resource Management Section, Arizona State Museum,
                University of Arizona, Tucson.

    n.d.   Archaeological Resources Report. MS, Arizona State Museum,
                University of Arizona, Tucson.

Arkin, Herbert and Raymond R. Colton
    1963   Tables for Statisticians. Second edition, Barnes and Noble,
                New York.

Bandelier, Adolf F.
    1892   Final Report on Investigations in the Southwest. Archaeological
                Institute of America Papers, American Series Vol. 4, Part 2.

    1970   The Southwestern Journals of Adolf F. Bandelier 1883-1884.
                Edited and annotated by C. H. Lange and C. L. Ripley, Univer-
                sity of New Mexico Press, Albuquerque.

Barsch, Dietrich and Chester F. Royse
    1971   A Model for the Development of Terraces and Pediment-Terraces
                in the Southwest. Zeitschrift für Geomorphologie Vol. 16,
                No. 1: 54-75.

Basso, Keith H.
    1970   The Cibeque Apache. Case Studies in Cultural Anthropology,
                Holt, Rinehart and Winston, Inc., New York.

Berry, Brian J. L.
    1961   City Size Distributions and Economic Development. Economic
                Development and Culture Change Vol. 9: 573-587.

    1964   Cities as Systems within Systems of Cities. Papers of the
                Regional Science Association Vol. 13: 147-163.

Berry, Brian J. L. and William L. Garrison
    1958   Alternate Explanations of Urban Rank-size Relationships.
                Annals of the Association of American Geographers Vol. 48: 83-91.

Blalock, Hubert M., Jr.
    1972   Social Statistics. Second edition. McGraw-Hill, New York.

Blouet, Brian W.
    1972   Factors influencing the evolution of settlement patterns.
              In Man, Settlement, and Urbanism, edited by Peter J. Ucko,
              Ruth Tringham, and G. W. Dimbleby, pp. 3-15. Schenkman
              Publishing Co., Cambridge, Massachusetts.

Bourke, John G.
    1891   On the Border with Crook. Charles Schribner's Sons, New York.

Brandes, Raymond S.
    1957   An Archaeological Survey within Gila County, Arizona. MS,
              Arizona State Museum, University of Arizona, Tucson.

    1960   Archaeological Awareness of the Southwest as Illustrated in
              Literature to 1890. Arizona and the West Vol. 2, No. 1: 6-25.

Breternitz, David A.
    1958   The Calkins Ranch Site, NA 2385: Preliminary Report. Plateau
              Vol. 31, No. 1: 19-20.

    1960   Excavations at Three Sites in the Verde Valley, Arizona.
              Museum of Northern Arizona Bulletin No. 34.

    1966   An Appraisal of Tree-ring Dated Pottery in the Southwest.
              Anthropological Papers of the University of Arizona No. 10.
              University of Arizona Press, Tucson.

Brown, David E.
    1973   Map of the Natural Vegetative Communities of Arizona (scale
              1:5000,000). Arizona Resources Information System. State of
              Arizona, Phoenix.

Brugge, David M.
    1965   A Linguistic Approach to Demographic Problems: The Tonto-
              Yavapai Boundary. Ethnohistory Vol. 12, No. 4: 355-372.

Bryan, Kirk
    1925   The Age of Channel Trenching (Arroyo Cutting) in the Arid
              Southwest. Science n.s. Vol. 62: 338-344.

Buskirk, Winfred
    1949   Western Apache Subsistence Economy. MS, Doctoral dissertation,
              Department of Anthropology, University of New Mexico, Albuquerque.

Canouts, Veletta K.
    1975   Archaeological Resources of the Orme Reservoir. Archaeological
              Series No. 92, Cultural Resource Management Section, Arizona
              State Museum, University of Arizona, Tucson.

Carlson, Roy L.
1970   White Mountain Redware. _Anthropological Papers of the University of Arizona_ No. 19. University of Arizona Press, Tucson.

Caywood, Louis R. and Edward H. Spicer
1935   _Tuzigoot: The Excavation and Repair of a Ruin on the Verde River near Clarkdale, Arizona._ Field Division of Education, National Park Service, Berkeley.

Chenhall, Robert G.
1967   The Silo Site: 1967. _Arizona Archaeologist_ No. 2.

1972   _Random Sampling in an Archaeological Survey._ Doctoral dissertation, Department of Anthropology, Arizona State University, Tempe, and University Microfilms, Ann Arbor.

Clark, J. Grahame D.
1960   _Archaeology and Society: Reconstructing the Prehistoric Past._ Metheun, London.

1970   _Aspects of Prehistory._ University of California Press, Berkeley.

Cochran, William G.
1963   _Sampling Techniques._ Second edition, John Wiley and Sons, New York.

Collier, Boyd D., George W. Cox, Albert W. Johnson, and Philip C. Miller
1973   _Dynamic Ecology._ Prentice-Hall, Englewood Cliffs, New Jersey.

Colton, Harold S.
1939   Prehistoric Culture Units and Their Relationships in Northern Arizona. _Museum of Northern Arizona Bulletin_ No. 17.

1941   Winona and Ridge Ruin: Part II, Notes on the Technology and Taxonomy of the Pottery. _Museum of Northern Arizona Bulletin_ No. 19.

1946   The Sinagua: A Summary of the Archaeology of the Region of Flagstaff, Arizona. _Museum of Northern Arizona Bulletin_ No. 22.

1956   Pottery Types of the Southwest, _Museum of Northern Arizona Ceramic Series_ No. 3C.

1958   Pottery Types of the Southwest, _Museum of Northern Arizona Ceramic Series_ No. 3D.

Colton, Harold S., and Lyndon L. Hargrave
1937   Handbook of Northern Arizona Pottery Wares. _Museum of Northern Arizona Bulletin_ No. 11.

Corbusier, William H.
    1886   The Apache-Yumas and Apache Mojaves. <u>American Antiquarian</u>
                Vol. 8: 276-284, 325-339.

Corbusier, William T.
    1969   <u>Verde to San Carlos</u>. Dale Stuart King, Tucson.

Cowgill, George L.
    1975   A Selection of Samplers: Comments on Archaeo-statistics.
                In <u>Sampling in Archaeology</u>, edited by James W. Mueller,
                pp. 258-274. University of Arizona Press, Tucson.

Dickerman, Robert W.
    1954   An Ecological Survey of the Three-Bar Game Management Unit
                Located near Roosevelt, Arizona. MS, Master's thesis,
                University of Arizona, Tucson.

DiPeso, Charles C.
    1968   <u>Casas Grandes and the Gran Chichimeca</u>. Museum of New Mexico
                Press, Santa Fe.

    1974   <u>Casas Grandes: A Fallen Trading Center of the Gran Chichimaca</u>,
                Vols. 1-3. The Amerind Foundation, Inc., Dragoon and Northland
                Press, Flagstaff.

Dixon, Keith A.
    1956   Hidden House, a Cliff Ruin in Sycamore Canyon, Central Arizona.
                <u>Museum of Northern Arizona Bulletin</u> No. 29.

Dixon, Wilfred J. and Frank J. Massey, Jr.
    1969   <u>Introduction to Statistical Analysis</u>. Third edition, McGraw-
                Hill, New York.

Doelle, William
    1975   Prehistoric Resource Exploitation Within the CONOCO Florence
                Project. <u>Archaeological Series</u> No. 62, Cultural Resource Man-
                agement Section, Arizona State Museum, University of Arizona,
                Tucson.

Douglass, Andrew E.
    1929   The Secret of the Southwest Solved by Talkative Tree Rings.
                <u>National Geographic Magazine</u> Vol. 56, No. 6: 736-770.

Doyel, David E.
    1972   Cultural and Ecological Aspects of Salado Prehistory. MS,
                Master's thesis, Department of Anthropology, California State
                University, Chico.

    1974a   Excavations in the Escalante Ruin Group, Southern Arizona.
                <u>Archaeological Series</u> No. 37, Cultural Resource Management
                Section, Arizona State Museum, University of Arizona, Tucson.

Doyel, David E.
    1974b   The Miami Wash Project: A Preliminary Report on Excavations
             in Hohokam and Salado Sites near Miami, Central Arizona.
             Arizona Highway Salvage Preliminary Report 11, Arizona State
             Museum, University of Arizona, Tucson.

    n.d.   Miami Wash Project: Hohokam and Salado in the Globe-Miami
             Area, Central Arizona. MS, Arizona State Museum, University
             of Arizona, Tucson.

Dunbier, Roger
    1968   The Sonoran Desert: Its Geography, Economy, and People.
             University of Arizona Press, Tucson.

Dziewoński, Kazimierz
    1972   General Theory of Rank-size Distributions in Regional Settle-
             ment Systems: Reappraisal and Reformulation of the Rank-size
             Rule. Papers of the Regional Science Association Vol. 29: 73-86.

    1975   The Role and Significance of Statistical Distributions in
             Studies of Settlement Systems. Papers of the Regional Science
             Association Vol. 34: 145-155.

Evenari, Michael, Leslie Shana, and Naphtali Tadmor
    1971   The Negev: The Challenge of a Desert. Harvard University
             Press, Cambridge.

Fenneman, Nevin M.
    1931   The Physiographic Provinces of the Western United States.
             McGraw-Hill, New York.

Fewkes, Jesse W.
    1898   Archaeological Expedition to Arizona in 1895. 17th Annual
             Report, Bureau of American Ethnology, pp. 519-744, Smithsonian
             Institution.

    1912   Antiquities of the Upper Verde River and Walnut Creek Valleyss,
             Arizona. 28th Annual Report, Bureau of American Ethnology,
             pp. 181-220, Smithsonian Institution.

Fisher, Ronald A. and Frank Yates
    1957   Statistical Tables for Biological, Agricultural and Medical
             Research. Fifth edition, Oliver and Boyd, Edinburgh.

Ford, Richard I.
    1973   Archeology Serving Humanity. In Research and Theory in Current
             Archeology, edited by Charles L. Redman, pp. 83-93. John Wiley
             and Sons, New York.

Gerald, Rex E.
1958   Two Wickiups on the San Carlos Indian Reservation, Arizona. The Kiva Vol. 23, No. 3: 5-11.

Gifford, E. W.
1932   The Southeastern Yavapai. University of California Publications in American Archaeology and Ethnology Vol. 29, No. 3: 177-252.

1936   Northeastern and Western Yavapai. University of California Publications in American Archaeology and Ethnology Vol. 34, No. 4: 247-354.

Gladwin, Harold S.
1957   A History of the Ancient Southwest. Bond Wheelwright Company, Portland, Maine.

Gladwin, Winifred and Harold S. Gladwin
1930   An Archaeological Survey of the Verde Valley. Medallion Papers No. 6, Gila Pueblo, Globe.

1935   The Eastern Range of the Red-on-buff Culture. Medallion Papers No. 16, Gila Pueblo, Globe.

Gladwin, Harold S., Emil W. Haury, E. B. Sayles, and Nora Gladwin
1937   Excavations at Snaketown, Material Culture. Medallion Papers No. 25, Gila Pueblo, Globe.

Goodwin, Grenville
1942   The Social Organization of the Western Apache. University of Chicago Press, Chicago.

1971   Western Apache Raiding and Warfare. Edited by Keith H. Basso, University of Arizona Press, Tucson.

Goodyear, Albert C., III
1975   Hecla II and III: An Interpretive Study of Archaeological Remains from the Lakeshore Project, Papago Reservation, South Central Arizona. Anthropological Research Paper No. 9, Arizona State University, Tempe.

Grady, Mark
1974   Archaeological Sites within the Copper Cities Mine Area: A Preliminary Report. Archaeological Series No. 55, Cultural Resource Management Section, Arizona State Museum, University of Arizona, Tucson.

n.d.   Mitigative Data Study. MS, Cultural Resource Management Section Arizona State Museum, University of Arizona, Tucson.

Grebinger, Paul and David P. Adam
    1974   Hard Times?: Classic Period Hohokam Cultural Development in
                the Tucson Basin, Arizona. World Archaeology Vol. 6, No. 2:
                226-241.

Green, Dee F.
    1974   Random Model Testing of Archaeological Site Locations in
                Allen and South Cottonwood Canyons, Southeastern Utah.
                The Kiva Vol. 39, Nos. 3-4: 289-299.

Greig-Smith, P.
    1964   Quantitative Plant Ecology. Second edition. Butterworths,
                London.

Gumerman, George J. (editor)
    1971   The Distribution of Prehistoric Population Aggregates.
                Prescott College Anthropological Reports No.1.

Gumerman, George J. and R. Roy Johnson
    1971   Prehistoric Human Population Distribution in a Biological
                Transition Zone. In "The Distribution of Prehistoric Popula-
                tion Aggregates," edited by George J. Gumerman, pp. 83-101,
                Prescott College Anthropological Reports No. 1.

Haas, Jonathan
    1971   The Ushklish Ruin; a Preliminary Report on Excavation of a
                Colonial Hohokam Period Site in the Lower Tonto Basin, Central
                Arizona. MS, Arizona State Museum, University of Arizona,
                Tucson.

Hammack, Laurens C.
    1969   Highway Salvage Excavations in the Upper Tonto Basin, Arizona.
                The Kiva Vol. 34, Nos. 2-3: 132-175.

    1970   Second Canyon Ruin: A Preliminary Report on the Salvage
                Excavations of an Archaeological Site near Redington, Arizona.
                MS, Arizona State Museum, University of Arizona, Tucson.

Hansen, Morris, William N. Hurwitz, and William G. Madow
    1953   Sample Survey Methods and Theory. Methods and Applications,
                Vol. 1. John Wiley and Sons, New York.

Hartman, G. W.
    1973   General Soil Map with Soil Interpretation for Land Use Planning,
                Maricopa County, Arizona. United States Department of Agri-
                culture, Soil Conservation Service.

Haury, Emil W.
    1932   Roosevelt 9:6, a Hohokam Site of the Colonial Period. Medallion
                Papers No. 11, Gila Pueblo, Globe.

Haury, Emil W.
    1934   The Canyon Creek Ruin and the Cliff Dwellings of the Sierra
            Ancha. <u>Medallion Papers</u> No. 14, Gila Pueblo, Globe.

    1945   The Excavation of Los Muertos and Neighboring Ruins in the
            Salt River Valley, Southern Arizona. <u>Papers of the Peabody
            Museum of Archaeology and Ethnography</u> Vol. 24, No. 1. Cambridge.

    1967   The Hohokam: First Masters of the Desert. <u>National Geographic
            Magazine</u> Vol. 131, No. 5: 670-695.

    1976   <u>The Hohokam: Desert Farmers and Craftsmen. Excavations at
            Snaketown 1964-1965.</u> University of Arizona Press, Tucson.

Haury, Emil W., Ernst Antevs, and John F. Lance
    1953   Artifacts with Mammoth Remains, Naco, Arizona. <u>American
            Antiquity</u> Vol. 19, No. 1: 1-24.

Haury, Emil W., E. B. Sayles, and William W. Wasley
    1959   The Lehner Mammoth Site, Southeastern Arizona. <u>American
            Antiquity</u> Vol. 25, No. 1: 2-30.

Haynes, C. Vance, Jr.
    1969   The Earliest Americans. <u>Science</u> Vol. 166: 709-716.

Hevly, Richard H.
    1964   Pollen Analysis of Quaternary Archaeological and Lacustrine
            Sediments from the Colorado Plateau. MS, Doctoral dissertation,
            Department of Anthropology, University of Arizona, Tucson.

Hill, James N.
    1970   Broken K Pueblo: Prehistoric Social Organization in the
            American Southwest. <u>Anthropological Papers of the University
            of Arizona</u> No. 18, University of Arizona Press, Tucson.

Huckell, Bruce B.
    1973a   Lake Pleasant II: A Preliminary Report on the Second Excava-
            tion at the Beardsley Canal Site, a Pioneer and Colonial
            Hohokam Site on the Lower Agua Fria River, Central Arizona.
            MS, Arizona State Museum, University of Arizona, Tucson.

    1973b   The Hardt Creek Site. <u>The Kiva</u> Vol. 39, No. 2: 171-197.

Hudson, J. C.
    1969   A Location Theory for Rural Settlement. <u>Annals of the Associ-
            ation of American Geographers</u> No. 59: 365-381.

Jackson, Earl
    1933   A Survey of the Verde Drainage. MS, Master's thesis, Depart-
            ment of Anthropology, University of Arizona, Tucson.

Jackson, Earl and Sallie P. Van Valkenburgh
    1954   Montezuma Castle Archeology, Part 1: Excavations. Southwestern
            Monuments Association, Technical Series Vol. 3, No. 1, Gila
            Pueblo, Globe.

Jennings, Jesse D.
    1968   Prehistory of North America. McGraw-Hill, New York.

Judge, W. James, James I. Ebert, and Robert K. Hitchcock
    1975   Sampling in Regional Archaeological Survey. In Sampling in
            Archaeology, edited by James W. Mueller, pp. 82-123. Univer-
            sity of Arizona Press, Tucson.

Kaut, Charles R.
    1957   The Western Apache Clan System: Its Origins and Development.
            University of New Mexico Publications in Anthropology No. 9.

Kayser, David W.
    1969   Screwtail Cave. The Kiva Vol. 34, Nos. 2-3: 124-131.

Kelly, Roger E.
    1969   An Archaeological Survey in the Payson Basin, Central Arizona.
            Plateau Vol. 42, No. 2: 46-65.

    1971   Diminishing Returns: Twelfth and Thirteenth Century Sinagua
            Environmental Adaptation in North Central Arizona. Doctoral
            dissertation, Department of Anthropology, University of Arizona,
            Tucson, and University Microfilms, Ann Arbor.

Kent, Kate Peck
    1954   Montezuma Castle Archeology, Part 2: Textiles. Southwestern
            Monuments Association, Technical Series Vol. 3, No. 2, Gila
            Pueblo, Globe.

Kershaw, Kenneth A.
    1964   Quantitative and Dynamic Ecology. Edward Arnold, London.

Kidder, Alfred V.
    1924   An Introduction to the Study of Southwestern Archaeology,
            with a Preliminary Account of the Excavations at Pecos. Papers
            of the Southwestern Expedition, Phillips Academy, New Haven.

    1931   The Pottery of Pecos. Volume 1, Papers of the Southwestern
            Expedition, Phillips Academy, New Haven.

Kish, Leslie
    1965   Survey Sampling. John Wiley and Sons, New York.

Kroeber, Alfred L.
    1916   Zuñi Potsherds. American Museum of Natural History Anthropo-
            logical Papers Vol. 18, Pt. 1: 7-37.

Lazerwitz, Bernard
    1968   Sampling Theory and Procedures. In <u>Methodology in Social</u>
            <u>Research</u>, edited by Hubert M. Blalock, Jr. and Ann B. Blalock,
            pp. 278-328. McGraw-Hill, New York.

Lee, Richard B. and Irven DeVore (editors)
    1968   <u>Man the Hunter</u>. Aldine Publishing Company, Chicago.

Leone, Mark P.
    1968a   <u>Economic Autonomy and Social Distance: Archaeological Evidence</u>.
            Doctoral dissertation, Department of Anthropology, University
            of Arizona, Tucson and University Microfilms, Ann Arbor.

    1968b   Neolithic Economic Authonomy and Social Distance. <u>Science</u> Vol.
            162: 1150-1151.

Ligner, J. J., Natalie D. White, and L. R. Kister
    1969   Part II: Water Resources. In "Mineral and Water Resources
            of Arizona," pp. 469-580. <u>The Arizona Bureau of Mines</u>
            <u>Bulletin</u> 180. University of Arizona Press, Tucson.

Lindsay, Alexander J., Jr. and Calvin H. Jennings
    1968   Salado Redware Conference. Ninth Southwestern Ceramic
            Seminar. <u>Museum of Northern Arizona Ceramic Series</u> No. 4.

Lipe, William D.
    1974   A Conservation Model for American Archaeology. <u>The Kiva</u>
            Vol. 39, Nos. 3-4: 213-235.

Lipe, William D. and Alexander J. Lindsay, Jr. (editors)
    1974   Proceedings of the 1974 Cultural Resource Management Conference,
            Federal Center, Denver, Colorado. <u>Museum of Northern Arizona</u>,
            <u>Technical Series</u> No. 14.

Longacre, William A.
    1970a   Archaeology as Anthropology: A Case Study. <u>Anthropological</u>
            <u>Papers of the University of Arizona</u> No. 17, University of
            Arizona Press, Tucson.

    1970b   A Historical Review. In <u>Reconstructing Prehistoric Pueblo</u>
            <u>Societies</u>, edited by William A. Longacre, pp. 1-10. Univer-
            sity of New Mexico Press, Albuquerque.

Longacre, William A. and James E. Ayres
    1968   Archaeological Lessons from an Apache Wickiup. In <u>New</u>
            <u>Perspectives in Archaeology</u>, edited by L. Binford and
             S. Binford, pp. 151-160. Aldine Publishing Company, Chicago.

Longacre, William A. and J. Jefferson Reid
    1975   The University of Arizona Archaeological Field School at
            Grasshopper: Eleven Years of Multidisciplinary Research and
            Teaching. <u>The Kiva</u> Vol. 40, Nos. 1-2: 3-38.

Martin, Paul Schultz
    1963   The Last 10,000 Years: A Fossil Pollen Record of the American
            Southwest. University of Arizona Press, Tucson.

Martin, Paul Sidney and Fred Plog
    1973   The Archaeology of Arizona: A Study of the Southwest Region.
            Doubleday/Natural History Press, Garden City, New York.

Matson, Richard G. and William D. Lipe
    1975   Regional Sampling: A Case Study of Cedar Mesa, Utah. In
            Sampling in Archaeology, edited by James W. Mueller, pp. 124-
            143. University of Arizona Press, Tucson.

McGimsey, Charles R., III
    1975   Peer Reviews. In "The Cache River Archeological Project:
            An Experiment in Contract Archeology." Assembled by
            Michael B. Schiffer and John H. House, pp. 325-6. Arkansas
            Archeological Survey Research Series No. 8.

McGimsey, Charles R., III and Hester A. Davis
    in press   Guidelines for the Profession: The Airlie House Reports.
            Special Publication, Society for American Archaeology.

McGregor, John C.
    1941   Winona and Ridge Ruin: Part 1, Architecture and Material
            Culture. Museum of Northern Arizona Bulletin No. 18.

    1965   Southwestern Archaeology. Second edition, University of
            Illinois Press, Urbana.

McGuire, Randall H.
    n.d.   Central Heights: A Small Salado Site near Globe. MS, Arizona
            State Museum, University of Arizona, Tucson.

Mearns, Edgar A.
    1890   Ancient Dwellings of the Rio Verde Valley. Popular Science
            Monthly Vol. 37: 745-763.

Mendenhall, William, Lyman Ott, and Richard L. Scheaffer
    1971   Elementary Survey Sampling. Wadsworth, Belmont, California.

Merriam, C. Hart
    1890   Results of a Biological Survey of the San Francisco Mountain
            Region and Desert of the Little Colorado in Arizona. North
            American Fauna No. 3, U.S. Department of Agriculture, Washington.

Mindeleff, Cosmos
    1896   Aboriginal Remains in the Verde Valley, Arizona. 13th Annual
            Report, Bureau of American Ethnology, pp. 179-261, Smithsonian
            Institution.

Mindeleff, Cosmos
    1900   Localization of Tusayan Clans. 19th Annual Report, Bureau of
            American Ethnology, pp. 635-653, Smithsonian Institution.

Moore, George C.
    1973   A Comparison of the Effectiveness of Social and Topical
            Criteria in Identifying Scholarly Communities. MS, Master's
            thesis, Department of Anthropology, Cornell University,
            Ithaca, New York.

Morris, Donald H.
    1970   Walnut Creek Village: A Ninth-century Hohokam-Anasazi Settle-
            ment in the Mountains of Central Arizona. American Antiquity
            Vol. 35, No. 1: 49-61.

Morris, Earl H.
    1928   An Aboriginal Salt Mine at Camp Verde, Arizona. American
            Museum of Natural History Anthropological Papers Vol. 30,
            Pt. 3: 75-97.

Mueller, James W.
    1974   The Use of Sampling in Archaeological Survey. Memoirs of the
            Society for American Archaeology No. 28.

    1975a   Archaeological Research as Cluster Sampling. In Sampling in
            Archaeology, edited by James W. Mueller, pp. 33-41. University
            of Arizona Press, Tucson.

    1975b   Sampling in Archaeology, edited by James W. Mueller, University
            of Arizona Press, Tucson.

Nelson, Nels C.
    1914   Pueblo Ruins of the Galisteo Basin. American Museum of Natural
            History Anthropological Papers Vol. 15, Pt. 1.

    1916   Chronology of the Tano Ruins, New Mexico. American Anthropologist
            Vol. 18, No. 2: 159-180.

Netting, Robert McC.
    1971   The Ecological Approach in Cultural Study. Module No. 6,
            Addison-Wesley Modular Publishing Co., Reading, Massachusetts.

Odum, Eugene P.
    1971   Fundamentals of Ecology. Third edition, W. B. Saunders Company,
            Philadelphia.

Olson, Alan P.
    1955   The Current Status of Athabascan Archaeology. MS, Arizona
            State Museum, University of Arizona, Tucson.

Olson, Alan P.
    1963   Some Archaeological Problems of Central and Northeastern
             Arizona. Plateau Vol. 35, No. 3: 93-106.

    1971   Archaeology of the Arizona Public Service Company 345 KV Line.
             Museum of Northern Arizona Bulletin No. 46.

Olson, Alan P. and Frances S. Olson
    n.d.   A Survey of the Pine-Payson Area, Central Arizona. MS,
             Arizona State Museum, University of Arizona, Tucson.

Parl, Boris
    1967   Basic Statistics. Doubleday, Garden City, New York.

Peck, Fred R.
    1956   An Archeological Reconnaissance of the East Verde River in
             Central Arizona. MS, Master's thesis, Department of Anthro-
             pology, University of Arizona, Tucson.

Pielou, E. C.
    1969   An Introduction to Mathematical Ecology. Wiley-Interscience,
             New York.

Pierson, Lloyd M.
    n.d.   NA 3945A, the Winneman Ranch Site. MS, Museum of Northern
             Arizona, Flagstaff.

Pinder, D. A. and M. E. Witherrick
    1972   The Principles, Practice and Pitfalls of Nearest-neighbor
             Analysis. Geography Vol. 57, No. 4: 277-288.

Plog, Fred
    1974   Settlement Patterns and Social History. In Frontiers of
             Anthropology, edited by Murray J. Leaf, pp. 68-91. D. Van
             Nostrand, New York.

Plog, Stephen
    n.d.   The Relative Efficiency of Sampling Techniques for Archaeo-
             logical Surveys. MS, Department of Anthropology, University
             of Michigan, Ann Arbor.

Pomeroy, John A.
    1974   A Study of Black-on-white Painted Pottery in the Tonto Basin,
             Arizona. Southwestern Lore Vol. 39, No. 4: 1-34.

Raab, L. Mark
    1974   Test Excavations at AZ. U:8:8 (ASM), Roosevelt lake, Arizona,
             Final Report. MS, Department of Anthropology, Arizona State
             University, Tempe.

Read, Dwight W.
    1975   Regional Sampling. In Sampling in Archaeology, edited by
                James W. Mueller, pp. 45-60. University of Arizona Press,
                Tucson.

Redman, Charles L.
    1974   Archeological Sampling Strategies. Module No. 55, Addison-
                Wesley Modular Publishing Co., Reading, Massachesetts.

Redman, Charles L. and Patty Jo Watson
    1970   Systematic, Intensive Surface Collection. American Antiquity
                Vol. 35, No. 3: 279-291.

Reid, J. Jefferson
    1973   Growth and Response to Stress at Grasshopper Pueblo, Arizona.
                Doctoral dissertation, Department of Anthropology, University
                of Arizona, Tucson, and University Microfilms, Ann Arbor.

Reid, J. Jefferson, Michael B. Schiffer, and Jeffrey M. Neff
    1975   Archaeological Considerations of Intrasite Sampling. In
                Sampling in Archaeology, edited by James W. Mueller, pp.
                209-224. University of Arizona Press, Tucson.

Rodgers, James B.
    1974   An Archaeological Survey of the Cave Buttes Dam Alternative
                Site and Reservoir, Arizona. Anthropological Research Paper
                No. 8, Arizona State University, Tempe.

Rootenberg, S.
    1964   Archaeological Field Sampling. American Antiquity Vol. 30,
                No. 2, Pt. 1: 181-188.

Royse, Chester F., Michael F. Sheridan, and H. Wesley Pierce
    1971   Geologic Guidebook 4 - Highways of Arizona: Arizona Highways
                87, 88, and 188. The Arizona Bureau of Mines Bulletin 184,
                University of Arizona, Tucson.

Sauer, Carl O. and Donald Brand
    1931   Prehistoric Settlements of Sonora with Special Reference to
                Cerros de Trincheras. University of California Publications
                in Geography Vol. 5, No. 3: 67-148.

Sayles, E. B. and Ernst Antevs
    1941   The Cochise Culture. Medallion Papers No. 29, Gila Pueblo,
                Globe.

Schiffer, Michael B.
    1972   Archaeological Context and Systematic Context. American
                Antiquity Vol. 37, No. 2: 156-165.

Schiffer, Michael B.
1975a   Archeological research and contract archeology. In "The Cache
         River Archeological Project: An Experiment in Contract Arch-
         eology," assembled by Michael B. Schiffer and John H. House,
         pp. 1-7, Arkansas Archeological Survey Research Series No. 8.

1975b   Archaeology as Behavioral Science. American Anthropologist
         Vol. 77, No. 4: 836-848.

Schiffer, Michael B. and John H. House (assemblers)
1975   The Cache River Archeological Project: An Experiment in
         Contract Archeology. Arkansas Archeological Survey Research
         Series No. 8.

Schmidt, Erich F.
1926   The Mrs. William Boyce Thompson Expedition. Natural History
         Vol. 26, No. 6: 635-644.

Schoenwetter, James
1962   The Pollen Analysis of Eighteen Archaeological Sites in
         Arizona and New Mexico. In "Chapters in the Prehistory of
         Eastern Arizona, I," by Paul S. Martin, John B. Rinaldo,
         William A. Longacre, Constance Cronin, Leslie G. Freeman, Jr.,
         and James Schoenwetter, pp. 168-209. Fieldiana: Anthropology
         Vol. 53. Chicago Natural History Museum, Chicago.

Schroeder, Albert H.
1947   Did the Sinagua of the Verde Valley Settle in the Salt River
         Valley? Southwestern Journal of Anthropology Vol. 3, No. 3:
         230-246.

1948   Montezuma Well. Plateau Vol. 20, No. 3: 37-40.

1949   A Preliminary Examination of the Sacred Mountain Ball Court.
         Plateau Vol. 21, NO. 4: 55-57.

1951   A New Ball Court Site in the Verde Valley. Plateau Vol. 23,
         No. 4: 61-63.

1952a   A Brief History of the Yavapai of the Middle Verde Valley.
         Plateau Vol. 24, No. 3: 111-118.

1952b   The Bearing of Ceramics on Developments in the Hohokam Classic
         Period. Southwestern Journal of Anthropology Vol. 8, No. 3:
         320-335.

1953   The Problem of Hohokam, Sinagua and Salado Relations in
         Southern Arizona. Plateau Vol. 26, No. 2: 75-83.

Schroeder, Albert H.
    1960   The Hohokam, Sinagua and the Hakataya. Archives of Archaeology
            No. 5. Society for American Archaeology and the University of
            Wisconsin Press, Madison.

    1963   A Study of the Apache Indians: Parts V-A through V-G for
            Western Apache Docket Number 22-D and Northern Tonto Docket
            Number 22-J before the Indian Claims Commission. MS, copy
            available at the Arizona State Museum, University of Arizona,
            Tucson.

    1965   Unregulated Diffusion from Mexico into the Southwest Prior to
            A.D. 700. American Antiquity Vol. 30, No. 3: 297-309.

Schumann, H. H. and B. W. Thomsen
    1972   Hydrologic Regimen of Lower Tonto Creek Basin, Gila County,
            Arizona: A REconnaissance Study. Arizona Water Commission
            Bulletin No. 3, Phoenix.

Schuyler, Robert L.
    1971   The History of American Archaeology: An Examination of
            Procedure. American Antiquity Vol. 36, No. 4: 383-409.

Scovill, Douglas H., Garland J. Gordon, and Keith M. Anderson
    1972   Guidelines for the Preparation of Statements of Environmental
            Impact on Archeological Resources. MS, Western Archeological
            Center, National Park Service, Tucson.

Sellers, William D. and Richard H. Hill (editors)
    1974   Arizona Climate. Second edition, University of Arizona Press,
            Tucson.
Shaffer, Jimmie Gray
    1972   Arizona U:2:29 (ASU): A Honanki Phase Site in the Southern
            Verde River, Arizona. MS, Master's thesis, Department of
            Anthropology, Arizona State University, Tempe.

Shiner, Joel L.
    1961   A Room at Gila Pueblo. The Kiva Vol. 27, No. 2: 3-11.

Shutler, Dick, Jr.
    1950   The Dry Creek Site: A Pre-pottery Lithic Horizon in the
            Verde Valley, Arizona. Plateau Vol. 23, No. 1: 1-10.

    1951   Two Pueblo Ruins in the Verde Valley, Arizona. Plateau
            Vol. 24, No. 1: 1-9.

Simon, Herbert A.
    1955   On a Class of Skew Distribution Functions. Biometrika
            Vol. 42: 425-440.

Simon, Herbert A.
    1962   The Architecture of Complexity. _American Philosophical Society Proceedings_ Vol. 106: 467-482.

    1972   The Sizes of Things. In _Statistics: A Guide to the Unknown,_ edited by Judith M. Tanur, pp. 195-202. Holden-Day, San Francisco.

Spicer, Edward H.
    1962   _Cycles of Conquest: The Impact of Spain, Mexico, and the United States on the Indians of the Southwest, 1533-1960._ University of Arizona Press, Tucson.

Spicer, Edward H. and Louis P. Caywood
    1936   Two Pueblo Ruins in West Central Arizona. _University of Arizona Bulletin_ Vol. 7, No. 1, _Social Science Bulletin_ No. 10. University of Arizona, Tucson.

Southwood, T. R. E.
    1966   _Ecological Methods._ Chapman and Hall, London.

Spier, Leslie
    1917   An Outline for a Chronology of Zuñi Ruins. _American Museum of Natural History Anthropological Papers_ Vol. 18, Pt. 3.

Steen, Charlie R., Lloyd Pierson, Vorsila Bohrer, and Kate Peck Kent
    1962   Archaeological Studies at Tonto National Monument, Arizona. _Southwestern Monuments Association Technical Series_ Vol. 2.

Steward, Julian
    1938   Basin-plateau Aboriginal Socio-political Groups. _Bureau of American Ethnology, Bulletin_ 120, Smithsonian Institution.

Sukhatme, Pandurang V. and Balkrishna V. Sukhatme
    1970   _Sampling Theory of Surveys with Applications._ Second edition, Iowa State University Press, Ames, Iowa.

Swedlund, Alan C.
    1975   Population Growth and Settlement Pattern in Franklin and Hampshire Counties, Massachusetts, 1650-1850. In "Population Studies in Archaeology and Biological Anthropology: A Symposium," edited by Alan C. Swedlund, pp. 22-33. _Society for American Archaeology Memoir_ 30.

Taylor, Walter W.
    1954   Southwestern Archaeology, Its History and Theory. _American Anthropologist_ Vol. 56, No. 1, Pt. 1: 561-575.

Thomas, David H.
    1973   An Empirical Test of Steward's Model of Great Basin Settlement Patterns. _American Antiquity_ Vol. 38, No. 2: 155-176.

Thomas, David H.
    1975   Nonsite Sampling in Archaeology: Up the Creek without a Site?
             In Sampling in Archaeology, edited by James W. Mueller, pp.
             61-81. University of Arizona Press, Tucson.

Trigger, Bruce G.
    1968   The Determinants of Settlement Patterns. In Settlement
             Archaeology, edited by Kwang-chih Chang, pp. 53-78. National
             Press Books, Palo Alto.

Tuohy, Donald R.
    1960   Two More Wickiups on the San Carlos Indian Reservation. The
             Kiva Vol. 26, No. 2: 27-30.

United States Department of Agriculture, Forest Service
    1957   National Forest Facts: Southwestern Region. Albuquerque.

United States Department of the Interior, Geological Survey
    1954   Compilations of Records of Surface Waters of the United States
             through September, 1950. Part 9: Colorado River Basin.
             Geological Survey Water-Supply Paper 1313. Washington.

    1964   Compilations of Records of Surface Waters of the United States,
             October 1950 to September 1960. Part 9: Colorado River
             Basin. Geological Survey Water-Supply Paper 1733. Washington.

    1970   Surface Water of the United States, 1961-1965. Part 9:
             Colorado River Basin, Vol. 3: Lower Colorado River Basin.
             Geological Survey Water-Supply Paper 1926. Washington.

United States Department of the Interior, Geological Survey, Water Resources
    Division
    1974   Water Resources Data for Arizona: 1973. Part 1, Surface
             Water Records. Washington.

University of Arizona, Hydrology Program
    1965   Map of Normal Annual Precipitation, 1931-1960, State of Arizona
             (scale 1:500,000). Department of Geology, Arizona Agricultural
             Experiment Station, and Institute of Atmospheric Physics,
             University of Arizona, Tucson.

Valehrach, Emil M.
    1967   A Site on the Verde. The Arizona Archaeologist No. 1: 25-34.

Valehrach, Emil M. and Bruce S. Valehrach
    1971   Excavations at Brazaletes Pueblo. The Arizona Archaeologist
             No. 6.

Vescelius, Gary S.
    1960   Archaeological Sampling: A Problem of Statistical Inference.
             In Essays in the Science of Culture, edited by Gertrude E. Dole
             and Robert L. Carneiro, pp. 457-470. Thomas Y. Crowell, New
             York.

Vickery, Irene S.
  1939   Besh-ba-gowah. The Kiva Vol. 4, No. 5: 19-22.

Vivian, R. Gwinn
  1975   Conservation and Diversion: Water Control Systems in the
            Anasazi Southwest. In "Irrigation's Impact Upon Society,"
            Anthropological Papers of the University of Arizona No. 25,
            edited by Theodore E. Downing and McGuire Gibson, pp. 95-112.
            University of Arizona Press, Tucson.

Vogt, K. D. and M. L. Richardson
  1974   General Soil Map of Gila County, Arizona. U.S. Department of
            Agriculture, Soil Conservation Service.

Wasley, William W.
  1957   Highway Salvage Archaeology by the Arizona State Museum,
            1956-57. The Kiva Vol. 23, No. 2: 17-19.

Wasley, William W. and Alfred E. Johnson
  1965   Salvage Archaeology in the Painted Rocks Reservoir, Western
            Arizona. Anthropological Papers of the University of Arizona
            No. 9. University of Arizona Press, Tucson.

Weaver, Donald E., Jr.
  1972   A Cultural-ecological Model for the Classic Period in the
            Lower Salt River Valley, Arizona. The Kiva Vol. 38, No. 1:
            43-52.

Weed, Carol S.
  1972   The Beardsley Canal Site. The Kiva Vol. 38, No. 2: 57-94.

  1974   A Model of Centralized Redistribution. Paper presented at the
            39th Annual Meeting of the Society for American Archaeology.
            Washington, D.C.

Weed, Carol S. and Albert E. Ward
  1970   The Henderson Site: Colonial Hohokam in North Central Arizona:
            A Preliminary Report. The Kiva Vol. 36, No. 2: 1-11.

Wendorf, Fred and Erik K. Reed
  1955   An Alternative Reconstruction of Northern Rio Grande Prehistory.
            El Palacio Vol. 62, Nos. 5-6: 131-173.

Wendt, G. E.
  1969   General Soil Map, Yavapai County, Arizona. United States
            Department of AGriculture, Soil Conservation Service.

Wilcox, David R.
  n.d.   The Entry of Athapascans into the American Southwest: The
            Problem Today. MS, Arizona State Museum, University of Arizona,
            Tucson.

Willey, Gordon R.
    1953   Prehistoric Settlement Patterns in the Virú Valley, Peru.
                <u>Bureau of American Ethnology, Bulletin</u> No. 155, Smithsonian
                Institution.

    1966   <u>An Introduction to American Archaeology. Volume 1: North and
                Middle America</u>. Prentice-Hall, Englewood Cliffs, New Jersey.

Willey, Gordon R. and Philip Phillips
    1958   <u>Method and Theory in American Archaeology</u>. University of
                Chicago Press, Chicago.

Willey, Gordon R. and Jeremy A. Sabloff
    1974   <u>A History of American Archaeology</u>. W. H. Freeman and Company,
                San Francisco.

Wilmsen, Edwin N.
    1970   Lithic Analysis and Cultural Inference: A Paleo-Indian Case.
                <u>Anthropological Papers of the University of Arizona</u> No. 16.
                University of Arizona Press, Tucson.

Wilson, Eldred D. and R. T. Moore
    1959   Structure of Basin and Range Province in Arizona. In "<u>Arizona
                Geological Society Guidebook II, Southern Arizona</u>," pp. 89-105,
                <u>Arizona Geological Society</u>.

Windmiller, Ric
    1971   A Partial Archaeological Survey of the Castle Dome-Pinto
                Creek Project Area, near Miami, Arizona. <u>Archaeological Series</u>
                No. 5, Cultural Resource Management Section, Arizona State
                Museum, University of Arizona, Tucson.

    1972a   Ta-E-Wun: A Colonial Period Hohokam Campsite in East-central
                Arizona. <u>The Kiva</u> Vol. 38, No. 1: 1-26.

    1972b   The Hagen Excavation: Pottery. MS, Western Archeological
                Center, National Park Service, Tucson.

    1973   An Archaeological Survey of the Castle Dome-Pinto Creek
                Project Area, near Miami, Arizona: Final Report. <u>Archaeo-
                logical Series</u> No. 22, Cultural Resource Management Section,
                Arizona State Museum, University of Arizona, Tucson.

    1974a   Archaeological Excavations at Scorpion Ridge Ruin, East-
                Central Arizona. <u>Archaeological Series</u> No. 48, Cultural
                Resource Management Section, Arizona State Museum, University
                of Arizona, Tucson.

    1974b   Contributions to Pinto Valley Archaeology. <u>Archaeological
                Series</u> No. 51, Cultural Resource Management Section, Arizona
                State Museum, University of Arizona. Tucson.

Windmiller, Ric
    1974c   Recent Archaeological Work in Salado Settlements. Paper read
             at the 18th Annual Meeting of the Arizona Academy of Science,
             Flagstaff.

Wood, Donald G.
    1972   Archaeological Reconnaissance of the Gila Indian Reservation:
             Second Action Year (Phase III). Archaeological Series No. 16,
             Cultural Resource Management Section, Arizona State Museum,
             University of Arizona, Tucson.

Wood, John J.
    1971   Fitting Discrete Probability Distributions to Prehistoric
             Settlement Patterns. In "The Distribution of Prehistoric
             Population Aggregates," edited by George J. Gumerman,
             pp. 63-82. Prescott College Studies in Anthropology No. 1.

Woodbury, Richard B.
    1961   Prehistoric Agriculture at Point of Pines, Arizona.   Memoirs
             of the Society for American Archaeology No. 17.

Yamane, Taro
    1967   Elementary Sampling Theory. Prentice-Hall, Englewood Cliffs,
             New Jersey.

Young, Jon N.
    1967   The Salado Culture in Southwestern Prehistory. Doctoral dis-
             sertation, Department of Anthropology, University of Arizona,
             Tucson, and University Microfilms, Ann Arbor.

    1972   The Hagen Site at Gila Pueblo. MS, Arizona State Museum,
             University of Arizona, Tucson.

Zipf, George K.
    1949   Human Behavior and the Principle of Least Effort. Addison-
             Wesley Press, Cambridge, Massachusetts.